Created and Directed by Han

D0193457

INSIGHT GUIDES
SOUTHAFRICA

Edited by Johannes Haape
Updated by Eberhard Gennrich
Managing Editor: Roger Williams

Editorial Director: Brian Bell

HOUGHTON MIFFLIN COMPANY

ABOUT THIS BOOK

Höfer

Many travellers longing to see South Africa, widely held to be one of the most beautiful countries on earth, were until recently put off by the country's political regime. But with black majority rule now in place, that inhibition had gone and tourism may even help accelerate change by forging links between a previously inward-looking South Africa and the world community.

Such a fascinating destination was a natural for Insight Guides the award-winning series created in 1970 by **Hans Höfer**, now chairman of Apa Publications. Each of the 190 titles encourages readers to celebrate the essence of a place rather than try to tailor it to their expectations, and is edited according to Höfer's conviction that, without insight, travel can narrow the mind rather than broaden it. To provide insight into South Africa, Apa Publications turned to more than 100 local writers, researchers and photographers, who were involved over a period of 18 months in creating what they determined would be the definitive guidebook to their country.

Haape

Coordinating this effort as project editor was **Johannes Haape**. Born in South Africa, he graduated from the University of Natal in zoology, psychology, religions and classics. He travelled widely in southern Africa and has a good working knowledge of four local languages. Today he owns a tour company in Germany specialising in subsaharan Africa.

van Heerden

Assisted by **Dries van Heerden**, formerly columnist and political editor of the *Sunday Times*, the country's largest-selling newspaper, Haape set about revising and supplementing contributions with an eye to presenting the fullest possible picture. Van Heerden also contributed several chapters, including those on Johannesburg, Pretoria and Natal.

Rodney Davenport, emeritus professor and editor of the standard work *A Modern History of South Africa*, made the major contribution to the historical narrative. He was assisted by **Francis Thackeray,** a Yale PhD and head of paleonthology at the Transvaal Museum.

Rautenbach

The "Performing Arts" chapter was a joint venture by **Gerold Maclim** of *The Star* and **Mariechen Waldner**, who reports for the Sunday newspaper *Rapport*. Waldner also teamed up with project editor Haape in compiling "A Mix of Cultures" and also wrote "Southwestern Transvaal", the "Orange Free State" and "Steam Locomotives". **Hugh Eley**, deputy sports editor of *The Star,* reported on South Africa's return to the international sports arena. **Peter Devereux**, whose childhood next to the Cape winelands predisposed him for his job as wine editor of *Style* magazine, wrote about food and wine.

Devereux

Naas Rautenbach, director of the Transvaal Museum and curator of mammals, wrote "The Call of the Wild". He feels that "South Africa is facing a green wave of environmental awareness and that its scientific community has to gear itself up to make suggestions to government and corporate bodies."

Maclean

Gordon Maclean, professor of zoology and editor of *Roberts Birds of South Africa,* wrote "Birds in the Bush", while **Dr Ian Macdonald**, director of the South African Nature Foundation, wrote "Nature Conservation and National Parks".

Piet Müller, deputy editor of the Afrikaans Sunday newspaper *Rap-*

Beckett

port, contributed the article about South Africa's people, "Living Together". Dr Müller believes "the dynamic process of change in the New South Africa will create a vibrant open society, enabling it to play its rightful role in Africa." **Dennis Beckett**, deputy editor of the *Sunday Star* and former editor and owner of the magazine *Frontline,* wrote the chapter "Facing the Future".

The economic scenario presented in "Rich Man, Poor Man" was written by **Sean Cleary**, director of Strategic Concepts. "The Spirit of Religion", conceived by Professor **Gerhardus Oosthuizen**, was written by his colleague **Hans-Jürgen Becken**, medic, theologian and the author of numerous books.

On the cultural level, **Christopher Till**, director of the Johannesburg Art Gallery and of the city's museums, wrote the chapter on art, **Jacques Malan**, emeritus professor of the University of Pretoria and general editor of the South Africa music encyclopedia, covered music, and **Steven Grey** supplied the contribution on literature. Professor Grey believes "that with a past of division, literature is an important medium for making acquaintance across barriers."

David Bristow, environmental scientist and author of well over a dozen books relating to Southern Africa's national heritage, contributed four major articles relating to tourist destinations in the Cape Province and Transkei. **Vincent Carruthers**, former executive director of the South Africa Wildlife Society, compiled "Northern and Eastern Transvaal" and "The Kruger National Park".

Carruthers

Bristow

Glaue

Other contributions came from an impressive variety of experts, including Zulu ethnic specialist **Sighart Bourquin**, astronomer **Professor Walter Wargau**, history professor **Joy Brain**, geologist **Dr Peter Booth**, architect **Professor Walter Peters**, marine biologist **Professor Anton Machlachlon**, entomologist **Professor Erik Holm**, vertebrate and invertebrate specialist **Wulf Haacke**, historian **At van Wyk**, economist **Dr Erich Leistner** and rock art specialist **Dr Thomas Dowson**; they all contributed informative panels.

The responsibility for compiling the reference section in "Travel Tips" was assigned to **Inge Glaue**, who amassed a huge amount of information, some of which is in print for the first time. Contributing researchers for "Travel Tips" were **Jill Blackwood-Murray**, **Petra Blunck**, **Lea Phillipps**, **Tanja** and **Paola Riemann**, **Thomas Schmidt** and **Dr E. Ukan**. This section was edited by **Werner Gordes** and **Tony Halliday**. Halliday and **Anne Midgette** also translated a number of contributions from German into English.

Special thanks are due to **Professor Tim Partridge** and **Professor A. C. Thembela**, who undertook important advisory functions, and to the **Anthony Bannister Photo Agency** which supplied many of the eye-catching photographs. Others who assisted at various stages were **Adelheid Gartler, Inge Grossmann, Heidi Stinnes, Professor Izak Rust**, and **Dr W. A. de Klerk**.

The book, which was proofread by **Carole Mansur** and **Mary Morton**, was completed in Insight Guides' London editorial office. For this edition, it was thoroughly revised on the spot by **Eberhard Gennrich**.

CONTENTS

CONTENTS

TRAVEL TIPS

THE SHAPE OF GOOD HOPE

"The news from [South] Africa is absorbingly interesting at the moment," wrote an observer after a visit. The writer was Matthew Arnold and the year was 1879, but Arnold's remark is particularly relevant today. Perhaps no country in the world is poised to change as dramatically as South Africa, as a clutch of cultures, interlinked but powerfully divergent, struggles to find a communal voice.

Contrast is nothing new in South Africa. For centuries people fleeing tribal conflict, natural disasters and European wars settled here in search of a new life. Isolated on the extremities of a sprawling continent removed from a changing world, its inhabitants never managed to assimilate, but have remained apart in language, culture and appearance. In many ways, South Africa is a microcosm of global differences.

Within this diverse community is a vibrant contrast of artistic expression. In the musical field, black hits such as *Saraphina* and *Woza Albert* thrive side by side with classical ballet and Wagner's *Ring*. The country has produced sports celebrities such as Gary Player and Jody Scheckter, several Nobel prize winners, and a world-famous heart surgeon, Christian Barnard. The fact that Barnard comes from a country where Zulu medicine men also practice is therefore hardly surprising.

The country's diversity reaches its fullest expression in nature. Nearly 2,000 miles of glistening beaches embrace wide open landscapes, snow-covered peaks and magnificent national parks teeming with flora and big game. Two consistent phenomena accompany a visit to South Africa. The first is the brilliance of its sunshine and endless blue skies, the blood-red horizons and shades of purple at sunset. The other is the natural responsiveness of its people, whether experienced in the towering skyscraper towns or the rarely visited languid backwaters.

Of all the faces which South Africa shows, that of the "New South Africa" is the most remarkable. Not long ago a small minority held the wheel of state and the majority of the citizens were excluded from the power game. Now there is a brave, new environment. Many prejudices of the past are being abandoned, forcing South Africans of various backgrounds to search together for common values and new forms of living together. It's a daunting task which, if successful, could become a model for conflict solving the world over. The news is indeed absorbingly interesting.

Preceding pages: Johannesburg skyscraper; a traditional Sotho dwelling; surfing the Natal Coast; springtime in Namaqualand; rural Natal; golden arches in the Cedarberg; springbok in the Kalahari. **Left,** black meets white.

Important evidence of man's early presence has been discovered in several caves in southern Africa. Fossils uncovered belong to the genus Australopithecus, commonly referred to as "the missing link" between ape and man which lived between 1 and 3 million years ago. Some sites have also provided remains of the extinct species of the genus Homo Australopithecus and other distant relatives of Homo sapiens, generally referred to as "hominids".

The first specimen of Australopithecus was described in 1925 by Raymond Dart, professor of anatomy at the University of the Witwatersrand. This specimen, a juvenile skull and mandible, had been found during lime-mining operations at Taung. Dart called it Australopithecus africanus. The hole at the base of the skull (the foramen magnum) indicated that the ape-man had walked upright. Estimates of cranial capacity suggested that this hominid had a tiny brain in adulthood (around 500 cc), comparable to the brain size of an adult chimpanzee. This challenged the prevailing view that man's early ancestors had a large brain.

Secrets of the skull: Many of the questions raised were answered at Sterkfontein, where fragmentary remains of an adult australopithecine were discovered in 1936. Robert Broom of the Transvaal Museum was encouraged by the prime minister, General Jan Smuts, to look for additional specimens at the site, and in April 1947 a very fine complete skull was found. Broom categorised the Sterkfontein fossils as Plesianthropus ("almost man"). The complete skull, whose cranial capacity corresponded closely to estimates based on "Dart's Child" from Taung, was around 2½ million years old and was nicknamed "Mrs Ples".

Sterkfontein cave deposits from later ages have yielded evidence of Homo habilis, a species of the same genus to which modern man (Homo sapiens) belongs. An almost complete skull of Homo habilis ("handy man") was discovered in 1976 by Alun

Hughes of the University of the Witwatersrand. Homo habilis is likely to have made the stone tools found at the site.

The discovery of blackened bones suggests that the controlled use of fire existed 1½ million years ago – the earliest such evidence anywhere in the world. Certainly, access to fire would have been a significant advantage when leopards and other carnivores sought shelter at cave sites such as Swartkrans. At least one australopithecine from this site was a victim of a leopard, judging by two promi-

nent holes on the skull of a juvenile hominid, punctured by the carnivore's canines.

Other sites have provided valuable evidence for the emergence of Homo sapiens in the Late Pleistocene era. An archaic form of modern man is represented by a skull from Florisbad, near Bloemfontein in the Orange Free State. A cave complex at Klasies River Mouth in the southern Cape has provided evidence of anatomically modern man in deposits thought to be at least 100,000 years old. Fossils from Border Cave, on the boundary between KwaZulu/Natal and Swaziland, and from Klasies River Mouth are of particular interest since they are the earliest known remains of anatomically modern man, who may well have evolved in Africa before radiating throughout the world.

Enter modern man: Scattered groups of San hunter-gatherers, or Bushmen, inhabited the southwestern parts of Africa 10,000 years ago and practised a hunter-gatherer economy. They have long since disappeared as social groups, having been persecuted by later settlers, and have left only rock paintings and engravings (see page 91).

The Bushmen's nomadic lifestyle brought them into contact with Khoikhoi cattle herders who, according to modern historians, migrated southwards from present-day northern Botswana. The Khoi lived a pasto-

dispute. Archaeologists think that Iron Age communities were established in the Transvaal and northern Natal as early as 1,500 years ago. They lived in settled communities with domesticated animals and cultivated crops – mostly grain and vegetables. Examples of their metalworking and pottery have been discovered at various sites, the best example being a number of beautifully preserved ceramic heads found near Lydenburg in the eastern Transvaal.

Initially, these early communities were largely confined to the northern and eastern savannah. By the mid-14th century, however, there was a marked expansion into the open grassland of the western Transvaal and

ral existence, often following a fixed migratory pattern in search of grazing according to seasonal changes. Their large cattle herds formed the basis of their economic and community life, and the long-horned oxen were even used defensively to shield warriors. This almost complete dependence on livestock rendered them vulnerable to natural disasters such as disease and droughts. Consequently, the arrival of the first European explorers in the mid-15th century found the Khoikhoi less able than other African societies to resist colonial encroachment.

The first arrival of Bantu-speaking communities in southern Africa is still a matter of

Free State. Large communities of Tswana and Sotho-speaking people settled in the Rustenburg region of the Magaliesberg mountain range and Nguni-speaking people fanned out into the Eastern Cape. Still, settlements remained dependent on a mean annual rainfall of more than 24 inches (600 mm) for the cultivation of their crops and good grazing for their livestock.

From about the middle of the 16th century, coastal communities came into contact with Portuguese traders at Delagoa Bay and survivors of shipwrecks often returned with vivid tales of well-organised chiefdoms living in areas rich in agricultural produce and livestock. These chiefdoms were relatively small, each enjoying political and economic autonomy although their heads were most often related through elaborate intermarriage. By 1600, however, Southern Nguni clans were trying to expand their power and influence by incorporating neighbouring tribes into larger political units.

Towards the end of the 18th century, similar loose confederations started to form in Natal, with larger kingdoms expanding through the incorporation of weaker neighbours. Territorial disputes arose over the lucrative trade routes to the Mthetwa and from the death of Dingiswayo.

Shaka, the chief of the Zulus, a minor tribe

the undisputed ruler of a vast Zulu empire stretching from the Pongola to the Tugela River and from the sea to the Buffalo River.

Shaka's conquests, wrote one historian, caused "a singular crisis that smashed tribes, scattered others and dashed the fragments into new combinations". His influence was felt far beyond the border of the Zulu empires. His military expeditions led to hordes of refugees fleeing the ravages of war, in turn wreaking their own form of devastation and destruction. The tremors of Shaka's wars were soon felt southwards into the Eastern Cape and across the Drakensberg into the Transvaal and Free State highveld.

Here the fleeing invaders cut a swathe of

in the Mthetwa confederation, took it upon himself to rebuild Dingiswayo's empire. Shaka's methods of expanding his power were ruthless and brutal. He sought to destroy enemies completely by eliminating their ruling family, killing most of the men and incorporating the survivors into his kingdom. Unlike his predecessor, his aim was not to create a loose confederacy, but rather a single, united kingdom. Eventually, his power enabled him to defeat his old enemy, the Ndwandwe. By 1819 Shaka was

Left, early Nguni settlement. **Above**, the 19th century was marked by tribal conflict.

destruction, smashing existing Sotho chiefdoms and incorporating the survivors. Between 1820 and 1825 the southern Sotho chiefdoms were almost wiped out by the invasions and the resultant destruction of livestock and crops. Thousands of Sotho tribesmen fled in all directions, causing another chain reaction of plunder and chaos.

Mzilikazi, a former Zulu general, fled from Natal with a few followers after a dispute with Shaka and settled in the Transvaal where he established his mighty Ndebele empire. This lasted until the firepower of the white Voortrekker forced him across the Limpopo into Zimbabwe.

THE COLONISATION OF THE CAPE

The first European settlement on Africa's southern tip was established as a result of trade between Europe and the Far East. The Dutch East India Company needed a reliable supply station for scurvy-ridden crews which ran out of fresh produce during a voyage often lasting four to six months. The Cape, halfway along the sea route, seemed an obvious choice.

A young merchant, Jan van Riebeeck, and a small contingent of 90 men, women and children set sail from Holland to establish a base. On 6 April 1652, van Riebeeck's flagship, the Drommedaris, dropped anchor in Table Bay. It quickly became apparent that a small settlement consisting mainly of soldiers couldn't provide both protection for itself and supplies for passing ships. Van Riebeeck was given permission by the company to let some of his men become commercial suppliers to the settlement. In 1657 the first nine vryburgers (free burghers) left the employ of the company to settle as farmers along the Liesbeeck River. They were to become the first Boers, a people upholding many European values and skills but considering themselves primarily African and not subjects of any European nation.

At first the settlement was confined to the immediate vicinity of the Cape peninsula. It produced mainly wheat and vegetables while the company bartered for cattle with the neighbouring Khoikhoi. But as demand for fresh meat grew from passing ships, the administration became more dependent on the local farmers.

The settlement's borders expanded rapidly, causing frequent clashes over grazing land and water resources. The Khoikhoi tried to resist intrusion into their territory but succumbed to superior firepower. A series of devastating smallpox epidemics severely depleted their numbers. The vanquished and now landless Khoikhoi were gradually drawn to the farms as indentured labourers or enlisted into the Hottentot corps.

The company decided to import slaves from other Dutch colonies in the East Indies,

and by 1795 more than 20,000 slaves worked at the Cape – the vast majority owned by burghers and labourers. Although regarded as property, slaves were given minor rights. Manumission was subject to approval by the administration and only a few slaves were freed annually. These settled in the towns and found employment as craftsmen, carpenters, tailors and teachers.

Meanwhile, the European population was constantly expanding. Dutch settlers, among them orphan girls from Rotterdam, arrived.

In 1688, the first of 220 French Huguenots fleeing religious persecution following the revocation of the Edict of Nantes sought a new life at the Cape. They brought with them valuable know-how, including the cultivation of wine. Germans and other immigrants in the 18th century kept up a constant flow.

In time, many of the crop-farmers turned to livestock. As the demand for grazing land increased, the "Trekboer" evolved. These itinerant farmers moved into the hinterland across the Drakensberg mountain range, finally reaching the Great Fish River, 600 miles (1,000 km) further on. Here they were destined to run into the formidable Xhosa.

Left, the whites arrived at the Cape in 1652.
Right, Boer frontier family with servants.

In his isolation, the Trekboer developed a vigorous sense of self-sufficiency, which eventually also manifested itself in a spirit of individualism and independence. Frontier life was harsh and primitive. Contact with the markets was infrequent and the Trekboers and their families had to rely on their own ingenuity to survive harsh conditions.

Attempts by the Cape authorities to extend their influence to these communities were treated with disdain. There were constant conflicts over taxes, land allocation, military service and low prices for farm produce. In 1705 this simmering tension spilt over into open hostility when a group of prominent farmers clashed with Governor Willem Adriaen van der Stel over officialdom's manipulation of the local markets to suit their own pockets. Some ring-leaders were arrested and thrown into the castle dungeon. Others, however, managed to bring their complaints to the notice of the Dutch authorities and, after an investigation, van der Stel was recalled.

The tension between the Cape authorities and its free-spirited subjects continued throughout the 18th century. Emboldened by the Enlightenment and by the spirit of independence that swept through Europe – notably the Patriot movement in the Netherlands which campaigned against the ruling House of Orange – the Trekboers staged their own revolts against auhtority.

At Graaff-Reinet, dissatisfaction over frontier policies led in 1795 to an uprising against the unpopular rule of the local magistrate. And at Swellendam the burghers established a revolutionary National Convention along the lines of the French revolution and declared the district a free republic. Both republics eventually had to surrender when the British took over control of the Cape for the first time later that year.

At the turn of the 18th century the Cape settlement was dominated by white merchant officials and free white settlers, ruling jointly over a slave population and the Khoikhoi whose loss of bargaining power reduced their status to effective rightlessness. The unequal status of these groups laid the basis of the system of apartheid institutionalised in the 20th century.

British control: The British presence at the Cape was initially strategic. During the War of American Independence, an increasing number of French vessels visited the Cape on their way to India. This development greatly disturbed the British government, then on the brink of hostilities with Napoleon. When the Dutch East Indian Company was finally liquidated in 1795, British forces took control of the Cape as allies of the Prince of Orange. Between 1802 and 1806 it reverted briefly back to the Dutch; but, after hostilities resumed in Europe, it was finally retaken by the British.

The government in London sought to integrate the Cape fully into the British colonial system. This had a direct impact on the nature of central and local government, the legal system, language policy, currency and laws of land tenure. Over 20 years, the whole administration was systematically anglicised. To accelerate this transformation, large numbers of British settlers were sent to the Cape. The decision to sponsor emigration served a dual purpose: it eased the pressure of unemployment in Britain and provided a cheap defence of the Cape colony's eastern frontier.

Buffer zone: Arriving in the Cape between 1820 and 1824, the British settlers were issued with basic rations, tents and farming tools and quickly dispatched to the frontier regions. The majority of the 1,000 men and their families were settled in the Zuurveld area, bordering on the Great Fish River. A buffer zone was created between the Fish and the Keiskamma to separate the settlers from the local Xhosa tribes.

Frontier life was harsh and uncompromising. Few of the settlers were farmers and many drifted towards towns such as Bathurst and Albany. Those who remained on the land had to contend with a fickle climate, regular crop failures and constant raids on their stock and herds by marauding groups of Xhosas. The settlers continuously petitioned the government in the Cape to provide adequate protection, but their pleas were mostly to no avail. The settlers themselves were organised into militia, which added to their grievances.

The 1820 settlers brought with them a heritage that still strongly influences South African society. Their contribution left an indelible mark on the development of education, religion, literature, press freedom and the legal system in the country. The new immigrants shared with their Afrikaner neighbours a common resentment against the administration in Cape Town. Much of it was focused on the legal and social reforms instituted to eradicate the inequalities that had developed during the Dutch period of rule. The abolition of slavery and the subsequent emancipation of slaves generated the most tension.

Turmoil on the frontier: By the start of the 19th century, the South African interior experienced a period of considerable turmoil. Tribal conflict pushed Bantu-speaking tribes deeper into the interior and southwards along the eastern coast where they came into contact with the European groups who were beginning to expand northwards.

to separate the settlers from the black tribes. This proved to be futile. The white farmers continued to expand eastwards, encroaching on tribal land and were in turn subjected to raids of devastating intensity.

The settlers, blaming the British administration for the lack of adequate protection, took matters into their own hands. Between 1819 and 1853 four frontier wars erupted in the border area, claiming the lives of thousands of Xhosas and debilitating traditional societies for generations to come.

Attempts by the British administration to reassert its authority were met by equally strong resistance from the farmers. Their feeling of alienation from the Cape was

On the eastern Cape frontier, these contacts were almost always confrontational. A shortage of land was the major cause of the trouble. Both the Xhosa and the white settlers were stock farmers, dependent on sufficient grazing. A series of devastating droughts aggravated the problems. By the 1830s it was clear that the eastern frontier region was grossly overpopulated.

The Cape government tried to restore a semblance of order by creating buffer zones

aggravated by their anger over lack of compensation for their losses. Moreover, farming activities were further restricted by a shortage of labourers and servants. The emancipation of slaves meant further financial losses, and the vagrancy of newly freed slaves added to the feeling of insecurity among the frontier population.

The vast majority of the Afrikaners were very conservative and drew strict distinctions between whites and blacks on the basis of race, social class and religion. The actions of the colonial government offended these deep-rooted convictions. They resented their lack of representation in the govern-

Above, Table Bay developed into an important replenishment station on the sea route between Europe and the Far East.

ment at the Cape and the fact that they were denied any say in the administration of their own affairs.

Much of the white resentment was focused on the activities of Protestant missionaries whose zeal for social reform clashed sharply with the ingrained conservative prejudices of the frontiersmen. Explaining their reasons to leave the colony one of the white leaders, Piet Retief, said it was a bid to get away from "dishonest persons masquerading under the cloak of religion" and "to preserve proper relations between master and servant".

By the mid-1830s the combination of these issues led a number of Afrikaner farmers to believe that there was little future for

them on the eastern frontier. Their dissatisfaction called for drastic solutions. The only remaining option was a mass emigration into the territories to the north and the northeast of the Cape Colony.

The Great Trek: The 15,000 Afrikaner men, women and children who embarked on the Great Trek faced an uncertain future in relatively uncharted territory. Exploratory expeditions had ventured into the interior but, for the most part, the wide expanses beyond the great Orange River were a daunting and unknown quantity in a land often emptied by tribal conflict.

The frontier farmer Piet Retief led one

grouping on an arduous journey with loaded ox-wagons across the trecherous Drakensberg mountain range into Natal. Accompanied by just 100 men, Retief continued on to the capital of the Zulu monarch, Dingaane, at Mgundgundhlovu. Here, agreement was reached to secede large parts of central and southern Natal to the Boer settlers.

But Dingaane's fears had been aroused. On 6 February 1838, as the trekkers were taking their leave, the Zulu king ordered them to be killed. Immediately, Zulu warriors fanned out, falling upon the unsuspecting Voortrekker settlements along the lower reaches of the Drakensberg, slaughtering 500 people and seizing more than 25,000 head of livestock. In turmoil and riven by disagreement, the Voortrekkers turned to Andries Pretorius, an eastern Cape farmer who had not undertaken the original expedition. Pretorius immediately set about reorganising the trekkers.

Finally, on 16 December 1838, the Voortrekker forces scored a clear victory against the Zulus at the Battle of Blood River. Pursuing the fleeing Zulu to their capital, they found it in ashes. Dingaane was eventually assassinated by conspirators in what is today Swaziland. The might of the proud Zulu empire built by Shaka had been broken. The Afrikaner, looking for an explanation for his victory, found it in divine intervention.

The Great Trek period between 1834 and 1840 was the seminal epoch in Afrikaner history. Romanticised by generations of Afrikaners, it shaped the constitutional thinking of successive governments. From any perspective, the Great Trek is a key event in South African history: within a short time the whole of the South African interior was opened up for European settlement and development. To this day its implications divide historians. For some, it represents resistance against British colonialism and oppression and the bringing of civilisation to the interior of a "dark continent". For others, it represents a new form of colonialism that led to the suppression of black communities and ultimate loss of their freedom.

The birth of Boer republics: After their victory, the Boers in Natal set up a new republic which proved short-lived. In 1842, British forces occupied the harbour settlement of Durban and annexed its hinterland as a crown colony. Faced with the prospect of

British administration, the Voortrekkers moved back across the Drakensberg range to join rival groups on the highveld. A final clash of arms between British and Zulu occurred nearly four decades later. The British, fearing a resurrected Zulu nation, invaded Zulu territory; in the resulting fighting, 1,200 British and colonial forces died.

The Zulu victory proved pyrrhic. At the end of the war Zulu social and economic life was disrupted and the Zulu kingdom carved into 13 chiefdoms. To this day, the province of KwaZulu/Natal remains culturally the most British part of South Africa, with still a dominant Zulu population and a sizeable Indian community which was introduced in

recognising Boer independence north of the Vaal in 1852, and south of the river in 1854. The move effectively awarded sovereignty to the two Boer republics of the Orange Free State and the Transvaal. Many Afrikaners considered the Great Trek now to be completed. South Africa was divided into a British colonial South and a predominantly Afrikaner North.

The constitutions of the newly independent states strongly emphasised popular sovereignty. The Orange Free State introduced a presidential system influenced by the American model, while the Transvaal, now the South African Republic, at one stage even insisted on a three-quarters majority

the second half of the 19th century to work in flourishing sugar plantations.

On the highveld, the independence of a sequence of Boer republics was challenged by a British law which extended British jurisdiction to the 26th south parallel. In 1848 a British invasion force annexed the entire territory between the Orange and the Vaal Rivers. A counter-offensive led by Pretorius was easily defeated at the Battle of Boomplats. Eventually, a change of government in London contributed to the British

Left, Boer leader Andries Pretorius. **Above**, Boers and Zulus were locked in a struggle for survival.

with a report-back system to constituents for every new law. Citizens' rights were restricted to white Afrikaners belonging to the Protestant faith.

Gradually, the power of neighbouring chiefdoms was eroded. Between 1840 and 1898 a series of conflicts with the Venda, Sotho, Pedi and Ndebele in the northern Transvaal and eastern Orange Free State ended in their defeat. This resulted in often large tracts of land being transferred for Boer settlement while the remaining black areas were being classified as "native reserves" which doubled up as reservoirs of labour for Boer farmers.

South Africa before the mid-19th century was a thinly populated land with limited economic resources and a small export trade in such items as wool, ivory and hides. Before 1848 there were few roads, before 1860 no substantial banks, and until 1880 almost no railway lines. Such towns as existed, apart from the ports, were either seats of magistracy like Graaff-Reinet, or meeting-places for the quarterly nachtmaal of the Dutch Reformed Church.

Diamond rush: All this changed after 1867,

when the first diamond was found north of the Orange River. Speculators from the Cape and Natal, a few Afrikaner farmers, and local Griqua and Tlhaping tribesmen sought to benefit from the river diggings on the Vaal and the dry diggings that soon turned into the vast prospectors' camp of Kimberley. The region became a bone of contention among the British, Free State and Transvaal governments because of its strategic position. That problem was resolved, amid much controversy, by an arbitration court which ordered the proclamation of the diamond fields as the crown colony of Griqualand West.

Successful diamond mining depended on the ability of the claim-holders to control marketing, and this necessity led between 1870 and 1888 to a step-by-step amalgamation of individual claims, which was made more urgent as the mines went deeper and the work became more expensive. Cecil John Rhodes's De Beers Company eventually emerged as the pre-eminent mining house, a position it still holds.

The Kimberley mines drew in the skills of well-paid immigrants and the manual labour of low-paid Africans. The latter were recruited on contract by labour touts in collusion with chiefs, who in turn required payment of their subjects in firearms as well as other goods. The black miners were in due course housed in compounds under strict control, and subjected to close body searches to prevent diamond smuggling. The white diggers won exemption from these searches. Thus there developed a pattern of labour differentiation and control which would set a precedent for much of the industrial life of South Africa in later years.

With the birth of Kimberley, industrial South Africa came into being. It provided an urban market for foodstuffs, at first supplied largely by African farmers. Kimberley's needs also set in motion the railway age.

Gold fever: Gold, like diamonds, had been discovered in 1867, at Tati on the Transvaal border of Bechuanaland, and subsequently in various parts of the eastern Transvaal from 1874. But it was only with the location of the main reef on the Witwatersrand in 1886 that South African gold mining began in earnest. Kimberley supplied the entrepreneurs, the initial capital and some of the expertise to set Rand mining going. But the monopoly conditions necessary for diamond mining did not develop on the Rand.

The Chamber of Mines, established in 1887, went some way to regulate the competition, above all by ensuring that labour was made extremely cheap, and housed in compounds as a control device. But by 1890 the Chamber found itself in opposition to Paul Kruger's republican government for both political and economic reasons.

The government resented the intrusion of foreigners (uitlanders), especially when they demanded political rights, which it was reluctant to grant. It sought to profit from gold mining but drove up production costs by, among other means, the inefficient taxing of explosives. By 1895 it was becoming clear to governments in Europe that the Transvaal had become a focal point of power, just at a moment when the international partition of Africa was moving towards a climax.

The imperial factor: The European occupation of southern Africa was a double process. On the one hand, there was the physical access to labour. (The choice territory was generally land already occupied, with a potential labour supply to hand.) This process had been completed by the end of the 19th century, when nearly all land in southern Africa was either owned by whites with surveyed titles, or at the disposal of governments, or occupied by blacks under traditional forms of communal tenure.

The first phase of the Anglo-Boer conflict over territory, which developed after the recognition of republican sovereignty by

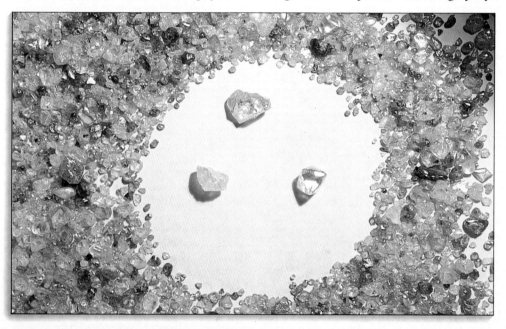

Left, a miner's life. Above, diamonds are forever.

appropriation of the greater part of the land by white colonists as they carved out farms and worked the mineral deposits they had acquired through victory in frontier wars. On the other, there was a contest between Great Britain as the paramount power in the region and the Boer republics for the political control of territory. These parallel movements can be helpfully distinguished.

The occupation of land was promoted by the fact that commandos sent against resisting chiefdoms received their rewards not in wages but in the form of land, cattle and

Britain, was a dispute between Britain and the Free State over the control of Basutoland (Lesotho) and the Diamond Fields. Both territories passed under British control, both were later transferred to the Cape Colony, but Basutoland was made a British protectorate in 1884, as were Bechuanaland (Botswana) in 1885 and Swaziland in 1902.

From 1868 it became a stated objective of British policy to amalgamate the South African territories politically for reasons of defence and economy. In 1875 Disraeli's Colonial Secretary, Lord Carnarvon, sought to do this, but he forced the pace, and failed to win the backing of the Cape government. He had, however, annexed the Transvaal by an adroit move designed to put pressure on the Free State. The annexation proved a fiasco, partly because of poor administration, partly because the Afrikaner leadership under Paul Kruger organised a successful rebellion in 1880–81 and persuaded Gladstone that it would be wise to withdraw. Conventions signed in 1881 and 1884 restored the Transvaal's independence on terms which gave Britain, at best, an ambiguous right to intervene in its affairs.

When gold mining was developed on the Witwatersrand, it became apparent that the economic balance had shifted to the north, and that whoever ruled the Transvaal would

dominate South Africa. Deep-level mining on the Rand produced only narrow profit margins, owing partly to Kruger's fiscal policy, and this created at least a temptation to overthrow his government.

Cecil Rhodes, prime minister of the Cape from 1890 to 1896, had already unsuccessfully attempted to incorporate the Transvaal in a South African railway and customs union, and then to encircle the republic by purchasing Lourenço Marques (Maputo) from the Portuguese. In 1895 he plotted a rebellion on the Rand to be assisted by an invasion by his British South Africa Company forces from across the border. But the

Jameson Raid, planned with the knowledge of the British Government, also failed, and seriously undermined Kruger's willingness to trust the British. Rhodes was discredited and resigned.

The Anglo-Boer War: In a sustained diplomatic face-off in 1899, the British drove Kruger to the brink of war by insisting on the full recognition of uitlander rights. Kruger yielded ground to the point at which his pride could yield no more, and anticipated a British ultimatum by invading the coastal colonies in October.

The Anglo-Boer War of 1899–1902 at first went well for the Boers, who scored major victories against a heavily equipped, well-trained enemy. Only when the main British forces arrived were they able to invade the allied republics, occupying Bloemfontein and Pretoria by June 1900. However, the war lasted two more years on account of successful Boer guerrilla tactics.

The conflict had a profound effect on the moulding of South African political attitudes. To start with, it was the first major conflict in South Africa between whites. The Afrikaner people suffered physically as well as in loss of dignity from the effects of the guerrilla war, through destruction of their homes and villages and their sufferings from sickness in the concentration camps, in which the mortality rate was high. Close on 28,000 Boers, the vast majority of them women and children, died from disease and lack of sanitary conditions.

Latter-day Afrikaner nationalism was born out of a determination to survive as a people. The myth that it was a "white man's war" which didn't affect blacks has little historical evidence to support it: blacks were recruited as labourers and scouts by both sides, though the Boers were more reluctant than the British to give them arms.

Blacks also suffered directly and in large numbers during the sieges and from the destruction of farms, as well as from living in concentration camps where more than 14,000 died. But their hardships went relatively unnoticed in the published accounts, and, when the war was over and the peace treaty signed, they had little to expect for their sufferings.

<u>Left</u>, **the Boers kept the British Empire at bay for three years.**

KRUGER AND RHODES

The Transvaal Boers were hardened pioneers, and none more so than their leader, Paul Kruger. In his youth he was known for his strength and marksmanship; in maturity for his rigid Calvinism and common-sense wisdom.

Kruger was of pure Voortrekker stock. As a young boy he accompanied the Potgieter trek that quarrelled so much with the other groups and eventually broke away from the mainstream to settle in the Western Transvaal. He earned his spurs during the battle of Vegkop where Mzilikazi's Ndebele warriors flung themselves against a Voortrekker laager in a desperate fight for control of the land. Towards the end of an eventful life, he was elected president of the Transvaal in 1883. Fiercely proud of the independence of his people and a Calvinist to the core, he saw a parallel between the history of the Boers and that of the Israelites of old. This view appealed to his followers and was to prevail for decades among their offspring in the emergence of Afrikaner nationalism.

It fell to Kruger to defend his land against the avarice of British imperialists wishing to add the gold-rich Transvaal to the laurels of their Empire. Biding his time, he staved off the grabbing hands of Cecil John Rhodes but eventually lost the game of war played with "devilish refinement" by the arch-imperialists in London. Realising that both the honour and the independence of his people were at stake, Kruger declared war on Great Britain on 11 October 1899. He rejoiced in the initial victories of the Boer army, but for his own safety had to go abroad, where he had a hero's welcome throughout the European continent.

In the meantime, his people fought with great valour. For more than three years small groups of Boer cavalrymen led by legendary leaders such as Christiaan de Wet and Koos de la Rey launched guerrilla-style attacks against the British lines.

In voluntary exile, Kruger, the "Wounded Lion" (as he was drawn by a French caricaturist), followed the war to the final surrender of the Boer forces in 1902. Refusing to submit to British rule he remained in exile and on 14 July 1904 died in Clarens, Switzerland, whence his remains were returned for interment in Pretoria.

If ever there was a bête noire almost custom-made for Kruger, it was Cecil John Rhodes –

Right, Paul Kruger, the "Wounded Lion".

"deputy God… deputy Satan", as he was dubbed by Mark Twain. A century ago he stood at the pinnacle of his power as diamond king, politician-statesman, British Empire-builder and international figure. Lionised and caricatured by the world press, he was a legend to people living as far apart as the Boers of Transvaal and peasants in the most remote corners of Imperial Russia.

The son of an English parish priest, he came to South Africa on his own in 1870, at the age of 17. Although sickly and living the life of a gypsy, he gained control of the diamond industry in Kimberley and added to his fortune from gold.

As prime minister of the Cape Colony, he used intrigue and war to grab the land of the

Matabele and Shona north of the Limpopo and established under Royal Charter his personal states of Northern and Southern Rhodesia (now Zambia and Zimbabwe). He also schemed with the German Kaiser to build a railroad from the Cape to Cairo. He was a British imperialist par excellence who, in his attempts to subvert the Transvaal to British rule, hatched the abortive Jameson Raid and so caused his own downfall. He fought back and, but for the Anglo-Boer War and his death in 1902, he might have regained the premiership of the Cape. He was an exceptional personality who thought himself omnipotent and died, in the words of his biographer, Robert Rotberg, "both genius and rogue". ■

The Peace of Vereeniging registered the victory of the Empire over the Boers shortly after the achievement of white domination. The 20th century would witness a speedy Afrikaner return to power and, after 90 years of assertive white dominance, at least the start of an impressive black resurgence.

Britain annexed the former republics in 1902, but made it possible for them to regain autonomy. This was largely the achievement of Generals Louis Botha and Jan Smuts, who saw the need for conciliation among whites – between Empire and Boer, Boer and English speaker, and rival groups within Afrikanerdom – but left the problem of dealing with blacks to the "stronger shoulders" of the future. The British government thought that extending the vote to blacks would jeopardise their aim of conciliating the whites.

Meanwhile, black political organisations watched resentfully as Britain first allowed the Transvaal and Orange River Colony to acquire white-controlled constitutions in 1907–08, and then agreed after the National Convention of 1908–09 to a constitution for a united South Africa which did substantially the same thing.

Britain aimed to restore the South African economy by bringing the mines back into production and resettling the uprooted on the land, and thus to coax the Afrikaner back into the imperial fold. Black labour might be essential for this task but not black voters. Reconstruction therefore happened, conciliation among whites began to work, and the Union of South Africa took its place with the other white dominions in the British Commonwealth of Nations.

As a member of that imperial system, South Africa took part in two world wars and played a leading role in the evolution of dominion autonomy between 1917 and 1934. The involvement of prime ministers Louis Botha, Jan Smuts and Barry Hertzog in the consultations of the Empire were themselves an indication of how well conciliation had worked. But it operated only on the surface, and could not contain the groundswell of opposition underneath.

The Union of South Africa in 1910 was an embryonic industrial state, with mineral exports (especially gold) far exceeding agricultural and with a developing manufacturing industry producing mainly for the local market. These years also witnessed a parallel townward movement by both Afrikaans- and Bantu-speaking people.

Resurgence of Afrikaner power: Afrikaner republicanism was reborn soon after union, on a platform of opposition to the imperial connection and a demand for the effective recognition of Afrikaans language rights. The former found expression in the rebellion of 1914, triggered by the government's decision to invade German South West Africa, while the founding of the secretive Afrikaner Broederbond in 1918 led to a spread of Afrikaner cultural and economic organisations, the latter with a focus on the rescue of poor whites. Both found a political mouthpiece in the National Party governments of General Barry Hertzog between 1924 and 1939: first in alliance with the white Labour Party and after 1932 in alliance with General Smuts (until their fused United Party was split asunder when Hertzog tried to keep South Africa neutral in World War II).

Hertzog's strident nationalism was toned down once he had seen that South Africa could remain within the British Commonwealth without the rights of the Afrikaner necessarily being threatened. But this wasn't the view of a new "purified" National Party which started to grow since 1934 under the leadership of Dr D. F. Malan.

Malan's party, the voice no longer simply of the poor whites but also of a new brand of Afrikaner entrepreneur out for economic power, won the 1948 election and remained in power without a break ever since, until the first democratic elections for all South Africans in April 1994. Until then Afrikaner voters, some of whom had been attracted to Leninism in their poverty of the 1920s, had entrenched themselves not only on the land but also in the civil service and the professions, and more recently in business too. English speakers, by contrast, remained politically marginal, though their hold in the business world remained strong.

South African politics have never been a simple confrontation between two rival elements. The "Coloured" people, forced by white man's laws to accept a distinctive ethnicity which many of them disown, had been prevented by paucity of numbers from exercising more than a marginal influence on public affairs.

Roots of black opposition: But the main catalyst for change, which gradually came to monopolise the attention of the white political establishment, was the numerical growth and townward movement of black Africans. A small minority in all urban areas at the time

1913 and 1936. Thus tied down, Africans found it hard to organise effectively to promote political or economic change.

It appeared briefly during World War II that the segregationist policies might wither away under the ideological pressures generated by the Atlantic Charter. The wartime government of General Smuts tried to ameliorate the conditions of urban Africans, ceased briefly to enforce the pass laws, began to build African secondary schools, made a start with African pensions and dis-

of union, Africans were in the majority in nearly all by mid-century, though required nearly everywhere to reside in "locations" away from the towns proper.

Africans were also effectively debarred by law from political and trade union activities, and controlled in their movements by pass laws. This ensured that many could not move from white-owned farms to towns. The majority, who remained in the tribal reserves, were also prohibited by law from acquiring land outside the reserves by the Land Acts of

ability benefits, and professed its rejection of the principle of segregation. But, in the run-up to the general elections of 1943 and 1948, the Smuts government could not contain the rising propaganda of the National Party.

Smuts's failure to initiate a change of direction led to a major confrontation with the African Mineworkers' Union in 1946, in which lives were lost. This broke African trust in Smuts. His government's attempts at policy changes, on the eve of the 1948 election, were neither sweeping enough to attract African backing nor cautious enough to prevent the white electorate from casting their votes decisively for Malan.

Above, Jan Smuts (left) and Barry Herzog dominated politics in the early 20th century.

The National Party headed by Dr Daniel François Malan, a preacher and journalist before he became a politician, won the 1948 general election against expectations and by a narrow margin. The bulk of their support came from recently urbanised whites who feared the challenge of blacks in the marketplace, especially as the African National Congress (ANC), in association with the African Mineworkers' Union, showed signs of growth during the 1940s.

The new government's response was to

bring out a legislative programme designed to entrench white (and by implication Afrikaner) dominance. The principles of apartheid (separateness) dominated the government's legislative programme from the start. It enacted a Population Registration Act to slot everybody into an appropriate race group, as well as to outlaw inter-racial matrimony or sexual relations, and a Group Areas Act to divide every town in South Africa into defined sectors where only members of particular groups could own or occupy property. This required the physical removal of many Coloured and Asian households, but few whites. Most resented of all were the

"pass laws" which restricted the movements of blacks. The legislation was buttressed by a series of laws designed to undercut political resistance, beginning with the Suppression of Communism Act. It was followed by measures which would restrict individuals and organisations, while denying them right of appeal to the courts.

After Dr Henrik Frensch Verwoerd, a chief promoter of apartheid legislation, became prime minister in 1958, the policy was developed to promote territorial partition so that the African reserves could be turned into "independent homelands" whose citizens could on that pretext be deprived of access to political rights in the South African heartland. Verwoerd tried to establish border industries to enable blacks living in the homelands to find employment in "white" South Africa with minimal daily travel; but he would not allow white capital to finance such development.

His successor, Balthazar Johannes Vorster, a lawyer and staunch supporter of traditional Boer principles, removed this restriction; but the policy was poorly conceived, and by 1970 it was clear that job creation in the homelands fell far short of providing a living for the number of Africans required by government policy to live there.

Growing black resistance: Such policies strengthened support for the ANC. The oldest existing political party in the country, it had formed for six decades the vanguard of black political aspirations. It was in January 1912 that representatives of the country's major African organisations met in Bloemfontein to form the Native National Congress. The movement, soon renamed African National Congress, had its agenda cut out. Two years earlier the Union of South Africa had been forged out of the ashes of the Boer-Brit struggle, but had ignored the position of the vast majority of the country's citizens.

The ANC spent its first years protesting the historical errors committed at Union. But its critics accused it of being an organisation of elderly men fighting to preserve their hard-won, middle-class privileges. Impatient activists joined the fledgling labour movements that advocated more radical action. In

1943 the ANC Youth League was formed by a group of young men whose political legacy is still being felt: the brilliant Anton Lembede, Oliver Tambo, Walter Sisulu and an enigmatic young lawyer, Nelson Mandela. They were soon strong enough to stage an internal coup and to get their candidate, Dr James Moroka, elected president. This marked the beginning of a new strategy of direct, non-violent confrontation with the government. A campaign against the pass laws during the war eventually led to the launching of a

trials" which marked the next 35 years.

The defendants were all found innocent in 1961, but in the meantime divisions opened up within the ANC. A group of "Africanists" led by Robert Sobukwe were disturbed by communist influences on ANC policy, arguing that if a racist government was in power the assertion of African nationalism was the real note to strike. They were driven out of the ANC in 1958, and broke away to form the Pan-Africanist Congress (PAC).

When the government launched its cam-

Defiance Campaign in 1952, a well-orchestrated passive resistance tactic by African, Asian and Coloured movements to offset the white tercentenary celebrations. Its forceful suppression led to the public adoption of a Freedom Charter at Klipfontein, near Johannesburg, in 1955 – a broad social democratic affirmation designed to achieve wide public support. Documents confiscated by the police when they broke up the gathering formed the basis for the first of a number of "treason

paign for a republic in 1960, the ANC and PAC were at daggers drawn, yet both were angling for mass support by promoting anti-pass demonstrations linked to wage demands. Some 30,000 Africans marched on the Houses of Parliament in Cape Town. Police bullets killed 67 protesters at Sharpeville, near Vereeniging on the south Rand, on 21 March, and the government, clearly frightened, banned both the PAC and the ANC, driving them underground. The world condemned the Sharpeville shootings, and the ostracisation of South Africa in world affairs began.

White responses: In a whites-only referendum, Dr Verwoerd obtained a narrow vic-

Left, Hendrik Verwoerd masterminded the 1960s Homeland Policy. **Above**, Sharpeville 1961: police bullets killed 67 people.

tory to proclaim a republic and his government subsequently decided to leave the British Commonwealth. Sharpeville had shown the inadequacy of passive resistance and drove the African resistance movements into violent opposition. In 1963, however, the police captured the underground leaders of the ANC, headed by Nelson Mandela, in Rivonia, outside Johannesburg, as they were planning to disrupt public life. After an eight-month trial, they received life sentences in the notorious Robben Island prison.

The ANC and the PAC set up bases in exile in Lusaka, Dar-es-Salaam and London, but they found it difficult to make much impact locally or internationally. For almost 10 years

the South African government managed to keep a lid on black political activity. Activists were rounded up and held under "90 Days" detention without trial. Some died in police custody. It seemed as if the back of black resistance had been broken.

In September 1966, Hendrik Verwoerd was stabbed to death in the House of Assembly by a parliamentary messenger. His amazing self-confidence was immediately missed. His successor, B. J. Vorster, was better at silencing opposition than developing strategies for change. But, when capital started to flow back into South Africa, he tried to revive the socio-economic aspects of the apartheid programme. Investment corporations were set up to develop the homelands. The expansion of black businesses, black housing, black schools and black immigration into the white area was made harder.

By 1970 the number of jobs created in the homelands was seen to be nowhere near that required if Africans were to be able to "flow back" from the white areas. The government decided to press ahead with homeland "independence", starting with the Transkei in 1976. The aim was to create alternative allegiances, thus depriving all citizens of "independent" homelands of their South African citizenship even if they still lived in the Republic.

The tide turns: On a cold winter's day, 16 June 1976, Soweto, the large African residential location outside Johannesburg, erupted after a government decision to enforce the use of Afrikaans as a language medium in schools, though the grievances were far wider and included objections to homeland independence. Much of the drive came from a new Black Consciousness Movement led by Steve Biko, an activist from the Eastern Cape.

Over a period of 18 months the burning of public buildings, schools, liquor outlets and motor vehicles had most of the African townships in flames and the conflagration soon also spread into Coloured and Indian residential areas. The government again clamped down heavily. On 18 August 1977, Biko was arrested by the security police. Twenty-six days later he was dead from massive head injuries sustained during interrogation.

Black consciousness was too well-rooted to be effectively extinguished; it re-emerged in other forms, linking Africanist aspirations to a socialist ideal. Many young activists fled the country, joining the waiting structures of the ANC in exile. This influx of new blood rejuvenated and strengthened the movement considerably. Led by Oliver Tambo, the ANC redoubled its onslaught against the government on two fronts: the military, where they achieved moderate successes with sabotage attacks on certain strategic installations; and international isolation, where they continuously pushed for strong punitive measures – economic sanctions, arms embargoes and cultural and sporting boycotts.

Internally, black opposition re-emerged in the formation of the United Democratic Front (UDF) – a loose federation of anti-apartheid movements, linked ideologically to the ANC. A new generation of black leadership – "the '76-generation" – came to the fore. When they were restricted, trade unions became a focal point of political activity, leading to the ·creation of the giant Congress of South African Trade Unions (COSATU). Church leaders emerged as vocal spokesmen for black aspirations, with men like Archbishop Desmond Tutu and Dr Allan Boesak becoming household names across the world. Tutu became the second South African to win the Nobel prize for peace (the first having been Albert Luthuli, a Natal teacher who had become leader of the ANC in the 1950s and was awarded the prize in 1960). More "moderate" leaders and movements also began to emerge. Some, like Chief Mangosuthu Buthelezi and his Inkatha Freedom Party and Enos Mabuza of the Kangwane-homeland, fought apartheid from "within the system".

World opinion: In the 1960s and '70s, Vorster's government had offended world opinion by refusing to support sanctions against the white rulers of Rhodesia, and by holding out against the transfer of power in South West Africa (present-day Namibia), in a running dispute with the United Nations which had started soon after World War II. Talk of international sanctions, beginning with an arms embargo in 1963, was spreading to include economic and cultural boycotts. Almost the whole world condemned the Republic's policies.

Vorster's government fell after disclosures of serious financial mismanagement in the running of its propaganda activities. The scandal divided the ruling National Party and propelled the Defence Minister, Pieter Willem Botha, to the premiership. Botha restored effective control over government. He also tried to rebuild the economy, which went into deep recession from 1982 as a result of a sustained drought and a dramatic

fall in the gold price, aggravated by a move among the world's banks to impose a stranglehold on South Africa's borrowing.

Far from trying to abolish apartheid, Botha attempted in 1983 to make it irremovable. He secured white electoral support for a new constitution which not only made him an executive president (as distinct from the largely formal office created in 1961) but also created ethnically distinct houses of parliament for whites, Coloured people and Indians, with no representation for Africans.

This led to renewed violence in the new Coloured and Indian constituencies when a general election was held in 1983. By then,

Left, Soweto, 1976. **Above,** violence swept through the townships for nearly two decades.

the ability of black organisations to conduct effective resistance had markedly increased as industrial workers and resistance leaders in the townships began to act together.

African trade unions, after more than 60 years of suppression under hostile laws, matured between 1973 (when successful strikes were organised in Natal) and 1991, by which time they had been fully legalised in successive stages.

Several large industrial federations, of which the Congress of South African Trade Unions was the most prominent, came into being. COSATU worked in close association with a new National Union of Mineworkers, which had acquired considerable experience

in negotiations with the Chamber of Mines.

A United Democratic Front consisting of representatives of over 600 movements of various kinds, emerged in 1985, and maintained a loose relationship outside South Africa with the ANC. The ANC, for its part, was now concentrating on building up its links with the international community, setting up missions in many parts of the world where the South African government was not represented, even acquiring diplomatic recognition in some.

Furthermore, the homeland structures, Verwoerd's brainchild, were beginning to collapse as "independent" states – in some instances through the exposure of corruption, in others through the overthrow of ruling dynasties – ground to a standstill. In Natal, even though KwaZulu's Inkatha movement had opposed independence, something like open warfare developed between Inkatha and ANC supporters as each side attempted to build up its constituency in anticipation of an eventual redistribution of political power.

Paralysed by a manifest inability to keep his economic and constitutional policies on course and in the face of a growing threat from a new Afrikaner right wing, P. W. Botha was forced out of office by a ministerial rebellion in September 1989. The future direction of the National Party was thus thrown into confusion on the eve of a general election which had been forced upon it by a deadlock with the Coloured House of Representatives arising out of the terms of the 1983 constitution.

Apartheid in reverse: Botha's mantle fell on the shoulders of the Transvaal leader of the National Party, Frederik Willem de Klerk, who won the 1989 white general election by an outright majority over opponents of both left and right after seeking a mandate for unspecified reform. Educated and confident, de Klerk was an example of a new generation of Afrikaners who came of age after the introduction of apartheid and began to question the very basis of the system they inherited from their ancestors.

Because he was known to be a supporter of narrow, white "group interests", many doubted his will to go for real change. But South Africa could no longer afford to maintain apartheid in an increasingly hostile world, with a weakened economy, and with a ruinously expensive war which had broken out on the South West African border against members of the South West African People's Organisation (SWAPO).

Opening the parliamentary session of 1990, de Klerk undertook to remove apartheid, promising sweeping reforms. He planned to move cautiously, consulting the ANC leadership step by step. On 11 February he unconditionally released Nelson Mandela, the last of the imprisoned ANC leaders, after he had served 27 years in jail. It was a momentous decision because it signalled to a world which had long regarded Mandela's imprisonment as a symbol of apartheid's evil that a milestone had been passed. Six weeks later de

Klerk removed another source of international protest: he attended the independence celebrations as South West Africa became Namibia, ending a deadlock that had lasted more than 40 years.

De Klerk found a willing negotiating partner in the pragmatic Mandela. Opening the South African Parliament in February 1990, he declared the government's willingness to negotiate a new constitution with equal political rights for all. The ban on political opponents was lifted and the leaders of the liberation movements released from jail or allowed to return from exile. Yet a groundswell of public violence was a constant reminder that the transition would not be easy.

Violence between rival African movements reached new levels of intensity, especially in Natal, where the conflict between Inkatha and the ANC/COSATU became endemic. In February 1991 a much publicised agreement between Mandela and Inkatha's Mangosuthu Buthelezi was immediately followed by further loss of life, although the ANC was now working much harder to patch up its differences with rival movements, including the PAC.

Much of the violence arose out of disputes related to local government, for the ANC-supported "civic" movement fought to discredit, and in some instances physically attacked, black councillors elected under the

The continued absence of substantial changes in the law gave the ANC a reason for not disbanding its military wing, Umkhonto we Sizwe (Spear of the Nation), so as to retain the possibility of resuming the armed struggle. De Klerk also failed to fulfil an undertaking to expose the activities of "hit squads" in the army and the police force, which had allegedly committed a number of unsolved political murders over the years.

Left, the unlikely architects of a revolution, F. W. de Klerk and Nelson Mandela. **Above**, a first-time voter proudly displays proof of her newly won democratic rights.

unpopular local government legislation of 1983. Nor would the ANC abandon its demand for continuing international sanctions before changes in the law had made the removal of apartheid irreversible – even though their opponents argued that the South African economy could not possibly recover without a greater foreign investment in view of the high growth of the population.

The negotiating process became tangible through the creation of a multi-party forum, named the Convention for a Democratic South Africa (Codessa). But right-wing resistance to de Klerk's moves increased and the Conservative Party opposition won a number of important by-elections. In a bold move, de Klerk called a whites-only referendum in March 1992 to obtain a new mandate for his political reforms. More than two-thirds of white voters endorsed his programme for the "New South Africa".

The odd couple: Hopes for the country's future centred to a remarkable degree around de Klerk and Mandela – a fact the outside world recognised by awarding them jointly the 1993 Nobel Peace Prize. But could de Klerk neutralise groups such as the Afrikaner Resistance Movement, who still referred to the ANC as "the AntiChrist"? And could Mandela reconcile the ethnic rivalries cemented by centuries of violence?

the country's voters. White intellectuals began to question whether South Africa was simply exchanging the tyranny of apartheid for the tyranny of authoritarian ANC rule. The Zulus, worried by the ANC's Xhosa leadership and by its socialist leanings, demanded an independent Zulu state or at least a meaningful degree of federal power. The Zulu leader, Chief Mangosuthu Buthelezi, said the Inkatha Freedom Party would not participate in the elections, and for a while it looked as if the poll in Natal might have to be postponed until a future date.

Just a week before the election, Inkatha agreed to take part, and millions of party logos had to be stuck to the already printed

Mandela called his election manifesto *A Better Life for All*. It promised 10 years of free education for all children, a million new homes, and a public works programme to provide jobs for 2½ million people. These were extravagant and unrealistic promises, said de Klerk, who realised better than most that there had been little significant investment in the country's infrastructure for years and that the annual 6 percent growth of the 1960s had turned into negative growth by the early 1990s.

As a three-month election campaign began early in 1994, it was clear that there were perilously few shared assumptions among

ballot papers. With an illiteracy rate approaching 50 percent among the 16 million black voters, it was important that the ballot papers, printed in 11 official languages, should also contain the logo of each party and a picture of its leader.

The three-day election was described by one official as "unmitigated chaos". Many ballot papers went missing. Fraud and malpractice were prevalent. But the wonder was that such an event was happening at all. People who had never seen a ballot paper queued for hours under a hot sun to cast their vote. Old women, some more than 100, were pushed in their wheelchairs to the booths.

White women lined up alongside their maids. Archbishop Desmond Tutu danced a jig for the cameras after voting in Cape Town. A Johannesburg radio station played Louis Armstrong's *What a Wonderful World*. After 342 years and 23 days, white rule had come to an end.

Despite the allegations of chicanery, the election had to be declared free and fair. The ANC emerged with 62 percent of the vote. This fell short of the 66 percent which would have allowed them unilaterally to rewrite the constitution, but it was still a respectable result. On 9 May 1994, Nelson Mandela, former prisoner 466/64, was elected president of the Republic of South Africa. F. W.

of government make the transition from rhetoric to effective reconstruction? He was at least assured of a honeymoon period and for a while it seemed almost unpatriotic to criticise him. After all, he had sacrificed 27 years of his life for his people and his generosity of spirit was admired throughout the world. But the government of national unity's first year seemed one of gentle drift, with ministers appearing to make decisions largely without reference to their cabinet colleagues. A debate over the extent to which a Truth Commission should identify and punish "war criminals" of the apartheid era led to the first visible rift between Mandela and de Klerk.

The big question was how long the black

de Klerk became one of two vice-presidents.

In one sense, the problems were only beginning. Capital had continued to flow out of the country, promised foreign investment failed to materialise, inflation was in double figures, more than half the black workforce was unemployed, allegations of corruption became more insistent, and crime and drug syndicates were increasing their power. Could a 75-year-old president with no experience

Left, in the historic 1994 election, people queued for hours under a blazing sun to get to the voting booths. **Above**, the long-awaited taste of victory for Nelson Mandela.

majority would wait for the president to make good his promises to improve their economic well-being. "The wheels of government grind slowly," said Mandela.

But at least they *were* grinding, and the transition to black majority rule, an event which only a few years before had seemed as improbable as the break-up of the Soviet Union, had been achieved without the predicted bloodbath. What's more, the South Africans, white and black, had in the end accomplished the miracle themselves, without the intervention of international tribunals or peace-keeping forces. Hope, although still fragile, began to bloom again.

Modern-day South Africa has often been called the laboratory of mankind: a country scarred by the policy of apartheid but also a place where all races on earth are represented and live cheek by jowl; a country where colonial cultures did not suppress the indigenous African cultures – turning the country into a melting-pot and forcing South Africans from various backgrounds to experiment with new forms of living together.

More nations, speaking more languages, and representing more racial groups, live within the borders of South Africa than in the notoriously politically unstable Balkan peninsula or the former Soviet Union. South Africans may lack a common heritage, identity or language, but the fact that the large majority regard themselves as Christians supplies a degree of shared values. They also share a common future – a realisation which has only lately begun to emerge, but has been powerful enough to initiate and sustain a process of political negotiation which led to common political structures for all.

Although 70 percent of South Africa's inhabitants are black, they represent various ethnic and language groups. So the country is often called a country of minorities. The most pressing problem was to establish a constitution which guarantees equal opportunities and the vote to all, but also safeguards the language and cultural rights of minorities. Whites feel threatened by the numerically more powerful black groups; but small black groups also feel threatened by larger groups – such as the Zulus, the Xhosas and the Afrikaners. Because the various groups live in such close proximity, a classical federal option, based on geographical separation, may not be feasible.

The tavern of the oceans: During the European Renaissance and ensuing voyages of discovery, South Africa became strategically important as a halfway station between Europe and the Far East. That made the Cape of Good Hope the ideal place for establishing

a victualling port, to supply the merchant fleets with fresh meat and vegetables at a time when scurvy was a dreaded scourge.

From this humble beginning, modern South Africa developed, especially after the Eighty Years' War between Spain and the people of the Low Lands, and later the Thirty Years' War in Germany, forced many Europeans to seek a new start in Africa. Later their ranks were swelled by Huguenots from France. Today Protestantism of the Calvinist variety is still the dominant religion.

South Africa's oldest city, Cape Town, has long been known as the "tavern of the oceans". And indeed, the country's position midway between the Orient and the Occident made it an ideal meeting-place for peoples and ideas from both hemispheres. Apart from an African population, whose ancestry goes back to the Great Lakes of Africa, there is a strong community of people of European descent, priding themselves that their history has made them just as "indigenous" as their black compatriots.

Although South Africans are supposed to be notoriously race-conscious, history proves that at various stages races mixed

Preceding pages: Sun City; downtown Durban; baptism in the Indian Ocean; Cape Town Coon Carnival. Left, Northern Cape farmer. Right, service with a smile.

freely. The blood of the ancient San (Bushman) flows in the veins of many black people, just as the blood of the Khoi (or Hottentot) and various races from the Orient flows in the veins of modern Afrikaners.

Afrikaans: It was inevitable that the small colony established in 1652 should soon spill over the Hottentots-Holland Mountains, its natural border. Settlers who left the Cape became nomadic cattle farmers and hunters. Under these extreme circumstances, a new language, called Afrikaans, was born out of the Dutch language of medieval Flanders and other European, African and Oriental additions. Contact with the new, strange land and its strange inhabitants gave birth to a

surprisingly "streamlined" Germanic language which, like English, rid itself of most of its declensions.

The new colonists soon called themselves Afrikaners. Their struggle for survival and a cultural identity shaped the course of South Africa's history for over 300 years. Afrikaners were the country's dominant political group, until April 1994. Afrikaans was, with English, recognised as one of the country's two official languages in 1923. It is the mother tongue of 5 million people and is daily used by 14 million. More than half of all whose mother tongue is Afrikaans are black or brown.

Afrikaans is the only language to arise out of the European colonial period and is still the only indigenous African language used for higher educational purposes. Although Afrikaans literature is little over a century old, it has already produced writers of international repute, such as the poets N. P. van Wyk Louw, Elizabeth Eybers and Breyten Breytenbach, and the novelists André P. Brink and Etienne Leroux.

Afrikaners are fiercely independent and much of their politics has revolved around national and cultural independence. The cattle farmers trekking across the interior over a period of a century and a half founded various independent republics which brought them more than once into conflict with a British Empire set on expanding its global influence. This led to two wars of independence, of which the second, the so-called Boer War, lasted from 1899 to 1902. The legacy of this war was racial bitterness between Afrikaners and English speakers, which lasted for more than half a century. Gradually, however, the two groups learned to accommodate each other.

The black tribes: Archaeological evidence suggests that black tribes inhabited parts of South Africa as far back as 2,000 years ago. However, the first contact between white cattle farmers and their black counterparts took place in the 18th century near the Fish River in the Eastern Cape Province. A series of bloody border wars ensued. The Xhosa-speaking tribes were the vanguard of a migration movement that started somewhere in Central Africa.

In contrast to black nations north of the Equator, who belong mainly to the Negro group of languages, these tribes are Bantu-speaking. They belong to two principal language families, the Nguni languages, comprising Zulu and Xhosa, and the Sotho languages, spoken mainly in the central part of South Africa. Zulu and Xhosa are South Africa's two largest language groups, closely followed by Afrikaans. Ten major black languages are spoken in South Africa, and the country's new constitution makers have been trying hard to find a practical way of recognising 11 official languages.

Of all the black tribes, the Zulus were militarily the most active. Their ambitious king, Shaka, succeeded in uniting the various Zulu tribes into one nation. He organised them along military lines, much like the Spartans in Greece, and created a war machine unequalled in the history of southern Africa. The Zulu king's military manoeuvres laid waste and decimated the local population in some parts of the South African interior, which enabled the white cattle farmers during the "Great Trek" to settle in large parts of the interior and to subjugate the black tribes.

The rivalry between Afrikaners and black tribes for living space was a principal reason for the system of apartheid or racial separation, which became official government policy in 1948. Only half a century later, in 1990, was impetus given to its abolition.

groupings about the creation of a new constitutional dispensation.

A process of rapid and continuous urbanisation has placed a tremendous burden on South African urban structures, with job opportunities and housing in short supply. South Africans, proud of their affluent cities, have only recently accepted the fact that "informal settlements", or squatter camps, will for a long time be part of the urban scene.

Education for blacks is still one of the most urgent issues facing South Africa but here, too, significant progress is being made. Already, there are annually more black children graduating from high school than there are matriculants of all other races combined.

Early trekkers into the interior often compared themselves with the tribes of Israel who migrated to a land populated by "heathens" with whom they were not allowed to integrate. The presence of the numerically superior black groups was interpreted as a threat to the Afrikaner's existence.

At the start of the 1990s, President F.W. de Klerk, took the bold and unexpected step of declaring apartheid a "failure", abolishing racial segregation and initiating negotiations with the country's major black political

Left, the Indian community is the largest outside South Africa. **Above**, arriving together.

The English: The Napoleonic wars in Europe altered the course of South Africa's history and brought new people and a new language to the country. In order to safeguard its interests, Britain took possession of the Cape towards the end of the 18th century. This prompted a large scale migration movement and the new arrivals were mostly settled in the Eastern Cape. Whereas Afrikaners were mostly stock farmers and hunters, the new immigrants included merchants and artisans. With the discovery of diamonds and gold, the English speakers were well equipped to develop the fledgling mining industry. Even today, the language of the business community is mainly English while the language of politics and administration is to a large extent Afrikaans.

Asians: As the proud Zulus were unwilling to work in the sugar plantations of the coastal province of Natal, Indian labourers were imported during the 19th century. These new immigrants brought with them their languages, cultures and religions. Hindu temples can be found in most of the larger cities in the country. The possibility of settling in South Africa where the traditional Indian caste system did not apply, and where a new country offered endless opportunities for enterprising businessmen, lured many Indian merchants to South Africa and they

Town. They gradually lost their language and adopted Afrikaans and English, although Arabic is still considered the language of the mosque and children learn to read it from an early age. The first Afrikaans-medium school in the country was established in 1863 in Cape Town by the Muslim community and Afrikaans was written in Arabic characters – a custom which prevails, albeit on a small scale, to the present day.

The Muslim community of Cape Town is world-renowned for its annual music festival which takes place around New Year. The actual competition is preceded by colourful parades of the various "troupes" through the streets of Cape Town. Their music has a

subsequently made an indelible impression on the country's economic life.

Cultural traditions are preserved through the practising of traditional festivals, dancing, cuisine and religious ceremonies. The voice of the Muslim muezzin (caller) can be heard five times a day summoning the faithful to prayer. The first Muslims had arrived in the early 18th century, as part of the court retinue of Sheikh Yusuf, a nobleman of Macassar in the East Indies who was banished to the Cape for his part in an uprising against the Dutch colonial government.

These Malay-speaking immigrants formed a hardworking colony in Cape

distinct, characteristic flavour, and shows traces of the musical tradition of the Orient.

New settlers: A group which made an indelible impression on South African economic life is the Jewish community. Men like Barney Barnato and Alfred Beit played an important part in the establishment of the prosperous diamond and gold mining industries. A large group of Jewish refugees from the Baltic settled in the country after World War I and became involved in trading and manufacturing, thus laying the foundations of one of the most prosperous sectors of the South African economy.

Jews also played an important role in

South African cultural life with names like Nadine Gordimer (writing), Lippy Lipshitz (sculpture), Irma Stern (painting) and the Afrikaans poetess Olga Kirsh gaining distinction in their fields.

The years immediately following World War II brought large numbers of new settlers from Europe to South Africa. These included Dutch immigrants of strict Reformed persuasion, searching for a new country where they could practise their beliefs; and large numbers of Germans – most of them highly skilled in engineering and the sciences – looking for an almost pristine land where they could start afresh, far away from their war-ravaged fatherland.

Czechoslovakia (1968) also brought a number of new immigrants from central Europe to South Africa. These immigrants played a vital part in the economy by supplying new skills and helping to create job opportunities.

Although most new immigrants soon blended into their surroundings, the Portuguese, because of their larger numbers (almost half a million), preferred to live together in typical Portuguese quarters of South African cities. Because so many of them had an agricultural background, they became the most important growers and suppliers of fresh produce in South Africa.

The Greek community, although much smaller in number, has made its mark, espe-

Without these skilled immigrants from central and western Europe, South Africa would probably not have succeeded in establishing a highly industrialised society with such technical achievements as its unique petro-chemical industry.

Since the 1960s, the numbers of immigrants were swelled by large numbers of Greek settlers, mainly from Cyprus, and Portuguese from the island of Madeira or the former Portuguese colonies in Africa. The Soviet invasions of Hungary (1956) and

Left, Engineroom on ship. **Above**, Examination delights, Johannesburg.

cially in retailing. Many supermarkets and most cafés are Greek-owned.

Cultural life: In spite of its years of racial tension that divided communities and individuals, South Africans in recent years have started to share a vibrant cultural life. The decades of struggle against apartheid produced (black) protest theatre of a high quality which gradually became part of mainstream theatrical life. Similarly the years of (white) "border wars" in Angola produced an amount of stridently anti-militaristic literature in Afrikaans, known as grensliteratuur (border literature).

South African music has developed a

"crossover style" with a distinct African flavour which has also found a lucrative export market. Crossover-artists like Johnny Clegg (Le Zulu blanc), Claire Johnstone and her back-up group, Mango Groove and Ladysmith Black Mambazo have built up a following that defies ethnic or racial categorisation. This has led to a revival in both local Afrikaans music and in that of the various African languages.

The welcome return of exiled South African artists such as Miriam Makeba and Dollar Band (Abdullah Ebrahim) has injected new vigour into the South African arts scene.

The 1980s proved to what extent the black and white cultures of South Africa are merg-

ing. This applies not only to music but particularly to the visual arts where a distinctly new "South African" art form has developed from the merger of European and African traditions. Artists such as Hudson Hlungwane (sculpture), Nicholas Maritz (painting), William Kentridge and Karel Nel are in the vanguard of this movement.

Sporting activities: With its blue skies and sunny weather, South Africa is the ideal country for outdoor activities and South Africans share a passion for sport. In spite of – or perhaps because of – decades of sporting isolation, the country's sportsmen and women were the first to start breaking down

the social and political barriers that separated them. Today, with the country returning to the international scene, most sporting codes are fully integrated.

Soccer is certainly the most popular sport among blacks, but unfortunately the sports boycott robbed stars such as Jomo Sono, Kaizer Motaung and Ace Ntselengoe of opportunities of displaying their skills to the outside world.

Among whites, rugby is the favourite sport, and the national team, the Springboks, is ranked with New Zealand's famed All Blacks as the best in the world. Again, one of the few undoubted geniuses of world rugby, Naas Botha, seldom had the opportunity to prove himself against the best in the world.

Rugby as a sport is dominated by Afrikaans speakers while the English community for long concentrated on cricket, producing such world greats as Mike Proctor, Graeme Pollock, Barry Richards and Clive Rice. With cricket at the forefront of sporting development in South Africa, it has in recent years seen a huge inflow of black talent which will drastically alter the composition of "traditional" teams.

Boxing and track and field athletics are already highly successful crossover-sports. South Africans of all races are equally proud of both black and white world boxing champions such as Brian Mitchell, Dingaan Thobela and Welcome Ncita. A South African track team combines the sprinting skills of white athletes such as Johan Rossouw and Evette de Klerk with the long-distance prowess of black runners such as Xolile Yawa and David Tsebe and Matthews Temane.

The future: For decades the political and social structures of the country emphasised that which divided and separated the various groups. This trend has now been reversed as South Africans are searching together for common values and symbols that unite them. The crucible of the urban community has brought home the fundamental truth that South Africans share a common destiny and their individual futures are inextricably linked. But the problems – not least the economic prospects – remain daunting, and the shape of that future will be decided only slowly as the 21st century approaches.

<u>Left</u>, **traditional headgear of a married Zulu woman. <u>Right</u>, tourists' campfire.**

Religion plays an important role in the lives of most people in South Africa. It affects daily family life; even in the smallest villages, steeples or minarets reach like fingers toward the sky; and in the shadow of the skyscrapers which shape the skylines of major cities, houses of worship stand ready for believers to congregate for devotions and prayers. Official decisions are strongly tied to religious convictions. Despite a softening of approach in recent years, strict Sunday observance laws are still in effect in the country, and they govern both trading hours and entertainment.

In the course of the country's fluctuating history, countless religions have taken root. The constitution guarantees freedom of religion to all; and each sector of the population has its own distinct belief. As in most other parts of Africa south of the Sahara, Christian denominations form the largest group: four out of five South Africans belong to a Christian church or organisation. But this hasn't always been the case.

African tribal religions: Before the beginnings of colonisation by whites in the middle of the 17th century, the indigenous tribes lived according to their various traditional beliefs. There was a common belief in a female deity in heaven, who once created everything, then withdrew into the nether distance. People on earth were able to contact her only through the agency of their dead ancestors; these "living dead" were already with the Godhood, and could pass along the requests of their earth-dwelling descendants concerning such matters as rain, health and fertility.

But the ancestors had to receive a sign. This was given by slaughtering an animal, which was then divided communally and consumed – the dead ancestors receiving their portion. The head of each household functioned as family priest; in matters concerning the whole tribe, the chief took the role. He killed the cow or goat with a spear reserved for the purpose, and conveyed the requests of the living to the ancestors.

Left, the Dutch Reformed church of Stellenbosch. **Right**, a Catholic ceremony.

Tribal religious specialists were once known as "medicine men"; today, they're usually called traditional healers, Sangomas or "doctor-priests". These are highly informed about herbal medicine, with a remarkable ability to cure illness as well as to set broken bones or inoculate against epidemics. Moreover, their task was to preserve and pass on religious traditions. For the African peoples lived in an unlettered culture: sacred writings, as known by most of the world's major religions, simply did not exist.

But these legend tellers, hierarchically organised in each tribe, saw to the maintenance of inherited traditions, and advised family and tribal priests as to the appropriate signs and actions.

These beliefs are characterised by holistic thinking – symbolised by the circle. For this reason, the huts and kraals of traditionalists are round; people sit in a circle at their gatherings. This holistic approach is manifest in the individual's involvement in the web of his relationships to himself and his family, to his society and environment, to the realm of spirits, good and evil – and ultimately to God. Religious practices, therefore, are aimed at the preservation and reinforcement of harmony in this network, at keeping damaging influences at bay or healing damaged relationships.

Conciliatory practices are accompanied by a wealth of symbolism. If, for example, two people have fought, they would sit opposite each other at the door of a hut, repeat the hurtful words they have said, and take ashes into their mouths as a sign that the words have now been burnt. They pour clean water over each other's hands, and extend them to each other as a sign of forgiveness.

Preventative measures are also deeply symbolic. To dwellers in grass huts, lightning is particularly dangerous; in order to

Thus burial rites are a solemn ceremony; birth and marriage rituals, too, are elaborate.

Today, tribal religions persist only in remote areas of the country, for the number of adherents is decreasing steadily: only one in five "tribal" South Africans still professes these beliefs. Yet it is important to recognise and understand these religions, for these ways of thinking are still evident throughout Africa, even if most people today can read and write and are accustomed to living with modern forms of economy and society.

Christian churches: South Africa's first encounter with Christianity occurred when Dutch settlers colonised the Cape of Good Hope, bringing with them their Calvinist

protect farmhouses from this danger, they do not put up iron lightning rods (unfamiliar to natives), but bury smooth stones from the river bed around the huts, from which lightning will theoretically slip off; they also use long thorns – today made of barbed wire and rusty nails – for protection. Ultimately, these symbols are only concrete manifestations of the plea to the ancestors to intercede with God so that lightning will not strike the kraal.

The wish to be near to God after death also strongly influences daily behaviour. A man who has led a bad life risks hovering eternally near his grave, as an ephemeral spirit.

beliefs. At first, they observed these so solemnly that they tolerated only the Reformed Church within their sphere of influence. As time progressed, countless mission societies came along, all competing for converts.

Today, South Africa contains followers of every kind of Christian belief. Most denominations have established their own churches in the country; yet, while safeguarding their own religious identity, they keep up strong ties with churches abroad and also work together economically within the country. The most important interdenominational organisation is the Council of Churches which has also played an important political role in protest against government actions in the apartheid days.

The Reformed churches: The family of Reformed churches is the oldest in the country. Three years after the arrival of Jan van Riebeeck at the Cape on 6 April 1652, the first Reformed church was founded. Its congregation was mainly Dutch, who remained true to their language in their religious life; their Dutch evolved into Afrikaans, still spoken at home and in church. Although the Church didn't formally engage in missionary work, its adherents found it natural that their native servants should sit with them in the morning and evening when the head of the family read from the Bible and held

in 1986. Its 3 ¾ million members and followers make the Reformed Church one of the country's largest denominations.

The Lutheran churches: The first missionary of the Lutheran family, Georg Schmidt, travelled from the Brotherhood of Count Zinzendorf to South Africa in 1737 and founded the Genadendaal Mission, near Cape Town. Today, congregations of the brotherhood are found predominantly in the Cape Province and Transkei. Although its followers are not numerous – around 100,000 – this movement exercises great influence in South Africa as a result of its book of proverbs, which many families use as a devotional text.

The first Lutheran congregation was es-

services for the members of his household.

It wasn't until 1826 that the first official mission was established, but it grew into a force that has since spread the gospel far beyond the borders of South Africa. Two smaller churches branched out of the Dutch Reformed Church in the middle of the 19th century; as segregation became more pronounced, "daughter churches" were set up for different racial groups. This initial support of trends which ultimately led to apartheid was publicly rescinded and repudiated

Left, a traditional church wedding. **Right**, Sundays are sacred.

tablished in Cape Town in 1779. In the early 19th century, the work of missionaries, most of whom came from Germany (Berlin and Hermannsburg) and Scandinavia, helped spread the religion rapidly through communities of natives and colonists alike; over the years, this led to the development of independent churches. The Lutherans set great store by their native tongue. In communities originally settled by Germans, one can go to German services even today.

English churches: As a result of political developments and a large population of English immigrants, as well as English and American missionary work, the entire spectrum of British churches is represented. Foremost is the Anglican Church, established in South Africa in 1749. The local diocese has been independent since 1876. In the controversy surrounding apartheid, Anglican bishops have often been in the forefront of resistance, with Archbishop Desmond Tutu emerging as a spokesman for black political aspirations.

The Scottish Presbyterians first arrived in 1806 during the second wave of English colonists. They were particularly concerned with academic and technical education for the young; while disputes about segregated education in South Africa were taking place, they developed their own school system.

administers other countries in southern Africa. The Catholic Church has been growing much faster than most other denominations. The reason is that it is more sympathetic than some to native ways of thinking; it also came out strongly against apartheid.

Also well established are the Baptists, the Salvation Army, and the Greek Orthodox Church. With over 2 million adherents, the charismatic and Pentecostal movements are the fastest-growing denominations.

The African Independent Churches: For 100 years, the African Independent Churches (AIC) have appeared throughout sub-Saharan Africa. Interestingly enough, their centres of concentration are in Nigeria and

The Methodists were known for their missionary work, which made a significant contribution to Christianising the natives.

The Roman Catholic Church: The Catholic Church's cross was raised in certain parts of South Africa long ago: Bartolomeu Dias did so on the island of Santa Cruz (Holy Cross) in Algoa Bay in 1486, as did Vasco da Gama in Mossel Bay in 1498. But no one was allowed actually to practise this religion here until 1806. Even after this, obstacles were set in the Church's way; it wasn't truly able to blossom until 1862. This denomination is governed by a council of bishops, under the jurisdiction of the Vatican. The council also

South Africa, where every third "African" belongs to one of their 5,000-plus congregations, small or large. The fact that there were only 900 branches 40 years ago gives some idea of Christianity's rapid growth.

Once the Bible had been translated into the native tongues of various tribes, these new Christians read it avidly. They were then able to see that the message which early missionaries had brought them was presented in terms of the interpretations current in the missionaries' own distant homelands: "bread of life, packaged in cellophane".

The great spiritual achievement of these Bible translations lay in their transferring the

Christian message directly into specific African cultures. After reading them, converts broke away from the mission churches and founded the AIC congregations. In 1883, Nehemiah Tile broke off from the Methodist Church and founded, with the support of his chief, the National Thembu Church. In 1885, the Native Independent Congregationalist Church separated from the London Missionary Society; in 1889, the Lutheran Bapedi Church declared its independence from the Berlin Mission, taking their missionary Johannes Winter with them.

Mangena Maake Mokone, who emancipated his followers from the Methodist Church in Pretoria in 1892, called his de-

movement. This is unrelated to the Israeli brand of Zionism; the name stems from an American Pentecostal church, the Christian Catholic Apostolic Church of Zion. Hereafter, African spirituality, with prayer healing and baptism by total immersion, was strongly emphasised; and the prohibition on tobacco, alcohol, medication and pork found widespread support among AIC members. Hundreds of small congregations, each with a different name and uniform, gathered under native leadership. On weekends, these worship services can be observed, in both city and countryside, throughout Africa.

A third development has been the formation of major African churches. Charismatic

nomination the Ethiopian Church. This became a catchword: Ethiopia, the symbol of African independence. And this first great flowering of the AIC became famous as the "Ethiopian" movement. Its followers established ties with the Afro-American churches which had been founded in America by descendants of the slaves. White South Africans perceived all this as "the black danger".

In 1910, the second great AIC movement spread throughout the country: the Zionist

Left, 20 percent of Indians and Cape Malays follow the Islamic faith. **Above**, an Indian fire walker gets ready to perform.

church leaders gather crowds of Christians, transcending tribal and country boundaries, in the course of intensive missionary work. Good examples of this trend in South Africa are the Nazareth Baptist Church, founded near Durban in 1910 by the prophet Isaiah Shembe, and the Zion Christian Church of the prophet Engenas Lekganyane, established in 1914 near Pietersburg. In the AIC, the African Reformation has found a vehicle with which to steer itself into the future.

Services in African: The incorporation of tradition has become an essential element of AIC services; for instance, the symbol of the circle in tribal religions as an expression of holistic thinking. As the AIC has to get by without large amounts of foreign aid, its financial means are adequate only for bare essentials, usually not for the erection of large churches and hospitals. "Temples" of this church often consist of a simple circle of whitewashed stones around a high tree which stands in for the church steeple.

When they congregate for sermon and prayers, church members sit in this circle on grass mats, singing their hymns in traditional native fashion, drumming and dancing all the while. If the weather's bad, a round hut accommodates the proceedings, its central pole replacing the tree. These "temples" aren't found only in rural areas; they can

indication of this can be seen on Sundays at sunrise on the beach at Durban, where this method of healing is practised.

Employers view AIC members as industrious and honest. In their congregations, harmony with God and fellow men is an important element, taken over from tribal religion; they are a peaceful people, who do not take part in the bloody conflicts between different political parties. A main belief is the human value of the individual. The movement has no all-encompassing parent organisation.

Indian religions: As well as the religions which have grown out of the encounters of natives and white settlers, the great religions of the East have settled in South Africa.

often be seen in big cities, to which many brown Christians migrate to find work.

Harking back to the "doctor-priests" of tribal religions, religion and healing are closely interrelated in the AIC. As Christians, however, members make it clear that they are neither praying to ancestors for intervention nor using medicines; rather, they are praying for the sick. Such a prayer service is held after every worship service, a part of the congregations' often touching concern and care for the sick. Some people also undertake long journeys to their central church, to sacred springs, or to the coast, where the sea is said to have particularly curative powers. An

Three-quarters of the first contracted labourers brought into the country in 1860 were Hindu; today, two out of three South Africans of Indian origin are Hindu. They have kept alive their native languages – Tamil, Hindi, Telegu and Gujarati – for use at worship or at home, and read Vedic literature. Their temples and ashrams, facilities resembling cloisters, are notably well attended. Because the religion's ethical standards are high, members of the Indian community have the lowest recorded crime (and divorce) rate per capita of any ethnic group.

As opposed to Hinduism, which has some 650,000 adherents in South Africa today, the

Indian religions of Buddhism and Jainism have remained small minorities. The Buddhists have erected an ashram in Ixopo, Natal, which is predominantly attended by whites. Jains exert a considerable influence through their policy of non-aggression. Their hero is Mahatma Gandhi, who spent two years in South Africa fighting for the rights of Indian contracted labourers.

Judaism: Until the middle of the 19th century, South African Jews were denied the right to practise their religion; they did not build their first synagogue until 1863. Gold and diamond mining and the growth of the cities resulted in an increase in the number of Jewish immigrants, especially from Eastern

Islam: Islam discovered the Cape as early as the 17th century, when Dutch settlers brought slaves, soldiers and convicts, many of them from Indonesia, to the Cape of Good Hope. Their descendants are known as Cape Malays. Among the Indian contracted labourers brought to South Africa were hundreds of Muslims; and most subsequent Indian immigrants were also followers of Islam. Hundreds of immigrants from other parts of Africa who came to South Africa to find work had the same beliefs.

Today, South Africa is home to some 350,000 Muslims; in nearly every city, the muezzin sounds from the minaret of the mosque five times a day, calling the faithful

Europe. Apart from a small group of reformed Jews, the Jewish population is predominantly Orthodox. Judaism is still a religion of immigrants.

Many synagogues today stand empty and abandoned. During the conflicts between Israelis and Palestinians, tension grew between Jews and Muslims in South Africa. Many Africans sympathised with the Palestinians, and some Jews left the country. Today, an estimated 100,000 Jews remain.

Left, the initiation ritual of a sangoma (diviner). **Right**, her lips are smeared with the gall bladder of a chicken.

to prayer – these days usually over a loudspeaker. As well as maintaining religious schools, the Muslims are eager to bring others into contact with their beliefs, and they campaign for Islam with a host of pamphlets, brochures and newspapers.

Alcohol and gambling are forbidden to the Muslim, but he may have as many as four wives. In South Africa, Muslims play an important economic role; many of them are tradesmen or skilled workers, while others have attained positions of privilege as doctors or lawyers. They are active participants in cultural and social programmes, and campaign vigorously for equality and justice.

Christian Barnard, whose fame has resulted in his parental home in the Cape being turned into a museum, dramatically extended the frontiers of medicine in 1967 when he performed the world's first successful heart transplant at Groote Schuur Hospital. Yet, despite such startling medical advances, an estimated 80 percent of the country's black population still ask the sangoma – or a variety of other traditional and faith healers – to diagnose and treat their ills.

Nothing illustrates more forcefully the di-

It would be idle, however, to pretend that such cooperation is typical. The first world and the third world have more often coexisted in a state of mutual distaste and distrust. Why, the outside world asks, is Africa's response to modernisation so different to that of other parts of the world? In South Africa itself, black authors have blamed apartheid for their group's low educational level and consequent socio-economic and political problems. Colonialism is blamed, too, because, in its narrow pursuit of profits,

vision of South Africa into two cultures. The surgeon's scalpel and the sangoma's bones, although they belong to apparently incompatible worlds, are equally valued by citizens of different heritages.

The cultures do not invariably clash. Traditional healing techniques, for example, are usually anathema to the medical establishment; yet, during an emergency in Soweto, a surgeon operating on a sangoma injured in a car accident agreed to let a healer bless the operation by "speaking to the ancestors". Horatio Zungu, a traditional healer, commented afterwards: "I was pleased to see that they respect our culture."

it neglected to train local people to accept responsibility or fulfil managerial roles.

But there are deeper reasons, to be found in tradition and culture. Africa still cherishes the "humanity" of the human being and, unlike the Westerner, reacts fiercely against the suffocating effects of the cold, rationalistic, techno-scientific approach.

The African thinks in terms of life-force or power. So long as one participates in life-force, one is at the pivot of reality. When life-force is present, action follows; force is being and being is force – the two are interrelated. Vital force is consecrated, mysterious energy. God is the most potent force, followed by the ancestors, who mediate the energy to their progeny. Among the living, too, the hierarchy is based on vital force. The chief is the sum and substance of his tribe; in the magical realm, anything originating from him is considered to be most powerful.

It is this attitude towards vital force that makes Africa's response to science and technology so different from that of, say, Asia. Unlike African belief, Asian religions have a strong contemplative, rational component. In pursuit of material wealth, Asia accepted

occur in a single isolated sphere of human existence. It takes place only if it touches a person's entire thinking, feeling and life.

The people of Europe were helped in their scientific endeavours by the analytical approach of their philosophical and religious beliefs. Primal religions have rendered no such assistance in Africa. Logic does not play a decisive role in African religious thought. Faith is not based on logical argument; it is a matter of trust, not rational belief. Behind everything are the continuous

the West's techno-scientific outlook, but largely rejected its religion. In contrast, Africa accepted the West's religion but failed to acquire its techno-scientific expertise. This would imply that science, technology and industry are culture-bound.

The human being's harmonious adaptation to new environments is related to the fact that an individual's whole life is affected on entering a new situation. If only a part of a person comprehends the process, problems arise because effective development cannot

Left, Ndebele women cooking in cast-iron *potjie*.
Above, Traditional wear from the past.

divine and ancestral acts, and other supernatural forces. Fear of these forces in nature, and the mythologies based on them, do not encourage people to regard nature as a force that can be moulded or manipulated.

Alien systems: Colonial rulers, not understanding such modes of thought, unwittingly held back the African personality's development. They introduced an overly restrictive version of Christianity which undermined the traditional, unifying belief systems. They imposed an alien economic system which undermined family life and attacked human dignity, glorifying competitiveness at any cost and introducing rapid urbanisation and a ruthless cash economy. Also, fearing opposition, they relied on political suppression, which culminated in apartheid. The masses were denied adequate education and their initiative was sapped.

Faced with such odds, blacks rejected innovation in favour of tradition. They regarded achievement as being less important than the fact that one had been born into a community. A culture of illiteracy developed, even among those who received some schooling. Outstanding individual excellence or creative achievement was suspect. Black youth often attacked the black middle class, accusing them of not being faithful to the group, of having prospered as a result of

black political influence. Official birth control programmes do have a measure of success in the black metropolitan areas, but the authorities remain concerned about the population growth in rural areas, where children are traditionally seen as a measure of a black man's wealth and contraception is totally unacceptable, especially to males.

It is in the area of healing that the chasm between the two cultures often seems at its widest. Traditional African medicine is closely tied to traditional and Christian religions. Traditional religion allows people to communicate with the Supreme Being through their ancestors. According to popular belief, people are most vulnerable to

a despised system – not in spite of the system, as is usually the case.

Education, for many forward-thinkers the brightest hope for the future, found it hard to shake off its old image as the preserve of a privileged class, a luxury status symbol unrelated to the needs of the modern world. Indeed, the educational system was a failure even before the black youth, regarding their schools as educational ghettoes, wrecked it.

Children as wealth: The two-cultures clash extended to such sensitive areas as birth control. This is a strongly politicised subject, regarded by some blacks as a white technique to contain black numbers and hence

illness caused by sorcery when their ancestors are "facing away". They go to healers to be instructed in the appropriate rituals to placate the ancestors and to ensure the good health of their families.

There are broadly two types of traditional healers: those specialising in herbal treatments and those who practise natural treatment methods. The inyanga (Zulu) is apprenticed to a practising healer for at least a year. The inyanga is usually a man. Diviners (sangoma) use supernatural diagnostic methods – throwing bones, mirrors, dreams, trances. A sangoma, usually a woman, also has a comprehensive knowledge of herbal medicines. She is apprenticed to a qualified sangoma for several years.

The most common treatments administered by indigenous healers are infusions, hot and cold, powders which are rubbed into the parts of the body where incisions have been made, poultices, lotions and ointments. Healers also prescribe vapour baths, enemas and emetics to flush out impurities.

Faith-healers (umthandazi) are professed Christians who work within the independent indigenous black churches, such as the Zionist Christian Church, the country's biggest church with a following of millions. The ZCC not only has a number of faith-healers with immense reputations and constantly overcrowded consulting rooms, but also has its own range of herbal treatments, coffee, tea and strict rules for healthy living. Faith-healers do not always undergo training.

Westerners, however, continue to put enormous faith in "training" and "qualifications" in all areas of life, and these concepts have yet to make the leap across the cultural divide. Sometimes, indeed, the gap seems scarcely bridgeable. In the West, for example, nature must be manipulated; in Africa, nature is a mother who provides. Westerners live much of their mental life in the future, planning their next moves; the traditional African emphasis is on the past with a passive, almost fatalistic, dimension.

So, given these differences, can a holistic world view be replaced by one that recognises and harnesses cultural diversity? Many liberals in South Africa put their faith in education. There must be greater stress, they say, on science and technology, less on ethnic loyalties which can lead to violent conflict; there must be more emphasis on discussion, participation and self-expression.

At the heart of South Africa's struggle is what Laurens van der Post described as "a battle about being and non-being; about having a soul of one's own or not having a soul at all". The African needs to reconcile the spiritual universe, which is felt to be true "being", with the material universe.

Coming together: Medicine, surprisingly enough, provides some hope that apparently irreconcilable approaches can be combined. Although liaison between traditional and modern medical practitioners is infrequent, there has always been unofficial contact, and many Western doctors believe that they can use the influence of traditional healers to encourage more effective treatment.

They have, for instance, begun to inform traditional healers of the symptoms of diseases like Aids and cancer in the hope that healers would learn to recognise these symptoms and refer cases to hospitals.

Although Western doctors still believe some traditional treatments to be extremely dangerous, they have started to acknowledge that traditional healing possesses a certain wisdom and understanding of social responses. Traditional healers are said to have

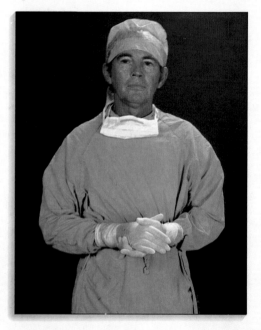

achieved miracle cures on mentally ill people and cancer patients. South Africa's National Convention on Holistic Health and Healing has tried to persuade cancer specialists to liaise with traditional healers.

Psychologists in particular believe that the traditional healer's holistic treatment of patients, incorporating psychological, societal, cultural, inter-personal and spiritual facets in the healing process, is worth researching. It is not impossible, therefore, that this synthesis represents an area in which South African medics will achieve a "first" of no less significance than Christian Barnard's breakthrough heart transplant operation.

Left, country medicines. **Right**, Dr Christian Barnard – from surgeon to international celebrity.

South Africa is often thought of as a rich country. An image of gold and diamonds, affluent lifestyles, Cape beaches flanked by luxury apartments, vineyards, elegant 18th-century dwellings and the skyscrapers of Johannesburg makes that impression inevitable. Tourist literature often reinforces it, and makes the other face of South Africa – that of political violence and racial segregation – that much more difficult for the outsider to understand.

In fact, however, South Africa, although

edge of progress, some of the best financial markets in the world, uranium enrichment and satellite manufacturing capability, world-class architecture and impressive public and private health services.

On the other hand, the shanty-towns on the verge of its cities and the efforts of poor peasants to scratch a living from eroded patches of land in several rural areas are reminiscent of the slums of São Paolo, Calcutta or Lagos, and the grinding poverty of rural subsistence elsewhere in Africa. South

not as poor as many countries on the continent, is not rich either, except in its natural beauty, cultural diversity and unusual mineral endowment. Its Gross Domestic Product (GDP) per capita places it, at US$2,290 a year, in the same league as Algeria or Uruguay, just ahead of Poland and Malaysia and behind Gabon.

The explanation for the discrepancy between truth and perception lies in an unequal distribution of wealth, opportunity and achievement between races and regions, and, of course, between urban and rural areas. South Africa's developed sector boasts mining technology on the cutting

Africa, despite its European – and North American – face, cannot escape the realities of its history or its geography.

South Africa's treasure house of minerals, advanced mining and manufacturing technology and sophisticated financial services give it the potential for striking economic success in the 21st century. To achieve this, it needs foreign capital investment equal to about 10 percent of gross domestic product; interest rates high enough to stimulate a sharp improvement in personal savings; greater domestic investment in manufacturing; continuing deregulation and lower personal and corporate tax rates to encourage entrepreneurial effort; and a better educational system, ensuring that mathematics, general science and technical skills are more widely available to the workforce. All this requires a measure of political stability.

A mining-based economy: Like that of most Third World countries, the South African economy is based on primary products: a wide range of metals and minerals capable of profitable extraction, given the historically low cost and skill structure of the labour market. As late as 1990, almost 70 percent of

active population, despite its great contribution to export earnings.

Until the mid-1980s, most skilled work was still restricted by law to non-blacks, to guarantee full employment to white adult voters. These restrictions have now been abolished, but the backlog will take decades to eliminate. There are disproportionately few blacks in white-collar jobs and almost no whites in unskilled positions. Black South Africans are still mostly on the lower rungs of employment and status, but they are now

the value of all exports derived from mining, with gold alone contributing 40 percent. The country is also a net exporter of agricultural products, with almost a third of production being sold abroad in years when drought does not limit the crop.

About one-quarter of all those in employment work in the services sector (including domestic service). They are followed by those in manufacturing, agriculture, forestry and fishing, commerce and finance, and then mining and quarrying. Mining provides jobs to fewer than 10 percent of the economically

Left, Johannesburg suburb. **Above**, Soweto.

on the ladder and the brightest and best are climbing it with speed.

For 18 years, however, the economy has not grown fast enough to keep pace with the growth of the population – some 2.4 percent – or to provide the jobs sought by the even more rapidly expanding ranks of school-leavers. Even if the economy were to grow at more than 3 percent a year in the 1990s, the formal sector will still be unable to provide jobs to more than 10 million adults in the year 2000, leaving some 8 million more to be accommodated elsewhere. Almost all these will be black.

Continuing high inflation – between 8 and

15 percent per year since 1974 – and unionisation of black workers for the first time in the 1980s combined to cause spiralling wages. Unemployment also went up as employers sought cost-saving, capital-intensive alternatives. Thanks to inflation, real personal disposable incomes per capita fell by about 18 percent during the 1980s.

Agriculture, too, has its problems. Forty percent of farm income is generated by 1 percent of all farmers. The government is committed to removing the subsidies which have long kept inefficient farming units in production. At the same time, pressures are rising for the unionisation of farm workers and experience in the mining and manufac-

turing sectors suggests that this will lead to rapid wage growth. Farmers who stay on the land, therefore, may well decide to replace labour with capital equipment.

Market garden to mining camp: South Africa in its modern guise came into being after 1652, because ships of the Dutch East India Company needed to take on fresh water, meat, fruit and vegetables at a halfway station between Holland and the East. The early colonial economy was therefore – like the indigenous economy which preceded it – pastoral and agricultural. Later settlements by Dutch, Germans and French Huguenots each added to the stock of agricultural skills,

the French, in particular, bringing viticulture and improving the quality of fruit and wine.

Even the British settlers, who arrived in 1820 with little or no previous farming experience, settled into a rural existence, raising livestock and crops on frontier farms. They brought some skills as artisans and a fresh breeze of ideas concerning freedom of the press, but their arrival had no appreciable impact on the national economy.

It was not until the discovery of diamonds near the Orange River in the 1870s and of gold a decade later in the South African Republic that mining skills developed much beyond the primitive level practised by the local tribes. Silver had been mined on a small scale on the Cape Peninsula since the 18th century, providing the raw material for local silversmiths to produce small items in the rococo and, later, neo-classical styles, but there was no industry to speak of.

Diamonds and gold changed all that. An influx of fortune-seekers brought instant shanty-towns and attracted those who would meet the needs of the diggers and traders. A new economy, based on mining and including services from engineering to banking, sprung up in response. A new era began.

Until World War II, this economy defined the character of South Africa. Agriculture was still of great importance, as food was needed in ever greater quantities in the burgeoning mining towns, but the catalyst of growth was gold and diamonds. The most successful of the original mining consortia later became the mining finance houses that controlled not only the mines and refineries, but also the banks, discount houses and industrial empires spawned by the needs of the mines and the opportunities for benefication of the minerals extracted from the ground.

Progress was sometimes agonisingly slow. Gold was the standard of monetary value for much of the century and its price was pegged at a fixed rate. Profitable production required low labour costs and high returns, as the capital needed to open new mines was enormous. South Africa's true industrialisation began only in the 1930s on a small scale and, driven by the government's desire for economic independence in respect of strategic goods, took off in the aftermath of World War II.

Impressive infrastructure: Tarred roads and railways criss-cross the country; microwave towers loom from many hills; there are over 5 million telephones, numerous radio stations, five television channels, four major harbours and numerous airports in operation throughout the country. The national carrier, South African Airways, flies over 45 million passengers a year. The economy still owes much to its roots. Agricultural exports were valued at R5,500million in 1989 while the value of minerals exported was R58,800 million, almost R20,000 million of which was due to gold sales. The value of platinum group, diamond and uranium sales in 1989, was almost R7,000 million. Coal exports were valued at R3,600 million.

On the other hand, low US dollar gold

ever, targeted by the sanctioneers. By developing new markets in the Far East and dropping prices to maintain market share in their traditional markets, South African coal exporters lost little ground and succeeded in 1989 in surpassing the previous export high of 46 million tonnes achieved in 1986. Similar, though less impressive, results were obtained with iron and steel sales.

The oil and gas sector will change considerably once all trade restrictions on South Africa are lifted. Threatened by a United Nations ban on oil sales, the government invested heavily in synthetic fuels technology and South Africa became the world leader in oil-from-coal conversion. Oil was

prices forcied many mines to cut back on unprofitable production and put thousands of jobs at risk. The mining houses hope that the R30,000 million development of new mines in the "Potchefstroom Gap" will give higher yields per tonne and help restore health to the industry.

South Africa's gold – excepting gold coins – and strategic mineral exports were proof against the economic sanctions imposed by the international community in the 1980s.

Coal, as well as iron and steel, were, how-

Left, the rewards of prosperity. **Above**, measures of progress, side by side.

also bought at a premium and stockpiled, and an extensive domestic exploration programme was undertaken. It was decided, in 1985, to go ahead with exploitation of the most promising find, a gas field off Mossel Bay, and to convert the gas into liquid fuel onshore. It is likely, however, that when this extremely expensive project is brought to fruition, oil sanctions may have been lifted and the facility will prove unnecessary.

The manufacturing sector includes food, chemicals, iron and steel, machinery and motor vehicle assembly and parts production, textiles and clothing. Exports are relatively small, though growing steadily in response to export incentives. The rate of growth in the volume of manufacturing output since the mid-1980s has been poor.

Tourism is potentially a growth industry, although, despite the country's great natural beauty, international marketing has been modest. Indeed, for years, it was felt that mass tourism ought to be discouraged. Just fewer than 1 million visitors came to South Africa in 1990, the majority from other African countries. Deregulation of the domestic tourism industry and more effective marketing abroad promise higher returns, provided reports of political violence do not harm the country's image further.

The decision of American banks to call up

their loans in 1985 had a greater impact on the economy than any other sanctions. While South Africa has traditionally been a net importer of capital, since 1985 it has had no option but to run continuous current account surpluses to meet its debt repayment obligations. This has distorted organic growth by forcing the fiscal authorities to take strong measures to discourage imports.

The challenge of the future: The rate of social and economic change in South Africa is still accelerating. The difference between the speed of change in the social and economic spheres and the difficulties in adapting to the exisiting political structures, helps explain

the instability which rocked South Africa in the 1980s. The country was transforming itself from its rural, traditional, tribal structures to those which make up an urban, industrial society. This change is nerve-wracking and often violent, but it is the only path to industrial democracy.

Western Europe travelled this route in the 19th and early 20th centuries. The revolutions and economic upheaval in the European empires were little different from the challenges South Africa faces today. Like all traditional societies, those whom we now call "Europeans" first banded together in tribes, defined by blood relationships and marriage. Only after industrial technology had forced people from different kinship groups together in the cities – often with violent consequences – and new interest groups had been forged in the urban crucible, did class interest and common ideologies begin to overtake the tribe as social bonding agents. Out of these new common cultures, industrial democracy was born.

How far has South Africa come? About 7 million black South Africans – about one-third of the total – lived in urban areas in 1980, as did 4 million whites. In 2000, there will be about 31 million blacks and only 5.3 million whites. By 2010, about 32 million blacks are likely to be urban residents, sharing the cities with 5.5 million whites, 4.2 million Coloureds and 1.2 million Asians.

In 1991, out of 10.1 million children at school, more than 8.1 million were black. In 1992, 60 percent of those passing out of high school were black children. In 1992, of 326,100 university students, 39 percent were blacks, 49 percent whites, 5 percent coloureds and 7 percent Asians, whereas in 1980 of a total of 152,400 students, only 12 percent had been blacks, 76 percent whites, 5 percent coloureds and 7 percent Asians.

South Africa has already come a long way and the pace of change is stepping up. Although there was urban violence, this will not destroy the country. Instead, its leaders have reached agreement on how, jointly, to manage the transition so as to build on the strength of the economy, take account of the social pressures, abandon the prejudices of the past and address the challenges and enormous opportunities of the future.

Left, feeding the poor

TRADE WITH NEIGHBOURS

Although occupying only 4 percent of the continent's surface, South Africa produces 53 percent of its electricity, 72 percent of its steel, 15 percent of its cement, and 98 percent of the coal. More than one-third of Africa's motor vehicles and an equal share of its tractors are in use in the country which is also responsible for 17 per cent of Africa's production and 20 per cent of its exports.

Among its immediate neighbours – Botswana, Lesotho, Swaziland, Namibia, Zimbabwe, Zambia, Malawi, Angola and Mozambique – the Republic is an economic giant, accounting for 88 per cent of electricity generated, 78 percent of GNP, 96 percent of steel and 82 percent of cement produced. South Africa boasts 63 per cent of the region's tarred roads, 89 per cent of the motor vehicles and telephones, 73 per cent of imports...

This regional powerhouse represents sub-equatorial Africa's foremost hope for economic progress and political stability. The World Bank has stated that economic cooperation with South Africa "will eventually transform the prospects for the whole of southern Africa". Several African leaders have since echoed this view. The early 1990s witnessed the termination of the boycotts which the Organisation of African Unity had decreed since its founding in 1963.

In 1993, of the total South African exports worth R78.3 billion, much went to other, mostly neighbouring, African countries. Its foodstuffs, agrochemicals, pharmaceutical products, motor vehicles, machinery, spare parts, building materials and other exports play an essential role throughout the region.

South African railways, air lines and road transport carry not only the country's trade with the rest of Africa but also a significant share of the neighbouring countries' overseas trade. An average of 75 percent of their imports and 18 percent of their exports are routed via South African ports and railways. More than three-quarters of Zimbabwe's imports and 63 per cent of its exports go through South Africa; the figures for far-off Zaire were 90 per cent and 35 per cent.

Eskom, South Africa's huge electricity utility, supplies power to six neighbouring countries (over 1,607 million KWh). The neighbours in the region direct 42 per cent of their international telephone calls to South Africa – three times as much as to each other. Over 80 percent of passengers travelling in the airlines of neighbouring states use the international airport in some fashion, making it a regional hub.

The country's modern hospitals, medical schools and research institutes attract patients from as far as Kenya. With its vaccines and diverse services, the Veterinary Research Institute at Onderstepoort near Pretoria helps to protect cattle and other animals throughout the region. The sophisticated research facilities of the Council for Scientific and Industrial Research, the norms and specifications of the Bureau of Standards, the work of specialised agricultural research institutes, the know-how of the Geological Service, the

expertise of engineers and hydrologists, the maintenance and repair shops of airways and railways – these and other facilities are widely utilised throughout the region and beyond.

South African investments in Africa amount to R4,000 million, mostly private investments in mining, manufacturing, agriculture and banking. The Anglo American Corporation and other local mining houses play a crucial role in exploring and mining the region's mineral resources. South African mining machinery and state-of-the-art technology are also proving to be indispensable. Given political stability, the country would have irresistible attractions for international investors seeking such Africa-related expertise. ∎

Right, Sasol oil refinery.

For a long time South Africa was, at core, a very simple place to understand. A minority of the people ran the show. The majority stood outside the gates of citizenship. Why did such a system, once common enough in the world, survive for so long in South Africa? Was there some oddity in the genes of the dominant white minority, or particularly in the genes of the Afrikaners, the dominant majority within that minority?

That sort of theory became widely held, and may contain a kernel of truth. The Afrikaners are among the world's smallest tribes, with one of the world's minor languages, and it may be that this brought subtle psychological factors into play.

But the real reason for South Africa's tardiness in getting into step is simpler and sounder: proportions. The dominant white segment was not – as it is in the US, for instance – so large that de-racialising was a question of who sat in the front of the bus. It was a question of who had their hands on the wheel of state. Nor was the dominant segment so small, as in Kenya, that it had to succumb to majority demands. It was small enough to be terrified of letting go of the reins, and big enough to hang on to the reins through a good deal of stormy riding.

History has known no clear parallel to South Africa's population proportions: a ruling segment of 20 percent; a category of 10 percent Indians and Coloureds; a 70 percent black majority. This was the formula for awkwardness. Moreover, the difference between the cultures, languages, and sheer appearances of the various parties was as great as it is possible to be. Plenty of countries have ethnic problems enough, between people who look the same and sound the same. But "black" and "white" are as opposite as you can get.

The terms are misnomers – "brown" and "pink" would be closer to truth – but the terms that symbolise opposites are those that people use. Even down to the most bizarre coincidences, symbols of oppositeness are everywhere. The main commemorative day

in the Afrikaner calendar is 16 December, a solstice away from its African equivalent, 16 June. The Zulu word for "father" is the same as the Afrikaans use for "baby". The portents for merger were not propitious.

In this light, it is scarcely surprising that South Africans on the whole grew up in the expectation that apocalypse loomed. The general idea was simple: first, there would be a revolution; and second, everything would become different.

It was widely taken as inevitable that the

state would coil even tighter, even more besieged, until finally it snapped. Then a new world would follow. Some white people took it for granted that the new world would mean their destruction; the end of survival. Some black people took it for granted that the new world would mean nirvana. In the middle, a huge bulk waited with caution, believing that apartheid was the source of ill, hoping that after apartheid things would be better, less than wholly confident.

But the revolution evaporated, as quietly as a puddle drying up. History will pinpoint a moment – 2 February 1990, when President F. W. de Klerk said in effect: "Oops,

Left and **right**, the future belongs to both blacks and whites.

reverse gear." But history is written in short sentences; the puddle had in fact been drying up for years.

Now we have a new environment, a new mode of thought, and a new task. It's an environment where, for instance, the children of today often live in a world as wide as their parents' was narrow. And the task is truly daunting: no longer a matter of fighting for or against the status quo, for or against the revolution, but of making a shared country a success against odds any bookmaker would laugh at. The national mood skids from high to low and back again. Much depends on the daily news. But not all is a hostage to the headlines, and that is the saving grace.

Little lives are lived amidst the grand morass, and not all are lived ill. Ben the gateman at the parking lot, for instance, has a new house with electricity and water and his last six months have been one long Christmas. Jonas the smiling milkman always answers the routine "How are you?" with a vigorous "Hundred percent!" Frank, the barman at the tennis club, is frantic about whether he's done everything right for his daughter's wedding next week.

These people – all of them, as it happens, black – are extraordinarily ordinary. They're more or less content. By and large, they see the white man more as a provider of jobs than as brutal oppressor. They pay practically zero attention to the great political issues of our times except when these things burst through their living-room doors, which has been happening recently more often than they might like.

Yet these people too want to live their lives in peace and security, and that is now the big issue, the binding issue, virtually the sole issue at a time that the prospect of chaos looms large before the eyes of the world.

Heartening people come in all shapes and colours. There has always been a solid supply of white people who put time and energy into such things as assisting at black night-schools, helping at clinics in squatter camps, and so on. South Africa is packed with people who long for peace, hunger for harmony. These are the real people, ignored behind the political squabbles.

The threats are gigantic, and all boil down to security or the lack of it. There's no such thing as a general view of how things are shaping. Clearly, the country is a living re-

buttal of the old adage that no ruling class relinquishes power without being vanquished. The state served probably the clearest advance notice in history that the ruling segment does intend to relinquish power, and the debate now is solely over whether the first administrators of majority rule can successfully tackle the daunting problems still facing South Africa.

It is accepted that the country's largely "Third World" nature spells hard times in the competitive world economy of today and tomorrow; that its situation is unique and wherever it's going is necessarily unprecedented; that the old model of a communist takeover is now ancient history. A few other features are widely held, such as the possibility of a descent into outright wheelspin. But, for the most part, predicting South Africa's future is an individual concern. No-one knows better than anyone else. The best interested outsiders can do is absorb a reasonable collection of disparate perspectives and form their own judgements.

So, absorb this one for a start. The old black-versus-white underlay of South African politics lives no longer. It's not that racial issues will disappear – not this century, presumably not the next – but that the racial divide will soon loosen its grip to a status not vastly greater than, say, the religious splits in Belgium or Germany. The country has acquired a thoroughly democratic political foundation – very probably a foundation more democratic than is conventional in the established, less pressured, democracies, in the sense that it looks for such things as a fuller and freer accountability to ordinary people, with a higher level of balancing of local, regional, and national interests and powers.

Given this foundation, the former, predemocratic, lines of allegiance largely fell away. There was for instance, a substantial upsurge of "conservative" and/or "cautious" black political expression, which had remained invisible during the era of the fight for black liberation.

Under this scenario, South Africa ended up with two dominant political parties: a centre-right faction that is essentially the successor to the National Party, and a centre-left faction derived from the African National Congress.

The so-called "route of Africa" – snap

replacement of a right-wing settler regime by a left-wing liberation movement which soon displays feet of clay – has thus have been short-circuited. The country entered the non-racial era guided by a government of national unity which was answerable to a mainly black electorate.

If stability could be reasonably assured, the economic decline of the past two decades could be checked. Investor confidence would return. Various of today's superficially central issues would become far less important. The quest for equality, for example, would be largely replaced by a quest for prosperity. A black electorate would give short shrift to such pre-democratic obses-

sale scrapping of community existence. This idea has spread terror among minorities who perceived their way of life being simply wiped out, but nowadays this notion is being replaced by maturer recognition of the need to seek justice and inter-racial respect rather than enforced denial of ethnic bonds.

A fully-fledged democratic electorate could, given strong and united leadership, remove much of the continuing violence. For the first time, the decision-making process now involves not a white state imposing its will on a black minority but a primarily black democracy in which the aggrieved will be contesting the decisions ratified by their own relatives and communities. But

sions as how many black faces take seats in corporate boardrooms, and would place heavy emphasis on what level of security and opportunity is available to the average voter.

The search for progress will be assisted by assorted built-in factors and extraneous co-incidences. The collapse of communism diminished the old stark left-right conflicts. The ebbing tide of what was once considered the holy grail of colour-blindness will also work to South Africa's benefit. Traditionally "non-racialism" was taken to mean a whole-

Above, working together will not be restricted to servicing machinery.

corruption, whether perpetrated by criminals or simply by various tribal groups trying to do the best for their own people, will prove difficult to root out. Also, the power-play of strong personalities, all keen to succeed Nelson Mandela after his self-imposed one-term presidency, began creating clear tensions within the first year of majority rule.

Yet South Africa has the potential to become the true powerhouse of Africa, and possibly the world's most dramatic case of a Third World country catapulting to a secure First World status. The pitfalls are many; but, if successfully reconnoitred, the outcome could be a resounding success.

THE CHANGING FACE OF ART

The art of southern Africa dates back to pre-history and, it has been argued, represents the human race's longest artistic tradition This claim is based on San (Bushman) rock art, which developed from this time right up to the second half of the 19th century.

The paintings and engravings of the San people are found mainly in the Drakensberg and its extension from the eastern Cape to Lesotho and Swaziland, as well as in the mountains of the northern Transvaal and sites on the inland plateau along the Vaal and Orange Rivers. The sensitive depictions of animals and human figures painted and engraved in rock shelters are thought to be shamanistic and a link between the real world and the spirit world. There are over 3,000 documented sites in South Africa.

Wood carving, beadwork, basket-making and pottery have for centuries been found here, serving both utilitarian and decorative purposes. You can still find carved sticks and head rests, initiation figures and decorative doors, stools and utensils.

Beadwork is produced by most African people in South Africa but most strikingly by Zulu speakers. This art, originally used to identify status, is increasingly aimed at a tourist market. Highly original patterns, using traditional beads alone, have given way to the combined use of plastic, safety-pins and other more modern material stitched on to decorative blankets.

Western influences: The influence of Western painters and art was first felt when early explorers recorded their adventures. The names of 19th-century chroniclers such as Thomas Baines (1820–75), Fredrick I'Ons (1802–87) and Thomas Bowler (1812–69) are synonymous with early South African painting. Their works can be seen in social history museums and art galleries. The influence of Europe remained strong, with the Dutch tradition of landscape painting predominating thanks to Dutch settlers such as Frans Oerder (1867–1944) and Pieter Wenning (1873–1921). They helped establish the South African-born painters J.E.A.

Volschenk (1853–1936) and Hugo Naude (1869–1941) and artists who reflected the British and French Impressionist landscape tradition, such as Robert Gwelo Goodman (1871–1938).

Anton van Wouw (1892–1945) is commonly regarded as the father of modern Western sculpture in South Africa. A Dutchman who arrived in 1890, his work followed a descriptive realist tradition. Moses Kottler (1896–1977) and Lippy Lipshitz (1903–80) followed a carving tradition, as did later artists such as Elsa Dziomba (1902–70) and Lucas Sithole (born 1931).

The influence of Expressionism reached the country in the early 1920s when Irma Stern (1904–66) and Maggie Laubser (1886–1973) returned from studies in Weimar and Berlin. The 1930s saw the New Group set out to explore Post-Impressionist influences, following what they believed to be progressive ideals. Gregoire Boonzaier (b. 1909), Terence MacCaw (1913–76) and Walter Battiss (1906–82) led the break away from what they perceived to be amateurism in South African art displayed by the naturalistic depiction of landscape.

Among the most prominent black artists of the early 1940s were Gerard Sekoto (b. 1913), who left to live in Paris in 1947, Ernest Mancoba (b. 1910), and George Pemba (b. 1920). All three painted scenes of people and places in a realistic manner.

Township art: Post-war developments saw a move towards abstract art theories current in Europe and the United States in the 1950s. But also present was a figurative expressive style, emanating from a growing body of black urban artists. Their subject matter of crowded black townships and distorted expressive human figures became known as Township art.

Mslaba Dumile (b. 1939) is the best-known exponent. Black sculptors such as Sydney Kumalo (1935–90) and Michael Zondi (b. 1926), became, together with Dumile, the first black artists to represent South Africa internationally.

A further attempt to combine a European approach and African symbolism took place during the 1960s with artists such as Edoardo

Preceding pages: taking part in art. Left, a Karel Nel painting.

Villa (b. 1920), Giuseppe Cattaneo (b. 1929) and Cecil Skotnes (b. 1952) featuring prominently. Villa settled in South Africa from Italy after World War II and introduced welded metal sculpture.

The 1970s saw the rise of an art which began to question the South African experience. Despite the country's enforced cultural isolation, black artists such as Leonard Matsoso (b. 1949) and Ezrom Legae (b. 1938) still achieved international recognition. Avant-garde artists tried to reflect the socio-political realities and challenge the social conscience.

A new generation of artists – such as William Kentridge (b. 1955), Penny Siopis

(b. 1953) and Keith Dietrich (b. 1950) – came to prominence in the mid-1980s and have used a figurative style in their interpretation of contemporary socio-political events. Personal iconography and exploration of other issues and subjects have been undertaken by artists like Karel Nel (b. 1955) and Paul Shelly (b. 1963).

The phenomenon of formally-untrained rural artists finding their way into the mainstream of South African art can be traced to the 1985 exhibition, "Tributaries". Black sculptors fron the Venda area in the northern Transvaal were introduced to the urban art world. Among the most original is Jackson

Hlungwani (b. 1923), whose religious cosmology and world view are translated through extraordinarily powerful and innovative sculptures.

Rorke's Drift, a mission station in Zululand, provided art instruction for black students in the 1970s, with printmaking the preferred medium. Many artists who are now teaching in a variety of situations, including community art centres in high-density townships such as Soweto (Funda), Kathlehong and Alexandra, are products of this important school, now closed.

People's art: The Community Arts Project in Cape Town and the Thupelo Art Project in Johannesburg are two non-formal collective projects which have adapted teaching to conditions in the townships, providing skills, training and access to resources. The Thupelo Art Project, which owes its origins to the Triangle artists' workshop in New York, saw the development of an abstract expressionist, non-figurative style. This caused controversy among those who felt a figurative socio-political style was more appropriate to the South African situation.

This found expression with the 1985 unrest in the black townships which saw the emergence of a spontaneous public art known as "people's parks". These were places where people could gather and conduct cultural and political activities. Symbols of work such as tools were juxtaposed in sculptures with common junk, maps of Africa and home-made wooden weapons. None of these "parks" remains.

Graffiti was another form of expression indicating the "cultural struggle". Posters and designs for T-shirts with political messages form a second area of "visual culture".

Many objects previously classified as craft or folk art have been culturally elevated. Wire, ceramic toys, soft sculpture and beaded blankets are to be found in museums, art galleries, and private collections. Artists such as Bonnie Ntshalintshali (b. 1967) and Fée Halsted Berning (b. 1958), who work together on a farm in KwaZulu/Natal producing ceramic sculptures, symbolise a new trend: their work shows how the artistic conventions of rural and urban experience are converging in a way which is helping to define a new South African identity.

Left, street art in a black township.

THE FIRST ARTISTS

A vast number of paintings and engravings found in rock shelters and on rocky outcrops are the only remaining archaeological traces of the Bushmen (San) who were southern Africa's only inhabitants until about 2,000 years ago.

The art is associated with the trance experiences and beliefs of medicine peoples (shamans). A central ritual for Bushmen groups was, and still is, among the Kalahari groups, the trance dance. During a dance, women clap and sing medicine songs named after things said to be powerful, such as the eland or giraffe, while men dance rhythmically, taking thudding steps around the women. Bushmen believe the singing and dancing activates a supernatural potency. Powerful animals are also said to contain this potency.

The task of the shamans in the group – about half of the men and about a third of the women – is to harness this potency and enter a trance state or, for the Bushmen, the spirit world. Once in the spirit world, shamans are said to cure the sick, resolve social conflict, and control the game as well as the rain-animal that brought rain. Such "work" guaranteed the existence of Bushman society. Shamans entering the spirit world experience a variety of physical and visual hallucinations, often using "death" and "underwater" as metaphors for trance experience.

Bushmen see similarities between a shaman entering a trance and a dying eland. Both bleed at the nose, froth at the mouth, stumble about and eventually collapse unconscious. For this reason shamans refer to trance as "half-death" or "little death". Each shaman's experience, no matter how contradictory, is accepted as authentic. The paintings depicting trance dances (women clapping and men dancing) symbolise supernatural potency (the most common and important of which is the eland), rain-animals, and the visual and physical hallucinations which shamans experience. They were also another means by which the shamans tried to communicate their experiences to their peers. The paintings and engravings were probably done by shaman-artists after the trance dance because they would lack control during it.

An interview with one of the last surviving descendants of a Bushman artist, a woman now in her eighties and living in Transkei, has shed new light on the probable ritual use of the paintings. She told how eland were driven up the valley and killed at a spot near the cave. Blood from the animals was carried to the cave, to be used as an ingredient in the paint. The eland's power was thus transferred from the animal's body to the paint and then to the paintings themselves. When dancing in the cave in front of the freshly executed paintings, the shamans, wanting to increase their level of potency, would turn to face the paintings, believing that the potency in the paintings would then flow into them. For the Bushmen, potency flowed from this animal, via its blood, to the paintings where it was stored, and then from the paintings to the trancing shamans.

Paintings and engravings can no longer be seen just as symbols of supernatural power and the experiences of the spirit world. They

were also regarded as powerful things in themselves, storehouses of the potency that made contact with the spirit world possible.

The Bushmen's way of life survived the coming of the Khoi herders, who migrated from the north; indeed, they developed good relations with them. But their society was harmed first by Bantu speaking farmers and then by the arrival of Europeans in the 17th century. The colonists looked down on the Bushmen, whom they saw as lacking religion and acceptable social values, and began pursuing them. Today, Bushmen groups are struggling to survive in parts of Botswana and Namibia, but have long since disappeared as separate social group in South Africa. ∎

Truly indigenous theatre in South Africa is inextricably linked to the country's political reality. The 1980s produced not only an abundance of "protest plays" focusing on the effects of apartheid but also saw the emergence of a new generation of black actors and playwrights, some of them achieving international acclaim.

Theatre complexes such as the Market Theatre in Johannesburg became known as politically daring centres for developing talent and lending expression to the political sentiments of the oppressed. It was a laborious process, often hampered by state censorship and not always artistically successful. But it has produced some acclaimed theatre that was exported to international stages.

In Johannesburg, variations of the protest theme spread to more conventional theatres such as the Windybrow as well as an exciting new venue catering for outrageous performances, the Black Sun. In Cape Town, the Baxter Theatre, owned by the University of Cape Town, has been the traditional venue for more "daring" productions, while Durban's Loft Theatre Company is also no stranger to controversy. Today, despite the introduction of far-reaching political reforms, indigenous theatre performances often remain confined to makeshift and unconventional venues.

Among the first to succeed abroad was playwright Athol Fugard (A Lesson from Aloes) and the very successful partnership of John Kani and Winston Ntshona (Sizwe Banzi Is Dead and The Island) who were both honoured with the American theatre's highest accolade, the Tony Award. An expatriate actor, Zakes Mokae, later won the award for his performance in Fugard's Master Harold and the Boys.

Often dubbed "the father of black theatre", Gibson Kente provided through his "theatre of the townships" numerous opportunities for aspiring writers and actors to become major stars. This provided the impetus to talented writers such as Mbongeni Ngema, Barney Simon and Percy Mtwa to take their

Left, a NAPAC **performance of** *Aurora's Wedding*.
Right, **modern drama**.

trail-blazing production Woza Albert on to the international stages.

Ngema's Asinamali wound up on Broadway in 1987 and won a Tony nomination for best director. In 1988, he took his hit musical Sarafina first to New York's Lincoln Theatre and then to Broadway where it played to capacity audiences for 11 months. Sarafina has also been made into a film which opened to great acclaim at the Cannes Film Festival in 1992.

Following in the wake of protest plays,

Afrikaans theatre made a resurgence in the second half of the 1980s. Its writers introduced vital impulses into the theatrical firmament with works such as God's Forgotten, Paradise Is Closing Down and the hugely popular Adapt or Die.

But indigenous protest theatre produced only part of South Africa's considerable talents on the stage. In the early 1970s, impresario Pieter Toerien was already an established stalwart of commercial theatre, even before his André Huguenet Theatre had come into being. Much of Toerien's early work was staged at the Intimate Theatre and later at the now defunct Barnato Theatre in

Johannesburg. After a lengthy battle in the early 1980s, Toerien saved the Alhambra from demolition, rebuilt the stage area, refurbished the auditorium and opened with a season of one of the most successful productions of a serious play in South African theatre history, Amadeus. The venue was immediately established as part of the counrty's drama circuit.

During the 1960s and early 1970s, the government-subsidised performing arts councils of the four provinces, Transvaal, Natal, the Cape and the Orange Free State were less daring in their approach to indigenous theatre, preferring to mount classical performances or well-tested modern theatre.

This has changed, however. Experimental drama, indigenous black protest theatre and an impressive wealth of other contemporary domestic plays have been produced on the subsidised stages of the performing arts councils' modern provincial theatre complexes: the State Theatre in Pretoria, the Nico Malan Theatre Centre in Cape Town, the Sand du Plessis Theatre in Bloemfontein and Durban's Playhouse.

In the area of musical theatre, Joan Brickhill and Louis Burke, Des and Dawn Lindberg, the late Taubie Kushlick (for her Brel works in particular) and the Performing Arts Council of the Transvaal (Pact) all had far greater access to the world's top musicals in the 1970s and early 1980s than, because of to the international boycott, they did later.

The four performing arts council complexes also produced lavish productions of evergreens, from The Great Waltz and The Pirates of Penzance to Hello, Dolly! and Evita. Largely through the efforts of these councils, the growth of the classical disciplines has also being fostered. The councils enabled classical companies to develop an identity and achieve so high a standard that they can now interchange performers with some of the world's top theatres.

Audiences in the major cities have been treated to lavish productions of many of the world's best-loved operas, and South African favourites such as Mimi Coertze, Carla Pohl, Emma Renzi, Marieta Napier, Hans van Heerden and Deon van der Walt are well-known on international stages. International stars such as Monserrat Caballe, Alfredo Kraus, Zankunaro, Denis Maszola and Martina Arroya performed in South African productions.

The country's oldest ballet school was established at the University of Cape Town in 1934, and still feeds the ballet company of the Cape Performing Arts Board (Capab) which developed in the 1960s. Both were pioneered by Dr Dulcie Howes, doyenne of South African ballet, who retired in 1969. The present director of UCT Ballet School and artistic adviser of Capab ballet, Professor David Poole, is another of South Africa's great ballet pioneers. Poole, who trained with Dame Ninette de Valois in London, was elected vice-chairman of the Royal Academy of Dancing in Britain. The Performing Arts Council of the Transvaal (PACT) runs South Africa's second major professional ballet company. Both have impressive repertoires which include not only classical works but also many short, indigenous ballets.

Both companies have brought international stars such as Errol Pickford and Nicola Roberts from the Royal Ballet, Alla Mikhalchenko from the Bolshoi Ballet and Patricia Neary from the Ballantine Ballet Company to South African stages.

All the performing arts councils have a symphony season, featuring not only the major South African orchestras, conductors and soloists, but also international musicians. Music lovers have lately been treated to the Radio Orchester Baden-Baden and the Bamberger Symphoniker. Conductors Louis Fremou, Wolfgang Bothe, Enrico Garcia de Ascusio and Reinhard Schwarz have performed on local stages, as have soloists such as violinist Pierre Amoyal and pianist Peter Francke.

The country's performing arts councils, however, are not the only centres with thriving theatre complexes. Welkom has its own sophisticated theatre complex which stages drama, opera and ballet. And Roodepoort, near Johannesburg in the Gauteng Province, has developed a well-deserved reputation. Its Pro Musica Orchestra performs up to eight symphony concerts a year, and the

Black Mambazo, who subsequently leapt to fame. From the late 1980s, South African groups and soloists have travelled Britain, America, Japan and Australia and have been greeted with pop-star enthusiasm. Political exiles such as Miriam Makeba, Hugh Masekela and Dollar Brand who have long been international stars, have now returned.

Two of the most famous events on South Africa's cultural diary are the Roodepoort Eisteddfod and the Grahamstown Festival.

The acclaimed Roodepoort Eisteddfod, the largest musical competition in the Southern Hemisphere, started in 1981 with 320 participants and has grown to a monumental event. Now as many as 8,000 participants,

Roodepoort City Opera is known for its ambitious productions. On its agenda for 1992 was one opera a year from Wagner's Ring cycle; all four will be staged in 1996.

South African music, too, has come to the fore, and names such as Johnny Clegg and Savuka, Mahlathini and the Mahotella Queens, Yvonne Chakachaka, Lucky Dube and Mango Groove are internationally known. Paul Simon recorded his Graceland album with the a capella group, Ladysmith

Left, *The Importance of Being Earnest*. **Above**, **Martha Haape in the Giordano opera**, *Andrea Chenier*, **about the French Revolution.**

600 from overseas, compete in a wide spectrum of categories: choral, vocal, instrumental, folk song and dance, bands and orchestras, composition.

The tremendous growth of the annual Grahamstown Festival has gone a long way towards proving that "local is lekker" in South African theatre. It features all the performing arts, from protest theatre to classical Shakespeare, ballet, mime, music, anything from the old to the new, from the traditional to the avant-garde. It has grown into a major cultural event and is the place to be seen by South Africa's playwrights, artists and the serious theatre-going public.

Music is, like life itself, what is made of it. White South Africans have a highly specialised musical culture requiring an educated appreciation – and so 13 university departments are turning out professional composers, performers and teachers, and four subsidised regional councils equipped with theatres, orchestras, dancers and actors bring the performing arts to the public. The complete European heritage has been transplanted to southern Africa and is tenderly cultivated.

African tradition: Rubbing shoulders with this European heritage is a completely different tradition, arising from a differing set of premises in which aesthetic considerations are subject to strong communal forces. African music is far more than an emotional response to sound patterns. It is vital in every respect and has to be "lived" if it is to answer to its purpose; it arises from the inner drive of people who are expressing not only a love of singing and dancing but also the inner forces which shape their being.

Music rises directly from life and is everybody's concern, from the earliest childhood right up to old age. It is not something to hear and listen to; it is experienced through active participation, singing, dancing, clapping hands, blowing on reeds or thumping a drum. Its impact on the community is dependent on participation and sharing.

To know their music is to gain insight into their innermost being. To know their music is to know Africa, since it expresses their most intimate experiences. A symbol of this unity is their language, which depends for its meaning on the pitch at which syllables are pronounced. The languages are "tonal" and are spoken with clear-cut melodic contour, remarkable volume, verve and expression. Speaking, in fact, is close to singing.

The communal spirit is at its strongest in the tribe, less strong in the nation and at its weakest in the relationship to other nations with different forms of speech. But it is never entirely absent. All recognise the validity of music which expresses seasonal activities, or occasions such as initiation of adolescent youths, exorcism of spirits, festival days, the

Left and **right**, same principle, different tones.

"amusements" of young people, beer drinking, and education through songs. The result is that there has always been extensive borrowing and adaptation between tribes and nations in southern Africa. This is not confined to the actual music, but applies especially to instruments and the forms in which they have been developed.

The San, who were among the earliest inhabitants of southern Africa, used the bow and arrow for hunting and warfare and adapted forms of the bow for making music.

Strangely enough, the black nations hardly ever used it for warfare but extensively copied the bows used for musical purposes. Cultural appreciation actually had precedence over hunting and war.

When, on 25 November 1497, the Portuguese discoverer Vasco da Gama landed at Mossel Bay on the southwest coast he was met on the beach by a band of Khoikhoi who treated the expedition to a performance on reed flutes. These can be regarded as a set of dismantled pan pipes, with each player blowing on one reed to produce a single tone at a set point of time. Probably da Gama heard a set of four different reeds playing a four-note melody. Five centuries later, the same principle is still used by the Venda in northern Transvaal. The only difference is that the Venda use a large number of players to each pitch and, since the reeds can not all have the exact bore commensurate with the pitch, the resulting impression is one of a conglomerate of microtonal pitches grouped around four notes.

Cape Malays: To solve the labour problems experienced by the Cape settlement during the 17th and 18th centuries, slaves were imported from Dutch possessions in the Far East, notably from Malaysia. These people have always been extremely musical and were often required to act as house musicians

microtonal decorations surrounding certain melody tones), and also by traditional vocal styles which have survived 300 years of estrangement from the original country.

Some of these are of a religious nature (for example, the pudjies, antiphonal singing divided between an imam and members of the congregation), while others are connected with wedding ceremonies (for instance, the antiphonal minnat songs which are sung at an extremely slow pace by a leader and a group of male guests.) But they have also preserved songs reflecting their two centuries of serfdom, which were absorbed from the old Dutch repertoire of folk songs.

In addition, they have cultivated a truly

and perform at banquets by their Dutch masters. Today around 150,000 of their descendants live in Cape Town, including many who have retained signs of their Eastern heritage in their religious and cultural life.

Their musical gift is still one of their main assets and is in fact inseparable from their daily lives. However, it is far more of a heritage than a talent which can be commercially exploited. It has marked Eastern characteristics which are easily isolated: for example, a couple of rhythmic instruments (the portable drum, ghomma, and the large tambourine, rebana), an Eastern singing style marked by karienkels ("sound wrinkles" of

South African style which might be described as Afrikaans, as far as the language and the general liveliness is concerned, but which also has a distinctive colouring due to improvisation, dynamic rhythms and a noticeably loud and extrovert (banjo) sound which combine to give it an exotic flavour. These colourful characteristics have become part and parcel of the South African scene. Many people regard them as being distinctively South African, but their impact can actually be enjoyed only when Cape Malays or their Coloured compatriots are the performers. Typical of these "picnic songs", as they are often called, are the ghomma songs, in which the gift of improvisation plays an important part in stringing together words and melodies without a recognisable context, and the moppies which excel in roguish words and rhythms.

The jazz revolution: Traditional music lags behind jazz in popularity among black people. Launched in South Africa by the technological advances represented by the gramophone and radio transmission, it soon swamped the multi-racial scene. It especially bewitched black musicians attracted by its emotional loudness and rhythmical irregularities. They heard the voice of Africa in an new way, with unusual instruments and saying new and complex things.

Its rise in South Africa became a triumphal march. At first untrained youngsters emulated their American counterparts, but soon developed a style of their own, variously called Township Jazz, Black Jazz or Marabi. One of its earliest and most successful pioneers was the extremely successful and idolised "Dollar" Brand, now known as Abdullah Ibrahim.

The quality of the music produced soon enabled gifted black musicians to break through on the international scene – an example followed in recent years by musical stage productions like King Kong, Ipi Tombi and Serafina but also by local artists combining their talents with major international

Jazz can be considered to be the art of continual change in the time dimension, a view providing a clue to its almost frightening impact on humanity in this century. It is highly volatile, also in its effect on devotees, which makes it the predestined art of peoples in transition, Western people as well as those of the Third World, and latterly also of India and the Far East. Jazz is a driving force which not only expresses change, but assists at its implementation.

Left, entertainers Johnny Clegg and Brenda Fasi in action. **Above**, a home band in Cape Town's Malay community.

stars as was the case with Ladysmith Black Mambazo teaming up with Paul Simon on his Graceland tour and album.

Most of the tensions which contributed to the rapid rise of jazz in South Africa are still there, but this has its positive aspects too. They are the spice of life to jazz, but also act as a hothouse in which new ideas can germinate. One of these is the possibility of a fusion between black traditional music and the European musical art represented in South Africa. Judging by the eminent success which a similar fusion has had in the field of jazz, the prospects for an entirely original South African art music are bright.

JUMP
AND OTHER
STORIES

NADINE
GORDIMER

BLOOMSBURY

The first European literature to deal with South African experience is the Portuguese. A significant part of Portugal's national epic, Luís de Camões's *The Lusiads* of 1572, deals with the early navigators' records of rounding the formidable Cape of Storms. Here the African land mass is portrayed as a hostile and dark giant, threatening to all but the most heroic Christian adventurers. He is given a mythological name, Adamastor, and a part of his body is Table Mountain that guards the entry to the land.

After the settlement of the Dutch there in 1652, the written records of the Cape are mostly in diary form. In the 18th century this small enclave had a considerable reputation in Europe as a botanical paradise and several travellers' records portray its slave-holding milieu. Inland over the frontier was an explorer's playground, of which a boastful adventurer like François le Vaillant in 1795 could publish his highly exaggerated accounts. Nevertheless, the travelogue of the Enlightenment included detailed records of the life and customs of indigenous peoples, together with accounts of hunting big-game.

British tradition: From the 1820s, with the British colonisation of Southern Africa, a systematic literature begins with the introduction of the press. On the Eastern frontier, the first Xhosa-language newspaper began in the 1840s, more or less at the time the emancipation of slaves became general. Missionary endeavour on many fronts, while translating the Bible, preserved the first accounts we have of the earliest oral literature in Xhosa, Zulu, Tswana and Sotho.

The even older poetry and folklore of the Khoisan peoples was first taken down and translated by the German philologist Wilhelm Bleek, whose collection for the South African Library in Cape Town has not yet been exhausted by scholars. The "Bushmen" and "Hottentots" – both now extinct – provide us in their mythology and history with an absorbing account of the European conqueror from the other side.

The British frontier produced two types of

writing which persist even today. Thomas Pringle (1789–1834) introduced a higher, romantic style of poetry which started a tradition which stays in touch with European models, while Andrew Geddes Bain (1797–1864) began a stream of popular songs and satires which used the far more earthy language of the market-place. In Bain's polyglot work we find early forms of Afrikaans, the African language that was to develop from Dutch, English, French and German (the languages of the early settlers), Malay and spoken black languages.

Continuing the Pringle line of high culture, we have by 1883 the publication of the novel, *The Story of an African Farm*, which was really the first great work to be written in the far-flung colonies. It was greeted in the motherland with amazement and controversy, for it was the first work which gave a realistic and credible portrait of the conditions of daily life on an establishment in the Karoo and of the cruel and difficult society, with its educational, commercial and religious institutions, on which it depended. The author, Olive Schreiner (1855–1920), was the daughter of a German missionary and his English wife but considered herself one of the first "South Africans", owing her inspiration to the modern nation she was so influential in building.

Adventure novels: The other popular stream of writing in the late 19th century was particularly productive and successful. With the appeal of British imperialism at its height, many earlier forms became concentrated in the adventure romance. In the hands of an exponent like H. Rider Haggard (1856–1925), this new form created one of the first modern bestsellers. *King Solomon's Mines* (1885) has been filmed at least five times.

What is so memorable about his original adventures is the skilful way Haggard wrote them. He used an endearing, self-effacing narrator, Allan Quatermain, who was a professional hunter, settled in Durban, always willing to guide newcomers into the interior of Africa. One must remember that it had not been so long since David Livingstone had set off from the Northern Cape to find the inland Okavango Swamps of Botswana and then

Left, one of the many works of Nadine Gordimer, South Africa's Nobel laureate.

the great Central Lakes of Africa, nor since Burton and Speke had located the source of the Nile. The imperial adventure romance has everything to do with glamorising these exploits for readers back home.

Industrial South Africa, with its sizable cities such as Cape Town, Durban and Johannesburg, has maintained a literature like any modern country's since the declaration of Union in 1910. After Schreiner, a distinctive tradition emerges in fiction, which includes writers like Nadine Gordimer – whose novels such as *Burger's Daughter* have been internationally acclaimed – and Breyten Breytenbach. J. M. Coetzee (*Life and Times of Michael K*) and André P. Brink (*A Dry White Season*) are equally well-known outside South Africa. Directly in the Haggard line is Wilbur Smith, whose adventures (such as *Where the Lion Feeds*) are very widely translated.

The oeuvre of many South African writers has tended to dwell on the burning racial and political issues that have confronted to country. But in the works of Sir Laurens van der Post (born 1906), such debates, if they have arisen at all, have played only a subordinate role. The essence of *The Lost World of the Kalahari* (1958), his famous book and documentary film on the Bushmen, or his gripping tales of adventure such as *Flamingo Feather*, *A Story like the Wind* (1972), and its sequel *A Far-Off Place* (1974), is far more the enduring culture of southern Africa's native people (particularly the Bushmen) and the mysteries and wonders of the vast landscape in which they live.

The black experience: Parts of this fiction-writing tradition are particularly African. A black writer, Sol T. Plaatjie (1876–1932), in Mhudi (1916), started to reformulate the Haggard-Schreiner heritage in ways that made it sympathetic to the portrayal of the black history that white writers had tended to ignore or even destroy. In the same line, magical Bessie Head (1937–86), who lived the second half of her life in Botswana, was able to recover whole areas of the black experience from oral sources. These she converted into short stories that, while remaining African in spirit, are very acceptable to white readers – *The Collector of Treasures* (1977) is a good example.

Those unfamiliar with South African writing should, however, beware of making too easy distinctions between "white" and "black" writing, as if these two categories existed apart from one another. Throughout the 20th century the great theme of the fiction writers has been precisely the relationship between blacks and whites, so that every writer to some extent has been studying and presenting the country as one in which inter-relationships are vitally important. The best example is Alan Paton's *Cry, the Beloved Country* (1948), still the widest-read South African work of all time.

Paton's novel first appeared while the apartheid system was becoming entrenched. It may be read as an outcry against what would happen in the country if the rural areas were to be allowed to deteriorate, if lawlessness in the overcrowded cities were encouraged by profiteers, and if good partriachal relations collapsed into violent revolution.

Afrikaans writing: Poetry in modern South Africa has also proved a distinguished area of its literature, particularly in Afrikaans. Indeed, it is through their poetry that many Afrikaans-language artists have shaped their tongue as a written language. Eugäne N. Marais (1871–1936), a founder of lyric verse in Afrikaans, was also a widely respected naturalist whose classic works such as Soul of the White Ant raised the science of zoological observation into an art form.

Another Afrikaans-language poet is C. Louis Leipoldt (1880–1947). Like Schreiner, he was born of German missionary stock. He wrote voluminously in several languages, particularly about Rhenish mission settlements which were such a feature of the development of the Western Cape. Like many other Afrikaans figures, Leipoldt was an all-round man who wrote histories of wine and of indigenous cooking as well.

For many years, the Afrikaner's struggle for language rights was almost indistinguishable from his political awakening. This found expression in the formation of the "Genootskap van Regte Afrikaners" (Institute of True Afrikaners) in 1875 and again in the 1930s when writers such as Totius, Jan F. E. Celliers and C. J. Langenhoven vividly described the plight of the thousands of "poor whites" driven to cities by a devastating drought and economic recession.

This overt form of political expression later matured in the work of poets such as N. P. van Wyk Louw and Dirk Opperman. In the 1960s a younger generation of writers – led by Breytenbach, Brink and Etienne Leroux – emerged, and their work represented a drastic departure from the conventional Afrikaans tradition.

Modern trends: Two further aspects of contemporary South African literature should be noted. The first is that, during apartheid times especially, when many artists were driven into exile in Europe and America, the form of autobiography became particularly rewarding among black writers. Peter Abrahams in 1954 published *Tell Freedom*, the first of many such works to recount the life-histories of black people.

Down Second Avenue (1959) by Es'kia

gave rise to a new generation of black writers such as Lewis Nkosi, Alex la Guma, Richard Rive, Casey Motsitsi and Can Themba, whose work was heavily influenced by the racy style of journalism.

The other aspect of South African literature that needs to be celebrated is its drama. Unlike in many other African countries, theatre life in South Africa is well established and commercially organised. Now that all cultural boycotts of South Africa have been lifted, productions of opera, ballet and musicals may be seen that compare with the world's best.

But during the deprived apartheid years a type of South African theatre has evolved

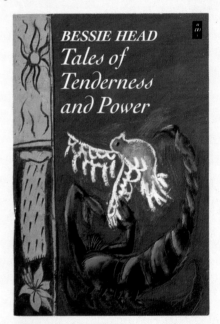

Mphahlele is another example of a black man's story of climbing out of a disadvantaged world of poverty and illiteracy to be educated and ultimately achieve the status of self-made writer. Mphahlele has also distinguished himself as a scholar and critic at universities in West Africa and the United States. South African autobiographers like these have given especially memorable testimony on the theme of freedom.

In the mid-1950s a number of ambitious young writers found expression in the pages of a black-oriented magazine, *Drum*. This

Above, taking cover in a literary world.

which uniquely knows how to make the maximum use of conditions of poverty. Athol Fugard's plays such as *Master Harold and the Boys* – very akin to Brecht's – have translated well into German, and many others in his style have been exported from the Market Theatre in Johannesburg, which until recently was his base.

Works of the playwright Mbongeni Ngema (Asinmali) have also been performed on stages across the world. Celebrating resilience and human survival, South African plays in many languages have become the form in which literature meets its audience most passionately and joyfully.

Remarkable yet true: the chief reason for South Africa's establishment was food and wine. Holland's domination of the East Indies' spice islands created heavy sea traffic past the Cape in the mid-1600s and, after three months at sea, crews stopped in Table Bay to take on fresh water from Table Mountain. The vegetable garden started by Jan van Riebeeck, first commander of the Cape, still exists at the top of Adderley Street, although it is now a botanical park.

As the primitive settlement grew first into a seaside village, then into a town, hearty and wholesome Dutch cooking held sway. Gradually culinary ideas from the East Indies were introduced. Stews were enhanced by cloves, cinnamon, pimiento, turmeric, anise and tamarind. Likewise cakes and homemade sweets, confectionery and preserves. It was not long before rice was a standard accompaniment to many dishes – a direct legacy of the Dutch/Indonesian rijstafel – as well as oriental pickles and condiments. All still play a big role in the ingredients of traditional cuisine.

As well as being moulded by the passing spice trade, Cape food was influenced by East Indian slaves, political hostages and exiles, whose families transformed old Dutch recipes with the flavours of Bengal, Java, Malabar, Ceylon and Malaya. To this day the Malay word piesang is Afrikaans for a banana; small cubes of meat grilled on a short skewer are called sosatie (a corruption of Indonesia's sate). A mouthwatering baked meat-loaf aromatic with mild curry, with a sweet/tart piquancy, enjoyed with a savoury sauce of dried fruit (blatjang), is called bobotie after its Javanese original and is a favourite in many homes.

French influence arrived in 1688 with the Huguenots, who were fleeing the revocation of the Edict of Nantes. They settled in the wonderfully scenic Franschhoek valley, where they harvested fruit and made wine. Their technique of preserving food by long slow simmering, confit, means that all fruits preserved in sugar syrup, including jam, are

Preceding pages: every visit to the country must include a seafood platter. **Left,** dinner at eight.

called konfyt in Afrikaans. To them, South Africa owes a rich heritage of biscuits, tarts, cookery with wine, pastries and even a bread roll called mosbolletjies using fermenting wine as a raising agent instead of yeast. Broken into pieces and dried in the oven, this fine-textured speciality is turned into hardish rusks – the standard accompaniment to early morning coffee all across the country, even in many hotels.

Traditional African cooking: In stark contrast to dishes derived from European settlers is the simple cuisine of southern Africa's original inhabitants. Comprising mostly roving tribes, these people subsisted for centuries on a diet based on grains – prepared usually as a porridge – cooked greens, depending on what was available, and the fortunes of the hunt. Today their descendants still follow this fundamental trinity of meat, porridge and cooked vegetables but with the modern enhancement of tinned fish, supermarket fast-foods, tea and coffee, cool drinks and commercial bread.

Gifts of the Southern Oceans: Until the 1800s when Europeans first settled widely in the interior, it was the southern and eastern coastline which saw development of villages and towns. Fine-textured fish, mussels, oysters, crabs, baby squid, and pilchards are still caught in abundance but the finest seafood is to be had only between November and April: this is high season for the Cape's world-famous rock lobster, a prized delicacy so sweet and tender that vast quantities are exported to top restaurants worldwide. Similar to North Sea lobster except that it has no claws, it is served in all the traditional ways such as thermidor, armoricaine, grilled or cold with mayonnaise. For many people, the pinnacle of the country's cuisine is curried lobster – a ravishing contrast of moist, hot lobster pieces in mild/aromatic Cape Malay curry, all served with fluffy white rice.

Other summer delicacies are the pelagic fish, arriving in shoals along the east coast in the warm Indian Ocean. Barracuda, yellowtail, katonkel and shad are all fighting fish popular amongst anglers, but they are overshadowed by the Cape's pungently flavoured snoek. Named by the early Dutch settlers after the European freshwater pike, this is a long (almost 3ft/1 metre) silvery fighter with firm flesh and prominent, captivating taste. Served fried, it is traditionally accompanied by sweet korrelkonfyt, a luscious jam made of honey-flavoured muscat grapes which complements the bracing saltiness of the snoek. Then there's snoeksmoor, a hot savoury mix of fried onions and potatoes with browned snoek chunks, sometimes with a little stewed tomato, always served with rice and tart blatjang.

Unfortunately, as with home cooking elsewhere in the world, such specialities are rarely recreated in restaurants. Yet there are several restaurants serving this type of food

with real pride. In Johannesburg, Leipoldt's serves dozens of dishes on its daily buffet, but most good restaurants are in the Cape. Best is probably the restaurant on Boschendal wine estate near Franschhoek, followed by Laborie restaurant in Paarl, the restaurant on Spier wine estate near Stellenbosch, the Jonkershuis restaurant on historical Groot Constantia wine estate and the tiny Kaapse Tafel restaurant near the museum in Cape Town itself.

Satisfactions of the hunt: South Africa is hunting country. Since the first Dutch farmers cleared the Cape of lion, elephant, buffalo and buck South Africans have relished the pleasures of the sunny outdoors, of meats and sausages grilled over wood coals, of sustaining air-dried venison called biltong, of fresh-brewed coffee around a camp fire under the Southern Cross. To this day in countless gardens every weekend wood fires are lit for the family braaivleis (braai = to grill or roast, vleis = meat). Lamb chops, curried sosaties, freshly picked corn on the cob, a coarse-minced sausage of well-spiced beef and pork fat called boerewors (boer = a farmer, wors = sausage) are the foundations of this outdoor meal, but it can also include beef fillet, or cuts of springbok, kudu, bush pig, eland or impala.

The fact that most of the population lives inland, far from the sea, is another reason why South Africans are heavy meat-eaters. Apart from the midwinter hunting months when venison becomes sought after, beef is preferred, followed by lamb. Pork and veal are the exception rather than the rule. First-class steak houses and chicken takeaways are found in almost every suburb, serving meat of a quality that few hotels or conventional restaurants can match.

Regional pleasures: In the Cape, seafood gets most attention, along with casual lunches on wine-farms and the sampling of homely traditional foods. There are also several very high-class restaurants for which bookings need to be made weeks in advance during summer.

Sub-tropical Natal also specialises in seafood. Not to be missed are Natal's famous curries, popularised by its Indian community. Unlike the Cape's mild Malay curries which work well with seafood, the Indian curries of Natal are usually reserved for beef, lamb, chicken or vegetarian dishes. Rice, sambals, masala, crackly poppadoms, rubbery roti bread, fried puri dough, coconut and sliced banana are the signatures of curry restaurants throughout the province. As Natal is close to Mozambique, its restaurants abound with prawns, calamari, cuttlefish, langoustines and deep-sea lobster.

Finally, Johannesburg and Pretoria, at the heart of South Africa's wealthiest region, offer a wealth of cosmopolitan restaurants. These provide all the polish, kitchen artistry and style of "special occasion" establishments in large cities anywhere.

Left, spicing up the stock national repertoire.

WORLD-CLASS WINE

Outside Europe and the Middle East the world's oldest vineyards are found at the Cape. Since February 1659, when the Cape's first grapes were pressed, wine has been as symbolic of the Cape as Table Mountain itself. Several of today's top wine estates have been producing sound wines for more than 300 years and today there are over 2,100 different wines to choose from, excluding vintage duplications.

Most are white wines made in the German style and are off-dry to semi-sweet but with a slightly higher alcohol content because of South Africa's sunnier climate. The best regularly win awards in Europe. The only Cape winemaker to be named "Winemaker of the Year", Günter Broezel, is famous for his Trockenbeerenauslese wines made 6,200 miles (10,000 km) south of his birthplace.

Blessed with a Mediterranean climate, the Cape's vineyards nevertheless enjoy widely varying conditions during the ripening period (January to April) from very hot inland areas to quite cool coastal and mountain regions. Thus, the vintage starts with early-ripening varieties such as Chardonnay, Rhine Riesling, Pinot Noir, and Sauvignon Blanc being picked before the end of January, and ends with late-ripeners like Cabernet Sauvignon which are sometimes not sufficiently ripe even by April. This extended vintage encourages many producers to keep their cellars occupied by handling many grape varieties in succession. The result is a wide range of wines coming off one farm – in some cases more than 20.

Apart from various German styles of white table wine, exceptional sherry-style wines are made, rich fortified muscatels, weighty ports and jerepigos. Cabernet Sauvignon is the best red wine, followed by Shiraz, Pinot Noir, Merlot, Cinsaut and many blends of these. Of course, the best-known red table wine is Pinotage, a crossing of Pinot Noir and Cinsaut (then mistakenly called Hermitage) which was invented at the Cape and first made headlines in 1959. Richly flavoured, often made in massive, muscular style, Pinotage is usually at its best appreciated after at least 10 years' bottle-maturation.

Indeed, many Cape red wines need this time to reach ripe mellowness and maturity – a fact rarely appreciated by South Africans who happily drink all wines as soon as they are available for sale. Collectors and connoisseurs there certainly are, but they're few and far between. It's usually the overseas wine-lovers who point out how much better wines are, reds especially, if they're given some years to ripen.

Until 1973 wine producers were relatively unregulated and could print what they liked on their labels – and sometimes even put a different wine into the bottle. But since then a strict control exercised by inspectors ensures that what's on the label is definitely what's in the bottle. Wines thus controlled carry a small "Wine of Origin" sticker on the neck of the bottle which tells if the label has been certified for a particular type of grape, a particular year, or a particular wine region. The coloured horizontal stripes – green, red and blue – on the sticker relate to these criteria. A wine can be certified for any one of these descriptions

or all three and, if the wine comes from a single farm (an estate), the word "estate" is printed in black above the top stripe.

Not all wines are certified, but this does not mean uncertified wines are sub-standard. It is a fact, however, that the Wine of Origin system has greatly improved standards – both of label accuracy and quality of wine.

Although sound everyday wines are available at some cooperative wineries for as little as R4 a bottle, you will usually pay between R15 and R25 for very good wines and perhaps R30 to R40 for a handful of real showpieces. As elsewhere in the world, of course, in most restaurants these figures will usually be at least doubled. ∎

South Africa, a country with a rich sporting tradition, is tailor-made for the enjoyment of tourists who are either active participants or avid spectators.

A friendly climate attracts the country's inhabitants to an outdoor lifestyle like iron filings to a magnet, while those of a more sedentary nature flock to impressive facilities such as the magnificent Ellis Park "super stadium" in Johannesburg, Pretoria's Loftus Versfeld, King's Park in Durban or Newlands in Cape Town to watch rugby which, with the aid of the adoring media, has been built up into the king of South African sport.

If rugby is king, at least among the white population, cricket is the crown prince, but you will not see too many black faces in the crowd. In keeping with the world-wide trend, soccer commands the fanatical support of South Africa's large black community, who are loyal to teams with delightfully exotic names like Kaizer Chiefs, Moroko Swallows, Mamelodi Sundowns and Orlando Pirates. As the largest participatory sport in the country, football has a showpiece stadium, Soccer City, an ultra-modern facility on the outskirts of Johannesburg which is an eye-opener to any visitor with a passion for the most popular game on the globe. There are also stadiums in every large township and the game is played almost year-long. Even rugby stadiums such as Ellis Park are utilised for the big occasion while barefoot enthusiasts in the rural areas display their skills on pitches hacked out of the bush.

But, for mass participation in a uniquely South African event, there is nothing to equal the Comrades Marathon, a 55-mile (90-km) pilgrimage made by more than 14,000 runners every year between the Natal cities of Durban and Maritzburg – "up" one year from Durban to Maritzburg and "down" the next to a finish near the beach.

On a day in May, the country comes to a standstill as millions of TV viewers watch the drama of a road race which has made a hero of Bruce Fordyce, the world's most accomplished ultra-distance runner, unfold.

Left, sailing off Durban. **Right**, the Olympic barefoot runner Zola Budd-Pieterse.

By winning the race a record nine times, Fordyce has become a legend in his own lifetime, although in 1991 he surrendered his crown to tough Nick Bester, who has also made a name for himself in triathlons and the increasingly popular duathlons. The Comrades Marathon has also made a superstar of glamorous Frith van der Merwe, a pencil-slim former teacher who is expected to take the world by storm since all restrictions on South Africans competing in international competitions have been lifted.

Road running has a huge following in South Africa and races that vary in distance from 6–26 miles (10–42 km) are held every weekend in a major city, often attracting fields of several thousand, while the country is in the grip of a cycling boom, both at the coast and inland, and Durban and Cape Town host international surfing and board sailing competitions.

Running and cycling make it natural for triathlons and duathlons to come to the fore – the triathlons incorporating a swim or canoe leg, a ride and a run, and duathlons usually swimming and running. Swimming triathlons are popular at the coast, while canoeing holds sway in the Transvaal, where the many dams and lakes in and around the major cities Johannesburg and Pretoria are dotted with paddlers every weekend. In fact South Africa is the venue for some exciting and testing canoe races, the most challenging of which is the four-day, 142-mile (228-km) Berg River marathon from Paarl to Veldrif, which includes stretches of "white water". This is usually held around July, with the two-day Orange River marathon in May and the Breede River and Fish River marathons later in the year, around September.

International isolation because of the country's apartheid policy, since dismantled in keeping with State President F.W. de

Klerk's vision of a "New South Africa", resulted in a powerful provincial sporting system and the "big six" are Northern Transvaal, based in the capital, Pretoria; Transvaal (Johannesburg), Western Province (Cape Town), Eastern Province (Port Elizabeth), KwaZulu/Natal (Durban) and the Orange Free State (Bloemfontein). In rugby and cricket, as well as in several other "minor" sports, the major prize is the Currie Cup, while soccer produces a National Soccer League champion and a number of cup competitions, just like those played in Europe or South America.

Since the moratorium on international

contact came to an end, there is the prospect of major tours again both to and from South Africa. The world has waited with bated breath to see the mighty Springboks in action again and stadiums across the country reverberate to rapturous applause as they host touring teams such as the All Blacks, British Lions and French Tricolours rugby sides and the English, West Indies, Australian and Indian cricket teams. The speed with which cricket has unified a racially divided administration has been a lesson to all other South African sporting codes and the new United Cricket Board of South Africa have launched an impressive development programme in the townships to uplift thousands of under-privileged black children.

World-class facilities do not, however, end with rugby, cricket and soccer. South Africa more than holds its own in almost every sphere and is well-placed to stage international events as diverse as motor racing, tennis, swimming, cycling, squash, gymnastics, power boating and bowls.

Kyalami race track, just outside Johannesburg, has been built to international Formula One specifications. The Standard Bank Arena in Johannesburg is a superb tennis venue. Every major city has modern synthetic athletics tracks, squash courts and fine golf courses.

Athletics is one sport which put South Africa on the world map, even during the days of isolation, when Zola Budd (now Pieterse) went to England on a British passport to pursue her Olympic dream. Nobody can forget her ill-fated tangle with Mary Decker-Slaney in the 1984 Los Angeles Games, but Zola is on the come-back trail and, together with little Elana Meyer from the small coastal town of George, will keep spectators enthralled well into the 1990s as they attempt to re-write the world record books at distances from 3,000 metres to the 13-mile (21-km) half-marathon.

Golf was one of the few sports to escape the bleak years of isolation, which in particular hamstrung rugby and cricket and forced South African administrators to organise highly publicised "rebel" tours against the likes of the New Zealand Cavaliers (rugby) and England and Sri Lanka (cricket) to sustain a public desperate to watch their beloved Springboks in action.

A nation which produced the world-beat-ing Bobby Lock, Gary Player and, more recently, World Series of Golf champion David Frost and Ernie Els continues to attract golfing superstars who either play on the multi million-rand Sunshine Tour or the Million Dollar Challenge at the sporting and entertainment Mecca of Sun City, where past winners include the popular Bernhard Langer and Welsh wizard Ian Woosnam and South Africans have been treated to the skills of Nick Faldo, Bernhard Langer, Curtis Strange, Sandy Lyle, Seve Ballesteros and José-Maria Olazabal in recent years.

The course hacked out of the bush at Sun City is a challenge no visitor can pass up – another equally demanding layout for the

South Africans have also proved their mettle. The junior lightweight Brian Mitchell has defended his world title more times than any other fighter in his division while Dingaan Thobela and Welcome Noita have both proved to be without peer in their weight categories in recent years.

The decades of international isolation came as a bitter blow to a country proud of its heritage as a major sporting nation. However, in recent years the doors to international competition have swung open. Unity between sporting bodies divided by political differences was achieved and South Africa has been readmitted as a participant in the Olympic Games.

million-rand Lost City leisure complex has been built at the same location – and there are many immaculately manicured courses around the country, including the plush Durban Country Club, which is rated as one of the top 100 courses in the world. For the more adventurous at heart, you can take a walk on the wild side at the Hans Merensky Golf Club on the edge of the Kruger National Park at Phalaborwa, where there are hippo in a water hazard and antelope on the fairways.

In the harsh world of professional boxing

Left, the Comrades Marathon. **Above**, the path to international competition starts in the clubs.

In a number of sports the standards have dropped alarmingly because of the lack of international competition. In others, South African sportsmen seemed to continue at the same high level where they left off. Despite more than two decades of isolation the country's cricketers reached the semi-finals at their first-ever appearance at the World Cup, while South Africa became the venue in 1995 for rugby's most prestigious international competition. There's still a lot of catching up to do, of course, but South African sportsmen and women are once again able to take their place with pride in the international arena.

What can match the magic of a starlit African night, when the monotonous pinging of a fruit-bat and the eerie call of a thick-tailed bush-baby in the forests accentuate the stillness? And later, as dawn approaches, the roar of a satiated lion attesting his presence and the cackling of hyenas carried on the early morning breeze stir all but the deepest sleepers, filling them with wonder.

Imagine lunch in the shade of a giant fig tree on the banks of a tropical river, with hippos snorting contentedly in the slow waters and an elephant bull lazily browsing in the reed beds. Baboons frolic and giraffes delicately crop the terminal shoots of an acacia tree. Few experiences are more intense or vivid than hearing the sound of thousands of buffaloes trampling the dust on their way to drink after a long day in the scorching African sun.

Great diversity: South Africa is endowed with a rich mammal fauna comprising some 230 land and 43 marine species. This means that 7 percent of the world's known extant mammals can be encountered in just 1 percent of the earth's land mass. This variety can be ascribed to the country's great ecological diversity, manifested in two major oceanic currents flowing along the coastline and in the presence of six major land biotic zones. These range from desert in the northwest, to Cape Macchia with its winter rainfall in the south, the central semi-arid Karoo, the grassland of the Orange Free State and southern Transvaal, the eastern montane and coastal forests, and the ecologically complex and diverse woodland savannah of lowland Natal and eastern and northern Transvaal.

Nearly all of Africa's classic big-game species can be found in South Africa's parks and reserves, though the Kruger National Park boasts the widest selection. Nevertheless, many of the country's smaller parks contain nearly as many species, often with peculiar regional specialities.

Unusual species: About 60 percent of species are small and have diversified into

Preceding pages: elephants have a well developed community life. Left, neck in neck. Right, the bird warns the buffalo of impending danger.

nearly all areas of the environment. Most remarkable of all are mammals adapted to existences underground or in space. The 20-plus species of mole found in the country are endemic to Africa and all have short, cigar-shaped bodies, underdeveloped eyes and no external ears. Their presence in an area is conspicuously confirmed by mounds of excavated earth pushed to the surface from newly constructed tunnels.

Bats are the only mammals to have achieved the ability of true flight and are the

masters of the night skies. Unlike birds, the elements of the bat's forelimbs became elongated instead of lost in evolution. A double layer of tough skin between the fingers and between the forearm and torso completes the wings. Bats cannot fly as fast as birds but are more agile and acrobatic.

All bats become active at night and the insectivorous species manage navigation by means of echolocation – emitting ultrasonic pulses through the mouth. In South Africa there are at least 75 species, which, eight fruit-eating species apart, feed on insects. Insectivorous bats remove thousands of tonnes of harmful insects from the environment and fruit-bats are important pollinators and seed dispersers of endemic trees.

Elephant shrews could easily be mistaken for rodents, were it not for their movable, elongated snouts, large eyes and soft pelts and the fact that they satisfy their voracious appetite on insects. These timid creatures are active during the cooler parts of the day, and their slender and elongated limbs facilitate lightning movement.

Rodents are distinguished by their protruding curved upper incisors and in South Africa the wide array of species have adapted to the diverse environments. At 55 lbs (25 kg), the porcupine is by far the largest African rodent, while cane rats can grow to

Popular primates: Primates are favourites amongst tourists, probably because they display so many humanlike qualities. Many an enjoyable hour can be spent in the heat of the day watching the antics of a baboon troop. Only five primates occur in South Africa. The chacma baboon, the samango monkey and the vervet monkey are diurnal and live in well-organised groups. Mutual grooming is an integral part of their social behaviour and helps maintain communal order.

The predominantly terrestrial chacma baboon is the largest of the three species and is found in game parks across the country. Dominant adults can give a good account of themselves in protecting their troop against

a mass of 6–11 lbs (3–5 kg), making them a delicacy among certain local peoples. The other species are small – less than 4 oz (100 gm) – and unobtrusive but they form an important link in the ecosystem both as consumers of large quantities of vegetable material and as prey to medium-sized carnivores.

Rock-dwelling hyraxes (or dassies) are found where there are suitable rock crevices for safe retreats, and boulders to provide basking places in the sun. Hares are also quite common – the plains species distinguishable by long, well-developed hindlegs. The riverine rabbit is very rare and only occurs in the semi-arid regions of the Karoo.

carnivores such as leopards. The smaller, pale-coloured vervet monkey prefers open woodland, whereas the medium-sized darker samango monkey is a forest dweller. The lesser bush-baby and the thick-tailed bush-baby are both nocturnal and entirely tree-living. Both bush-babies are exceptionally agile and capable of enormous jumps when moving from tree to tree foraging for fruit and gum.

Meat-eaters: Modern man has always been fascinated by carnivores, perhaps since his ancestors had to struggle to protect human lives and livestock from predatory raids. Many human behavioural traits are likened to those of carnivores – the cunning of a jackal, the voraciousness of the honey-badger, the bravery of a lion, the cowardliness of a hyena. Few sights on earth can match the majesty and confidence of a lion strolling to water at dusk after a long day at rest, or the steady stealth of a pride of lions on the hunt. Tales about confrontations with lions abound throughout southern Africa.

In earlier times lions were widely distributed throughout the region but because of poaching they are now largely confined to the low veld of the eastern Transvaal, northern Natal and the arid northern Cape. A large male may weigh up to 400 lbs (180 kg) while the lioness, who does most of the killing, is

cheetah breeding stations have been established at the Hartebeespoort Dam near Pretoria and north of Nelspruit in the Eastern Transvaal.

The teamwork, dogged determination and ability to select the weakest prey are often overlooked by critics of the hunting dog's method of wearing down the stamina of its quarry in a protracted chase. It is not commonly appreciated that the spotted hyena, unlike its close relative, the brown hyena, is not exclusively a scavenger but an effective hunter in its own right.

Perhaps not as captivating, but no less interesting to observe are the many smaller carnivores like jackal, caracal and the serval

somewhat smaller and without the distinguishing mane.

Only the secretive leopard can match the lion in stealth, and its fluidity of movement its agility and its strength required to carry large prey into a tree with no more than a few easy bounds – are amazing. The *pièce de résistance* of many wildlife films is the cheetah chasing its prey at speeds of up to 75 mph (120 kph) over open plains. To ensure the continued survival of this graceful feline,

Left, the Steenbuck antelope. Above, the hippopotamus spends its days in the water and comes out to graze at night.

cat. The close collaboration and intricate social system of the dwarf and banded mongoose of the woodland savannahs and the suricate in the arid regions have been the subject of several rewarding studies.

African plains are dotted with termite mounds, and it stands to reason that some mammals will utilise this abundant and rich source of nourishment. Although the aardwolf, the scaly ant-eater and the aardvark are not related, they are all nocturnal with retiring habits and all rely on termites and formicid ants for nourishment. The pangolin – colloquially known as the *ietermago* – rolls in a tight ball when disturbed, relying on its scales for protection. The ant-bear can justifiably be regarded as nature's building contractor, as a large array of other animals rely on their numerous burrows for refuge.

The African elephant: Local elephants are much larger than the Indian variety with an average bull measuring up to 11 ft (3.5 metres) at the shoulder with tusks weighing between 65 and 100 lb (30 and 45 kg) each – although a mass of 236 lb (107 kg) has been recorded. Recent research has shown that lone elephant bulls remain in touch with herds led by matriarchs by means of infrasonic sound. Such solitary bulls are therefore not outcasts or rogues, but often the prime breeding bulls and very much part of the

social system of an elephant population.

The international ban on the ivory trade has sparked heated international debate. Whereas this embargo was justifiably aimed at curbing ruthless poaching of elephants elsewhere in Africa it did not allow for decades of responsible and effective conservation in South Africa where, paradoxically, elephant populations have to be culled in the continued interest of their environment and survival. The loss in revenue from elephant products caused by such sustained yield and scientifically based culling-schemes is sorely missed since it has traditionally been reinvested in conservation.

Rhinos: Both species of rhinoceri were on the verge of extinction. At one stage a group of only 60 square-lipped (white) rhinos remained in the Umfolozi Game Reserve. Thanks to an extensive conservation campaign their numbers have grown steadily and rhinos are now exported to zoos and game parks all over the world. The smaller, but more aggressive, hook-lipped (black) rhinoceros is a browser, and is still subject to intensive conservation measures.

Large rhinos can weigh up to 5 tons (5,000 kg) and despite their ferocious appearance are inoffensive and myopic creatures that would rather turn and lumber off than charge. The horn – it can grow to more than 3 ft (1 metre) in length – is composed of tightly packed fibre growing from the skin and resting on a hollow base in the skull. Coveted by poachers for their so-called aphrodisiac qualities, they are also sometimes knocked off in fights or accidents.

Two species of pig occur in the country. The aptly named warthog, with its characteristic curved tusks and aerial-like tail when in flight, is least likely to win a beauty contest. Characterised by an ungainly body and large head, the hippopotamus is capable of large-scale destruction in cultivated fields and is consequently found mostly in conservation areas, although a few wanderers remain in permanent water sources in remote areas.

Hooved animals: Zebras are best known for their dramatic black and white striping, with the Burchell's zebra of the woodland plains distinguishable by the shadow stripe in the white. The mountain zebra is considered an endangered species and is specially protected in the Mountain Zebra National Park near Cradock. The extinct quagga now only exists on the pages of yellowed manuscripts.

The giraffe, with its greatly elongated neck and reticulate colour pattern, is unmistakable. Among the bovids, kudu, impala and springbok are common game species, but the buffalo is most renowned and features prominently in the writings of early explorers and adventurers, which recounted large herds trekking across the plains of the interior. Anybody would be hard-pressed to choose the most stately among the arid adapted oryx (gemsbok) – thought by some to be the origin of the myth of the "unicorn" because in profile only one of its curved horns can be seen – or the sable and roan antelopes frequenting woodland savannahs.

Herds of blue wildebeest are often observed grazing in close association with Burchell's zebra or waterbuck – easily distinguishable by the white circles around their tails – in open woodlands. The black wildebeest prefers the grassland plains of the highveld and Natal. The grace and spryness of the springbok on the open central and western arid plains have so inspired South Africans that it has been adopted as the national emblem of the country's sportsmen.

Early explorers wrote vivid accounts of springboks moving across the plains in their "millions" in search of grazing, often springing into the air in its characteristic "pronk".

South African coastline – are believed to be highly intelligent, a claim easily accepted when their performances in dolphinariums in Port Elizabeth and Durban are observed.

The number of sperm whales has increased since whaling was stopped around the South African coastline in the early 1970s. These 50-ft (15-metre) long whales have perfected the ability to remain under water for extended periods – often remaining submerged for up to 90 minutes. Like dolphins, they communicate with each other by means of clicks and whistles. They normally give birth to single, well-developed young that can immediately swim well and follow the mother. The giant blue whale – the larg-

Of the smaller antelope, the grey duiker and steenbok still occur in healthy numbers throughout the country. However, the plight of the petit grysbok and especially the oribi is less secure. The nyala is a beautiful but very elusive antelope that can be spotted occasionally in the game reserves of Natal and Kruger National Park.

Marine mammals: Schools of bottle-nosed dolphins are often seen off beaches as they relish playing in the surf. These creatures – one of 43 marine mammals occurring off the

Left, family resemblance. **Above**, the cheetah is the fastest animal on land.

est mammal ever on the face of the earth – are also sometimes seen.

Special "whale-spotting tours" are organised, starting in False Bay and moving along the southern coastline to Cape Agulhas. The best time for whale watching is from the beginning of June till mid-November. The wildlife enthusiast visiting South Africa will find ample opportunities – whether through hunting, photography or merely observing and appreciating the fauna. Opportunities exist for one and all, whether in the relative comfort of a tour bus or motor-car or on a hiking trail under the guidance and protection of an experienced game ranger.

The ecological diversity of South Africa ensures a large number of amphibian and reptile species – a majority of them exclusive to the subcontinent.

As amphibians are mostly nocturnal it is hard to find any of the 120 known species. However, during spring and early summer, visitors are often treated to the diversity of the night sounds made by frogs. Some species occur in huge numbers, creating deafening choruses. But more often the abundance of species is reflected in the variety of sounds

opment takes place until a small froglet hatches from each egg.

No salamanders occur in Africa south of the Sahara and caecilians are only known as far south as Malawi. Although South Africa's frog species are well documented, new ones are still being discovered.

The potential danger of some reptiles should not be underestimated but, if treated with respect, confrontations with humans can largely be avoided. The fear-inspiring Nile crocodile is nowadays largely restricted

– from the booming call of the African bull frog, to the snoring rasps of certain toads, from the ringing chorus of reed frogs to a cacophony of noises described by experts as "raucous cackle", "wooden tapping", "rapid chattering", or "explosive ticks".

Toads, too are rarely encountered. Some, like the aquatic clawed-toad or platanna, – which, in the past, was often used for pregnancy tests – are not often seen, as they mostly keep to the water. At the other extreme are the short-headed frogs which are quite independent of water, even for reproduction purposes. They make their nests underground where the entire larval devel-

to game reserves. In recent years crocodile farming has become a popular and prosperous venture which helps to reduce the pressure on natural populations.

Southern Africa has an exceptional variety of tortoise fauna. It includes five marine turtles and five side-necked, freshwater terrapins. The importation of the American red-eared terrapin, to be sold to customers of pet shops, has led to the establishment of isolated populations of discarded purchases.

Twelve species of land tortoise are found – the highest number in any one country. The smallest species of all of them, doesn't quite reach 4 inches (10 cm) in length when fully grown. The geometric tortoise, which occurs on the Cape Flats, is currently the country's most threatened reptile species.

Amongst the lizards, the geckos predominate. Most are nocturnal. Many have adhesive pads under their toes enabling them to hang upside-down against a ceiling or walk up a window pane. Geckos are usually welcome house guests because of their voracious appetite for insects. The tropical house gecko, a common lizard, may be seen at night around lights in the Kruger Park.

Snakes, which are represented by about 130 species on this sub-continent, hold a morbid fascination for many people. With the exception of the very large – and immensely strong – varieties of rock python which may be dangerous to man, only 14 species possess a potentially fatal bite. This means that the vast majority of snakes are harmless or not seriously dangerous.

Many species, such as the dwarf adders, the harmless egg-eating snakes and also the dangerous varieties of cobras, are in fair

Chameleons are encountered but in South Africa they are restricted to two genera, the one egg-laying, the other live bearing. One of the strangest creatures is the Namaqua chameleon, whose habitat is in the western area and which lives on the arid ground.

Girdled and plated lizards are indigenous and firm favourites in terrariums. Most common are armadillo lizards, crag lizards and the brightly coloured flat rock lizards. If lucky, one may even see the country's largest lizard species, the Nile monitor, a timorous creature that keeps to rivers and dams.

Left and above, the hunter and the hunted.

demand with snake keepers. Stringent measures have been introduced by conservation authorities to curb the commercial exploitation and illegal exporting of snakes which threatened to deplete the sparse resources.

Cases of snake-bite are rare and mostly result from people accidentally treading on a member of the adder family. These snakes – short, fat and lethargic – are not aggressive but do bite when trampled upon. Adder bites can be lethal but their venom acts slowly and allows time for treatment. The dangers of snake-bite have been greatly reduced by improved first-aid measures and by the excellent quality of anti snake-bite serum.

Visitors interested in bird-watching can spend hours enjoying a rich variety – from the lush woodlands in the east where birds of prey soar effortlessly on the thermals, through the arid interior where some species have developed special adaptations to cope with the semi-desert conditions, to the Western Cape with its floral wealth sustaining large numbers of unique birds.

South Africa's birdlife, being at the southern end of one of the world's largest landmasses, has evolved many unique forms,

some of which have since penetrated to other continents. Among the endemic families are hamerkop, shoebill, secretary bird, louries, wood hoopoes, sugar-birds and whydahs.

Eastern woodlands: More than half of the 718 bird species found in South Africa can be observed in the Kruger National Park, making it one of the most productive birding spots in the world. For the serious bird-watcher, this is an ornithological paradise; but even the casual visitor can enjoy the captivating splendour of the feathered beauties. About 60 percent of the African continent is savannah – or "bushveld" – so it is not surprising that most of its special birds occur

in this type of country – many birds of prey, the bustards and korhaans, kingfishers, bee-eaters, rollers, hornbills and bush shrikes.

Africa is home to some of the most spectacular birds of prey in the world, ranging in size from the huge martial eagle down to the smaller falcons and kestrels. In the lowveld it is possible to see most of the South African species in the course of a normal day's drive. Perhaps the most striking is the bateleur, a rather unusual kind of snake eagle with a black body, white underwings and bright red face and legs. It glides hour after hour against the blue sky, searching for its prey of small mammals, gamebirds, reptiles and carrion. The most spectacular scavengers are the vultures which can be seen soaring in the hot midday hours on the lookout for the carcasses of big game killed by lions or dead through other causes. In fact, lion kills make up only a small fraction of the food of vultures, contrary to what most people believe.

Other large birds of prey include the tawny eagle of the more open savannahs and the somewhat smaller African hawk eagle living in denser woodland along the rivers. Riverine trees often include giant figs which attract fruit-eating birds like the green pigeon, louries, hornbills, barbets and bulbuls. Some of the most colourful are the bee-eaters. These graceful birds usually perch conspicuously on top of leafless twigs of bushes or trees (or on telephone wires), and so are easy to photograph from a vehicle.

Surprisingly, most of Africa's kingfishers are woodland birds. At the waterside, along the major rivers, both giant and pied king-fishers are common, but in the woodlands one can see at least five species including the grey-headed and the uncommon pygmy kingfisher. Their distinctive ringing calls are very much a feature of the bushveld. Another essentially African group includes the rollers and hornbills. All five southern African roller species occur in the Kruger Park – easily recognised by their brilliant blue wings. Like the bee-eaters, they perch conspicuously in the open. The lilac-breasted roller, exceptionally beautiful, is the most characteristic bird of the Kruger Park.

Hornbills are common over most of the

park, especially the yellow-billed and red-billed varieties. One to watch out for in particular is the unusual ground hornbill, a very big black bird with white wings and a rather grotesque red-wattled face. It walks about in solemn groups of 5 to 10 birds feeding on insects, reptiles and other small animals. Often seen at camp-sites, scavenging for hand-outs from visitors, are the metallic blue starlings with their glossy plumage and yellow button eyes. The distinctive sound of the redchested cuckoo or *Piet-my-*

long-tailed widow or sakabula can often be seen sweeping across the grasslands while the snow-white cattle egret can be seen riding on the backs of grazing herds, picking at the grasshoppers that the cattle disturb.

A sight to behold is the secretary bird with long plumes resembling quill feathers at the back of its head. Sometimes visitors are lucky enough to witness the dramatic spectacle of a battle between a secretary bird and a snake, the bird using its long legs to stamp the reptile to death.

vrou – its local, onomatopoeic name – can be heard in the spring and summer.

The highveld: In the open grasslands of the Transvaal and Free State highveld, a large variety of species can easily be spotted from the road. A distinctive bird is the beautiful blue korhaan, one of the rarer members of the bustard family in Africa but still quite common here. The korhaan as well as the bigger Kori bustard are sometimes hunted for their meat – as are francolins and quails.

The magnificent, if somewhat ponderous,

Quite a few highveld birds can be found in the mountains to the east and in the Karoo to the west. Several of the chats fall into this distributional pattern and so does the endemic ground woodpecker, a curious bird that never perches in trees and finds all its food of ants on the ground. It nests in an earth burrow in a vertical bank or a steep hillside. Orang-breasted rock-jumpers and Drakensberg siskins are endemic to the mountains of the eastern escarpment.

Natal, from mountains to sea: The eastern slopes of the Drakensberg mountain range and the dense evergreen forests and deep valleys at its foothills provide a grandiose

Left, the yellow-billed hornbill. **Above**, the popular African hoopoo.

backdrop to a rich birdlife. A number of hotels, chalets and camp-sites provide convenient stopping places. The forests harbour sunbirds, flycatchers and the shy bush blackcap, a species that extends down the bushy valleys bordering clear mountain streams.

Down the grassy slopes are grey-wing francolins, yellow-breasted pipits and cisticolas. If there are protea bushes around, it is likely that one can catch a glimpse of Gurney's sugarbird, whose squeaky song breaks the mountain silence. The brightly-coloured forest weaver, emerald cuckoo and purple-crested lourie are found here and in the Tsitsikamma Forest National Park.

South Africa's national bird, the blue crowned eagle, which can sometimes be seen hiding in ambush in a tree waiting for an unsuspecting victim. It swoops down on its prey suddenly, carrying it off with its strong claws and the aid of its massive wings.

The Natal Midlands are largely given over to farming but provide some excellent birding spots. Close to the Natal capital, Pietermaritzburg, is Game Valley (formerly Karkloof Falls Game Reserve) which boasts about 300 bird species, including waterbirds (kingfishers, wagtails and the hamerkop), grassland birds (longclaws, cisticolas and guineafowl) and forest birds (trogons, robins, bush shrikes and many more). It is one of the best birding places in the Natal Midlands.

crane, nests on the flatter tops of these grassy spurs, laying two mottled eggs on the bare ground or rock. Overhead, the bearded vulture, black eagle and Cape vulture wheel about in search of food. At Giant's Castle Game Reserve a "vulture restaurant" provides carrion for the birds in winter and the opportunity for bird-watchers to photograph from a comfortable hide fitted with one-way glass and ports for telephoto lenses. The South African population of the bearded vulture – or lammergeier – numbers only about 200 pairs, so this is certainly a sight not to be missed.

Another majestic sight is that of the

Tracts of bushveld in the northern parts of Natal are much like the Kruger Park in vegetation and avifauna. The game reserves on the Natal North Coast are rich havens for waterfowl, herons, pelicans, flamingos and the majestic fish eagle. In Ndumu Game Reserve bordering Mozambique, one can find such subtropical specialities as purple-banded sunbird, yellow-spotted nicator and Pel's fishing owl. Here, too, is the place to see many of the tropical waterbirds, such as the African finfoot and all kinds of storks, herons, and bitterns. Other game reserves like Umfolozi, Hluhluwe, Mkuzi and Lake St Lucia also boast prolific birdlife.

The arid lands: For the keen bird-watcher no visit would be complete without a trip through the Karoo and the arid western parts of the country. Bird-watching is relatively easy in this dry, open habitat. Perhaps the most eye-catching birds here are Ludwig's bustard and the Karoo korhaan. A roadside stop will almost certainly produce some arid-zone specialities, like the rufouseared warbler, Layard's titbabbler and chat flycatcher. As one goes westward, chances improve of seeing some of the endemic larks, such as Sclater's lark (around Vanwyksvlei and Brandvlei) and the red lark (in the red sand dunes near Kenhardt and Aggenys).

The Karoo National Park near Beaufort West makes a convenient and comfortable stopping place if one is travelling by road to Cape Town from upcountry. Here one can step out of the front door of a chalet and be greeted by whitebacked mousebirds, Karoo robins and the ubiquitous bokmakierie, a member of the endemic African family of bush shrikes.

The region's best known inhabitant is the ostrich, the world's biggest bird whose males reach a height of about 8 ft (2.5 metres) and weigh up to 300 lbs (135 kg). Although the birds are generally docile, the male – distinguished by its black plumage – can be temperamental during the mating season. Its skin may turn a bright pink and it is likely to make a roaring sound – not unlike that of a lion – when approached by intruders. If all else fails, it may deliver a formidable kick with deft accuracy.

Ostriches are known for their speed and can reach up to 30 mph (50 kph) – an attribute often displayed to visitors at an "ostrich derby" at farms in the Oudtshoorn area. A major part of the economy of the region is dependent on the ostrich industry, the skin of the bird being used for leatherware such as handbags and shoes, the feathers for dusters, the meat for dried *biltong* and the massive eggshells sold as curios.

The Kalahari, a region of sandveld dotted with low shrubs and some bigger acacia bushes and trees, has an abundant supply of small and large mammals, which make birds of prey a feature of the avifauna.

Undoubtedly the most astonishing avian spectacle in the Kalahari are the huge nests

of the sociable weaver in the bigger camel-thorn trees. Looking like thatched roofs, these communally built structures can be up to four metres in diameter and house anything up to 200 weavers. They live in these nest masses all year round, breeding there after suitably good rains. The dainty pygmy falcon, Africa's smallest raptor, makes its home here too. A pair of falcons may take over one or two chambers in the weaver's nest, the two species living side-by-side. The nests are very cool but also vulnerable to attacks by predators such as snakes and honey badgers who frequently raid the nests in search of eggs and young birds.

At water-holes provided by the conserva-

tion authorities one can see remarkable flocks of sand grouse flying in to drink shortly after sunrise, sometimes in their hundreds or even thousands. Sand grouse are unique in their habit of carrying water in their belly feathers for their young to drink, the feathers being specially designed to take up large amounts of water in the manner of a sponge. The males wade into the water to soak before flying back to their thirsty chicks which drink the water from the feathers.

The fynbos area: Large tracts of land in the southern Cape hillsides and mountains are covered by a characteristic growth of low shrubs and bushes, many of them with small

Left, secretary birds. **Right**, a pelican poses.

leaves – hence the name fynbos, meaning "fine bush". It is among the richest floral regions in the world, containing over 8,500 species of plants, many of them pollinated by birds which come to the flowers to feed on the abundant nectar, especially of the proteas and heaths. Two of the endemic nectar-feeders are the Cape sugarbird and the orange-breasted sunbird. Also endemic to the region are the protea canary, a seed-eater, and the insectivorous Victorin's warbler.

Further north, into Namaqualand (famous for its show of spring flowers), the fynbos assumes a more arid character. This is where one can find the cinnamon-breasted warbler and the fairy flycatcher, but bird-spotters

must take a scramble into the dry, rocky hills for these special birds.

Coastal birds: The Benguela current along the southern and southwestern coastline supports a rich supply of fish which in turn attracts large numbers of seabirds. Large flocks of cormorants can often be seen perching on rocks or flying in a characteristic V-formation in search of shoals. When one is spotted, the whole flock descends upon it in a frenzy, diving into the water to gorge on their catch.

Some garrulous and noisy gulls inhabit the shores, the most impressive being the kelp. These large birds often drop molluscs from great heights on to the rocks below, thus exposing the edible animals inside.

Large colonies of Cape gannets are found at Lambert's Bay and on small islets such as Bird Island and Malgas along the coast. This beautiful bird with creamy plumage and distinctive black markings on the face can often be seen swooping down on fish in the waves below. Arctic terns or sea swallows migrate from the Arctic to the Antarctic every year using the South African coastline as a stopover. Other smaller birds that can be spotted are the African black oystercatcher, the sanderling and the white-fronted plover.

Bird migration: Every summer more than 100 species of bird migrate from the northern hemisphere to the South African shores. Some like the ringed plover fly more than 6,000 miles (10,000 km) from its northern breeding grounds in Siberia to the western Cape. The most common migrants are waders of the sandpiper family but they also include other birds ranging in size from herons to shrikes.

The journey from South Africa to Europe may take a small bird five to seven weeks to complete. They travel at ground speeds of 25–45 mph (40–75 kph) and often fly for up to 100 hours non-stop over inhospitable stretches of ocean and desert. Small birds must use flapping flight, but larger species such as storks and eagles can soar and glide. This is much slower, but this way they expend less energy – a useful method of travel for birds whose size does not allow them to store a great deal of fat. Travelling these vast distances a bird may burn up to 40 percent of its body mass.

Big soaring birds migrate by day when the heat of the sun generates thermals from the ground below, and they can utilise the rising warm air for lift. Small birds usually migrate at night at heights of up to 6,500 ft (2,000 metres) above the ground.

For navigation, they make use of the position of the sun by day and the stars by night, assisted by other environmental factors such as magnetism, wind direction, smell and landmarks. However, this process remains one of nature's great mysteries: young birds instinctively know how to find the correct migration route even in the absence of experienced adults.

Left, the white-fronted bee-eater with dragonfly.

INSECTS

With an estimated 50,000 species of insect, South Africa is a haven for entomologists, professional or amateur, photographers, collectors, or mere "bug-watchers". The tropical bushveld savannah is in the far northern part of the country and is home to the largest variety. Found in great abundance are giant termites, huge – but harmless – baboon spiders, fascinating stick insects, emperor moths and butterflies. An astounding and colourful variety of dung-beetles perform curious antics with their "meals-on-wheels". Praying mantises with weird camouflage-shapes and colours ambush their

Touring south one enters an entirely different world of nature – the famous Cape, well-known for the greatest variety of plants in the world. In tandem with this ancient and isolated plant community, equally enigmatic forms of insect life are found. The world-famous wingless Colophon beetles inhabit the high mountain peaks and they are so rare that some species are only known from the fragments of a solitary dead beetle. The exquisite protea, South Africa's national flower, plays host to a variety of equally beautiful chafer beetles of innumerable shapes and sizes. In the forests the most primitive living arthropod, the velvet worm, has survived almost unchanged over the past 400 million years.

Well-known for its kaleidoscope of colour in

prey and columns of matabele-ants set out to raid the termite nests – they themselves in danger of being waylaid by robber flies. The variety of insect life with amazing habits teems in every acre of this vast natural veld.

The tropical coastal region of the Natal east coast harbours a unique and endemic fauna of truly tropical forms. From mangrove-crabs to web-throwing spiders; from multi-coloured tropical fruitchafers to the famous glamour of tropical butterflies of all are concentrated in this narrow strip of coastal paradise. Here unique species – with relatives to be found only in central and west Africa – can be observed in the comfortable surroundings of a holiday resort or tourist camp.

the flowering season, the arid western region of Namaqualand is as highly regarded among entomologists for its wealth of insects and other arthropods. Best known is the colourful bottlebrush beetle, but many large oarabids, spiders, scorpions and hymenopterans are also found.

South Africa is an insect collector's paradise. Popular groups such as Cetoniinae (about 200 species) and butterflies (about 800 species) sport a far greater variety in South Africa than anywhere else on the continent. With the large variety of habitat and the excellent infrastructure the country has to offer, South Africa is most definitely the continent's most inviting country for insect enthusiasts. ■

The flora of southern Africa is one of the most varied in the world. Here, you can find nearly one-tenth of all known flowering plants – some 24,000 species in all.

Many of these indigenous plants have now become familiar to gardeners, thanks to plant hunters (especially the Dutch) who scoured the Cape area for colourful flowers suited to colder climates. Among the plants they introduced were the pelargoniums (commonly called geraniums) which brighten house fronts, balconies and window-boxes all over the world, and which were first brought to Europe in 1690.

Many heathers (ericas) originate from southern Africa, along with other popular plants, such as red-hot poker, agapanthus, gladiolus, kaffir lilies, crocosmias and sweet-scented freesias. Although most of these were first discovered in the 18th century, new plants from southern Africa have found favour more recently, including the richly coloured gazanias and the shy osteospermums, which open their petals only when the sun shines.

Officially, southern Africa is subdivided into seven floral regions, each with its own, fascinating flora.

1. The region of the Cape Plant Kingdom, located around Cape Town on the southwestern tip of the continent, is about 27,000 sq. miles (70,000 sq. km) in area – the size of the Republic of Ireland – and is home to 8,600 kinds of flowering plants. On the 200 sq. miles (500 sq. km) of Cape Peninsula, alone, 2,600 indigenous species have been counted: more than in many considerably larger countries.

This area receives most of its rainfall in the cold seasons of the year, between April and October. The region is renowned for its heathers (over 600 species) and South Africa's most famous orchid, known as the "pride of Table Mountain".

2. The Karru Succulent region (from the Hottentot word *kuru*, meaning dry or sparse) forms a broad band running parallel to the west coast of the Cape, north of the Cape

Floral Kingdom. It covers some 43,300 sq. miles (111,000 sq. km – a little smaller than the state of New York. Here, too, rainfall occurs primarily in the winter months, but the yearly average total is only 9–11 inches (23–28 cm). The name, therefore, reveals its nature: this is a dry, semi-desert land, dominated by succulents, especially shrubs with fleshy leaves.

Mesembryanthemums, known to rock gardeners throughout the world for their colourful, daisy-like flowers, grow here in abundance. Other natives include the pebble plant (Lithops) and plants of the similar Conophytum and Argyrodema families. All these produce splendid blossoms of shimmering, metallic red-violet, yellow, white, or copper-coloured petals. These tend to appear in one burst around September and October.

Trees are, in general, rare in this region; but the tree-like *Aloe arborescens* (candelabra plant) can be found in large quantities in certain parts of the north. The best time to visit this region is in spring (from September), when the meadows are flooded with a red-yellow-orange sea of flowering annuals. The Botanical Garden of the National Botanical Institute, near Worcester, presents a wonderful introduction to the local flora.

3. The Nama Karru, some 211,000 sq. miles (541,000 sq. km) in area – almost as large as France – is the second-largest plant region in southern Africa. Located on the central plateau, its terrain is mainly flat or gently rolling, broken in places by hills and mesas (table-lands). The annual rainfall of 4–20 inches (10–50 cm) occurs during the summer months, while the lowest winter temperatures range between 32°F and 48°F (0°–9°C). Vegetation in this area is dominated by small shrubs (known as karru bushes) and, in years of good rainfall, long-lived grass species. Predominant among the small bushes are members of the family Compositae, such as camellia bushes, kapok (silk-cotton) bushes and quassia bushes.

The great silvery plumes of feather grass and ostrich grass are a common sight. There is also a certain type of catalpa bush, which reaches heights of up to 8 ft (2.5 metres) and has large white trumpet-shaped blossoms –

Left, the endangered cycad has been around for millions of years.

that is a characteristic of broad expanses of level ground, particularly in the north.

In the deeper dry valleys, you will often encounter the sweet thistle, whose myriad yellow blossoms enchant the eye of the beholder in the summer months.

4. The savannah extends across the entire Kalahari basin to the east coast, with a narrow strip reaching down into the southern Cape region. Some 374,000 sq. miles (959,000 sq. km) in area – about as big as Germany, France, the Netherlands and Belgium combined, it is the largest vegetal region of the subcontinent. Rainfall, which occurs primarily in summer, averages about 10 inches (25 cm) a year.

eral feet. In the eastern Transvaal, Natal, and the eastern Cape, you will find many spurges (euphorbias) and tree-aloes.

Eye-catching grass varieties, such as red grass, pepper grass and ostrich grass, are all common. During the dry season – when many trees and bushes lose their leaves – these grasses take on a yellow or reddish colour, which has a corresponding effect on the overall landscape. Each year, large areas are burned off; but at the beginning of the rainy season, these bleak patches of burnt black are covered virtually overnight with a colourful carpet of spring flowers and fresh green shoots. In the Botanical Garden of the National Botanical Institute in Pretoria, lo-

"Savannah" denotes an area of mixed vegetation consisting mainly of grassland with scattered trees and drought-resistant undergrowth. Although isolated trees and shrubs are the norm, you can also encounter large patches of savannah forest forming the so-called "Bosveld" (bushveld) – as, for example, in many areas of the Kruger Park in East Transvaal.

Thorny acacia trees, often with a distinctive umbrella crown, are characteristic in dry areas of the region. The bizarre baobab, which can be found in the extreme north and belongs to the silk-cotton family, has a mighty trunk which often attains a diameter of sev-

cated in an area where savannah gives way to grassland, you can see typical examples of the plant life of both regions.

5. The grassland, with an area of 133,770 sq. miles (343,000 sq. km) – almost as large as Germany – is confined to the high Central Plateau, and encompasses Lesotho, western Swasiland, and large regions of the Orange Free State and Transvaal. Rain falls virtually only in summer, while frost occurs on most nights in winter. Even so, approximately one-tenth of the world's 10,000 species of grass are indigenous to the area.

The grassland can be roughly divided into a western and an eastern region; of these, the western receives, on average, less than 26 inches (66 cm) of rainfall annually, while the eastern receives more. The grasses of the west are generally designated "sweet" or "white", while the eastern, moister region produces "sour" or "purple" grasses. As you might gather from these terms, the former range from a light straw colour to an off-white when dry, while the latter are reddish or violet. The descriptions "sweet" and "sour" refer to their value as fodder.

6. Forests are in short supply in southern Africa; only in the southern Cape, in the vicinity of George, will you find extensive woodland. There are, however, small, generally isolated areas of forest in the belt which

Among the peripheral ranges – the long chain of the Drakensberg mountains, for example, which extend northwards from the eastern Cape up into the Transvaal – there are many patches of what was once a larger forest, above all in gorges and on humid slopes. Such areas are dominated by coniferous species, such as Podocarpus (known locally as yellow wood). These trees can grow into forest giants, reaching heights of up to 130 ft (40 metres). Species of the Olea (olive) family also grow here, as well as the so-called stinkwood, which is highly valued in the furniture trade.

The Namib, a true desert, lies to the north of South Africa, stretching parallel to the

extends between the coast and the mountain ranges on the periphery of the continent, from the southwest Cape north of Cape Town, east and then on up to the north through Natal and Mozambique. Despite the relative lack of forest, there are nearly 1,000 types of tree.

Along Natal's east coast, you can still see isolated remnants of mangrove forest, growing in mud and sand. Further inland, you can see the remains of evergreen forests, where milkwood, ebony and wild bananas grow.

Left, the red disa, famous orchid of Table Mountain; red-hot poker. **Above**, the protea is the country's national flower.

coast of Namibia. In this region, almost entirely without rainfall, vegetation is scarce or entirely absent. On the rare occasions when rain does fall, the sand and pebble soil of the Namib comes alive with annual grasses and herbs whose seeds have lain dormant for years, waiting for just such an event.

In places, you will also see the Namib's most famous plant, the welwitschia; this resembles a giant carrot with two broad flat leathery leaves growing out of the top. The welwitschia is an extremely long-lived plant, often surviving for centuries, and its appearance is all the more weird because of the way the desert wind can etch and erode its leaves.

A recent survey of overseas visitors to South Africa revealed that 9 out of 10 came primarily to experience its wildlife and unspoiled natural areas. When one realises what a wide variety of wild plants animals and ecosystems the country has to offer, this statistic is not at all surprising. However, although wildlife is extremely significant as the cornerstone of the rapidly growing tourist industry, the importance of conserving it does not rest on this consideration alone.

Why conserve?: Nature conservation is also essential for the preservation of one of the world's richest centres of genetic diversity and for the maintenance of natural resources on which many of the country's people depend for their livelihood. Nature conservation is accordingly taken very seriously and South Africans have much to be proud of, at least in recent times.

Although covering only 4 percent of Africa and approximately 0.8 percent of the world's land area, South Africa holds more than 10 percent of the world's higher plants (24,000 of the total of 250,000 species), 8 percent of its birds (718 of 9,000), 5.8 percent of its mammals (227 of 3,927) and 4.6 percent of its reptiles (286 of 6,214). By comparison, France, about half the size of South Africa, has only 4,400 native plant species, while Canada, more than seven times its size, has only 3,160 plant species. Australia, six times its size, has only 17,500 plant species, 656 regularly occurring bird species and 224 mammal species.

Not only is the area exceptionally rich in species but many of these species are found nowhere else (these are called "endemic species"). Thus about a third of the plants and reptiles are endemic to South Africa, 15 percent of the mammals and 6 percent of the 600 bird species breeding in the country. The plants of the southernmost tip of the continent are actually so different from those found anywhere else that the area has been defined as one of the six floral kingdoms of the world – the Cape Kingdom. This tiny area, only 18,000 sq. miles (46,000 sq. km) in extent, is thus considered equivalent, for example, to the Boreal Kingdom which includes all of Europe, North America and northern Asia, an area of more than 20 million sq. miles (53 million sq. km).

This high concentration of unique wild species places South Africa on a par with the much discussed tropical rainforest areas, such as those of the Amazon Basin or Southeast Asia as an area of international significance for conservation.

The conservation record: Africa, and thus South Africa, is most famous for its amazing variety of antelopes and other grazing mammals and the large carnivores that prey on them. These herds of antelope used to graze from the Cape Peninsula in the south to the Limpopo Valley on the northern border.

However, in the south, the huge herds of springbok and quagga (a now-extinct subspecies of the still widespread plains zebra) that used to roam the fertile plains of the Karoo, soon disappeared before the guns of the European colonists. Those dark days before the dawning of the conservation ethic also saw the extinction of the endemic blue buck, a relative of the sable and roan antelope that was restricted to the southern Cape Province. This is the only endemic vertebrate animal known to have become totally extinct in South Africa.

The conservation record is not so good for native plants: at least 39 species or subspecies have become extinct since their discovery. Several additional plant species probably became extinct without ever having been described, particularly in the lowland areas of the southwestern Cape where localised endemics abound and the conversion of natural vegetation for agriculture and urbanisation has removed over 90 percent of the original area of certain vegetation types.

As the herds of wild ungulates were decimated in the 17th and 18th centuries, they were replaced by flocks of sheep and herds of cattle when the European colonists expanded into the interior of the country. The larger carnivores – lions, spotted and brown hyenas, cheetahs and Cape hunting dogs – came increasingly into conflict with live-

Preceding pages: drives in open Land-Rovers are a special feature of the private game reserves. **Left,** a zebra crossing the river.

stock farmers. Soon these species became restricted to the remaining unoccupied or sparsely occupied portions of the country. Of all the larger carnivores, only the wily leopard has managed to persist in reasonable numbers outside the larger national parks and nature reserves, mainly in mountainous areas where it is able to avoid persecution.

Today the large carnivores, the elephants, the rhinoceroses and the large herds of wild antelopes, are restricted in main to the larger protected areas, particularly those in the country's northern savannahs. The greatest of these is the Kruger National Park. At 7,500 sq. miles (19,485 sq. km), this park is almost as large as the state of Israel and

wildlife and full complement of large predators is a "must" for every visitor who hasn't yet experienced the wonders of the African savannahs. It is undoubtedly one of the best managed national parks in the world – not that the everyday visitor will see much sign of the intensive research, monitoring and management that goes into its running. Although this management is sometimes intensive, with aspects such as the supply of water to artificial watering-holes, the burning of the grasslands and savannahs and the stocking rate of large herbivores, all being carefully manipulated to ensure the park's ecosystems are not degraded, it is sensitively implemented so as not to destroy the wilder-

larger than Kuwait or the nearby kingdom of Swaziland. This enormous savannah park constitutes a quarter of the country's total area under formal protection for nature conservation. The total of 28,000 sq. miles (72,700 sq. km) that enjoy such protection are in more than 580 reserves scattered throughout the country. This area sounds large, yet only 5.8 percent of South Africa's surface area is protected for conservation – far less than the 10 percent set as the minimum national requirement by the International Union for the Conservation of Nature.

The Kruger National Park with its intact savannah landscapes, magnificent herds of

ness qualities of the place.

The result is a park in which visitors can view from their own vehicles or from a variety of hides some of the finest spectacles of African wildlife still available to the average tourist anywhere on the continent. It is now even possible to undertake wilderness walking trails within the park under the supervision of park rangers. However, the demand for places on such trails far exceeds the supply and one should book well in advance.

The park itself encompasses a range of different savannah types and the well-prepared visitor can spend many days exploring its vastness, its diversity and its unending series of wildlife interactions, without ever becoming bored. Within this park alone, it is possible to see up to 132 native mammal species, 438 species of birds, 104 reptile species and 1,771 plant species, including 357 species of trees and shrubs.

One outstanding sanctuary where one can stay during a visit to Kruger is the Olifants Rest Camp. Here, in the evening, one can relax on the hilltop and watch elephants and giraffes moving through the savannah far below. In the Olifants River, which flows quietly over sandbanks far below at the base of the hill on which the rest camp is situated, maybe a lone buffalo bull is drinking while a pair of black storks look on uninterestedly.

Gemsbok National Park in the more arid west and to at least one of the many excellent game reserves in the well-watered savannahs on the eastern seaboard in Natal.

Kalahari Gemsbok National Park is the country's second largest national park (at 3,700 sq. miles or 9,600 sq. km). Situated in the far north of the Cape Province, the park is bordered by Namibia on the west and Botswana on the east. The latter border is along the normally dry bed of the Nossob River and is unfenced, the Botswana side of the border being the western boundary of that country's even larger Gemsbok National Park (9,500 sq. miles or 24,800 sq. km). The stark beauty of this semi-desert

As the sun sets and the first bats start flickering through the red-tinged sky, it is possible to look out over a vast landscape with no sign of people as far as the eye can see.

Kalahari Gemsbok Park: A visit to Kruger National Park, splendid though it is, will not be enough to show the visitor the full range of the country's wildlife and wild places. For those who wish to savour the full variety of the savannah, no visit will be complete unless it also includes trips to the Kalahari

Left, preparing tranquilliser darts for elephants. Above, without man's help, the black rhino faces extinction in Africa.

area with its red Kalahari sand dunes, dotted with low thorn trees and covered in good rainfall seasons with vast waving strands of sunbleached grasses, is remarkable. The Kalahari Gemsbok is crossed from north to south by the Auob and Nossob Rivers and it is along these fertile riverbeds that most of the grazing animals congregate.

Here can be seen such dry country specialists as the majestic gemsbok, the red hartebeest and the springbok. Amongst the birds, the social weavers are probably the most characteristic. Their enormous communal nests not only provide accommodation for themselves but also harbour a whole community of "hangers-on", including the diminutive pygmy falcon which appropriates and then nests in one of the many individual chambers that are built into the nest.

The tall acacia trees that grow in these riverbeds concentrate the larger birds of prey that abound in the open savannahs. There are few places in Africa where one can meet with such densities of large eagles, vultures, falcons, hawks and owls. Family parties of ostriches are frequently met with as they slowly pick their way across the dune veld or run energetically along a shimmering pan. In the dry heat of midday the pace of life slows right down in these silent savannahs. At this time Kori bustards, Africa's largest flying

including Africa's oldest surviving game reserves, Hluhluwe and Umfolozi. Both were proclaimed in 1895, just 13 years after Yellowstone National Park was established in the United States as the world's first. Proclaimed primarily to protect the last remaining populations of rhinoceros in Natal, these parks have succeeded beyond their originators' wildest expectations.

The square-lipped rhinoceros found its last sanctuary in the Umfolozi Reserve and this population was thought to have been reduced to fewer than 20 individuals early in the 20th century. By careful protection and through the development of methods to capture safely and transport these enormous

bird species, fly in from the surrounding dune veld to stand gasping in the shade of a knarled old "kameeldoring" tree.

Mammalian predators are also easily located along these sparsely vegetated riverbeds and this is probably one of the best places in South Africa to observe the cheetah hunting. This is also the major sanctuary for the only large carnivore which is endemic to southern Africa, the brown hyena. However, one will have to be up very early to catch a glimpse of this mainly nocturnal predator and scavenger.

Jewels of the east: In the east of the country there are many smaller savannah reserves,

creatures, the Natal Parks Board, which administers these reserves, has built up the world population of this species to its current total of more than 7,000 individuals. There are 1,800 to 2,000 of these rhinos in the Hluhluwe and Umfolozi Reserves.

More than 3 500 have been captured and safely transferred to other conservation areas in Africa and to zoos and parks throughout the world. The population of more than 900 individuals currently in the Kruger National Park all stem from individuals translocated from these two remarkable little reserves. This is one of the few instances world-wide where conservation measures have been so successful that it has been possible to remove a species from the IUCN Red Data Book of endangered species.

These two Natal reserves have also played a significant role in the conservation of the South African population of the black or hook-lipped rhinoceros. With the current deterioration of nature conservation programmes elsewhere in Africa, what was once the relatively insignificant population of about 600 black rhinos held by South Africa has suddenly become the only relatively secure wild population in existence. A massive conservation effort is continuing.

These reserves are not only famous for their rhinoceros populations. Other mam-

different conservation areas to visit. Africa's largest estuary, Lake St Lucia, holds the country's most important hippopotamus and Nile crocodile populations. Waterbirds inhabit this enormous shallow lake, including large breeding colonies of white pelicans and the striking caspian tern. If the water levels are low vast flocks of flamingoes can be seen on this unique water body. Rest camps are located at several points around this lake. South of the estuary mouth, Mapelaan Nature Reserve preserves a diverse dune forest on what are said to be the world's highest forested sand dunes.

North of the estuary mouth stretches a series of coastal reserves with a proclaimed

mals abound, including the most attractive of the African antelope, the nyala, found only in the dense thickets of the southeastern lowlands. The variety of birdlife is astounding, and breathtaking hours spent in the hides at waterholes in these reserves during the winter dry season will never be forgotten. The nearby Mkuzi Game Reserve is also renowned for its hides.

Maputaland: On the northeastern coastal plain of Maputaland there are a variety of

Left, famous game wardens Dr Ian Player and Magqubu Ntombela. **Above**, Laura Stanton in her clinic with a rehabilitated black eagle.

marine reserve preserving the adjacent offshore wonders. Submerged coral reefs and the associated myriad tropical fish species and other sealife abound in the crystal clear waters of the warm Mozambique Current that washes these golden beaches fringed by lush dune forests. Each summer, hundreds of loggerhead and leatherback turtles haul themselves up these beaches to bury their clutches of eggs in these protected sands. After 25 years of strict protection by the Natal Parks Board, which each year monitors and safeguards their breeding activity, the populations are thriving.

To witness a huge turtle heave herself out

of the surf and up the beach, the moonlight glistening off her wet carapace as it must have done each year for countless millennia, and then to silently watch her go about this age-old ritual of reproduction, is to experience something which cannot fail to confirm the importance of maintaining the full diversity of life on earth. There is something in the turtle's heroic exertions which drives home the message that this tenacious life-force must not be summarily terminated through mankind's exploitation or pollution.

The coastal lakes of Sibayi and Kosi Bay lie close behind the forested dunes that back the turtle-nesting beaches of the Tongaland Marine Reserve. Rest camps situated on the

sq. km) hold a great variety of birdlife. More than 390 species have been recorded from the reserve and in the summer wet season (November to March) when migrant species are present, one may easily record upwards of 200 species within a few days. The reserve's only rest camp has limited accommodation and bookings must be made well in advance. Ndumu has the added advantage of allowing access to much of the reserve on foot under the supervision of a trained game guard; many of these guards are expert fieldsmen and will much improve the visitor's ability to detect the often unobtrusive birds and mammals in the reserve's dense forests.

shores of these lakes are administered by the Kwazulu Bureau of Natural Resource. Also run by this conservation agency is the Ndumu Game Reserve, located an hour's drive inland on the Usutu River, the country's border with Mozambique. This, the most tropical of the Natal reserves, is probably the premier bird reserve in South Africa. A series of pans lined with the yellow-barked fever trees are filled with an amazing variety of waterfowl and provide sanctuary for many hippopotamuses and crocodiles.

The fig forests that fringe the rivers and pans and the thickets that cover most of this relatively small reserve (42 sq. miles or 110

The high grasslands conservation areas have much else to offer and these few examples do not do justice to the wealth of ecosystems and protected areas that can be visited. Certain ecosystems deserve brief mention. For instance, the high grasslands of the Drakensberg mountain range that form Natal's inland boundary with the mountainous kingdom of Lesotho are virtually all included in various reserves and wilderness areas. Here are found many of the country's most beautiful landscapes – huge towering amphitheatres set above rolling grassy slopes,with numerous sparkling mountain streams running through tranquil forested gorges to fall tumbling over cascading waterfalls.

These mountains and grasslands are home to a fabulous variety of wild flowers and several of the country's endemic bird species, such as the yellow pipit and the Drakensberg siskin. The majestic lammergeyer is still secure in these high mountains.

The arid interior: Further west one can visit the Mountain Zebra National Park or the Karoo National Park as well as several provincial reserves, such as the Hester Malan Nature Reserve or Rolfontein Nature Reserve, to obtain a glimpse of the semi-arid Karoo ecosystem, now mainly used for sheep farming. The Karoo is probably the

host of insects and flocks of nomadic birds breeding in such an area provide an unforgettable spectacle.

Ironically, whereas in most other countries it is the sem-desert ecosystem which are best conserved in national parks, in South Africa the converse applies. This situation may soon be rectified, and the planned Richtersveld National Park (in the arid mountainous region just south of the Orange River border with Namibia) could go some way to ameliorating this current inadequacy of conservation coverage of the drier portions of the country. The existing Augrabies Falls National Park, higher up the Orange River, is certainly worth a visit but it is not

most characteristic of South Africa's ecosystems. For those who enjoy wide-open spaces and stark semi-desert landscapes, a trip through the Karoo, with planned stopovers at several of the relatively small reserves found here, will be well worthwhile.

Most of the Karoo's animal and plant life is unique to this area. Those visiting the region soon after good rains can witness levels of biological activity unsurpassed in any of the other ecosystems of South Africa. The fields of brightly coloured flowers, a

<u>Left</u> and <u>right</u>, a feature of any stay in the bush is the distinctive character of the safari camps.

large enough to ensure the long-term survival of the rich semi-desert fauna and flora of the country's western arid zone.

Forests, lakes and fynbos: Further south still, one has the well-watered coastal strip of the southern Cape Province. Here are found the country's largest evergreen forests. The Tsitsikamma Forest National Park, as well as the nearby Tsitsikamma Coastal National Park, allow the visitor a chance to see the region's dense temperate forests. The enormous yellowwood trees, their canopies often festooned with "old man's beard" lichens and the forest floor beneath them damp and mossy, are a far cry from the semi-desert

Karoo ecosystems which are located only a few hours drive inland. The Coastal Park not only boasts a spectacular five-day hiking trail – called the "Otter Trail" after the Cape clawless otters which can sometimes be seen feeding along this coastline – but also has an underwater trail for skindivers or scuba divers to follow within the marine portion of the reserve.

The Knysna Lagoon and the Wilderness Lakes System both have been recently proclaimed as "Contractual National Parks". This means that while people still continue to live in places within these parks future development is controlled so as to prevent any further deterioration in these important natural ecosystems. Both these systems fall within the major temperate rainforest areas of the southern Cape and the verdant forest landscapes add to the beauty of these water bodies.

The mountains in these southern Cape areas are almost all located within proclaimed and protected mountain catchment areas or state forest areas. Clad with the fynbos vegetation that holds the proteas ericas and other renowned plants of the Cape floral kingdom, these mountains are traversed by a series of hiking trails.

To take a four or five-day hike along one of these is to get to know one of the most spectacular ecosystems of the world. One can virtually walk from one end of the fynbos biome to the other if the route is carefully planned and the necessary bookings are made for the overnight huts studded at intervals along the various routes.

The number of people on these trails at any one time is carefully controlled in order to ensure that everyone has an opportunity to undergo a real wilderness experience. For those who prefer not to do a lot of walking, there are numerous reserves which can be visited by car.

At the tip of the Cape Peninsula is located the remarkable Cape of Good Hope Nature Reserve. This relatively tiny reserve (30 sq.

miles or 77 sq. km) holds a good representative sample of the Cape flora. It has 1,052 native plant species recorded within its boundaries, this total being more than two thirds that of the entire British Isles (which has 1,492 species in its land area of 9,330 sq. miles or 24,160 sq. km). Eleven of these plant species are found nowhere else except in this reserve.

The world-famous Table Mountain which forms the backdrop to the country's mother city, Cape Town, is itself a proclaimed nature reserve. Visitors can take relatively easy day walks some way up this mountain or use a cable car to reach the summit.

The future: Sitting on the top of Table Mountain and looking down on to the seemingly never-ending suburbs of Greater Cape Town one cannot help feeling uneasy about the conservation future in South Africa. Within a single life time the Cape Flats, which lie between the Cape Peninsula and the Hottentots-Hollands Mountains to the east, have been engulfed by a spreading wave of humanity. What used to be an area of exceptional wetlands and a veritable garden of wild flowers, is now virtually completely covered by factory land, suburbia and small agricultural holdings.

Wattles introduced from Australia choke the native vegetation on the last remaining

1960 to 35.8 million in 1989 and is expected to exceed 45 million in the year 2000) all the pressures on the natural environment are intensifying.

It is essential that conservation agencies continue to receive the necessary funds to carry out their important task of protecting the natural resources of South Africa for the benefit of all its peoples, including the generations still to be born. A visitor who, having enjoyed the wonderful country and its superb national parks, wishes to do something constructive to assure the future of conservation might consider taking out membership in one of the many local conservation societies.

scraps of uncultivated land. Many of the plants and animals of this area and the adjacent Cape Peninsula are now threatened with extinction. Five species have already been lost on the Cape Peninsula alone. About 1,500 South African plant species are thought to be facing extinction unless current trends in habitat destruction are halted or reversed.

With a human population which is currently growing extremely rapidly (the population increased from about 18.3 million in

Left, at the end of a day's walkabout. Above, rain falls on the Kalahari.

The oldest and largest of these is the Wildlife Society of Southern Africa, which came into existence during the campaign to establish the Kruger Park. It now has over 50,000 members and runs a variety of conservation education programmes (*see the Travel Tips section for contact numbers*).

Visitors can do the country's conservation agencies a favour if on their return they tell others of their experience and urge them to pay these wonderful reserves a visit. Nothing will assure their future existence more than a continuing high level of foreign tourism. So, even by simply visiting these parks, a positive step has already been taken.

Visitors have long been captivated by the beauty of South Africa. "Lofty Table Mountain with its beautiful table cloth of fleecy clouds," wrote David Livingstone in 1841. Sir Francis Drake observed that the Cape of Good Hope was "a most stately thing and the fairest Cape we saw in the whole circumference of the Earth." Bloemfontein was seen as a "quiet, smiling village," while Anthony Trollope, who roamed the country in 1878, was struck by the power of the diamond mine at Kimberley. A visitor should, he said, "take an opportunity of looking down upon the mine by moonlight. It is a weird and wonderful sight, and may almost be called sublime in its peculiar strangeness."

The most logical place to begin a tour of South Africa is Johannesburg, with its international airport and busy, modern skyscrapers. It is a town not without its problems, but with an improving political situation and a ready eye trained on the global marketplace, Johannesburg might well become Africa's city of the future.

Visitors on the look-out for winter sunshine will appreciate the "Mother City", Cape Town, reputedly one of the three most beautiful cities in the world, with its surrounding area of winelands, and the Cape of Good Hope. The most common connection from Cape Town to the eastern regions is via the Garden Route, well-known for its fishing hamlets, wide beaches and sub-tropical forests. Further up the coast is Natal, home to South Africa's fun-loving bathing resort, Durban, and the Umhlanga Rocks. Located in the Eastern Transvaal is the Kruger National Park , plus a host of excellently run private game reserves that will satisfy not only nature lovers but also the most selective visitor.

The variety of South Africa's landscape is equalled only by the multitude of interests it can accommodate. From teeming skyscraper towns to wide-sweeping clifftop vistas, the country offers something for every visitor, whether travelling in groups or exploring individually like Cecil Rhodes, who made special trips to The Veld to be "alone with the Alone".

Preceding pages: the grasslands of the Kalahari Gemsbok National Park; the southern skies darken; the South African sunset. **Left**, Zulu magic.

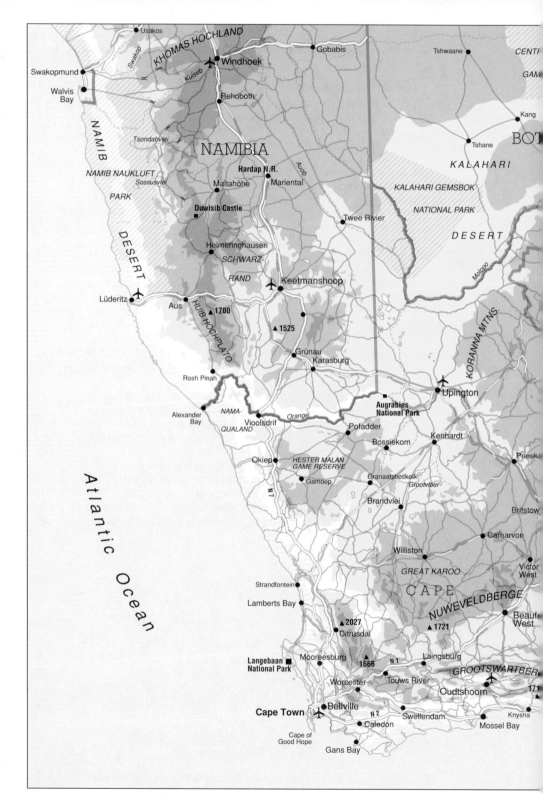

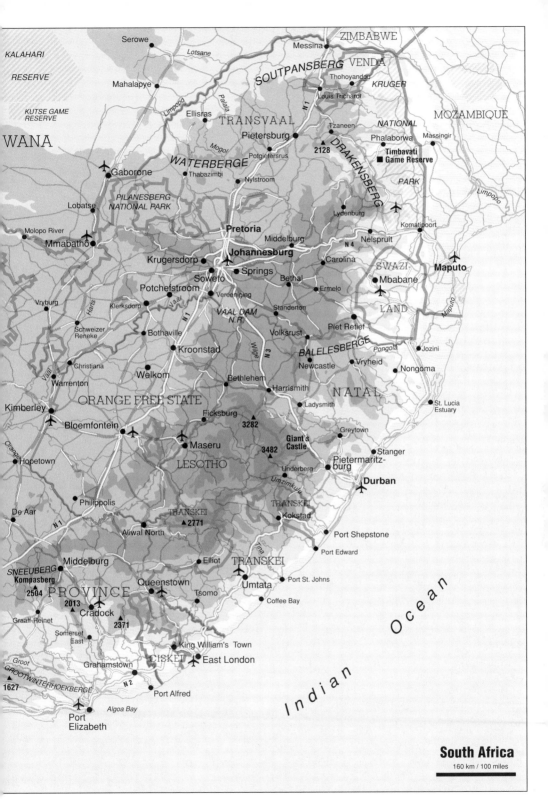

South Africa

160 km / 100 miles

155

JOHANNESBURG

e'Goli, it is called by the locals – the City of Gold. **Johannesburg** is the pulsating heart of South Africa's industrial and commercial life where, more than a mile below the bustling city traffic, miners dig for the world's most precious metal. At street level, high-powered businessmen and ambitious young stockbrokers rub shoulders daily with street vendors and traditional herbalists. Ultra-modern corporate towers dwarf noisy pavement stalls. It is now also the capital of the Gauteng province.

Ever since a fateful day in 1886 when George Harrison, a humble prospector, stumbled upon an outcrop of gold-bearing rock, the region's economy and life have been driven by the pulsating rhythm of the mining industry. The effects are inescapable. Stand on the top floor of the Carlton Centre, the city's highest building, and you see golden mine dumps and shaft headgears dotting the skyline. Walk down the avenues of downtown Johannesburg and you find streets, buildings and museums that evoke vivid memories of the days of "gold fever" and the "Randlords".

Harrison's discovery sparked off a gold rush never experienced before or since anywhere in the world. Prospectors and fortune-seekers descended on the area in search of instant wealth. Makeshift shelters and tents were pitched all over the once tranquil veld. A massive, sprawling, rough and raucous shanty-town sprang up overnight. Within three years, Johannesburg was the largest town in South Africa. A rudimentary stock exchange was established. Men outnumbered women three to one. Hotels and canteens, brothels and music halls were erected throughout the town to satisfy the needs of the boisterous, community.

Soon, however, major mining corporations moved in to take control of the industry and swallow up individual claims. The "Randlords" emerged on the scene, and soon dominated it. Men like Cecil John Rhodes, Barney Barnato,

J.B. Robinson, Alfred Beit and Julius Wehrner quickly accumulated huge fortunes and imposed a semblance of order on the unruly mining town and its polyglot community.

The Golden City still displays all the characteristics it acquired in those tumultuous days. Less than 5 minutes' drive from the bustling and throbbing downtown lie the quiet, elegant suburbs of Houghton and Parktown where the Randlords once held sway and built their opulent mansions.

Johannesburg is today the hub of a sprawling metropolis called the Witwatersrand (Ridge of White Waters) stretching more than 75 miles (120 km) from Springs in the east to Randfontein in the west with a rapidly growing population of almost 4 million. Through the years the small towns that sprang up haphazardly along the reef were landscaped and beautified, becoming popular tourist attractions.

Downtown: By world standards, Johannesburg is a medium-sized city, but in the African context it is a giant, en-

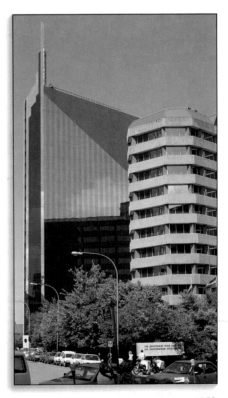

Preceding pages: city of the future.
Left, go-ahead Jo'burg.
Right, the Johannesburg Stock Exchange.

compassing some of the continent's best hotels and shopping opportunities. The **Carlton Hotel and Shopping Mall** is usually a visitor's first destination. Its 50th-floor **Panorama** provides the ideal vantage point from which to observe the Golden City's skyline. Just across the road is the **Small Street Mall** with its wide array of shops selling African curios, jewellery, electronic equipment and fashion and accessories.

Nowhere are the contrasts that typify Johannesburg so forcefully experienced as in its downtown area. Here, modern stores offering the latest in international fashions rub shoulders with traditional shops displaying skins, herbs, witch-doctor's bones and other unidentified objects. At the **Oriental Plaza** in Fordsburg, shoppers can bargain for the best prices on fabric and haberdashery as well as aromatic herbs and spices.

Hillbrow is a noisy, bustling, never-sleeping meeting point of the entire spectrum of South African cultures – at once exotic and chaotic. The densely populated 'Brow is cosmopolitan, offering a vivid miscellany of shops, restaurants, theatres and nightspots. At weekends flea markets spring up all over town. In front of the **Market Theatre** one can browse for hours while being entertained by street performers, musicians and buskers.

However, unwary visitors should be warned that Johannesburg – and especially the downtown area – can be dangerous. As in most big cities, skilled pickpockets, petty thieves and muggers are on the look-out for easy victims and it is not advisable to walk alone after dark. A special police unit has been established to protect tourists in the country's major cities.

For shopping, many visitors prefer to visit the quieter, more affluent northern suburbs. The **Rosebank Mall**, **Hyde Park Corner** and **Sandton City** – the largest shopping centre in the country – are the most conveniently located.

Wherever you go, street names reflect the pioneer days – Claim, Prospect, Nugget, Main Reef. A visit to a working gold mine can be arranged through the Chamber of Mines – but be forewarned, you need to be fit to undertake the arduous journey deep into the sweltering belly of the earth.

A more leisurely way of observing the gold mining industry at close hand would be a visit to **Gold Reef City** at Crown Mines, just 4 miles (6 km) from the city centre. Here, too, visitors are taken down a mineshaft and can watch the complete mining process from the extraction of the ore to the pouring of the molten gold into ingot-moulds. Above ground, the rumbustious pioneer days of the "gold rush" have been recreated in the form of a Victorian funfair, an old brewery and pub, and an old-fashioned apothecary.

Museums and galleries: The city's museums and galleries cover a wide range of interests – from the tribal and traditional to modern South African art work. At the **Africana Museum in Progress**, an ethnological exhibition is on display with replicas of huts and examples of beadwork, domestic equipment and artefacts. Housed in the Johannesburg Public Library is the

Africana Museum with exhibitions on the early history of South Africa and an impressive collection of early Cape furniture, silverware, coins and glassware. In the same building is the **Geological Museum** with a vast collection of the country's unique mineral wealth on display. Guided tours and lectures are available at all these venues.

The **Johannesburg Art Gallery** in Joubert Park is situated in a fascinating building combining old and modern architecture. It has representative collections of international and South African art and a print cabinet containing over 2,500 items. African tribal art is on display at the **Gertrude Posel Galley** at the University of the Witwatersrand and includes valuable examples of vanishing African art forms such as masks, head-dresses and beadwork.

The **Museum of South African Rock Art** (to be seen at the Johannesburg Zoo) is an open-air exhibition of rock engravings created by Bushmen and other nomadic tribes dating back to several centuries ago.

South Africa is one of the last developed countries in the world where steam railway locomotives are still in operation – although here, too, the tradition is fading fast to make way for modern electrical engines. For the steam enthusiast, however, there are still plenty of

Johannesburg

500 m / 0.3 miles

the graceful machines to be seen, particularly at the **Railway Museum** in the station concourse. The **James Hall Museum of Transport** in Pioneers' Park tells the story of land transport in South Africa, displaying trams, horse drawn carriages, ox-wagons and vintage motor-cars and fire engines.

The **Johannesburg Planetarium** is a fascinating place to view the southern skies from a fresh angle. Audio-visual shows and multi-media displays take visitors on a thrilling astrological journey to distant galaxies.

Two major centres for higher learning are situated within the borders of Johannesburg. The **University of Witwatersrand** was started in 1896 as a training institute for the mining industry. Today it is the largest English-language university in South Africa. The **Rand Afrikaans University** with its modern buildings followed three-quarters of a century later but has already established itself as a major academic institution. Visitors can take guided tours to both universities by arrangement.

On the wild side: More than anything else South Africa as a tourist destination is known for its wide and exquisite variety of wildlife. Nothing beats the experience of visiting one of the large game parks in the country to see lions, elephants, giraffes and antelopes in their natural habitat. But those less fortunate are able to enjoy scaled-down versions close to the city centres. The **Lion Park** at **Honeydew** and the **Krugersdorp Game Reserve** nearby – less than half an hour's drive from the city – have scores of lions and antelopes.

The **Johannesburg Zoo** houses more than 3,000 varieties of mammals, birds and reptiles. Enclosures for the big cats, elephants, giraffes, and large apes, guarded only by moats and free of iron bars, are popular tourist attractions as are the new polar bear habitat and walk-through aviary. At **Midrand**, just north of Johannesburg, the **Transvaal Snake Park** displays a large variety of African snakes in an attractive setting. Some of the world's most poisonous vipers are milked for visitors, twice a day.

Left, Civic Centre. **Right**, chess in Joubert Park.

Johannesburg is a birdwatcher's paradise. The **Florence Bloom Bird Sanctuary** is sited within the 250-acre (100-hectare) Delta Park. Two dams are included within its area and a large variety of birds can be watched from two viewing hides. The **Melrose Bird Sanctuary** includes a dam surrounded by extensive reed beds providing nests for a large variety of weavers while the **Koersman Bird Sanctuary** in **Westdene** specialises in water birds, guineafowl, ostriches and flamingos.

Ethnic dancing can be enjoyed at various venues scattered across the Witwatersrand. Dance troupes from various mines on the Reef often perform at **Gold Reef City**.

An amusing feature usually included is the *isicathulo* or gumboot dances. The famed Mzumbe dancers perform ancient legends and ethnic dances accompanied by tribal drums at the Heia Safari Ranch (only on Sundays), where a traditional South African *braai* can also be savoured.

At **Phumangena uMuzi** near **Aloe Ridge**, visitors can stay overnight in a traditional Zulu village complete with Zulu food, bone-throwing by a *sangoma* (witchdoctor) and tribal dancing. African herbalist shops where visitors can buy *muti* to cure every imaginable illness and affliction are to be found in downtown Johannesburg – nestling somewhat incongruously in the shadow of the ultra-modern new stock exchange building.

Guided tours of **Soweto** (SOuth WEstern TOwnships), the sprawling city with close on 2 million inhabitants, depart from the Carlton Hotel at regular intervals and include stopovers at a "cultural kraal", a nursery school and a sheltered workshop for the handicapped people. Other major black towns on the Rand are Alexandra, Kagiso, Kathlehong and Sebokeng.

The wide outdoors: For people who enjoy outdoor activities the Johannesburg area provides ample opportunities all the year round for entertainment. Myriad man-made lakes scattered across the Reef have been transformed into

pleasant recreational venues, popular for fishing, boating and birdwatching.

Visitors to the very popular **Zoo Lake** can hire rowing boats while the Emmarentia Dam adjoining the Botanical Gardens is a haven for water enthusiasts, providing facilities for boardsailing, canoeing, yachting, scuba diving and model boats. **Wemmer Pan** is an ideal place for a quiet afternoon picnic or a walk along several marked routes. It provides a superb panoramic view of the Johannesburg skyline.

At the adjoining **Pioneer Park** visitors can see the Santarama Midland, a miniature-scale version of Johannesburg, or watch the multi-coloured Musical Fountain propel streams of water into the air synchronised to the beat of popular tunes.

There is a growing number of self-guided walking trails which utilise the streams and ridges of metropolitan Johannesburg and provide facilities for picnics. Places of historical, archaeological and ecological interest are incorporated and clearly marked on detailed maps which can be obtained from the Johannesburg Publicity Association.

The **Braamfontein Spruit Trail** meanders through central Johannesburg, Randburg and Sandton to the Klein Jukskei River. It can be joined at any point. Other trails include the **Bloubos Trail**, the **Parktown Urban Walk** and the **Sandspruit Trail**. The **Randlords Heritage Trail** is an historic urban walk through areas where many of the original homes of the Gold Rush pioneers and other places of historical and architectural interest can still be seen.

The **Sterkfontein Caves** near **Krugersdorp** on the West Rand consist of six chambers with an underground lake said to have special healing powers. It was here that in 1936 Dr Robert Broom discovered the skull of the female of the genus *Plesianthropus transvaalensis* (affectionately known as "Mrs Ples"), estimated to be 1 million years old. Conducted tours of the cave complex take place every 30 minutes.

A day trip growing in popularity is the **Crocodile River Ramble**, visiting the

Dancers rest at flea market in Bruma Lake.

artists' colony on its banks. Some of the country's top artists participate in this venture. Visitors can watch them work and buy a wide variety of artwork, paintings, sculptures, hand-made jewellery and custom-built furniture.

At the **National Equestrian Centre** at Kyalami, a team of Lippizaner horses give performances of choreographed classical riding every Sunday. The beautiful white stallions are trained to perform in the style of the world renowned Spanish Riding School in Vienna. For the sports lover, Johannesburg and its vicinity provide a wide selection of facilities. They provide a number of world-class golf courses, 28 swimming pools (including a heated indoor pool in Hillbrow), public tennis courts, ice-skating rinks and indoor ten-pin bowling lanes scattered across the region.

Major sporting events are staged right through the year and in most instances tickets are easy to obtain. The **Air Show** at Rand Airport is always a favourite with visitors and residents alike, while the **Rand Show** held over Easter at Nasrec, just south of Johannesburg, attracts more than 500,000 visitors a year.

Day tours to various interesting tourist destinations are conducted by qualified and experienced tour guides. Private tours can also be arranged on request. Information can be obtained at the Johannesburg Publicity Association or at hotel reception desks.

Nightlife: Judged by international standards, Johannesburg's nightlife may not be all that glittering. The one exception is theatre, where local productions of a very high standard are staged regularly. The **Civic Theatre** has recently undergone extensive renovations and compares favourably with some of the major theatres of the world.

The vibrant local theatre scene is best experienced at the **Market Complex** where five theatres specialise in experimental and contemporary local productions. The Windybrow, the Leonard Rayne, the Alexander and the Alhambra are other popular theatres. The latest movie releases can be seen in cinemas throughout the town. For film and thea-

Gold Reef City.

tre events, consult the local newspapers and the monthly magazine, *Hello Johannesburg*, or the "Tonight" section of the *Star* newspaper.

For lovers of good food, Johannesburg offers a wide selection of top-class restaurants catering for every imaginable taste: Italian, French, Cajun, Indian, Oriental… Among the restaurants favoured by local critics are Le Canard and Les Marquis in Sandown, and Chapters in the Sandton Sun Hotel, the Ile the France in Randburg, the Zoo Lake restaurant with a beautiful view over the lake, Herbert Baker in Parktown and the Three Ships in the Carlton Hotel – just to name a few.

However, no visit would be complete without a dinner at restaurants such as Anton van Wouw, Leipoldt's or Grammadoela's where traditional South African dishes such as *bobotie*, *sosaties* and *potjiekos* can be savoured with a selection of local white and red wines.

For the best in jazz, the places to go are Kippies, Rakes, the Coconut Grove and the Roxy Rhythm Bar. Cabaret shows are staged nightly at No. 58 in Hillbrow and Sardi's by Night in downtown Johannesburg.

For a relaxing evening of dinner and dance it is hard to beat Caesar's Palace in Braamfontein and Grayston and the Villa in Sandton while the younger set can dance the night away at late-night spots such as Junction, Foxy's and Rumours.

Those interested in visiting some of the nightspots or restaurants should bear in mind that Johannesburg does not have an especially effective public transport system. There is no underground railway or light rail system and buses run on fixed routes and at irregular times. The network of taxis is not as extensive as in Europe or America but enquiries about reputable taxi companies can be made at hotel desks.

One final reminder: it's worth reiterating that, as in any big city, tourists should watch out for pickpockets and thieves, particularly downtown. The police can sometimes provide escorts for groups of visitors.

Group effort, Johannesburg.

THE LURE OF GOLD

Think of South Africa and you think of gold. From time immemorial, gold has been the symbol of earthly riches. Its rarity, its rich golden colour, resistance to corrosion, and ease of working make it the most precious of the world's precious metals.

Of the 112,000 tons of gold estimated to have been mined in the world to date, 50,000 tons have come from the African continent, the bulk of it from South Africa. Today, about half of the new gold found in the world each year comes from the "golden arc" – a 300-mile (500-km) stretch from Evander in the Eastern Transvaal, through Johannesburg, along the Wes Wits line to Klerksdorp and south to Welkom and the Free State goldfields. This makes South Africa the world's largest producer of gold, contributing about 36 percent of present production. Its mines can probably produce a further 42,000 tons of gold before they are completely worked out.

Gold's amazing properties add to its intrinsic value. It is so ductile it can be hammered into very thin foil – so thin, in fact, that green light waves will pass through it. As a medium of currency it is a hedge against political and economic disaster. In the jewellery industry it is treasured for its beauty and durability, and in electronics for its non-corrosive properties.

Pure gold is too soft for use in the manufacture of jewellery so it is alloyed with other metals (mostly copper and silver) to harden it and make it more durable. The degree of purity is expressed in terms of carats: 24-carat gold is pure gold, whereas 18-carat gold indicates an alloy consisting of 18 parts gold plus 6 parts other metals.

Nearly all of South Africa's gold comes from very old placer deposits known as the Witwatersrand conglomerate. Placers are essentially ancient stream deposits in which heavy gold particles have become trapped between the sand and gravel. The Witwatersrand conglomerate contains gold and pyrite, an ore known as "fool's gold" that looks very much like the "real thing" but lacks the bold yellow colour and is much harder than natural gold.

To get to the precious metal vertical shafts are sunk from which horizontal tunnels or stopes are bored to intersect the sloping gold reef at various levels. The ERPM mine on the Rand is the world's deepest mine sinking to a depth of over 3 miles (5 km). Horizontal tunnels stretch for 6 miles (10 km) underneath the bustling Johannesburg traffic. Down in the mine the heat is almost unbearable, with temperatures rising by more than 1°C for every 100 yards of descent. Massive ventilation plants have been installed to cool the 500,000 miners descending into the bowels of the earth every working day.

Gold mining is an expensive undertaking. The richness of gold-bearing ore is described in the term "grade". In placer deposits the gold is distributed in such minute particles that it is usually not visible to the naked eye. In a typical Witwatersrand gold mine the grade varies between 5 to as much as 200 grams per ton, but the average value is of the order 10 grams. For every million tons of ore, only about 7 tons of gold will be recovered – all of which would fit into the boot of an ordinary car. West Driefontein, the world's richest gold mine, produces about 45 tons of gold each year. ∎

Molten millions.

PRETORIA

The relative sedateness of **Pretoria**, the "City of the Voortrekkers", just a 50-km (31-mile) drive to the north of Johannesburg, disguises its influence as the centre of political decision-making and administrative capital of South Africa. Money may do the talking in the Golden City, but it is in Pretoria where the strings of power are held. Each October it lives up to its name, the Jacaranda City, when its tree-lined streets and sidewalks turn into a mauve carpet as the distinctive jacaranda mimosifolia trees start to blossom. In the city centre alone, 55,000 trees line the streets.

Pretoria is often unjustly referred to as a dull city with limited entertainment facilities and little nightlife. However, this has changed considerably as the "City of the Voortrekkers" has acquired a more cosmopolitan character.

Established in 1855, the city was named after two famous Voortrekker leaders, Andries Pretorius – the hero of the Battle of Blood River – and his son M.W. Pretorius. Their statues stand in front of the stately City Hall. Much of the Afrikaner history in the late 19th century was made here and numerous buildings of great historical significance bear witness to these turbulent times.

Today it is the administrative and executive capital of the country and the city where all the major governmental decisions are made; all state departments and para-statal bodies have their head offices in Pretoria. But it is also a green city of parks and gardens where an astonishing display of exotic and indigenous flora, flowering trees and shrubs can be found.

Historic Pretoria: Guarding the southern entrance to the city is the **Voortrekker Monument**, an imposing granite structure visible from almost everywhere. This national shrine of Afrikaners commemorates the Great Trek (1834–40), the seminal event in Afrikaner history that opened up the interior of South Africa for white occupation (*see panel on page 175*).

The city centre of Pretoria was first laid out on a rectangular pattern with streets wide enough to enable a cattle-drawn wagon to turn around. In the heart of the city is Church Square, around which the first settlements in Pretoria developed. Skirting the square are the **Old Raadzaal** – seat of the Zuid Afrikaansche Republic government; the **Palace of Justice** and the original **South African Reserve Bank**.

Dominating the centre of the square is a massive **statue of President Paul Kruger** designed by the famous sculptor, Anton van Wouw, and guarded by four bronze statues resembling burghers of the old Republic. A short walk down **Church Street** – at 2.7 miles (4.3 km), one of the longest straight streets in the world – brings the visitor to **Strijdom Square**, commemorating more recent history. A massive bust of former South African prime minister, J.G. Strijdom, and a statuary group of charging horses, symbolising the efforts to establish a Republic, dominate this square.

The administrative headquarters of

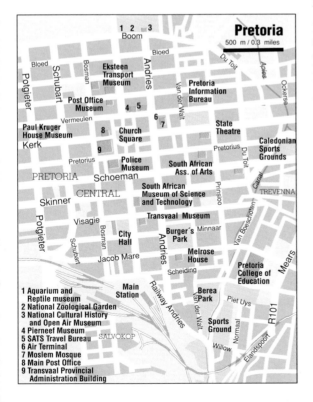

Pretoria

500 m / 0.3 miles

1 Aquarium and Reptile museum
2 National Zoological Garden
3 National Cultural History and Open Air Museum
4 Pierneef Museum
5 SATS Travel Bureau
6 Air Terminal
7 Moslem Mosque
8 Main Post Office
9 Transvaal Provincial Administration Building

the government is situated in the **Union Buildings** on Meintjieskop. This impressive red sandstone building designed by Sir Herbert Baker also provides a panoramic view of Pretoria. In the beautifully maintained gardens one also finds the **Delville Wood War Memorial** – a tribute to South African troops who fought in Europe during World War I – the **Police Memorial** and statues of three notable South African prime ministers, Gen. Louis Botha, Field Marshall J.C. Smuts and Gen. J.B.M. Hertzog. **Doornkloof**, the restored home of General Smuts – who served in the British War Cabinet during both world wars and later helped to draft the Charter of the United Nations – can be visited at Irene just outside Pretoria.

Many of the historic sites commemorate the heyday of the old Zuid-Afrikaansche Republic at the turn of the 20th century. **President Paul Kruger's House**, which he occupied during his term of office (1883–1900), has been restored to its former splendour. It contains relics and personal belongings of President Kruger as well as his private railway carriage and official State coach.

At the nearby **Heroes' Acre** the graves of famous Afrikaner leaders such as Andries Pretorius and Paul Kruger can be seen. **Melrose House**, an historical museum in Jacob Maré Street, opposite the Burgers Park, is where the peace treaty ending the Anglo-Boer War was signed. The house, designed and built in 1886, is one of South Africa's finest surviving examples of Victorian architecture. A number of strongly barricaded forts built to protect Pretoria during the Anglo-Boer War have survived and two, **Fort Skanskop** and **Fort Klapperkop**, have subsequently been turned into military museums – the former depicting the period between the Great Trek (1836) and the Anglo-Boer War (1902) and the latter from World War I to modern-day warfare.

Museums and exhibitions: The **Transvaal Museum** opposite the City Hall specialises in natural history with an extensive collection of fossils and geological and archaeological material. The

The Union Buildings are the centre of South African government.

National Cultural History and Open-air Museum boasts an impressive collection of rock art and an ethnological exhibition depicting the early history of the region. The **Pioneer Museum** is a tranquil open-air exhibition situated on the banks of the Moreleta Spruit. It consists of a restored thatched cottage depicting pioneer life in the mid-19th century and a reconstructed farmyard showing typical activities dating from the period. A similar exhibition can be seen at the **Willem Prinsloo Agricultural Museum** where regular demonstrations of farming activities are given.

The **University of Pretoria** is the largest residential university in the country with 12 faculties and more than 23,000 students. University staff members lead conducted tours of the campus. Easily visible at the southern entrance to Pretoria is the headquarters of the **University of South Africa**, known among locals as Unisa. With more than 105,000 students from across the globe, Unisa is the largest correspondence university in the world. Pretoria is the city with the greatest concentration of research institutes in the Republic, with the **Veterinary Research Institute** at **Onderstepoort** the best-known. Tours to this and other research centres such as the **Council for Scientific and Industrial Research** (CSIR), the **Uranium Enrichment Corporation** and the **South Africa Bureau of Standards** can be arranged.

The outdoor life: With its mild climate throughout the year, Pretoria is an ideal venue for visitors who like to spend their time in the open. The **Moreleta Spruit Hiking Trail** – a 5-mile (8-km) trail winding its way through Pretoria's eastern suburbs – offers the hiker tranquil surroundings and an opportunity to observe at close range a wide variety of indigenous trees and bird life.

Another haven for bird-watchers is the **Austin Roberts Bird Sanctuary** in Muckleneuck, where more than 100 indigenous bird species, including blue cranes, herons, ostriches and waterbirds, can be viewed.

The **National Zoo** is one of the largest of its kind in the world and about 150 mammal species can be seen. An overhead cableway provides the visitor with a panoramic view of the zoo and the surrounding city. A separate **aquarium** houses both freshwater and marine fish and a large collection of snakes, lizards and other reptiles are displayed in the adjacent **Reptile Park**.

At the **National Botanical Gardens** a large variety of indigenous plants are on display. Conducted tours include a slide show and visit to the nursery.

The **Fountains Valley** is Pretoria's most popular weekend retreat and picnic spot. Apart from hiking trails, playgrounds and swimming pools, it offers a miniature railway ride along a picturesque route through the valley. Just to the north of Pretoria is the **Roodeplaat Dam**, a popular spot for fishing, yachting, water sports and swimming. The **Wonderboom Nature Reserve** is situated in the Magaliesberg mountain range on the northern outskirts of the city. This area is dominated by the massive *Wonderboom* (miracle tree) – a 1,000-year-old fig tree, measuring 75 ft (23

Late-night café in Pretoria.

metres) in height and 160 ft (50 metres) in diameter with 13 trunks spread over a hectare (2½ acres).

The **Verwoerdburg Dam** is a modern development with a man-made lake right in the centre of a large shopping complex. This is a very popular spot for board-sailors and canoeists. The nearby **Atlantis Waterpark** offers fun-filled hours of swimming, water slides and aqua-rides. Apart from excellent golf courses and swimming pools, leisure facilities include an ice-rink at the Sterland Cine Complex, a 10-pin bowling alley at the Kingsley Centre across the road, and a newly developed mini-golf complex less than a block away.

Arts and entertainment: The **Pretoria Art Museum** in Arcadia Park houses the best collection of South African artists in the country including work by renowned local artists such as Frans Oerder, Maggie Laubscher and Walter Battis. Two smaller galleries are specifically devoted to the work of two well-known local artists: the **Pierneef Museum**, with an impressive collection of paintings and graphic art, and the **Van Wouw Museum**, housing work of the great sculptor, Anton van Wouw.

A novel development growing in popularity is the **Art in the Park** exhibitions held on Saturdays in the picturesque Magnolia Dell. Professional and amateur artists exhibit various forms of arts and crafts in the scenic and placid surroundings of a suburban park.

The **State Theatre** is the centre of cultural life in Pretoria. Five separate auditoriums in the modern complex provide facilities for opera, drama, ballet and symphony concerts. Guided tours of the complex, including the backstage areas, can be arranged. Symphony concerts are also held at the City Hall while plays are regularly staged at the **Breytenbach Theatre** in Sunnyside, the **Kleinteater** in the city centre and the **Aula** at the University of Pretoria.

Cinema complexes are scattered across town, though the biggest concentration is in Sunnyside. The newly refurbished Sterland has 14 cinemas and an ice-rink. The local daily newspaper,

The Kruger Monument on Church Square.

172

the *Pretoria News*, carries complete listings of cinemas, theatres, restaurants and special events such as art exhibitions, public lectures and flea markets.

As yet, Pretoria's nightlife cannot be compared with that of Johannesburg but the demand for high-quality entertainment has led to the establishment of popular nightspots such as After Dark for nightly cabaret shows and Jacqueline's and Kansas City, where one can dance the night away.

Many quality restaurants cater to tastes ranging from international cuisine to informal steakhouse. Among those favoured by locals are La Perla, the Oude Kaap Restaurant, Camelot, Diep in die Berg, and the Godfather. A drive to the Idle Winds country restaurant near Hartebeespoort Dam (Route 511) is well worth the trouble.

Special events: Details of conducted tours in and around the city can be obtained from the **Visitors' Information Bureau** at the Pretoria Municipal building on the corner of Van der Walt and Vermeulen streets. It also publishes regular guides to the city and its attractions. An interesting trip is a visit to the town of **Cullinan**, some 25 miles (40 km) east of the city.

This town grew around the diamond mining industry and has retained many of its original cottage-style terraced houses. It was here that in 1905 the world's largest diamond, the 3,106-carat **Cullinan diamond** was discovered. This massive diamond was cut into no fewer than 105 smaller gems of which the biggest now form part of the British Crown Jewels. Annual happenings include the **Jacaranda Carnival**, held each October, the **Pretoria Show**, at the Showgrounds in Pretoria West in August, and the **Wine and Food Festival**, held at the same venue a month later.

The Magaliesberg mountain range: Named after Magali, a local tribal chief, the Magaliesberg offers picturesque mountain scenery within easy reach of Pretoria and Johannesburg. Winding its way through the area is the Hennops River, supporting the tobacco and citrus industries in the vicinity and providing

Pretoria is also known as the "Jacaranda City".

the setting for numerous holiday resorts and walking trails. The ridge of the Magalies stretches for about 80 miles (130 km), its sheer cliffs providing an excellent breeding ground for the rare Cape vulture of which approximately 500 can be found in the area. Often these magnificent birds can be seen floating on the warm air currents. Shelters have been built to protect the birds from poachers, and volunteers brave the rocky ledges to get to nests to ring the chicks.

The **Hartebeespoort Dam**, 22 miles (35 km) to the west of Pretoria, (R27) is the most popular place of recreation in the area. The dam, covering 4½ sq. miles (12 sq. km), formed by two rivers — the Crocodile and Magalies — hosts a variety of watersports and is very popular among anglers. There are beautiful views from the winding road which skirts the dam and crosses the dam wall via a mountain tunnel.

The **Hartebeespoort Nature Reserve** is situated on the southeastern shores of the dam and offers walking trails through indigenous vegetation and a unique opportunity to observe birdlife and small buck from close range. A cableway connects the highest point on the Magalies with the dam and provides a thrilling ride and magnificent view.

Close by is the **Hartebeespoort Zoo and Snake Park**, a small and intimate facility with an interesting variety of animals, reptiles and birds. Snake, seal and chimpanzee shows are held over weekends and on public holidays. Special fun trains, departing from Pretoria and Johannesburg, are chartered for a sightseeing trip to the area.

A recent innovation is a **hot-air balloon safari** hovering over the Hartebeespoort Dam area. The flights last around 90 minutes and include a champagne brunch en route.

Rustenburg, the "town of rest", is a picturesque town at the centre of the local farming and mining communities. On its outskirts are pleasant and well-kept holiday resorts such as the **Kloof** and **Buffelspoort**, and to its south is the village of Magaliesburg and the very popular Mount Grace Hotel.

The house where Paul Kruger lived is now a museum.

THE VOORTREKKER MONUMENT

Dominating the Pretoria skyline is a massive, awe-inspring landmark that has become a shrine to most Afrikaners: the Voortrekker Monument. The 200-ft (61-metre) high chunk of granite commemorates the seminal event in Afrikaner history: the Great Trek (1834–40) from the Cape into the unknown interior.

Planning for the centennial anniversary of the Trek, a government commission in 1936 called for architects from all over the world to submit designs. It was to symbolise the courage and indomitable spirit of the trekkers and yet blend in with the vastness and solitude of the highveld landscape.

Eventually, the designs of a local architect, Gerhard Moerdijk, were chosen. He utilised building concepts also used by medieval black tribes at places like the Great Zimbabwe where flat stones were piled on top of one another. For the monument he used granite slabs from a local quarry.

In 1938 the gripping history of hardship and strife was vividly commemorated with a symbolic ox-wagon trek from Cape Town into the interior. Thousands of Afrikaners converged on Pretoria to witness the laying of the monument's cornerstone. World War II delayed construction but on 16 December 1949 the doors of the monument swung open during another mass celebration.

Surrounding the monument is a wall of 64 ox-wagons carved out of stone. This depicts the Voortrekker laager at the Battle of Blood River, scene of the decisive battle against the Zulu army of Dingaane on 16 December 1838. At the entrance are the bronze figures of a Voortrekker woman and two children, sculptured by the famous South African artist, Anton van Wouw. Nearby are the looming figures of two wildebeest, depicting the dangers confronting the pioneers. Guarding the four corners and cut out of the granite are the massive busts of the three most important Trek-leaders, Pretorius, Hendrik Potgieter and Piet Retief as well as the fourth figure of "the unknown trekker".

The main chamber inside is the impressive Hall of Heroes with a 100-ft (30-metre) square marble floor, surrounded by an historic frieze 300 ft long and 6 ft high (90 by 2 metres). On the 27 marble panels the highlights of the Trek are depicted in vivid detail. A number of South African sculptors were commissioned to work on the frieze. Meticulous care was taken to get every detail correct down to the smallest item of furniture or clothing. In many instances direct descendants of some of the Voortrekker heroes were used as models.

In the monument's lower hall attention is focused on a huge cenotaph of polished granite – the Altar of Sacrifice – on which the words *Ons vir jou, Suid-Afrika* (We for thee, South Africa) were carved out. Close by is the Eternal Flame, lit from a torch carried by youths in a relay from Cape Town in 1938. From the main hall a winding staircase leads up to the domed ceiling and the roof with a panoramic view of Pretoria and its surroundings. At exactly noon on each 16 December a shaft of sunlight penetrates an opening in the dome to fall on the cenotaph below.

The museum at the monument has an exhibition of Voortrekker relics and a reconstruction of a pioneer home. ∎

SUN CITY

To the north and west of Rustenburg lies the patchwork of the former homeland of **Bophuthatswana**. Any form of organised gambling was prohibited in South Africa until 1994 but the new "independence" of places such as Bophu-thatswana, Ciskei, Venda and the Transkei had provided a loophole for imaginative entrepreneurs. Thousands of visitors flock from the Witwatersrand to the round-the-clock wonderland of **Sun City**. Busloads of aspiring millionaires descend on the complex daily, hoping for the jackpot.

The resort nestles in the tranquil surroundings of an ancient volcanic crater, the Pilanesberg mountain, with its excellent National Park – the fourth largest game reserve in southern Africa. The reserve became famous for its "Operation Genesis" which involved the reintroduction of a large number of wildlife species such as leopard, kudu, rhino, lion and elephant. Day trips are taken from Sun City but there are also overnight facilities at luxury resorts such as Kwa-Maritane and Tshukudu. Small groups are accommodated at exclusive camps such as Mankwe or Metswedi.

Sun City comprises four of the most luxurious hotels to be found on the continent of Africa, a sprawling entertainment complex, a huge lake for a vast variety of watersports and two international standard golf courses. All are within easy walking distance from one another but a network of buses and a monorail train provide quicker access.

The Sun City Hotel is an international playground overlooking a magnificent landscape of sub-tropical gardens and sparkling swimming pools. It boasts a spacious pool terrace where refreshing cocktails can be ordered. The restaurants range from classic French cuisine and a carvery in the Calabash to the sophisticated atmosphere and upbeat elegance of Raffles.

By night the hotel explodes with shows featuring international entertainment **The lure of Sun City.**

stars and extravagant productions with high-kicking dancers. The Regency Club or the Salon Privé offer all-night facilities for the serious gambler.

The Cascades is another five-star hotel with luxurious rooms and exquisite restaurants. The Peninsula restaurant looks out on a lagoon with walkways and waterfalls which pink flamingos and black swans have made their home. A stroll through this topical paradise will reveal a host of exotic birds from golden pheasants to loeries.

The Cabanas caters more for family groups with rooms situated away from the main hotel building. Special features to entertain the younger generation include a mini-golf course, an adventure playground and **Animal World**, where they can get more closely acquainted with a variety of farm animals. Nearby is the **Kwena Gardens** with over 300 crocodiles, ranging from small hatchlings to the world's largest captive Nile crocodile.

The **Gary Player Country Club** is considered to be among the most spec-

Gambling is not only legal, but encouraged.

tacular – and challenging – golf courses in the world. For those interested in other sports there are 12 tennis courts – some floodlit – three squash courts, a bowling green and bowling alleys.

At **Waterworld**, just about any watersport imaginable can be enjoyed, from parasailing and jet-skiing to more gentle activities such as motor boat cruising.

The **entertainment centre** is a kaleidoscope of sight and sound with slot machines offering record-breaking jackpots, restaurants, boutiques and bars. In the middle of this is the famous 7,000-seat Superbowl auditorium where some of the world's greatest stars entertain capacity audiences.

But the most ambitious and glittering complex is the **Lost City**, a fantasy world in which a spectacular palace rises from the lakes and rainforests of ancient Africa. Features include a major new hotel and entertainment centre, a second golf course, a surfing basin with 6-ft (2-metre) high waves and a tropical beach where guests can laze in the sun or try out the world's highest waterslide.

NORTHERN AND EASTERN TRANSVAAL

North of the Witwatersrand and Pretoria lies a vast, flat, woodland plain covered in thorn trees – the Transvaal bushveld. Aeons ago the Great Rift Valley in East Africa cracked open, pumping vast masses of molten rock southwards, eventually creating the **bushveld igneous complex**, today regarded as one of the world's richest mineral areas.

Leaving Pretoria the Great North Road (N1) takes one past a number of small towns to Pietersburg. From there the road gently descends into the savannah bushveld crossing the **Tropic of Capricorn** just before it reaches the imposing slopes of the Soutpansberg Mountains. To the north, a vast sub-tropical expanse stretches to the **Limpopo Valley** and into **Zimbabwe**.

Also from Pretoria, the N4 leads steadily eastwards through wide open grasslands to the hauntingly beautiful eastern escarpment. Then it rapidly descends by way of winding mountain passes into the **lowveld**, which, not too long ago, was almost inaccessible because of fever and the deadly malaria mosquito.

The Southeastern Transvaal: From Johannesburg the R29 runs through the rolling plains and seemingly endless maizefields of the **eastern Transvaal highveld** to the **Swaziland** border while the R23 goes past Volksrust into northern Kwazulu/Natal.

Heidelberg, a picturesque town at the foot of the **Suikerbosrand** (Ridge of sugar bushes) was named by a German businessman after his alma mater. For a short time during the Anglo-Transvaal War (1880–81) it was the seat of the Boer government. A small nature reserve provides sleepover facilities and the railway museum in town is well worth a visit. Further east, **Standerton**, **Bethal** and **Ermelo** are the major towns of the southeastern Transvaal highveld which is dominated by the **Vaal River** system, making it one of the country's richest farming areas – maize, potatoes, sunflower seeds, beans, wool and dairy.

With its plentiful water and rich coal deposits, the region is also the power-house of the subcontinents. Dotting the skyline are the distinctive water-cooling towers of the 24 thermal **power stations** which send electricity along an extended grid of power lines to the Witwatersrand metropolis and further to the outlying areas.

The eastern grasslands: Initially the journey eastwards on the N4 show little promise of the exciting scenery which later is to be encountered. The undulating grassland of the district once teemed with vast herds of wildlife, particularly black wildebeest, zebra and antelope but these have now been displaced by cattle and sheep farming as well as intensive maize and sunflower monoculture. Occasionally, domesticated blesbok can be seen grazing in game-fenced ranches along the roadside.

The largest coal deposits in the country are found at **Witbank**, providing fuel for nearby power stations. The seemingly inexhaustible supply of coal is found in horizontal strata quite near the surface (not deeper than 1,000 ft/300

metres) and mined at 22 collieries in the area. Unfortunately the mining and smoke billowing out of the power stacks have given rise to growing problems with air pollution and acid rain.

It was near Witbank that in December 1899 a captured British war-correspondent, just escaped from a Boer prison, asked assistance from a local mine manager. The man was Winston Churchill, who was later smuggled on a train to Lourenço Marques; he ended up in Durban, where he had a hero's welcome.

The region is the ancestral home of the **Southern Ndebele**, famous for their love of colourful and symbolic decoration. Exquisite examples of geometrically patterned homes and intricate beadwork on women's costumes can be seen at **Botshabelo Mission** near Fort Merensky, 8 miles (13 km) north of Middelburg. The fort, built in 1865 by the Berlin missionary, Alexander Merensky, as a defence against Pedi raiders from the east, is open to visitors throughout the day.

Belfast and **Machadodorp** are two towns that played a pivotal role in the history of the Zuid-Afrikaansche Republic during the Anglo-Boer War. After the evacuation of Pretoria in 1900 the government of President Paul Kruger moved to the railway town of Machadodorp. Later that same year the last

Northern and Eastern Transvaal

80 km / 50 miles

major set-piece battle of the war was fought at **Bergendal** near Belfast. A small memorial marks the battlefield.

On the edge of the escarpment are the two little railway towns of **Waterval Boven** and **Waterval Onder** which lie on the rail link between Pretoria and Mozambique. In the mid-1890s, Dutch contractors employed considerable engineering skills in bringing the railway across the escarpment at the point where the Elands River plunges over a spectacular waterfall. The steeply inclined tunnel and rack-rail can be viewed along the roadside and a further short walk leads to a lovely view of the waterfall.

The area is also associated with the "Kruger Millions" rumoured to have been the contents of the Transvaal treasury taken along by the evacuating government. Despite there being no historical evidence to support this, many a fortune-seeker has combed the hills around Waterval Boven in vain, searching for the "missing millions".

An alternative route (R539) over the escarpment can be taken just before reaching Waterval Boven. This follows the course of the Crocodile River through the precipitous **Schoemanskloof**. The route meets with the N4 again at the confluence of the Elands and Crocodile Rivers which then tumble down over the beautiful **Montrose Falls**. The Montrose Hotel has an attractive tea garden overlooking the waterfall. The road leads through lush farmland towards Nelspurit and wayside stalls sell tropical fruits, nuts and curios.

Dullstroom, a little town 19 miles (30 km) north of Belfast holds much of the original beauty of the highveld. The region is dominated by **Die Berg**, the highest point in the Transvaal. Numerous small streams rise in these hills and drain towards the escarpment to the east. All are stocked with trout; fishing is as important in the area as farming. Advice on good fishing spots can be obtained at the Dullstroom Inn as most of the trout streams are privately owned.

The **Steenkampsberg Nature Reserve** outside Dullstroom provides sanctuary for the rare wattled crane. The

Recycled beer cans.

wetland habitats of this beautiful large bird have been so reduced that the species is now severely endangered. The wild flowers are magnificent. The highveld enjoys warm summers, cooled by refreshing regular thunderstorms which are usually short in duration. Winters are clear, dry and dusty and very cold at night. The Dullstroom area is wetter and colder than elsewhere on the highveld and cool mists are common even in summer.

Lydenburg (Place of Suffering) is a beautiful town that belies the name given to it by the few survivors of the malaria-stricken settlements in the lowveld. Later it became the capital of an independent Boer republic and the oldest surviving school building in the Transvaal and the old Dutch Reformed church date from this period. A British garrison was besieged here during the Transvaal War of 1880 and the powder magazine of the time has been preserved. A fish-breeding station has been established in the town supplies trout and other fish to dams in other parts of the country.

In the local museum examples of the "Lydenburg Heads" can be seen. A rich source of pottery fragments dating from AD500 was found in the area and was painstakingly assembled at the University of Cape Town. It turned out to be a number of "masks" resembling bizarre human-like heads.

From Lydenburg, the road crosses the **Mauchberg** and leads via the **Long Tom Pass** to Sabie. This was originally a route used by transport drivers but its name dates from the Anglo-Boer War. During their retreat before the British forces, the Boers defended the pass with several 150-mm Creusot guns taken from the forts around Pretoria. Nicknamed "Long Tom" these heavy artillery pieces were cumbersome but effective in slowing the British advance over the rugged mountain terrain. Sites of the last battle positions of the guns and of shell craters are marked along the road.

The descriptive names given to parts of the pass by transport drivers have survived. It includes Whiskyspruit – from the belief that the water from the

Scenes from a Ndebele village.

stream, mixed with Scottish liquids, make for an excellent drink; Koffie-hoogte at the summit where a coffee break was enjoyed and the self-descriptive Devil's Knuckles, a series of treacherous hillocks on the downslope.

The panorama route: Throughout the length of Natal and the eastern Transvaal the edge of the huge inland plateau of southern Africa swoops abruptly down providing breathtaking scenic views with opportunities for hiking and motoring. The **escarpment** or **Transvaal Drakensberg** is a spectacular cragged mountain range running south to north for nearly 200 miles (320 km). Its resistant quartzites formed impressive peaks such as Mariepskop and Mt Anderson while the softer shales between the quartzites were eroded into deep valleys. The escarpment intercepts moist air sweeping in from the Indian Ocean, making rainfall high; it can reach 80 inches (2,000 mm). Mists are frequent. Perennial streams abound and impressive falls tumble down rock faces.

Traversing the escarpment are many passes, all of which offer their own interest and excitement. Many of these routes were pioneered by the transport riders of the late 19th century who provided a vital economic link between the land-locked Zuid-Afrikaanshce Republic and the Portuguese port of Lourenço Marques (Maputo). Best known of these intrepid pioneers was Sir Percy Fitzpatrick and his dog, Jock. Monuments commemorating the hero-dog are to be found alongside many of the roads in the eastern Transvaal. The book Jock of the Bushveld recounts real-life episodes of hunting and adventure in the then untamed lowveld.

The town of **Sabie** lies on the southern reaches of the panorama route and is well suited as a base from which to explore the magnificent scenery in the vicinity. Sabie is the centre of the timber industry in the region and a little forest museum in the town is of interest. Timber plantations cover the hillsides around Sabie and the country's major paper mills are situated here. This is waterfall country and numerous short drives lead

This Ndebele village is near Middelburg.

from the town to picnic sites and view sites such as **Sabie Falls**, **Horseshoe Falls**, **Lone Creek Falls**, **Bridal Veil Falls** and **MacMac Falls** (named after all the Scots prospectors who camped in the area during the gold rush). Visitors interested in photography should remember that almost all of the waterfalls face east and should therefore best be visited before midday.

The road northwards from Sabie via **Graskop** to the **Blyde River Canyon** should be taken at a leisurely pace so that the breathtaking views can be enjoyed. **Pinnacle Rock**, **Jock's View**, **God's Window** and **Wonderview** are some of the spots where the traveller can stop to look out from sheer cliff outposts over the expanse of the lowveld. Further north lie the Lisbon Falls and the Berlin Falls before the view-drunk motorist reaches **Bourke's Luck potholes**. Here paths and footbridges take visitors to viewing sites overlooking the extraordinary example of river erosion.

More is to come. Northwards the Blyde River has carved a magnificent

gorge through the mountains. Viewing sites have been created at several points along the gorge providing a magnificent view of the winding river some 2,600 ft (800 metres) below the summit.

The canyon is dominated by three similarly shaped peaks, the **Three Rondavels**, and by **Mariepskop**, the highest point of the Transvaal Drakensberg. In the early 19th century the local Pedi and Pulana tribes were often under attack from the much stronger Swazis to the south. Eventually a united army was formed under Maripe Mashile of the Pulana; he led his warriors up the steep slopes to take up defensive positions on the mountain later named after him. The Swazi attack was thwarted when Maripe ordered his men to roll down huge boulders on to the advancing warriors.

The canyon itself is a nature reserve and is accessible only on foot. Numerous well-marked trails of varying lengths from half a mile to several days' hiking lead the visitor through this paradise of tumbling waterfalls and unusual flora. Cycads, giant ferns and rare orchids are among the unique variety of plant life to be found in the reserve. The tarred road follows the western lip of the gorge to the **Aventura Blydepoort Resort**, with comfortable chalets, a restaurant, nature trails and horses for hire.

An alternative trip from Sabie would be over the **Bonnet Pass** along the R533 to **Pilgrim's Rest**, the first gold-mining town in South Africa. Legend ascribes the discovery of gold in this valley to Alec "Wheelbarrow" Patterson, so called because he roamed the hills pushing all his possessions in a wheelbarrow. In 1873 his discovery and that of numerous others who rushed to establish their claims along the river banks, gave birth to the shanty-town of Pilgrim's Rest. At the time, **Pilgrim's Creek** was the richest alluvial deposit of gold discovered in the subcontinent and it attracted a motley assortment of fortune-seekers. By 1876, however, the gravels were all but worked out and the diggers left for the newly discovered gold fields of the Witwatersrand.

Today the entire town is preserved as a national monument and living mu- **Lone Creek Falls.**

seum. Delightful hours can be spent exploring the old hotel, printing press, miners' houses and other relics.

Hiking trails: Perhaps the most rewarding viewing of this picturesque countryside is via the network of hiking trails which traverses the eastern Transvaal escarpment. The **Fanie Botha Trail** was the first National Hiking Way trail to be opened in 1973. It covers almost 50 miles (80 km) of magnificent mountain countryside between the Ceylon Forest near Sabie to God's Window north of Graskop. Short sections of the five-day trail can be taken at a time.

At God's Window, the Fanie Botha trail merges with the 40-mile (65-km) **Blyderivierspoort Hiking Trail**, offering a series of much more leisurely walks along the canyon ending up at the Three Rondavels.

The region's early mining history can be traced along the **Prospector's Hiking Trail** which links up with the Fanie Botha Trail at MacMac Falls and leads northwards for 43 miles (70 km) through the historic mining villages of Pilgrim's Rest and north to Bourke's Luck potholes. One of the most attractive drives leads east from Graskop down the **Kowyn's Pass** into the lowveld. The Kowyn Hotel, at the foot of the pass, is an excellent base from which to explore the region. Pilgrim's Rest is also the starting point for two other routes, the **Morgenzon Trail** and the **Rambler's Trail** offering a selection of short walks.

The lowveld: Nelspruit, the capital of the eastern Transvaal, is sub-tropical; its attractive streets are festooned with bougainvillaea and frangipani. The Botanical Garden is laid out along the Crocodile River and is well worth a few hours' visit. This is the base of the escarpment and, as soon as one reaches the lower altitude, the heavily scented tropical air of the lowveld is noticeable.

The area around Nelspruit has a climate ideal for the cultivation of exotic sub-tropical fruit. Avocados, bananas, citrus fruit, litchis, mangoes, passion fruit, pawpaws and tomatoes are all produced for local and export markets.

The lowveld was the site of the major

The Three Rondavels at Blyde River Canyon.

pre-Witwatersrand gold rush. **Barberton**, near the Swaziland border, is the product of those wild days of fortunes made and lost overnight. Founded in 1883, it expanded rapidly as rich gold deposits were unearthed in the surrounding hills. Nearby Sheba Mine was once the richest mine in the world, and a separate town, **Eureka City**, grew up beside it. Eureka is now a ghost town and an interesting half-hour drive from Barberton leads to the ruins past old excavations and mining gear. The exciting history of Barberton and the surrounding area is preserved in a small museum in the library building and is well worth visiting.

The hills surrounding Barberton are rich in botany as well as gold and this floral wealth is preserved in several nature reserves. The **Cythna Letty Nature Reserve** is the locality where the original **Barberton daisy** was first discovered. These daisies are now in cultivation in gardens throughout the world and are almost as well known to gardeners as the Cape proteas.

The **Nelshoogte Pass** leads west from Barberton to the health spa at **Badplaas**. The roadside is festooned with orange-pink Pride of de Kaap (Bauhinia galpinii). Saddleback Pass climbs steeply up wooded slopes to the Swaziland border. Another attractive drive follows the Kaap River to the southern gates of the Kruger National Park.

To the north of Nelspruit (on the R40) are the attractive little towns of **White River** and **Hazyview**. Banana, pawpaw and mango plantations line the roadside and numbers of little stalls sell fruit, honey and other farm produce and handicrafts along the way. Close by are some pleasant country hotels, ideally positioned for exploring the escarpment and the game reserves to the east.

Another interesting drive from Nelspruit is along the R539 back into the hills of the escarpment to the **Sudwala Caves**. The chambers around the entrance to the caves are open to the public daily and one can explore on one's own for about 1,600 ft (500 metres) underground. Some of the dripstone

Rural community in the Eastern Transvaal.

formations resemble strange characters which gave rise to evocative names such as "Weeping Woman", "Screaming Monster", "Little Red Riding Hood" and "The Cunning Fox". The full depth is unknown, but once a month an expedition goes much deeper into the caves; this makes an exciting day's excursion.

An extraordinary feature of the caves is a continuous flow of air at a comfortable 68°F (20°C) at all times of the year. In the gardens of the caves is an exhibition of full-sized model dinosaurs and the caves themselves are steeped in geological and historical interest. Accommodation is available in cottages below the cave entrance. Refreshments and an array of curios are sold at the caves.

To the east of Nelspruit is **Komatipoort**, a small town sweltering in the heat of the lowveld at the confluence of the Komati and Crocodile Rivers. Two decades ago the town was a busy border post handling commerce and tourism between the hinterland and the Mozambican port of Maputo. With the collapse of the Mozambique economy after independence, however, the traffic has slowed to almost nothing. Lately, it is on the increase again, since the warring factions there seem to have "buried the hatchet" following national elections in November 1994.

During the Anglo-Boer War, Komatipoort was the base for Steinacker's Horse, a notorious irregular force under the flamboyant leadership of Colonel Ludwig von Steinacker, who claimed to be a Silesian baron. At the outbreak of the war he persuaded the British to assign him 40 men – later nicknamed the Forty Thieves – to hold the border and disrupt Boer communications.

Nearly all of the northern and eastern Transvaal owes its comparatively unspoilt nature to the fact that malaria nagana (sleeping sickness) and other livestock diseases prevented white settlement. At a place like **Ohrigstad**, a whole Voortrekker community was almost wiped out by malaria, forcing the survivors to abandon the town and move to Lydenburg.

Today these diseases have been

The Sabie River, lifeblood to big game.

brought under control but have not been eradicated. Malaria is still widespread in Mozambique and Swaziland and the Anopheles mosquitoes breed quickly in the summer rainy season. Although the disease is seldom lethal if properly treated, it can be seriously debilitating and often recurs persistently. Visitors to the Kruger National Park and northern Transvaal are well-advised to take anti-malaria tablets. Another disease, bilharzia, is even more widespread today than a century ago. Almost all rivers flowing towards the Indian Ocean most and dams in the Transvaal province are potentially contaminated: never bathe in or drink water in the open, which has not been sterilised.

Land of the Rain Queen: From Lydenburg on the R36 a winding pass penetrates the steep Drakensberg cliffs through the **Abel Erasmus Tunnel** leading ultimately into the hot baobab-studded flats of the northern Transvaal.

The great Drakensberg escarpment terminates in the well-wooded slopes around **Tzaneen**. This is a prosperous fruit-farming region with tea and timber plantations also abundant. From Tzaneen a number of interesting day trips can be undertaken. The **Fanie Botha Dam** is a major recreational spot located in the area and adjoining it is the Hans Merensky Dam.

The **Magoebaskloof Pass** meanders through indigenous forest up the slopes of the **Wolkberg**. The spectacularly beautiful pass is one of the most popular scenic drives in southern Africa. Roadside viewing sites and excursion paths provide ample opportunities to observe the magnificent countryside. The valley slopes are mostly covered by plantations, but there are also areas with indigenous trees such as ironwood, rooi hout and stinkwood.

A walk through the forest brings one to **Debengeni Falls**, a wonderful cascade tumbling into a natural swimming pool. Two hotels offering stunning mountain views are the Magoebaskloof Hotel and the luxury Coach House Inn.

Close by, towards **Duiwelskloof**, is the homeland of the Lobedu people,

The early days of gold prospecting at Pilgrim's Rest.

ruled by the mysterious queen Modajadji. For decades a dynasty of queens held sway over the region commanding awe and respect even from the warrior tribes among the Zulus and Swazis. In dry seasons she was sent gifts and offerings, together with heartfelt requests to use her secret powers to bring on the much-needed rain.

The adventure novelist H. Rider Haggard, who lived in South Africa for some time, based his novel *She* on the person of Modjadji. To this day the mystique of the "Rain Queen" remains and the reigning monarch can still only been seen and visited by favoured guests.

Baobab country: The **Soutpansberg** is a relatively small but very impressive mountain range just north of Louis Trichardt. A large variety of small antelopes and birds, including raptors, are found on the richly forested slopes. On its northern slopes are rock shelters with wall paintings indicating that San (Bushman) and Khoikhoi people may have inhabited the area during the Later Stone Age Preiod. The very popular

Soutpansberg Hiking Trail takes one on a five-day trip through the mountain.

At the foot of the mountain lies the town of **Louis Trichardt**, named after the pioneer Voortrekker, who led the first trek into the interior and on to the Mozambique coastal port of Lourenço Marques (Maputo). However, half of the party – including Trichardt himself – succumbed to the fever.

North of the Soutpansberg, in the far northern Transvaal, lies the traditional homeland of the **Venda-tribe**. The people of Venda are unique in the South African context being more closely related to the Shona of Zimbabwe than to any of the other indigenous people. Unlike most Africans, their traditional concept of wealth is not focused on cattle alone, but more on agriculture and metal products such as hoes and axes. In earlier times, the Venda were skilled iron and copper smelters and their connections with Arab traders of the African east coast have given Semitic features to many of their faces.

In these remote areas traditional ritu-

Today, Pilgrim's Rest is a national monument.

als continue to survive and ancestral spirits guard many of the pools and forests in the beautiful Soutpansberg mountains. Most important of these holy places is **Lake Fundudzi**. The best way to reach this quiet and beautiful spot is to hike the **Mabuda-Shango Hiking Trail** which leads through spectacular scenery and sacred forests.

The **Soutpansberg Trail** is another beautiful walk. But it can also be reached in a pleasant journey by car from Louis Trichardt along the R528. Swimming and washing in the lake is forbidden.

From time to time initiation ceremonies take place in Venda villages and visitors may, by special arrangement, witness the famous python dance, part of the domba or initiation ceremony. Lining up closely behind one another, young girls of the village mime the serpentine movement of a python to the beat of sacred drums. At **Thohoyandou**, the capital of Venda, fine carvings and other curios can be bought from traders along the roadside.

South Africa's northern border with Zimbabwe is the **Limpopo River** about 60 miles (100 km) to the north. Copper has been mined in the Limpopo valley since pre-historic times and the district is rich in archaeological relics.

The bulbous baobab: African legend has it that in a moment of humour, the gods planted baobab upside-down with its roots exposed to the sky. Certainly the bulbous branches and spindly extremities give that impression.

But the role of these bulbous monsters is far more important than their weird shape suggests. They grow in the hot, semi-arid parts of Africa, mostly north of the Soutpansberg Mountains and Olifants River. Their grotesque shape allows them to store huge volumes of water in their fibrous wood. When chewed by animals, particularly elephants, this offers critical relief in times of drought. The perpetual supply of water ensures an abundance of leaves every spring and these provide both shade and nourishment to animals and insects. The soft, well-insulated stems are ideal for hole-nesting birds such as **Vernacular creation...**

barbets and hornbills. After they have been vacated the nests are often re-employed as beehives or retreats for snakes and lizards so that every baobab is always abuzz with the comings and goings of its many residents.

In spring the sweet scent of the huge white pendulous flowers attract fruit-bats and these pollinate the plants as they seek out the nectar from flower to flower. The egg-shaped fruits are filled with seeds embedded in a white "cream of tartar" pulp much loved by monkeys, baboons and humans, Rich in vitamin C, the pulp has a sharp, refreshing taste and can be made into a pleasant dish or eaten raw. People of the Limpopo River valley attribute fertility properties to the fruits; rock paintings in that region often portray women with baobab fruits instead of breasts.

Baobabs can live for 3,000 to 4,000 years. Fires, weather and constant tunnelling and chewing by animals and birds leave them deeply scarred. Fibrous tissue heals the wounds but old trees are frequently hollowed and disfigured. Even in this state their ecological impact is significant. Hollow trees form natural water tanks, sometimes storing 1,300 gallons (5,000 litres) of water, and have saved the lives of many thirsty travellers in the past. One famous tree served as a bar in the gold rush days and another was fitted out with a flushing lavatory.

In spite of their durability, old baobabs do eventually die. When they do so, the end is swift and dramatic. In a few months the fibres which have lasted for thousands of years disintegrate and the great monarch tree simply collapses in on itself, disappearing so suddenly that it was once thought that they ignited spontaneously and burned away.

The bushveld: Turning south on the Great North Road in the direction of Pretoria one reaches the flourishing commercial centre of **Pietersburg**, the major town in the bushveld area. A popular stopover for visitors en route to the Kruger Park or Magoebaskloof, it also boasts the **Percy Fyfe Nature Reserve** and a recreation park.

...in a rural community.

This is also the headquarters of the **Zion Christian Church**, one of the largest of the 3,000 independent African churches in the country. Every Easter more than a million pilgrims travel to the open-air stadium outside the town to hear the charismatic Bishop Lekganyane preaching. Allow for the enormous influx of buses, mini-buses and other vehicles when travelling at that time.

Driving along the N1 through the bushveld, one is constantly aware of a distant mountain massif on the western horizon. This is the **Waterberg** – until recently, a remote retreat seldom visited by tourists. In recent years, however, some exciting nature reserves have been developed in these beautiful mountains.

Among the best of these is **Lapalala Wilderness**. This privately run reserve was a pioneer in environmental education and children from all walks of life regularly visit the well-equipped outdoor school.

Small timber and thatch camps are situated along the spectacular Palala River gorge, each spaced miles from the

next. Visitors reserve a camp to themselves and they enjoy complete isolation from any disturbance to hike, view game and swim in the clean, clear river.

The remoteness of the Waterberg has kept many of the local farmers unexposed to political development and in the small towns such as **Vaalwater** and **Ellisras** some of the old rural traditions and prejudices still survive.

At the southern end of the Waterberg is the "iron mountain" of **Thabazimbi**. Part of the largest deposit of iron ore in the world, this entire mountain is being mined away. The vivid red scar and ubiquitous dust deposits are both impressive and disturbing. The magnetic field surrounding these great iron deposits render conventional compasses useless in the area and some electronic equipment becomes unreliable.

Within easy reach from Pretoria are the small towns of **Naboomspruit** and **Nylstroom**. According to folklore, the Voortrekkers, having spent months on end travelling in their ox-wagons, reached a small river running north to south. This they believed to be the origins of the Nile River and promptly dubbed their new settlement Nylstroom.

Birdlife in the area is among the richest in the country, both in numbers and in the variety of species, and bird-watchers flock to the small **Nylsvlei Reserve** which conserves some of the marshland. No accommodation is available in the reserve but day visits can be arranged through the Provincial Administration.

The ancient subterranean origins of the bushveld – that created the mineral-rich igneous complex – are still evident at **Warmbath**, largest of several hot springs which erupt from the flat savannah. The mineral-rich spa waters are channelled into well-appointed public and private baths and a variety of medicinal treatments are available. A small town – less than 90 minutes' drive from Pretoria – with a number of hotels, a camping ground and golf course, has grown up around the spa. Nearby is the luxurious game reserve Mabula, which has comfortable accommodation, conference facilities and even offers game viewing on horseback.

Left, lunchtime. Right, the baobab – a giant of the African savannah.

THE KRUGER NATIONAL PARK

In a roundabout way, the diminutive mosquito and the tsetse fly safeguarded the vast herds of wild game which are today the highlight of a visit to South Africa. All attempts to settle or civilise the area were doomed and hunting parties were restricted to the disease-free winter months.

However, at the end of the 19th century the game populations diminished rapidly as the profits from hunting attracted increasing numbers of hunters. Under pressure from Barberton and Pilgrim's Rest inhabitants, President Kruger allowed the proclamation of the Sabie Game Reserve in 1898. It was later extended into what is now the Kruger National Park. Soon the agricultural worthlessness of private farms adjacent to the park acquired renewed value as they were made into game farms and private nature reserves.

Sabi-Sands is a block of such private properties, each independent but operating under cooperative environmental management. Among them are the famous **MalaMala**, **Londolozi** and **Sabi Sabi Game Reserves**. Each offers luxurious bush accommodation and unforgettable game-watching experiences.

Further north is **Manyaleti Game Reserve** and **Timbavati**, which is famous for its pride of white lions. Other private lodges in the area are **Tanda Tula**, **Inkasi**, **Matumi**, **Khoka Moya Trails**, **Ngala** and **Motswari**. All have remote but comfortable accommodation surrounded by the African bush, superb open-air cuisine and game drives and trails.

Lekkerlag, near Timbavati, is one of several game farms offering hunting safaris conducted under the supervision of professional hunters. Licences must be arranged in advance through the offices Directorate of Nature Conservation in Pretoria.

There is a considerable difference in

Preceding pages: the lion's share. **Left,** bush-babies don't sleep at night.

cost between the private game reserves mentioned and the state-run **Kruger National Park**. But there are also considerable differences in the service. The private reserves generally arrange game drives in four-wheel-drive vehicles with an experienced game guide in attendance. Not only does this mean that more game is seen, but much can be learned from the guides, who explain the behaviour of animals, how to track their spoor and how they integrate with the natural environment. The less obvious things in the veld – trees, geology, small animals and birds – will all be shown and explained to the interested visitor.

At night the private reserves set out dinner around a camp-fire *boma* and guests exchange their experiences of the day. Night drives are also arranged and many reserves will take visitors to a known lion or leopard kill after dark. On the other hand, it is often argued that game watching at the private parks is just *too* organised and comfortable, compared to the greater ruggedness of the Kruger Park.

One of the world's great game reserves, the Kruger National Park is probably without equal in its richness of animal life. Although it is served by an extensive network of roads and rest camps, this infrastructure barely affects the natural wildness. Regulations governing visitors' activities may seem onerous, but are directed mainly at safety and the wellbeing of the wildlife.

Many coach tours operate into the Kruger National Park, but game-viewing from a private car is just as enjoyable – and you can proceed at your own pace. Cars can be hired from Skukuza and various towns bordering the park. Skukuza and Nelspruit both have airstrips serviced by light aircraft arriving mainly from Johannesburg.

The speed limit of 25 mph (40 kph) should never be exceeded, not merely because of the threat of fines (which are rigorously imposed) but because game-spotting is seldom successful when travelling above this speed. For similar reasons it is unwise to attempt to cover large areas in a short time. It can be a very rewarding experience simply sit-

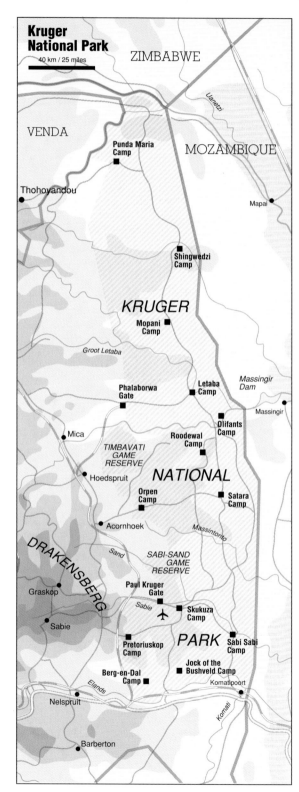

ting quietly at a water-hole rather than driving around in the hot sun.

The best game-viewing is in the morning until about 10 o'clock and in the late afternoon. Camps open at dawn (ranging from 4.30am in mid-summer to 6.30am in winter) and it is well worth rising at this hour to get the best sightings. The hot midday hours can be spent enjoying a leisurely picnic at a water-hole or in camp. Camp gates and entrance gates to the park close at sunset (6.30pm in summer and 5.30pm in winter) and late-comers are fined. Unfortunately, this early closing time often means abandoning a game drive just when it holds most promise.

Most animals are found throughout the park, but the frequency of sightings is determined by the topography and vegetation. Near southern rivers and watering-holes (Skukuza, Pretoriuskop, Lower Sabie, and Crocodile Bridge) hippo, elephant, crocodile, buffalo and small herds of giraffe are often spotted. The central parts (Satara, Olifants, Letaba) are inhabited by large herds of

antelope which in turn attack the larger predators. This is also a good place to see larger antelope such as kudu and waterbuck. In the north (Shingwedzi, Punda Maria, Pafuri) large herds of elephant and buffalo are often spotted, as well as leopard and the elusive nyala.

The 18 rest camps vary in size and character. Five camps – **Boulders**, **Mopani**, **Jock of the Bushveld**, **Nwanedzi** and **Roodewaal** – are private and must be taken in their entirety by a single party. They accommodate a maximum of 15 people and are mostly well designed. No catering is provided.

Three other camps are small and lacking in restaurant facilities: **Orpen**, **Malelane** and **Crocodile Bridge** are entry gates and used mostly by people arriving in the late afternoon. **Balule** is a small group of somewhat spartan rondavels on the Olifants River.

Skukuza is the largest camp and the headquarters of the park administration. The driving force behind the development of the park was Major James Stevenson-Hamilton, appointed chief

The Letaba rest camp.

game warden in 1902. His zeal in catching poachers and developing the park earned him the honoured name siKhukhuza – "the man who sweeps clean". Although comfortably appointed, the 200 huts and other buildings in the camp contrast with the primitive wilderness one expects in the bush.

Pretoriuskop is an old camp with a swimming pool, set in the southwest grasslands. Cheetah, sable antelope and **white rhinoceros** are frequently seen in this habitat. The white rhinoceros has a broad wide mouth suitable for grazing grass, unlike the hook-lipped, **black rhinoceros** which browses on trees.

Lower Sabie is an attractive camp located in the heart of the prime viewing areas of the park. Elephants are numerous in this part and can often be seen from the camp as they visit the Sabi River. An attractive drive along the river towards Skukuza usually rewards the viewer with sightings of buffalo, lion and bushbuck. Opportunities for birdwatching are excellent in this area.

The modern design of **Berg-en-Dal**

near the southern border of the park is unlike the traditional white African rondavels of other camps. Its extensive, well-fenced grounds are among the few places where one can walk in the park and enjoy the veld and flora at close quarters, as well as a swimming pool.

Satara is set in the open grassland of the central region of the park. **Lion** and **leopard** can be spotted in this part and large herds of zebra and wildebeest will also be seen. **Letaba** and **Olifants** camps are both sited on promontories looking out over a wide river frontage. Game-viewing from the restaurants and verandas of these camps is a truly African experience. The northern part of the park is served by two camps, **Shingwedzi** and **Punda Maria**. The latter is especially quaint having preserved some of the atmosphere of the 1920s when this part of the park was first proclaimed.

Although camp restaurants do serve meals, guests often prefer to cook their own on open-air fireplaces provided at the accommodation huts. Food and fuel are sold in the shops in the larger camps. Cutlery and crockery are not provided. In the quiet of evening the sounds of lion, hyena and other nocturnal animals can be heard in the surrounding bush.

Wilderness hiking trails are conducted under the supervision of an experienced ranger. Trails operate permanently out of four base camps: Wolhuter and Bushman in the south and Olifants and Nyala in the north. The number of hikers on each trail is limited to ten for reasons of safety and enjoyment so book well in advance. A face-to-face encounter with big game in the wild is something one will never forget.

Most people try to visit the park during the winter months – July to August. Temperatures are more moderate and the dry veld drives the animals to the water-holes where they can be seen more easily. However, other seasons have many compensating aspects – not least of which is the reduced number of tourists. In spring and summer the trees and veld flowers are at their best. Birdlife is abundant because of the influx of migratory species, and many of the animals are nursing their new-born young.

Left, Kruger in the Kruger. **Right,** *Panthera pardus:* the leopard.

KWAZULU/NATAL

Although the smallest province in South Africa, **KwaZulu/Natal** is in many respects a microcosm of the country's scenery. The Great Escarpment, or Natal Drakensberg, forms an enormous rampart along its northwestern border while its hinterland is a landscape of rolling hills and spectacular gorges carved by several major rivers making their way to the Indian Ocean.

The coastline has a sub-tropical climate and this, in combination with the influence of the warm southward-flowing Mozambique current, has ensured that the province offers South Africa's finest all-year seaside resorts.

The port city of Durban is the natural gateway to the Garden Province. It is easily accessible along the N3 from the Witwatersrand, or, alternatively, from the eastern Transvaal past Ermelo and Vryheid to northern Zululand. The region is also served by the modern **International Airport**, just 20 minutes' drive from the city centre.

Durban: The bustling port city of **Durban** lives up to its longstanding reputation as the fun-seeker's capital of South Africa. With its sub-tropical climate, its uninterrupted stretch of golden beaches lapped by the warm waters of the Indian Ocean and its sophisticated infrastructure, it is the fun-in-the-sun destination for the hundreds of thousands of tourists who pour in every year.

Durban is one of Africa's busiest harbour cities – a cosmopolitan metropolis where modern Western facilities blend harmoniously with African tribal traditions and Oriental customs. The centre of attraction is the **Golden Mile**, a 3½-mile (6-km) stretch along the city's main beachfront containing amusement parks, shops and restaurants

Funworld on the **Marine Parade** and **Waterland** near Country Club Beach Hotel offer a wide selection of motor chutes, boat rides, aerial cableways and go-carts. **Seaworld**, at the bottom of West Street, is the country's premier aquarium and dolphinarium.

The daily highlight is to watch divers descending into the massive shark tank to hand-feed these massive predators.

On the opposite end of the Marine Parade is the **Fithsimons Snake Park** which houses more than 80 species of snake and an intriguing collection of crocodiles, lizards, iguanas and other reptiles. A minute's walk away is **Minitown**, a charming scaled-down version of the city with replicas of all the major buildings, the harbour development, airport and railway station.

As a rule, the beaches along the Golden Mile are not overcrowded by European standards. The exceptions are on public holidays or over long weekends when thousands of up-country visitors descend on the famous **North** or **South Beaches**. Durbanites – and smart visitors – know which days to avoid downtown Durban and divert their activities to a wide selection of comfortable and safe locations in the suburbs such as **Brighton** or **Anstey's Beaches**. All Durban beaches have lifeguards and are protected by shark nets

Preceding pages: the country's playground at the sea. Left, cooling off on the Marine Parade. Right, winter means summer sunshine.

which are regularly serviced by the Natal Anti-Shark Measures Board.

But Durban is more than sun and surf. For those interested in South African history, this pulsating city has a lot to offer. The equestrian statue of **Dick King** stands at the bay end of the Victoria Embankment. It commemorates an historic rescue ride of more than 600 miles (1,000 km) to Grahamstown when, in 1842, the British garrison was besieged by Boer forces.

The **Natural History Museum** is housed on the first floor of the historic **City Hall**. It has a rich display of indigenous mammals, reptiles and birds – including a skeleton of the famous, flightless and extinct Indian Ocean island bird, the dodo.

The **Killie Campbell Museum** on Berea Ridge holds an acclaimed Africana library, a fine collection of rare furniture, and the renowned Mashu collection of Zulu arts and crafts.

Other museums include the **Local History Museum** in Aliwal Street, which offers an insight into the early history of Durban and Natal; the **Old House Museum** in St Andrew's Street, which has been restored to its Victorian splendour; **Warrior's Gate** with its fine collection of militaria, and the **Old Fort** erected on the site of the British camp during the Battle of Congella in

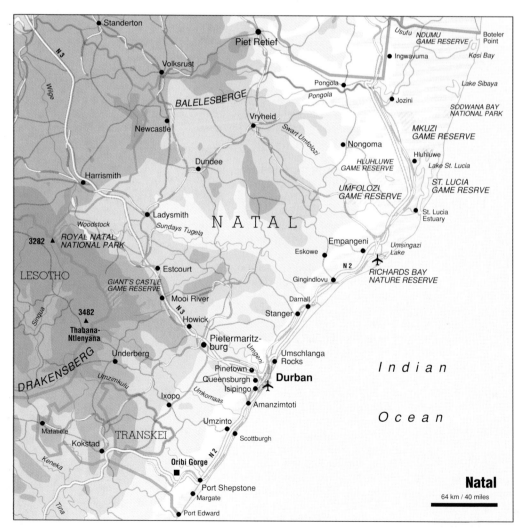

Natal

64 km / 40 miles

1842. For nautical enthusiasts, there is the **Port Natal Maritime Museum** comprising the naval minesweeper *SAS Durban* and the tugboat *J. R. More*, berthed at the small crafts' basin.

The **Durban Art Museum** on the second floor of the City Hall is one of the country's best formal galleries. It houses a permanent collection of work by local and international artists as well as modern graphics and Oriental art.

Scattered across the city are a number of richly adorned Hindu temples – the most interesting being the one at Bellair near the University of Natal. The **Hare Krishna Temple of Understanding** in Chatsworth is well worth a visit because of its striking combination of Eastern and Western architectural styles. The **Juma Mosque** in Grey Street, reputed to be the largest in the Southern Hemisphere, can be visited by arrangement.

The performing arts in Natal are well served by the ultra-modern **Natal Playhouse**. This stylish complex offers all-year-round theatre, symphony concerts, ballet and opera performances.

The **Durban Exhibition Centre** is an extensive complex which hosts a wide variety of shows, exhibitions, and sports events. A highlight of the cultural year is October's **Durban Tattoo**.

For the finest shopping in Durban the place to visit is **The Wheel**, within easy walking distance of the Marine Parade. Named because of its resemblance to a gigantic ferris wheel, it is a kaleidoscope of close on 150 speciality shops augmented by restaurants, department stores and cinemas. **The Workshop** in Pine Street – with 120-plus speciality shops – is a similar centre, with a Victorian theme, in the railways workshop.

A taste of the Orient – spices, curry, curios and knick-knacks – awaits the visitor in Warwick Avenue while flea markets do a brisk trade at various venues in the city.

Despite rapid urban development in recent years, Durban has maintained its lush, green character. Many public gardens, parks and small conservation reserves – most within walking distance of the beach – provide peace and tran-

The Mozambique Current warms Natal's Indian Ocean.

quillity for those weary of the bustle of the city and the hot, crowded beaches.

The **Botanic Gardens** in Lower Berea are known for their rare collection of cycads, a fine orchid house and a "scent-garden" for the blind.

A number of self-guided walking trails have been established, including the **Burman Bush Nature Reserve**, the **Kenneth Stainbank Reserve** – which also contains rhinos and antelopes; **Pigeon Valley Park** – renowned for its trees and the **Umgeni River Bird Park**.

The South Coast: Durban remains the ideal vantage point from which to explore the rest of the Garden Province. To its south stretches the Sunshine Coast – a string of safe, golden beaches, often hidden away amidst lush forest, sugar-cane fields and plantations of bananas, pawpaws and mangoes.

Close to Durban are two major holiday centres, **Amanzimtoti** and **Scottburgh**, plus other smaller resorts such as Warner Beach, Winklespruit, Illovo and Umkomaas.

Port Shepstone is situated at the mouth of the Umzimkulu River, the largest of southern Natal's watercourses navigable by small craft for about 5 miles (8 km) upstream. It is the largest town on the south coast and boasts a number of tree-shaded caravan parks, hotels, tidal pools and one of South Africa's finest golf courses.

South of Port Shepstone, the N2 turns inland, taking the visitor to one of Natal's top sights, **Oribi Gorge**. Here the Umzimkulwana River has carved a spectacular canyon, 15 miles (24 km) long, out of the sandstone cliffs. From the vantage point of the **Overhanging Rock** one can look down at the river more than 1,200 ft (370 metres) below.

The more conventional route between Port Shepstone and Port Edward is the R61 along the coast. The most popular resorts on the south coast are here. The **Umnini Craft Stalls**, between Umgababa and Widenham, have good-quality Zulu basketwork, pottery and handcrafted beadwork.

Shelly Beach is considered the best spot for ski-boat angling; the lagoon at

Tuc-tuc taxi and walk-walk

St Michael's-on-Sea is favoured by board sailors, while **Uvongo** with its pleasant lagoon in the estuary of the Vungu River is fast gaining popularity.

Margate is the main resort on what is known as the Hibiscus Coast and is served by a commercial airport. It is a lively and bustling town, offering all the standard holiday attractions.

South of Port Edward is the **Umtamvuna Nature Reserve**, a 7,400-acre (3,000-hectare) sanctuary for wildlife and birds and home to the endangered Cape vulture. On the other side is the Wild Coast Sun, a luxury hotel and gambling resort with excellent water sport facilities and one of the best golf courses in the country.

The North Coast: Like the area south of Durban the North Coast is studded with seaside resorts, for the most part built on the estuaries of numerous small rivers flowing into the Indian Ocean. The Dolphin Coast, as locals often call it, offers wide, unspoilt beaches nestling in sheltered coves surrounded by tropical lala palms, bougainvillaea and hibiscus.

A good way to explore the coastline is to follow R627 northwards from Durban. Alternatively, take the N2 highway and detour to the various resort towns.

Umhlanga Rocks is a fast-growing seaside resort with some of the province's best hotels, restaurants and shops. A special feature on the outskirts of town is the headquarters of the Natal Sharks Board, which offers demonstrations of shark control techniques.

Among the other resorts on the north coast are **Umdloti**, **Ballito**, **Willard Beach**, **Shaka's Rock**, **Salt Rock** and **Zinkwazi**, a delightful lagoon resort.

Close to Ballito, the R102 veers towards the interior, passing through Shaka's Kraal, Groutville – home of South Africa's first recipient of the Nobel peace prize, the late Dr Albert Luthuli – until it reaches **Stanger**, an old colonial town built on the site where the great Zulu king, Shaka, built his capital. Off the N2 on the road to Eshowe lie two reconstructed Zulu villages well worth visiting.

The deep-water harbour at **Richard's**

Theatre Lane in Pietermaritzburg.

SETTLERS FROM INDIA

Most of South Africa's Indian people are descended from one of the two groups that migrated from India in the 19th and early 20th centuries. The larger of these groups, the 152,184 indentured migrants, arrived at Port Natal between 1860 and 1911. Two-thirds of these were from south India and the remainder from the north. The second of the groups were the independent migrants, or "passenger" Indians, so called because they paid their own fare. Most were traders, and many who disembarked at Delagoa Bay made their way to the Transvaal after the discovery of gold.

Indian settlers have never been a homogeneous group, differing in caste and class, in religion and culture, in language spoken, in occupation and in political outlook. Even after nearly 150 years they have not been assimilated into the general population.

Almost 70 percent are Hindus; their women are easily distinguishable on festive occasions by their beautiful and colourful saris, the sindar or forehead dot worn by married women, and their gold jewellery. For everyday wear the sari is giving way to Western dress; the young especially dress in jeans and T-shirts. But the sari remains an essential part of the Hindu woman's wardrobe.

Muslim women wear Punjabi suits with the distinctive long silk scarf while the men cover their heads with a topee. An increasing number of Muslim fundamentalists are to be seen in Natal, covering their bodies and sometimes the face in black garments. Muslims comprise nearly 20 percent of Indians in South Africa.

Christians – about 13 percent of the Indian population – were Christians before they arrived in Natal or are more recent converts from the Hinduism; most belong to the Roman Catholic, Anglican and Pentecostal churches.

The original traders came from the Surat, in western India, and the majority were Gujarati-speaking Muslims. Many of the men had some capital and much business acumen which they used to establish themselves as merchants or storekeepers. It was to undertake a case for one of the large merchants that Mahatma Gandhi came to South Africa in 1893 as a young lawyer.

The Indian community varies also in its wealth and prosperity. There are many wealthy families, living in luxurious homes furnished with taste and comfort. There are also poor families living below the bread-line in cottages and shacks, and all levels between. Indian merchants and businessmen invest heavily in landed property, especially in the towns; professional men are prominent in medicine and related disciplines, law, accountancy and teaching.

Factories and small businesses depend on the Indian community for their artisans, clerks, factory workers, especially in the manufacturing sector, labourers and a host of other jobs of all kinds. Women began to enter the labour market in numbers in the 1960s and as they became better educated and earned their own living the extended family system came under increasing pressure. Today many young couples have moved out of the parental home and live in homes of their own. Nevertheless the system still operates and most working mothers are happy enough to leave their children in the security of the extended family.

Many of South Africa's Indians settled in ■ Natal.

Bay was developed in the 1970s to handle the bulk of the country's mineral exports – particularly coal extracted from the highveld.

Lake St Lucia is one of Africa's largest and most remarkable marine wilderness areas. The central feature is the 40-mile (64-km) lake – in fact, a huge estuary surrounded by dense forests, mangrove swamps and massive sand dunes. The shallow waters of the lake is home to an estimated 700 hippos and 2,000 crocodiles, resulting in a ban on all swimming and water sports. On the eastern shores, reedbuck, buffalo, waterbuck and kudu are often observed, as well as the odd cheetah or hyena. But it is as a haven for spectacular birdlife that St Lucia has become famous. Close on 400 species have been recorded. The large number of fish and crustaceans make it an angler's paradise.

The Natal Parks Board operates 10 overnight camps, including hutted accommodation at **Fanie's Island** – the most popular angling spot; **Charter's Creek** – the departure point for boat rides; **Mapelane** and **Cape Vidal**. The latter, situated on the ocean side of the lake offers excellent underwater and surf fishing opportunities. Bird-watchers usually prefer the rustic facilities at **False Bay Park**, the best vantage point from which to observe the vast colonies of pink-backed flamingos and pelicans.

St Lucia village has excellent hotels and holiday flats and is often used as a base to explore the entire region.

Four of the finest game reserves have made the northern Natal one of the region's most favoured tourist destinations. All the reserves offer clean, comfortable accommodation and basic facilities but visitors should bring along their own food and drink. The food is prepared by trained staff who then serve it in the respective huts, except in the luxurious Itala camp, which also has a fine restaurant.

The **Umfolozi Game Reserve**, the largest of the four, teems with wildlife with more than 85 mammal species – including the Big Five – elephant, rhino, lion, leopard and buffalo. More

The botanical gardens in Pietermaritzburg.

than any other game reserve in the country, the Umfolozi has retained its wildness. Over half of its area is preserved as a wilderness area which is accessible only on foot.

But the reserve is best known for the success achieved in saving the white (or wide-lipped) rhinoceros from extinction. In the early 1930s there were only about 150 white rhinos in southern Africa. A breeding programme launched by the Natal Parks Board has succeeded in raising the population to more than 1,000, while a further 3,000 of these magnificent animals have been exported to parks around the world.

Today, there is a similar battle taking place to save its cousin, the black rhino – distinguishable only by its narrow upper lip. Poachers, scavenging for its prized horn, have succeeded in depleting the African population of black rhinos from an estimated 55,000 in the mid-1980s to fewer than 4,500.

Game-spotting is at its best along the banks of the two major rivers flowing through the reserve, the Black and the White Umfolozi, as well as at the Bekapanzi water-hole where visitors can get out of their cars to observe the animals from a conveniently situated hide.

The Umfolozi's close neighbour, the **Hluhluwe Game Reserve**, is a stunningly beautiful park nestling in the foothills rising from the coastal plains. Situated in the Hluhluwe River valley, the 59,000-acre (23,900-hectare) park offers a variety of landscape – from misty mountain forests to thornveld, to savannah grassland to dense thickets.

Here, too, wide variety of mammals can be seen – including black and white rhino – but Hluhluwe is known for the nyala, one of Africa's most beautiful but elusive animals. At the Gujaneni Gate there is an fine reconstruction of a traditional Zulu homestead.

The **Mkuzi Game Reserve** on the lower reaches of the Lebombo Mountains is a photographer's dream come true. The 74,000-acre (30,000-hectare) reserve is bisected by the Mkuzi River and its Nsumu Pan – habitat of an astonishing variety of water birds – fish ea-

The monument to the Battle of Blood River.

gles, pelicans, herons and wild geese. Specially constructed hides provide close access to the large herds of blue wildebeest, reedbuck, waterbuck and black rhino.

Northeast of Mkuzi is the smallish but unique **Ndumu Game Reserve**, the jewel in the crown of the northern Natal. It is situated around picturesque pans in the flood plain of the Pongola River. The area is awash with birdlife, hippo, crocodile and antelope, including the elusive and beautiful bushbuck.

The **Sodwana Bay National Park** is an immensely popular resort among ski-boat fishermen and scuba-diving enthusiasts. Accommodation is provided in 450 camp-sites and 30 self-contained log cabins. Directly to its north is the country's largest freshwater lake, **Sibaya**, a popular spot for boating, game-fishing and skin-diving.

A number of privately-run game reserves have recently been established in northern Natal. Accommodation varies from luxury apartments to rustic, self-contained huts. These reserves offer excellent opportunities for game-spotting, bird-watching and leisurely walks. Among the best known are Rocktail Bay, the Bonamanzi Game Park, the Bushlands Game Lodge and the Nyala Safari Lodge.

Northern Natal: Some of the most epic battles that shaped South Africa's history took place on the misty, rolling hills and deep valleys of northern Natal. The **Battlefield Route** has in recent years become a feature for the region's tourists. It includes stopovers at Vryheid, once the capital of an independent Boer Republic; the Blood River Monument on the site where a small contingent of Voortrekkers staved off an attack by 13,000 Zulu warriors; Talana Hill overlooking Dundee, where the first battle of the Anglo-Boer War was fought, and two important sites of bloody encounters between British forces and the Zulus in the late 19th century – Isandhlawana and Rorke's Drift.

The Natal Midlands: From Durban the N8 leads east to Pietermaritzburg. It is along this 55-mile (90-km) route that

From the mountains to the sea: riding is always popular.

the Comrades Marathon takes place each May. Nineteen miles (30 km) outside Durban off the N3 is the spectacular Valley of a Thousand Hills with attractions such as **Phelulu**, a reconstructed Zulu village.

Pietermaritzburg, founded in 1838 and named after two prominent Voortrekker leaders, Piet Retief and Gerrit Maritz, is considered one of the world's best-preserved Victorian cities. Visitors can follow a self-guided trail through the historic heart of the town, often referred to as Heritage City and City of Flowers.

The elaborately decorated **City Hall**, the largest all-brick building in the southern hemisphere, was built in 1893 on the site of the old Voortrekker Parliament. Facing it, on the opposite side of Commercial Street, are two other historic buildings: the old Supreme Court and the Legislative Assembly.

The Voortrekker Museum, situated in the **Church of the Vow,** offers unique insights into frontier life in the mid-19th century. The small, white-ga-

bled building was erected in 1841 to fulfil a promise made to God before the Battle of Blood River. Next door is the restored house of the most important Voortrekker hero, Andries Pretorius.

The **Natal Museum** in Loop Street has sections devoted to natural history, paleontology, and ethnology, and has an excellent reconstruction of a Victorian Pietermaritzburg street.

Outside of Pietermaritzburg is **Midmar Dam**, the country's most popular spot for inland watersports. Not far off, the Umgeni River plunges more than 300 ft (100 metres) over the **Howick Falls** into a spectacular gorge below. The falls are easily visible from the small town of Howick which once played host to Mark Twain and the explorer Henry Morton Stanley.

Below the falls is the Umgeni Valley Nature Reserve and above it the Umgeni cuts through the beautiful but often overlooked **Karkloof Valley,** surrounded by a superb nature reserve, **Safariworld**. North of Howick the N3 rises steeply towards the lower reaches of the Drakensberg past picturesque towns such as Mooi River, Estcourt, Colenso and Ladismith.

Drakensberg: The Great Escarpment separates the coastal plains of Natal from the interior plateau. It reaches its highest peaks in Lesotho (where it is known as the Malutis), but nowhere is it more spectacular than in the east where jagged cliffs tower high above the Natal grassland. The Berg offers scenic beauty unsurpassed by anywhere in southern Africa.

Dominating the Royal Natal National Park is the **Amphitheatre**, a 5-mile (8-km) crescent-shaped stretch of the escarpment wall, providing a magnificent vista of the surrounding area.

A rewarding experience is a climb up **Mont-aux-Sources**, the country's highest peak (10,770ft/3,282 metres). The "Mountain of Beginnings" is so named because five of the country's major river systems – including the Tugela and the Elands – have their sources here.

A steep two-hour walk, with sturdy chain ladders to ease the ascent, brings

The white rhino is also known as the "square-lipped" rhino.

one to the summit. For experienced mountaineers there are longer and more challenging routes available.

Within a few miles of its source, the Tugela plunges for almost 1 mile (2 km) over a series of cascades and falls to the valley floor below. The combined drop of the **Tugela Falls** (2,790 ft/850 metres) makes it the second highest waterfall in the world.

The climate at the local resorts and hotels is generally mild all year round. However, as one ascends, the temperature may drop sharply and visitors should be prepared for unexpected heavy snowfalls during the winter months (May to September). Sudden thunderstorms or a blinding mist that can rapidly envelop the mountains may also make the journey hazardous for the inexperienced climber.

Cathedral Peak – and its surrounding nature reserve – is the centrepiece of a series of prominent free-standing peaks which present interesting challenges for the serious climber. Others in the range include the Bell, the Inner and Outer Horn, the Monk's Cowl and the very demanding **Cathkin Peak**.

Originally established to provide sanctuary to the eland – the largest antelope species – the **Giant's Castle Nature Reserve** is also considered the best venue in the country to observe raptors such as the majestic Cape vulture, the Lanner falcon, the snake eagle and endangered bearded vulture.

Hundreds of years ago San (Bushmen) communities settled along the massive basalt wall of the Drakensberg range. More than 5,000 examples of their rock paintings have been recorded and can be seen at sites such as "Bottle Cave" at Injasuti and a mere 1-mile (2-km) walk away from the base camp at the Giant's Castle Game Reserve. (*See "The First Artists" on page 91.*)

In the southern Berg, the **Sani Pass** (named after these hunter-gatherer communities) provides the only road access from the east to the independent state of Lesotho. Poor road conditions and treacherous hair-pin bends make four-wheel-drive vehicles essential.

Natal's north coast has high-wandering dunes.

ZULU LIFE AND CUSTOMS

The Zulus are the largest black nation in South Africa, sharing a common prehistoric origin and background with the many other so-called Nguni nations in the region. Little is known about their prehistory because neither the Zulu, nor any of the other Nguni people, ever evolved a written language. The first written accounts date from their first contact with whites in the 1820s.

For many decades that contact was limited to relatively small sections of the black communities and only at the end of the 19th century did increasing numbers come under Western influences. In the remoter parts of the country, old customs, traditions and beliefs are being observed in a more or less pure form; but education, conversion to Christianity, employment on farms and in villages, and large-scale urbanisation all encourage new customs and beliefs to evolve.

The indigenous religion of the Zulu and related groups is a belief in the survival of the spirit after death and a consequent ancestor worship. The line of descent is traced back to a common male ancestor whose name is adopted as a surname of the family from which the clan developed. The surname is therefore of some religious significance. Everyone is proud of his surname and prefers to be known and called by it in preference to a personal name; and everyone having the same surname is regarded as a blood-relation.

The creator of all things and the arch-ancestor is known by the name of *Unkulunkulu* – "the great-great-one". Each family will worship its own more recent ancestral spirits; a chief or the king will worship those of his forebears, which means those of the clan or the nation. The Zulu "paradise" is believed to be in the bowels of the earth. There the spirits lead much the same life that they enjoyed on earth. A rich man's spirit will have many cattle, many wives and much beer; a poor one will remain poor.

However, in relation to the living, family spirits are all-powerful, capable of overcoming all the ills and sufferings of mankind, and likewise can mete out punishment if offended or neglected. Consequently, they have always been relied upon as the mainstay for curing the sick and needy. A survey carried out in Soweto has shown that, notwithstanding urbanisation and Christianity, 83 percent of the respondents still believed in ancestral spirits. Prayers and appeals are often accompanied by the sacrificial offering of a beast or goat, the only sacred animals so used by the Zulu.

To help interpret the wishes of spirits the services of *isangoma* (diviners) are called upon while *inyanga* (medicine men) cure ailments with the help of *muti* (medicine).

Among the Zulu, as in most African societies, the bonds of kinship are extensive and knit into a group people who in Western society would not be regarded as directly related, or indeed even related at all. This "extended family" system, and the relationship established by a common surname, provide every Zulu with a number of so-called fathers and mothers, and many brothers and sisters. Although polygamy still is the basic traditional marriage system, economic circumstances and changed living conditions have made polygamous unions the exception rather than the rule.

The migratory labour system and increasing urbanisation have dramatically

A diviner (sangoma).

changed traditional domestic life. The careful distribution of labour between men and women, the rearing of children, relationships between the sexes... all these things are changing fundamentally.

One of the most deeply-rooted customs is the payment by a man of a certain number of cattle to his future father-in-law as a so-called "bride-price" for the girl he wishes to marry. This practice, *ilobolo* (or just lobolo), is determined by many factors but amounts, on average, to anything from seven to 14 head of cattle.

In urban communities where cattle are not always readily available, all or part of the lobolo may be paid in cash. The present rate is not much less than R1,000 and may be sometimes more than R3,000.

The payment of lobolo constitutes a token or symbol providing proof of the ratification of the marriage, and although the transaction cannot be regarded as one of purchase and sale, it nevertheless represents compensation for the loss of the woman's services in her father's home. Suggestions that the lobolo custom is outdated and should be abolished has met with massive opposition, both from men and women. A survey conducted some years ago in Soweto has indicated that in that year 98 percent of the marriages were preceded and concluded by the giving of lobolo.

A fundamental degree of acculturation has also taken place in the lives of urbanised Zulu women. Traditionally a Zulu woman remains a minor throughout her life. She resorts at all times under the guardianship of a male member of her family, be it her father, husband, uncle or even her own eldest son. With changes in family composition and a relocation of functions and duties as a result of many males working elsewhere, the women had to accept new responsibilities and thus experienced an awakening of a sense of independence.

Their entry into commerce and industry, nursing and teaching, social work, community service and even politics has enabled them to become more fully Westernised – often at a faster rate than most men. Zulu businesswomen are often more successful than men. Zulu women take most of the credit for ensuring that their children go to school and acquire some education. ■

The role of Zulu women is changing.

CAPE TOWN AND THE SOUTHWESTERN CAPE

"The fairest Cape we saw in the whole circumference of the earth," the great navigator Sir Francis Drake exclaimed when in 1580 he sailed into Table Bay aboard the *Golden Hind*. To this day, the Cape is a place of majestic splendour and stunning contrasts, with the bustling "Mother City", Cape Town, cradled against the imposing Table Mountain, flanked by Devil's Peak and Lion's Head.

Through the centuries it has been called many names: the Cape of Storms, by the Portuguese soldiers who first navigated their way around the treacherous shores at Cape Point; the Cape of Good Hope, by those who survived the journey to enter into the calmer waters of False Bay; the Tavern of the Seas, when fresh produce was shipped in here to enable fleets to continue on their arduous journey to the East. For South Africans it is simply "the Cape" – an acknowledgement both of its status as the Mother City, and of its uniqueness.

In many ways the southwestern Cape is a fresh and fertile world apart – divorced from its cultural roots in Europe and the East, and apart from the harshness that characterises the rest of Africa. Certainly, the feeling here is not African, but cosmopolitan; the weather is quite unlike that on the rest of the continent; the landscape differs starkly from that to be observed elsewhere.

For most of the year the Cape experiences weather that wafts between pleasant and sublime, but it earned its sobriquet Cape of Storms not without reason. The southwestern Cape is the only section of Africa that falls within a temperate weather zone and it enjoys a typically Mediterranean climate with long, hot summers and cold, wet winters. The howling southeaster is aptly called the "Cape Doctor": it sweeps away every loose object in its path, cleansing the city of dust and pollution and making its atmosphere one of the healthiest.

The sense of being physically cut off from the rest of the country is most obviously caused by the all-pervading barrier of serrated peaks that surrounds Cape Town. At the time when the southern land mass of Gondwanaland started to break up – around 300 million years ago – the southern rim that would emerge as Africa was grotesquely buckled and twisted. These great folds have since been weathered and ground down with few peaks rising higher than 6,500 ft (2,000 metres) and the resultant valleys have rich, clayey soils derived from softer shales. They are the nation's storehouse, the centre of its deciduous fruit, wheat, grape and wine industries.

History: Early Portuguese navigators were the first people known to have rounded the Cape of Good Hope, late in the 15th century. The appellation "Cape of Good Hope" was intended to encourage early sailors on their voyages around the often stormy Cape Point. First came Bartolomeu Dias, making his way as far east as Mossel Bay, and, a decade later, Vasco da Gama, who managed to reach India. Over the next century ships from many nations used

Preceding pages: Table Mountain. *Left,* Cape Town avant-garde. *Right,* the Mother City has the most statues of any South African town.

Table Bay as a safe anchorage and watering place, but it was the commercially-minded Dutch who first perceived that the Cape had strategic value.

In 1652 the Dutch East India Company (VOC) dispatched Jan van Riebeeck to establish a victualling station at the Cape, to supply fresh food and water to the scurvy-ridden crews of passing ships. It was never intended by his bosses in Amsterdam that the settlement should be more than a temporary halfway station to the East. But at this tiny settlement the foundations of the modern South Africa were laid. The Dutch first called the supply post the "Vleck van den Kaap" (Cape Hamlet).

Such was the success of this venture that the small settlement on Africa's southern tip soon grew to outstrip van Riebeeck's original purpose. Under successive governors, a castle-like fort was built, and watering canals, official buildings and elegant townhouses constructed. It was not long before the Dutch began trading with the local Hottentots as their need for cattle, sheep and minerals outstripped their own production. By the time of van Riebeeck's departure, 10 years later, former officials were already declared free burghers and established as small-scale farmers to till vineyards, vegetable gardens and fruit orchards to supply the growing

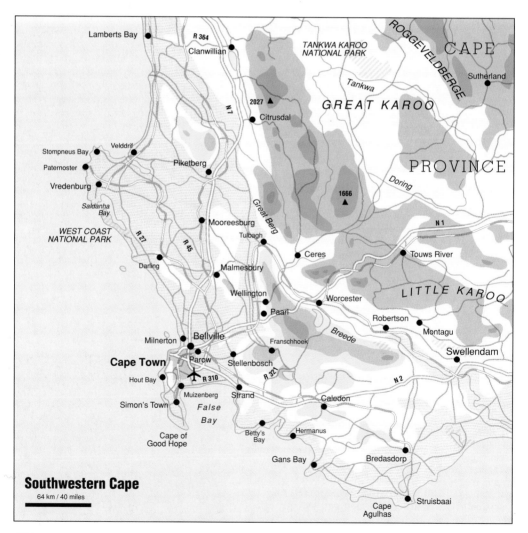

Southwestern Cape

64 km / 40 miles

demand. As the colony grew and prospered, with farmlands being opened up further and further inland of Table Bay, the Cape's reputation as the Tavern of the Seas spread across the world.

The historic town: The romantic setting of sea and mountains lends **Cape Town** a character similar to that of Rio de Janeiro, Hong Kong or Vancouver. Yet, by being manageably small and charmingly ethnic by international standards, the main downtown area can be quite comfortably explored on foot.

An obvious and tranquil place to begin a walking tour of the city is in its green lung, the **Company Gardens**, at the top of the bustling **Adderley Street**.

Originally established by van Riebeeck to grow fresh produce, the cool and well-shaded gardens form the heart of the Mother City – a place where children can feed the squirrels and doves in the sylvan parks and up the oak tree-lined avenue. Tucked into various secluded corners diverse buildings, at once grand and welcoming, house the **South African Natural History Museum** and its attached **planetarium**; the **Jewish Museum** and **synagogue**; and the Anglican **St George's Cathedral** (the diocese of Nobel peace laureate Archbishop Desmond Tutu).

Inside the garden is a **statue** of industrialist and empire-builder, **Cecil John**

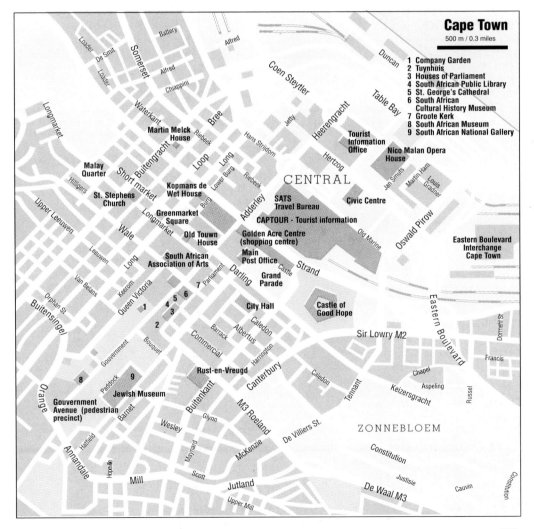

Rhodes, with a finger pointing northwards. The inscription on the statue reads: "Your hinterland lies there," a clear reference to Rhodes's life-long ambition to extend British influence "from the Cape to Cairo". At the southern entrance is a statue of another of South Africa's greatest sons, **General Jan Smuts**, war hero, prime minister and member of the British War Cabinet during both world wars. Dominating the area, however, are the Houses of Parliament, built in grand High Victorian style and facing on to Government Avenue. Next to it is Stalplein with Tuynhuys, the office and residence of South Africa's State President.

Walking down Adderley Street towards the harbour one passes the historic **Groote Kerk**, the oldest church in South Africa, containing an elaborately carved pulpit made by one of the country's premier sculptors, Anton Anreith. Still further down is the **Golden Acre shopping centre**. During excavations for the building of this modern complex the ruins of a stone-and-brick reservoir

built in 1663 were uncovered. This is now effectively protected behind illuminated glass panels.

At the bottom end of the street are the statues of **Jan van Riebeeck** and his wife, **Maria**. Close by is the **City Hall** with its baroque embellishments and honey-marble facade. It faces **The Parade**, originally intended to train military troops but now a bustling and colourful open-air market where visitors can bargain with street vendors for fruit and flowers.

On the eastern side of the Parade is the sturdy stone structure of the **Castle of Good Hope**, completed in 1697, making it the oldest remaining structure in South Africa. With its 30-ft (10-metre) walls and five corner bastions, each named after a title of the Prince of Orange, the Castle is today a military headquarters also housing a military and maritime museum.

Among its striking features are the moats and entrance gate with its klompie-brick bell tower. The inscription on the bell reads: "May the land **City Hall**.

worship the Lord, praise and exalt Him through all ages" – a theme taken up in recent years by a German immigrant, Heinrich Haape, and woven into an oratorio of the same name.

Cutting across the courtyard of the castle is the kat or balcony where the high society in the early days – most notably the socialite, Lady Anne Barnard – held their grandiose parties. Much more sombre and ominous are the dungeons, or "Black Holes" where criminals were imprisoned and tortured. One such occupant in the early 18th century was the legendary Adam Tas who led a burghers' revolt against the corrupt regime of the then governor, Willem Adriaan van der Stel.

In the centre of the city is **Greenmarket Square**, which to this day accommodates a thriving flea market where stalls trade anything from trendy shoes and clothing to finely crafted jewellery, ornaments and art. Two blocks west of the square is **Long Street**, well worth a stroll for window-shopping and bargain-hunting. It is an emporium of pawnshops and boutiques, knick-knack outlets and well-stocked secondhand bookshops specialising in Africana and first editions. Running the length of Long Street are fine Georgian and Victorian buildings, housing banks and churches, apartments and offices.

Those with a taste for the exotic will be drawn by the muezzin's cry beyond **Buitengracht Street** into the Bo-Kaap or **Malay Quarter**, an area of winding, narrow streets flanked by restored early 19th-century cottages. It is here where the descendants of the Batavian slaves imported by the Dutch colonists still continue to live.

Until 1933 the city reached right down to the golden beaches of Table Bay and Woodstock, where fishing boats berthed, children frolicked and people could promenade down Long Street right on to the pier. Then the harbour was enlarged and the foreshore area reclaimed. The **Victoria and Albert basin** area, the oldest section of the harbour, had fallen into disrepair, but wide-scale renovation and redevel-

The Greenmarket Square always has a flea market.

opment started in 1990 in an attempt to reunite the city with its maritime origins. Where decaying buildings once stood rotting, hotels, restaurants and pubs, museums and theatres now crowd together with a theme that is unmistakably nautical. Today it is one of the most interesting spots to be visited, either by day or by night.

On a clear day, **Robben Island** is clearly visible from across the bay. Originally started as a penal colony for errant slaves, it later became one of the most notorious prisons in the world where some of South Africa's best-known political prisoners were held. The prison has recently been closed and investigations into the commercial development of the island are presently being undertaken.

Cutting across the foreshore is **Table Bay Boulevard** – the start of the major N1 Highway that bisects the country 1,200 miles (2,000 km) from the south to the northernmost boundary point at Messina in the Northern Transvaal.

Museums and galleries: The **National Museum** is found at the top of Adderley Street, opposite the Gardens. Once the slave quarters and supreme court, it now houses collections of Cape silverware and furniture, weapons from all over the world, and coins, glassware and other interesting relics.

Associated with this museum is a collection of houses throughout the city that have been restored and preserved as outstanding examples of different architectural periods and lifestyles. Among these are **Bertrams House** in the Gardens, **Rust-en-Vreugd** in Buitenkant Street and the **Koopmans de Wet House** in Strand Street. At 71 Wale Street, the **Bo-Kaap Museum** portrays in detail the lifestyle of a 19th-century Malay family, complete with prayer room.

The **South African Natural History Museum** at the top of the Gardens has evocative displays of man's prehistory and evolution, indigenous people and their cultures, and animals, insects, birds, shells and geology. Among the most appealing displays are those of the

The South African Museum.

Bushman hunter-gatherer cultures, including original examples of their tools, rock art and engravings.

Close by is the **National Gallery** with an impressive collection of work by local artists and internationally acclaimed masters such as Gainsborough, Reynolds and Rodin. The **South African Library** contains a collection of some 400,000 books, including some very rare Africana.

Dining out: To this day, Cape Town lives up to its reputation as the Tavern of the Seas with the proverbial "restaurant on every corner". Eating places cater for most tastes, from the usual array of European fare to the various Eastern styles of classic Japanese and spicy Indian. It is difficult to single out individual restaurants and word of mouth is often the visitor's best guide.

However, generally considered to be outstanding is the **Buitenverwagting restaurant**, on the wine estate of the same name in Constantia; **Champers** in Highlands Estate is all roses and crystal, crayfish and quails; **Floris Smit Huis** in town is quirky and provocative, but its fare is unfalteringly gourmet; **Leinster Hall** provides an air and table to suit its gentle Victorian Gardens setting; and the *cognoscenti* flock to **Truffles** in Heathfield for the chef's dedicated and passionate cooking. A mere half-star below these are the **Almondbury** at Lakeside, **Blakes** in the Nico Malan Opera house complete with cabaret, **Farthings** in Kenilworth, **Freda's and Rozenhof** in Gardens, the **Swiss Chalet** in Pinelands and, for its accent on authentic Japanese cuisine, **Kamakura** in Sea Point.

The local culinary speciality is known as Cape-Malay – spicy with fruit, but seldom hot. Fruit and chutney-enhanced *boboties*, skewered-meat *sosaties*, *frikkadel* patties and tomato-based *bredie* with *blatjang* – you will find these delicacies at the Cape Sun's **Riempies**, the **Kaapse Tafel** in the Gardens, and **Biesmiellah** in the Bo-Kaap – the latter an authentic Islamic institution where no alcohol is allowed.

Those fancying seafood should re-

The Houses of Parliament.

ARCHITECTURAL STYLES

The oldest remaining building in South Africa is the Castle of Good Hope in Cape Town, dating from 1666. A bastioned structure originally on the water's edge, it is being restored. The Dutch East India Company, which established the castle, laid out A garden and a tiny settlement.

Around these gardens are located the most important cultural historic buildings of the Mother City: the slave quarters (today the Cultural History Museum); the Houses of Parliament; the Company's guest house, Tuynhuys (today office and residence of the State President); the South African Museum and the South African Library.

The Cape Dutch style is a vernacular architecture unique to South Africa and in particular to the Cape. It is characterised by a thatched roof; a main plaster-decorated gable, usually white; and large, shuttered, many-paned windows symmetrically disposed around a central door with fanlight. A *stoep*, an uncovered platform in front of the build-ing and usually terminated by built-in seats, is typical. Groot Constantia, home-stead and wine farm of the Dutch gover-nor Simon van der Stel, is a fine example of the style. The famous pediment on its wine cellar is the work of master sculptor Anton Anreith.

Cape Dutch, Georgian and Victorian buildings stand astride the oak-lined and water-furrowed Dorp Street in Stellenbosch, one of the oldest and most beautiful streets in South Africa.

As the frontiers of settlement pressed forward, a derivative of the Cape Dutch vernacular developed in the harsh, arid interior. The Karoo house is a flat-roofed yet pedimented building with stoep, and later verandah. The town of Graaff-Reinet is resplendent in Cape Dutch and Karoo contributions. Due to the scarcity of wood, a stone cobelled house style developed in the Great Karoo.

Vestiges of English settlement are terraced houses with Georgian and Re-gency verandahs such as those in Port Elizabeth. Grahamstown fuses the build-ing traditions of the Cape and those of the English settlers, who liked bay and bow windows. Some of the most splen-did English colonial buildings are in Na-tal, with Pietermarizburg as the finest repository of corrugated-iron roofed and verandahed red-brick buildings.

Architect to the imperialist Cecil Rhodes was Sir Herbert Baker, who blended the English concepts with the vernacular of the Cape. His crowning achievement remains the 1912 Union Buildings in Pretoria.

During the period of union, South Af-rica became receptive to the modern movement as espoused in Brazil. The climate of Durban, so similar to Brazil's, saw a ready transmutation; in Pretoria it significantly contributed towards the es-tablishment of a regional style in domes-tic architecture in the 1950s.

Today imported concepts crown the city centre of Johannesburg, the modern Stock Exchange, de Beers' head office, Standard Bank and Carlton Centre pre-vailing. Durban is dominated by the high-tech 88 Field Street building.

Housing its population is one of the most pressing needs facing South Af-rica. The economical, thermally sound and aesthetically satisfying properties of indigenous shelters may suggest solu-tions, for they embody important princi-ples of design. ∎

member that almost every restaurant has daily fresh catches of crayfish and perlemoen (abalone), black mussels and oysters, prawns and linefish. Places to dine which also provide scenic views are the **Brass Bell**, **Blues**, the **Wooden Bridge** and **Onse Huisie**, **Beachcomber**, **Wharfside Grill** and **Chapman's Peak Hotel**. In the Victoria and Albert basin area where tugs toot, sails flutter and seals frolic, one can quaff beer or wine and savour seafood at **Quay Four**, the **Fisherman's Tavern**, the **Green Dolphin** or **Bertie's Landing** – named after the country's premier yachtsman, "Biltong" Bertie Reed.

Sports and entertainment: Aided by the mild Mediterranean climate, Capetonians enjoy an active outdoor lifestyle. What with the 60-mile (100 km) peninsula and its myriad beaches, its mountains and forest paths, wild flower gardens and playful ocean, its sunny summer days and sea breezes, there is something to amuse the visitor every day of the year. However, visitors are often shocked by the near-freezing temperatures at the famous bikini bathing beaches of Clifton, Camps Bay and Llandudno, and the nudist beach at Sandy Bay.

For those who enjoy swimming in the sea, **Muizenberg** and **Fish Hoek** on the warmer False Bay coastline can provide the best spots. The secret is to choose a beach according to the wind direction: if there is a cloud cloth on Table Mountain it means the southeaster is blowing and one should head straight for **Clifton** or **Llandudno**; but if there is a northwesterly sea fog brewing go to Muizenberg and environs.

The reason for the Atlantic's chilly waters is more complex than most people realise. It has a lot to do with the whims of the "southeaster". When this wind pushes the warm surface-water away from the western shore, the water is replaced from underneath. This phenomenon is called "upwelling", bringing with it the cold Antarctic Middle Water of the Benguela Current. Small wonder water temperature can be as low as 54° or even 50°F (12–10°C) after a

Table Mountain with "cloth".

strong "blow". Ironically, it is in winter when the southeaster abates that the Atlantic beaches experience their warmest sea temperatures.

For those who do not want to brave the sea there are numerous public swimming-pools in the city, the most notable being the one at Newlands. For sporting mad Capetonians, Newlands has acquired mythical status as home of their beloved Western Province rugby team while in the summer an enjoyable game of cricket can be watched from under "the oaks" at the Newlands grounds.

Capetonians are rightfully proud of their performing arts tradition which has been sustained at a very high level in spite of a relative small population and the ravages of international isolation in recent years. Nowhere can this be better experienced than in the **Nico Malan Opera House** with its annual programme packed with ballet, opera, drama and musical shows of an international calibre. The Cape Town Symphony Orchestra gives weekly concerts in the City Hall, as well as providing the scores at the Opera House. Local talent is fostered by a strong tradition of performing arts at the universities, while lead roles and solos in major productions are often given to established international stars.

"Shakespeare in the Park" is virtually a festival in itself for local theatre. Large casts and flamboyant sets congregate under the oak trees in Maynardville Park every summer and spectators can picnic around the small lake while watching the performances.

During the **Cape Town Festival** season in late March and early April, the arts offering is bolstered by street performances of the widest variety: buskers and piano recitals are attractions in Greenmarket Square or the Harbour; symphony concerts play in the Gardens. Other theatre complexes in the city include the **Baxter** where students of the University of Cape Town performing arts department often perform the work of local playwrights.

Musical shows at the Baxter or **Good**

Simon's Town, a naval base on the Cape.

232

Hope Centre range from ethnic African bands, to local favourite crooner David Kramer. Jazz fans can hear the internationally acclaimed Abdullah Ibrahim (Dollar Brand) tinkling the ivories, Basil "Mannenberg" Coetzee blowing the brass or Jonathan Butler plucking the strings.

Table Mountain: The mountain that grandly greets one's arrival at the Cape is a massive block of horizontally bedded sandstone that dominates the city and Table Bay. For Capetonians it is a symbol that they hold dear. The cableway ferries on average 1,500 people a day up to the 3,300-ft (1,000-metre) summit, and certainly no visit to the "fairest Cape" is complete without gaining a view from the top of this famous landmark.

For those with enough determination there is another way – actually hundreds of ways – of getting to the top of the mountain by walking or climbing. Those keen enough to undertake this rewarding journey can consult one of many hiking guides that can be bought in bookstores, or contact the Mountain Club of South Africa for information.

Flanking Table Mountain are the imposing peaks of **Lion's Head** and **Devil's Peak**. It was on the slopes of the latter, that according to legend, a retired soldier named van Hunk was challenged by the devil to a smoking contest. The result of their showdown can be seen in the summertime by the blanket of smoke or "tablecloth" – hovering over Table Mountain.

On the eastern slopes of Table Mountain is the **National Botanic Gardens** at **Kirstenbosch**, open to the public throughout the week to come and marvel at the country's floral beauty. At present about 10,000 different species are cultivated in the garden covering 1,380 acres (560 hectares).

Situated on the slopes of Devil's Peak is the **Groote Schuur estate**, bequeathed to the South African nation after the death of Cecil Rhodes in 1902. It includes a number of ministerial residences as well as the campus of the University of Cape Town. The Groote

Table cable-car.

Schuur hospital and medical school was the scene for the world's first heart transplant, performed by Professor Christian Barnard in 1967.

The Peninsula: Cape Town's urban area spreads across the extreme northern end of a 60-mile (100 km) sliver of land, whose southern tip is the famous "Cape of Good Hope" which ignites the romance and dreams of everyone who ventures there. Precipitous mountain drives link up the innumerable coves and wide sandy beaches, villages and fishing communities, like beads on a littoral necklace.

To make the most of a circumnavigation of the Peninsula, one should set out early, just as the sun breaches the jagged **Hottentots-Holland Mountains** and dapples the surface of **False Bay** with a soft, warm palette. Staying with the sun the journey along the M4 begins at Muizenberg corner. This bustling seaside town was a popular resort in Victorian times, and it was in a small cottage here that Cecil John Rhodes chose to spend his last years when his health

prematurely failed him. The British gentry eagerly sought its moderate climate to cleanse their bodies of damp English winters and city smog. Thus the southeaster that blows almost constantly here during summer was dubbed the "Cape Doctor".

Down the False Bay coast the narrow road follows closely alongside the railway line, with **Muizenberg Mountain** crowding in on the left; it passes the quaint fishing harbour at **Kalk Bay** and on through **Fish Hoek** – both traditional fishing settlements. Winding through **Glencairn**, the road enters the historic port settlement of **Simon's Town**, established during Simon van der Stel's governorship, as a safe winter anchorage. From the time of the second British occupation of the Cape in 1806 it became a Royal Navy base until it was handed over to the South African Navy in 1957.

Many historic buildings on the main street's "historic mile" have been declared national monuments. The **Martello Tower** – the oldest of its kind in the world and one of two in this country – houses the **South African Naval Museum** display.

Leaving Simon's Town, the road winds up past **Miller's Point** and **Smitswinkel Bay**, where one can glance down to the sea far below. This is a route well-known to local cyclists – often numbering more than 15,000 – who every year, rain or shine, ride the 65-mile (105-km) Argus Cycle Tour around the Peninsula.

A short turn-off takes one to the **Cape of Good Hope Nature Reserve**. Amazingly, this small park is the second most visited reserve in the country, after the Kruger National Park. Standing in front of the old lighthouse and peering out across the great curve of ocean, one could almost imagine seeing South America to the right, Australia to the left and, yes, far to the south the thin white sliver of the Antarctic. The reserve was actually proclaimed to preserve a chunk of natural fynbos close to the city and to protect some rare plant species here. It also serves as a breeding ground for rare antelope and the visitor will invariably

Surfing at Llandudno.

see some Cape mountain zebra, bontebok and eland on the sandy plateau.

Turning back on the M6, just past the charming fishing village of **Kommetjie**, one is confronted with the massive chunk of mountain that is the back side of Table Mountain. The road veers steeply upwards on a nerve-racking 7-mile (11-km) journey up **Chapman's Peak** – arguably one of the world's most spectacular scenic drives. Above the road vertical sandstone cliffs rise some 2,300 ft (700 metres) to the summit, while below the rounded forms of granite boulders and domes hold the road suspended above Hout Bay. At the top of the pass one can stop to appreciate the impressive panorama of the silvery bay and its enfolding mountain arms.

Hout Bay is a popular stopover place for a tranquil lunch at any one of the many charming restaurants specialising in local fish dishes. Moving north, one crosses **Suikerbossie Hill** to peer down into postcard **Llandudno**, with its perfect sickle-shaped beach and rocky points. The imaginative houses that cling to the rocky slopes above the bay like surrealistic barnacles are the homes of the very wealthy.

By now the sun will be dropping down on its westward arc, maybe slipping into a bank of cloud just before it sinks into the ocean, as one heads for **Camps Bay**. This is near the journey's end, but some of the best is still to come. As one passes Hottentot's Huisie and Koeelbaai, the **Twelve Apostles** begin to glow in various shades of pink and red. The massive buttresses jut out like the prows of gigantic ships lined up along the shore. When the wind whips clouds around their ramparts it is easy to imagine it to be sea swells frothing around the tightly berthed hulls. With one last look at this glorious scene, great crags an idyllic shore, one re-enters the city bowl, either over panoramic Kloof Nek or by way of Sea Point's bustling promenades and boulevards.

Mountain passes: The 19th century was the country's great age of road-building, with no fewer than 15 major passes being hewn from the folded mountains

Hout Bay.

and out along precipitous ravines. Today most of these are tarred arteries connecting the many Boland towns, and the visitor is most likely to venture along at least some of the more spectacular ones that bear the name of their makers. Most dramatic are **Bain's Kloof Pass** between Wellington and Wolseley, **Michell's Pass** from there to Ceres, and the old **Du Toit's Kloof Pass** between Paarl and Worcester.

A popular day outing is to travel along the **Four Passes Drive** connecting Cape Town with Stellenbosch, Grabouw and Franschhoek. Starting off along the N2 the road meanders over the scenic **Sir Lowry's Pass** before a turn-off on to the R321 takes one across **Vijoen's Pass**. From here another turn-off leads to the **Franschhoek Pass** on the R45 and finally the R310 takes one down the **Hellshoogte Pass** which leads to Stellenbosch.

Hiking: Those planning to go hiking in the mountains should take care to consult the Mountain Club or a reliable guidebook for information about the viable routes. Whichever is chosen, one should never set off without enough food, water and warm, waterproof clothing to see you safely through a sudden Cape blizzard.

To Jan van Riebeeck they were the unassailable "Mountains of Africa" but today hiking trials and climbing routes are found throughout these rugged mountains. Table Mountain is criss-crossed with walks of varying degrees of difficulty; the Limietberg and Slanghoek Mountains between the Bain's and Du Toit's Kloof passes, the Hottentots-Holland Mountains between Stellenbosch, Franschhoek and Grabouw and the Langeberg above Swellendam each have two to six-day hiking trails with marked paths and log-cabin shelters. Booking is essential and can be done through the National Hikingway Board.

The **Cedarberg** is the northern-most of the folded ranges, the most remote and most rugged. It is maintained as a mountaineering wilderness area and leopard sanctuary, with only caves and a few rudimentary huts for shelter.

Mostert's Mill on the Groote Schuur.

There are, however, numerous camp-sites and bungalow resorts around the fringe of the wilderness area. Right in the middle of the fantastically weathered, huge carving-knife ridges is **Algeria Forestry Station**, with its green meadow and tranquil camp-site – something like a miniature Yosemite without the crowds.

The winelands: Today the Cape's wine industry, as well as the historic estate homesteads, are one of the country's most highly treasured assets and a principal tourist attraction.

At estates like **Boschendal, Delheim, Fairview, Blaauwklippen, Speirs, Neethlingshof** and **Lanzerac**, one can sip wine and take an *al fresco* lunch beneath spreading oaks while taking in the stunning beauty of pale mountains, russet and emerald vines and gracious white buildings.

Those estates which welcome visits by members of the public are indicated by road signs bearing the distinctive wine route logo. The principal wine routes are to be found at **Stellenbosch** and **Franschhoek**, **Paarl** and **Wellington**, with a lesser one located in the **Worcester Robertson** area.

The grandest of the many Cape Dutch homesteads found in the area, **Groot Constantia**, was once the home of Governor Simon van der Stel, the founder of viticulture at the Cape. The house has been superbly preserved and is today a living monument depicting social and cultural life of the residents of the Cape during its early years.

The Boland: Stellenbosch, the second town to be established at the Cape, was named after Simon van der Stel. At first, the farmers in the Eerste River valley produced wheat, but this was soon supplanted by vineyards. The town now forms the heart of the country's wine region, while the well-preserved historic town is its cultural jewel.

A walk from Die Braak commonage and up Dorp Street reveals an unbroken record of the town's various period styles, where many of the buildings are monuments and museums.

On or facing Die Braak are the **Rhenisch Church**, the Kruithuis or munitions magazine, and the neo-classical Cape Dutch museum of the Burgerhuis. Up Dorp Street one passes the Wine Museum and Art Gallery, the old drostdy, Oom Samie se Winkel (uncle's Samie's store – an old-fashioned shop), the Lutheran church, and, finally, the four period houses forming the Museum Complex. These are the rather primitive Schreuderhuis cottage, the elegant Cape Dutch Blettermanhuis, Georgian-styled Grosvenor House and mid-Victorian Murray House.

Stellenbosch, often called "the town of oaks", is also known for its university, the first Afrikaans language institution of higher education to have been established in the country. Its botanical garden in Van Riebeeck Street houses many interesting plants including the *Welwitschia mirabilis* from the Namib Desert, bonsai trees and orchids.

Across the Hellshoogte Pass lies the tranquil town of **Franschhoek**, founded by the French Huguenot settlers who fled from religious persecution in Europe after the revoking of the Edict of

Lanzerac wine estate in Stellenbosch.

Nantes in 1688. Its stately homesteads on sprawling wine estates best typify that romantic era. The **Huguenot Monument** commemorates these intrepid settlers who gave their names to many of South Africa's leading families such as Du Plessis, Malan and Joubert.

Paarl and Wellington are separated by the polished granite domes of **Paarl Mountain** and its surrounding nature reserve. Both towns have many fine historic Cape Dutch buildings, while Paarl has become an important commercial centre for the region. The granite "pearls" dominate the landscape and have been declared a national monument. Locals call it "Tortoise Mountain" because its domed oval summit looks like a tortoise shell. On its southern slope the imposing granite needle of the **Afrikaans Language monument** is clearly visible. It was erected in 1975 to commemorate the centenary of a movement started in the Paarl that eventually led to the recognition of Afrikaans as an official language.

From Wellington the road passes

over the most magnificent of all mountain passes, Bain's Kloof Pass, over the Slanghoek Mountains and into the wheat-golden and vine-red **Valley of Waveren**. At the far end of the valley is found **Tulbagh**, a miniature historic gem and small wine centre. Following a series of earthquakes in 1968 that virtually demolished the town, the main historic area of Church Street was rebuilt in the style of its former Cape Dutch glory. The whole street, its houses, church and museum is now a national monument.

Worcester and **Robertson** are the furthest outlying towns of the winelands, lying on a Karoo floor at the extreme northeastern end of Du Toit's Kloof Pass. The mighty **Hex River Mountain**s, highest in the Western Cape – snow-dusted in winter and set in a seething heat mirage through summer – loom in an almost oppressive way over Worcester. The drostdy (court house) is probably the finest example of Regency architecture in the country. The **Worcester Wild Flower Reserve** preserves both fynbos and Karoo vegetation, especially succulents.

The southeast coast is a weekend getaway-playground favoured by many Capetonians for its varied charms. It has mountains and ocean drives and scenery to match those of the Peninsula. There are large rural tracts and picturesque villages; small lakes and large estuaries; farm stalls sagging under an abundance of fruit, vegetables, preserves and baked goods, and country inns providing warmth and comfort.

And then there are the glorious beaches and river estuaries that even in summer are virtually deserted. **Hermanus** is the main resort town which can be reached from the N2, with a harbour and hotel, beaches and lagoon, sea and mountains all concentrated in a small area. At **Betty's Bay** is one of the finest bathing beaches, and an exquisite wild flower and mountain reserve.

The West Coast: The gem of this barren but invigorating coastal strip along the R27 from Cape Town is undoubtedly the **West Coast National Park** and its lagoon at **Langebaan** – a wetland wonder that is one of the world's most im-

The Cape's fertile land yields an abundance of produce.

portant conservation areas for paleo-arctic migrant birds. But most people who journey to these shores do so to marvel at another natural phenomenon the glorious eruption of wild flowers each spring.

The **Postberg** area of Langebaan is the favourite stopover for wild flower enthusiasts where, during the spring flower season, one is permitted to walk across any private land or track.

En route to Postberg, one passes **Church Haven**, a traditional Cape fishing village hugging the salt marsh shoreline of the **Langebaan Lagoon**. On its eastern shore, the village of Langebaan caters for an array of water sports such as angling, swimming, water skiing, yachting and board-sailing.

The other small settlements in the area all possess a charm of a bygone age. Time certainly seems to have passed by places like **Paternoster**, **Eland's Bay** and **Lambert's Bay**. With the virtual collapse of the fishing industry here due to over exploitation by commercial interests, the very fabric of these communities has become frayed. They have a romantic charm for tourists, but daily life here is as hard as the sea is cold. The soil is often cracked and dry like the fisherman's hands, but the smiles on the Sandvelders' faces are like the wild flowers that soften the ground in spring.

In Lambert's Bay – often referred to as the "heart of the crayfish route" – there is a fish factory, a most scenic fishing harbour, the **Sandveld Museum** and, an accessible Bird Island, the largest breeding colony of Cape gannets. Inland are numerous seasonal pans such as those at **Wagendrift and Rocher Pan Nature Reserve**, whose transient brackish waters attract many thousands of migrant wading birds. Flamingos are the most spectacular.

Lambert's Bay can also be reached by car, travelling along the N7 highway from Cape Town with a turn-off on the R364. The N7 also gives access to the two picturesque towns of **Clanwilliam** and **Citrusdal**, ideally situated for excursions into the Cedarberg Mountains.

Classic Cape wine country in the Hex River valley.

THE GARDEN ROUTE TO PORT ELIZABETH

The "Garden Route" takes a sweeping tour through a land of lushness and bountiful nature. This is very much an African garden – not the manicured lawns of Europe with their neat and formal layouts, but one of rugged coastline and sombre rainforests, glorious sweeps of beaches between rocky points, parallel rows of serrated mountain peaks and cosy hamlets nestling between sea and land, or in the folds of mountains shrouded in mist.

Travelling along superb highways, it can be easy to forget that it is also a delicate world, its natural tapestry woven with myriad threads and patterns. It is only by staying over for some days – at least – or to travel along its byways and coastal and forest tracks that the complexity and contrasts of this wild and wonderful garden can truly be appreciated by the visitor.

The Garden Route (N2) is one of the focal points of South Africa's holiday industry, where revellers come to enjoy the year-round temperate climate, the mostly warm seas, and a rural charm that is no longer to be found in the larger cities. The journey leads through hamlets and villages separated by miles of virgin nature, until it finally reaches Port Elizabeth – a port town rather than a big city by international standards. The Cape Folded Mountains and the coastline running parallel, are the most important landscape features.

The weather is pleasant almost year-round, with some snow on the higher peaks in winter and temperatures seldom reaching beyond the mid-30s in summer. This is the only area in the country which enjoys all year rainfall contributing to the "garden" aspect of its name.

The southern tip: As one travels east along the N2 highway from Cape Town, the first sign of a change in landscape is perceived as one passes Caledon, heading for Swellendam. This undulating area of the Southern Cape is almost totally given over to the cultivation of winter wheat – the country's principal winter cereal crop – on a wide coastal plain that stretches between the green, pleated Langeberg and the sea.

Caledon is known for its seven springs (six hot, one cold) that reach the surface there. On the outskirts of the town is a botanical garden that has acquired an international reputation for its floral beauty. A delightful detour from Caledon is to take the R320 through the "Hemel-en-Aarde-vallei" (Heaven-and-Earth-Valley) to the small fishing village of Hermanus and from there along the coast to **Cape Agulhas**.

This is the southernmost tip of Africa where the Atlantic and Indian Oceans meet. Portuguese sailors gave it the name Agulhas, meaning "needles", because it is at this point that the needle of a compass points due north, with no deviation. Huge waves pound the rocky coast while a 18 million-candlepower lighthouse guides shipping around the treacherous shores.

Nearby, the fishing village of **Arniston** (also known as Waenhuiskrans)

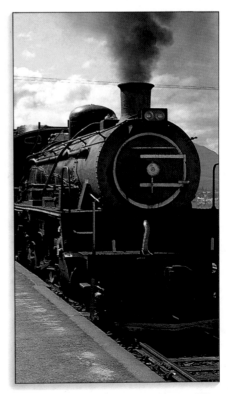

encapsulates all the romance of the area. A small but attractive hotel allows visitors to sample a traditional coastal lifestyle fast vanishing all around the world. Here, some of that spirit and the fisherfolk's traditional white-washed cottages have been preserved for posterity.

Set against the majestic backdrop of the **Langeberge**, **Swellendam** is one of the oldest and most gracious of the southern Cape's many historical towns. Close to the town is the **Bontebok National Park**, home to several species of buck – including the vari-coloured bontebok – and a large, varied population of birds.

To the northeast of Swellendam the R324 takes one straight into the **Tradouw Pass** that crosses the Langeberge to **Barrydale**. From here, the R62 can be followed to scenic towns and villages that have been changed little by the beat of the 20th century.

Places like **Montagu, Bonnievale, Ashton** and **Robertson** have buildings and streets of historical and architectural interest. East of Barrydale lies the **Little Karoo** and towns like **Ladismith** and **Calitzdorp** which form the centre of the country's decidous fruit industry.

Mossel Bay: Driving eastwards along N2 the looming Outeniqua mountains and the coastline slowly begin to converge until, at Mossel (mussel) Bay, the road rejoins the coast.

Once a quiet fishing hamlet and holiday resort – exporting aloe juice and ochre – **Mossel Bay** is rapidly being transformed into a sprawling industrial town, following the discovery of natural gas and oil deposits off its coast.

But it was water – fresh drinking water – that brought the first Europeans ever to step on southern African soil to this scenic coastline. In 1488, Bartolomeu Dias, searching for a sea route to India around the southern tip of Africa, anchored here to replenish. The large milkwood trees that can still be seen along the shore were first put to use as **"post office" trees**. The first letter posted in South Africa is thought to be one left hanging from a tree in an old boot by Pedro d'Ataide in 1500. A section of the town's museum is devoted to the area's maritime history, and also contains an extensive seashell collection.

The hub of activity during the holiday season are the town's beaches, sandy pearls separated by rocky ridges. Munro's Bay, Santos Beach and Dias Strand are the places to go for sun-worshippers and swimmers, and the Point and Die Bakke for surfers.

George and Oudtshoorn: Outeniqua, the name given to the mountains dominating the area east of Mossel Bay, is derived from a local phrase meaning "man laden with honey". In a sense, this *is* the "land of milk and honey", for here the high peaks trap the moist sea air to bathe the surrounding countryside in year-round rainfall, ensuring that everything is always green and lush.

The town of **George** (originally Georgetown) was established at the foot of the **Outeniqua Mountains** in 1811. The novelist Anthony Trollope, visiting the area over a century ago, declared it "the prettiest village in the world". The rural charms, the quiet and stunning

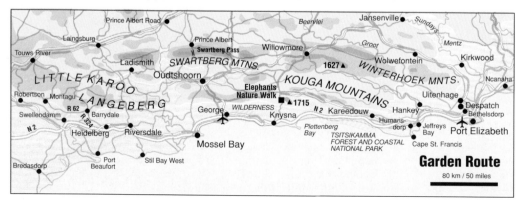

Garden Route

80 km / 50 miles

setting and the easy-going pace that so enraptured him has remained very much intact to charm modern tourists. Today this "land of milk and honey" is a major dairy-producing area, the source of most of the country's fresh vegetables as well as hops for the beer industry.

The town was named after King George III who reigned in England at the time of its founding. Then, it was essentially a timber-producing area where plots were granted to woodcutters on condition that they supplied timber for public buildings in town. Today it is the principal town on the Garden Route and a fine place to use as a base if some time is to be spent in the vicinity.

A walk through the old section of town provides a fascinating glimpse into the past – an imposing oak tree, under whose spreading boughs slaves were bought and sold, stands outside the library in York Street. Pieces of chain are still seen embedded in its trunk. At the top of York Street is the old drostdy, now the town museum. The first thing noticeable on entering the building is a cross-section of a giant, 1,220-year-old yellowwood tree.

A leisurely stroll around the town will reveal a combination of Cape Dutch architecture and the neo-classical European styles of the 18th and 19th centuries. Interesting churches that can be visited include the Dutch Reformed "Moederkerk"; the church of St Peter and St Paul, the country's oldest Catholic church; and the church of St Mark, the smallest Anglican cathedral in the country. On the outskirts of town is a small crocodile farm, where Nile crocodiles, the world's largest reptile species, are kept in a controlled environment.

Big bird-country: Although not strictly part of the Garden Route, two almost compulsory tourist stopovers are the **ostrich farms** of **Oudtshoorn**, and the nearby **Cango Caves**. The trip is a pleasant one, over the Outeniqua Pass and into the rain shadow of the Little Karoo – a generally arid valley relieved by flowing rivers and irrigated agriculture.

During the Victorian era Oudtshoorn was the centre of the ostrich-feather

Swellendam is the third oldest city in the country.

industry for the world's fashion markets. This generated vast riches – one kilogram of tail feathers could fetch up to R200. The revenue pouring into what was hitherto a small hamlet helped to build the "feather palaces" of the town, several of which have survived the decline in the market.

Today the ostrich industry still thrives, but the feathers are now used more for dusters than for the hats and boas of high fashion. But, while the feather market took a dip the skins of this wondrous bird have become part and parcel of the world of high fashion. Ostrich skins used in the manufacturing of expensive shoes, handbags and purses now command prices comparable to the highly prized skins of baby crocodiles.

Lunchtime at an ostrich farm means an opportunity to dine on an ostrich steak. Then the intrepid visitor can try his riding skills on the back of the world's largest bird or watch some "jockeys" spur on their mounts in the local "Ostrich Derby".

Ostrich-skin products – garments and accessories such as belts, bags and wallets – are very popular fashion and souvenir items. The massive hollow ostrich eggs (with a capacity equivalent to 24 hens' eggs) and feather dusters are also popular purchases. A rare treat is ostrich biltong, the spicy dried meat delicacy first prepared by the Voortrekker pioneers still savoured by all meat-eating South Africans.

In town one entire hall of the C. P. Nel Museum, is devoted to those heady days when ostrich feathers dusted the spirits of the community. Other exhibits include weapons, medals, and the history of local transport.

Wonderland: An even greater attraction is the Cango Caves, a series of vast underground dolomite caverns, transformed into a fairyland by huge and extensive stalactite and stalagmite formations. Their unique shapes resemble Gothic castles and grotesque creatures. The system of caves reaches deep into the Swartberg mountain range, but for safety and conservation reasons only a small part of it is open to the public. A

Oudtshoorn's ostrich farms...

local farmer, Soon van Zyl, is generally credited with first exploring the caves in 1780 while out hunting buck. But a rich find of stone tools and rock paintings suggested that early-Bushmen first dwelled in the cave opening, through which thousands of tourists now stream each month.

What can be seen at Cango is spectacularly impressive but is really only a minute section of an extensive cave system that extends under the Swartberg Mountains. There are at least four major chamber systems, of which only 800 yards of the 28 chambers comprising Cango One are accessible to the public. In 1972 Cango Two was discovered, followed by Cango Three in 1975, while Cango Four is presently being explored by speleologists. Gusts of wind flowing through the caves suggest a second, yet undiscovered entrance.

A second system of caves, closed to the public, has recently been found nearby and it is now thought to be even more extensive than Cango. However, exploring the caves is decidedly not a

...are a major tourist attraction.

pastime to be undertaken by novice adventurers, for even experienced cavers have been lost in those subterranean chambers.

Crossing the mountains: Lying at the hub of numerous mountain passes, George is an ideal place from which to undertake scenic drives. A circular trip up the **Montagu Pass**, or nearly parallel to it via the R29 over the **Outeniqua Pass** to Oudtshoorn and back, can be undertaken in a morning.

Once in Oudtshoorn, it is possible to carry on past the Cango Caves towards Prince Albert, taking one of the most beautiful of all mountain passes in South Africa, the **Swartberg Pass**. This is a gravel road, running over the mighty Swartberg range, with tight doublebacks leading down into the Great Karoo.

Alternative routes across the mountain can be taken along the **Seweweekspoort Pass** or by the main road (R29) through **Meiringspoort**.

A variation for the return trip from Outshoorn to George could be via **Robinson's Pass**. A luxuriant scenic

drive is the **Old Passes Road** from George to Knysna. It takes one along the original wagon road through the largest forest tracts in the country.

The lake district: The Old Passes route, spectacular as it is, should, however, not be considered seriously as an alternative to the major N2 route, for then one would miss one of the most scenic attractions in the region. Just outside George, across the chasmic Kaaimans River gorge, is the town of **Wilderness**.

Stretching from this mist-washed little holiday village all the way up the coast to the Goukamma Nature Reserve is the **Wilderness National Lake Area**, the first nationally proclaimed lake area in the country. Its wide open waterways, reed beds and marshes, as well as the fringing bush and forests, create a rich source of food and varied habitat for a wide array of birdlife. Most attractive are the large wading birds that scour the shallows for food; pockets of pink flamingos, drifting across the metallic water, straining the surface for tiny algae and crustaceans, and African spoon-

bills that rake the mud with their peculiar shaped bills. Of the 95 species of waterfowl recorded in South Africa, 75 can be seen bobbing on one of the lakes.

The charming coastal town of **Knysna** has long been the centre of South Africa's hardwood timber industry. Few would argue that Knysna, with its bounteous resources of tranquil lagoons, surrounding forests and mountain backdrop, its rugged coast and its historic villages, is one of the truly treasured gems of the Garden Route – and a haven for the visitor.

The town was founded by the enigmatic George Rex – once thought to be an illegitimate son of England's George III. It has the feel of a charming holiday village, and will reward strollers looking for interesting places. Among the historic buildings worth visiting are **Millwood House Museum**, which depicts the early history of Knysna.

The place to go to see and buy pottery and woven fabrics is Thesen House, a historic town building named after one of the town's influential families. The **British colonial influences left their mark.**

248

area is chiefly known for its natural wood products. This includes fine quality hardwood furniture manufactured by hand by master craftsmen, using yellowwood, dark stinkwood and ironwood judiciously culled from the surrounding forests.

No visit to Knysna is complete without a trip to **The Heads**. This pair of huge, orange sandstone cliffs flank a deep, potentially treacherous channel through which the sea pours to flood the Knysna Lagoon. The westernmost headland is a private nature reserve, called **Featherbed** and can be reached by a short ferry ride across the lagoon.

Between Knysna and George a steam train, the **Outeniqua Tjoe Choo**, runs on a narrow-gauge line, stopping at quaint country stations along the way. The line crosses the Knysna Lagoon, by girder bridges, before coming to its most dramatic section – weaving across the cliffs towering above Wilderness. Where the Kaaimans River cuts a deep gorge into the coastal cliffs, the railway line runs, suspended high above the waves

across a bridge fording the river mouth. A view site on the N2, above the river mouth, allows road travellers to admire this magnificent scene.

Forest giants: The surrounding rainforest was once but a small part of a vast coastal forest stretching from Swellendam in the west to as far east as Humansdorp. But it was largely destroyed by a series of fires, culminating in a massive blaze in 1856. Injudicious cutting during the 19th century further denuded the area. Today, the entire forest biome is under conservation management.

Walking through forest areas such as **Diepwalle** or at the Storms River Mouth one encounters a rich variety of lower plant forms thriving on the decay of the damp forests. This includes plants like dripping ferns as well as an abundance of sponge-like mosses, fungi, algae, lichens and liverworts. To gain fine views of the forests, the Passes Road can be taken to the **King Edward VII "big tree"** – one of a few giant yellowwoods that was spared by woodcutters of old.

A short turn-off to **Millwood** will

Angling for dinner.

take you even deeper into the forests, to a ghost town dating from the short-lived gold rush in the area over a century ago. Where once banks and houses, bars and brothels plied there busy trade, the giants of the forest – stinkwood, yellowwood, bastard saffron, and beechwood – have reclaimed their original habitat.

Of the herds of elephants that once roamed these murky sylvan ways, only five great pachyderms – called "bigfoot" – remain as a reminder of man's greed. A trip along the sinuous **Prince Alfred's Pass** brings one to the Diepwalle State Forest and its picturesque **Elephant Nature Walk**. This area has been the subject of some of the country's best-known literary works, notably *Fiela's Child* and *Circles in the Forest*, written by the renowned authoress, Dalene Matthee, and translated into several other languages.

About 19 miles (30 km) from Knysna, towards Plettenberg Bay, are the **Kranshoek** and **Harkerville forests**, ideal places for nature walks or picnics and swimming in the natural rivers.

Plettenberg Bay and Tsitsikamma: Historians often point out that Plettenberg Bay and not Cape Town was in fact the site of South Africa's first European occupation – survivors of the shipwrecked *Harlem* stayed here for about eight months in 1630. Today "Plett" is one of the country's most exclusive holiday resorts. But even the ostentatious, often gaudy new homes of wealthy up-country holidaymakers can't entirely detract from the natural beauty of the resort.

Every natural element here seems to achieve its most sublime form, whether it is the golden crescents of sand, the river mouths, the foaming surf or the wild, rocky shores. There are nature walks aplenty here, but for those who prefer to spend the day in bed and only come alive after sunset, Plett's nightlife – particularly in the holiday season – centres on the Beacon Isle Hotel, the rocky island berth which was once the site of a whaling station.

The **Robberg** (seal mountain) peninsula is a wild, windswept nature re-

Manicured lawns and churning seas.

serve. Although the massive colonies of seal that once converged there have been all but depleted, a few have survived, and the richness of the birdlife, intertidal life and coastal vegetation goes some way towards making up for the absence of these velvety creatures. On the Robberg, where it forms a distinctive saddle, a large cave overlooks a cove on the western side.

The floor of the cave and the approaching slope are littered with deep shell deposits that have puzzled experts for ages. The shell deposits are called middens, and they once provide subsistence to the groups of "Strandlopers" (or beachcombers) who lived along the the Cape coast at the time of the first white settlement at the Cape. The legacy of this nomadic Khoi-group is to this day preserved in the nomenclature encountered along the route – Outeniqua, Tsitsikamma, Kareedouw, Karatara, Goukamma and Knysna.

From Plettenberg Bay one can take either the N2 toll road that cuts a fairly straight path through forests and across the high coastal plain, or the meandering byway (R102) that winds downwards past the Grootrivier and Bloukrans gorges, and through the secretive **Nature's Valley**. The single span arch concrete bridges over the Storms-, Groot- and Bloukrans- rivers had the distinction, at their respective times of completion, of being the biggest such structures in the world.

Those who take the backroad through Coldstream will be rewarded by the experience of sinking deep down into the forest's cool microclimate, where monkeys clamber about in the branches; vividly coloured loerie birds dart through the canopy, and shy duiker and bushbuck creep through the undergrowth.

Both options bring one to the turn-off to **Storms River Mouth**, with its forests and unspoilt, rocky shore, its log cabins and suspension bridge, and the **Tsitsikamma National Park**, which includes the first marine national park in Africa.

Hiking trails: The extensive countrywide hiking system with its numerous trails scattered throughout the land con-

verges in the Southern Cape. Here exciting choices for multi-day hikes can be made – either the strenuous, eight-day trail through the Outeniqua Mountains, the five-day **Tsisikamma Trail**, or a three-day hike through the Harkerville forests and along its rocky coastline. But by far the most popular trail in South Africa is the five-day **Otter Trail**, that begins at Storms River Mouth and follows the rugged coastline to Nature's Valley. For the more casual walker there are a plethora of nature walks to choose from such as the **Kingfisher Hiking Trail**, a circular nature walk on the Touws River, as well as numerous short and long walks at Storms River Mouth.

Sunswept beaches: Its unique combination of beaches, rivers and lakes makes the Garden Route an obvious venue for a multiplicity of water sports. Angling is considered to be the most popular outdoor recreation in South Africa and in this area fish are found in abundance. Mossel Bay is the heartland for powerboating and deep-sea angling. Sea

Landing a big fish.

EXPLORING THE COAST

South Africa's spectacular 2,500-mile (4,000-km) coastline is dominated by sandy beaches broken by estuaries and rocky shores. It has a great variety of landforms and climate and is uniquely exposed to wave energy.

Bathed by the warm Agulhas current on the east coast and the cool upwelling waters of the Benguela system on the west, its shores embrace three biological provinces: subtropical, temperate and warm temperate. Spanning the south coast, the warm temperate region along the scenic "Garden Route" has the greatest proportion of endemic marine invertebrate species.

The golden-white beaches harbour abundant fauna attracted by the rich blooms of microscopic plants in the surf zones. Sand mussels, feeding on these diatoms, are widely collected for bait and often serve as a tasty delicacy for the more adventurous connoisseur. The mussels are certainly worth sampling, baked on the coals or fried. The upper shore above the driftline may harbour

sand hoppers or ghost crabs in warm areas. Whelks and swimming crabs can easily be enticed to the surface by dragging bait along the sand.

A rich variety of shore birds frequent the sandy beaches. These include resident back oystercatchers, sand-plovers and kelp gulls, as well as European migrants such as sanderlings and some terns. Many species of fish are found in surf zones; smaller forms use them as nursery areas and sand-sharks, skates and rays feed on the sand mussels.

Rocky shores are prominent features of the Cape south coast. Many large molluscs, including limpets, turban shells and abalones can be found. Rock pools also provide shelter for octopus, cuttle-fish, urchins, anemonies, shore crabs, chitons, snails, mussels and oysters. The nutrient rich waters of the west coast support extensive beds of kelp.

South Africa has limited fresh water inputs, so estuaries are small. Many are open to the sea only seasonally, and several have had their fresh water inflow reduced by new dams. Despite this, the country has numerous small but scenic estuaries. Prominent features are salt marshes on the south coast and mangrove swamps further eastwards. The fauna of the sand and mud flats of estuaries is dominated by burrowing prawns. Crabs are common in the salt marshes and numerous fish utilise the estuaries as feeding grounds and nursery areas. Amongst these, mullet and whitebait are the most typical.

A wide variety of shells wash up on South African shores. The most famous spot to collect these shells is in the shallow rock pools and on the beaches of Jeffreys Bay. These beaches accumulate a variety of shells, from intricately patterned cones and cowries to littorinids, nerites, key-hole limpets, venus shells and even the rare pansy shells.

The biggest array of intertidal habitats is along the eastern segment of the "Garden Route". The area around Port Elizabeth includes outstanding beaches, as well as the beaches of Jeffreys and St Francis Bays. To the west, the magnificent cliffs of the Tsitsikamma National Park frame a narrow stretch of rocky coast rich in intertidal life.

Further west, the shores of the Knysna lagoon support typical estuarine fauna and a variety of bird-life. Short boat trips or overnight cruises are available. ∎

cruises can be taken from the harbour which stop off at historic spots along the coast and then head out to Seal Island.

But most ordinary holidaymakers are content with merely swimming or lazing about in the sun. For this, the list of places to go to is endless and most local experts will differ: around Mossel Bay the best spots are **Munro's Bay** and **Santos Beach**, **Hartenbos**, the **Little** and **Great Brak** rivers, **Herold's** and **Victoria Bays**. From Wilderness to Knysna the only really safe spot to swim in the sea is **Walker Point** at Buffelsbaai and at **Brenton-on-Sea**. But the entire lakes area and the shallows of **Knysna Lagoon** are all safe.

Practically the entire 4-mile (7-km) "golden arc" of Plettenberg Bay is a swimmer's paradise with wide beaches and secluded coves, rolling breakers and calm bays. Once past Storms River Mouth, the beaches get even better. Next to "Plett", **St Francis Bay** has perhaps the finest and most unspoilt bathing and tanning area in South Africa.

Canoeing is most popular on the Great Brak River, on any of the lakes, and up the Knysna River while board sailing is usually done on Swartvlei, the largest of the Wilderness lakes. A diving training centre at Santos Beach provides scuba equipment and lessons on this most rewarding of pastimes, while at the Storms River Mouth snorkel and scuba enthusiasts can proceed along an underwater trail.

Off the Beacon Isle Hotel there is a reef conserved for diving only, resulting in the marine life becoming used to man's intrusion, often venturing close to the divers. Other diving spots, such as the one off Whale Rock, are for very experienced divers only.

The surfing spots of the southern Cape have become renowned throughout the world and a number of international competitions take place here annually. Lookout Beach at "Plett" and the Keurbooms and Robberg beaches are perhaps the most popular, but local fanatics will argue that the breakers at "Vic Bay" are the best.

The beautiful Garden Route finally

The Cango Caves are well-known for their acoustics.

reaches its end at the picturesque town of Humansdorp. From here roads lead to the the small and mostly private resorts on St Francis Bay, and to **Jeffreys Bay**, legendary among the world's surfing community but to non-surfers a fairly unremarkable place.

Other places of interest in the area include **Van Staden's Wild Flower Reserve and Bird Sanctuary**, the **Seaview Game Park and Animal Shelter** and the **Island State Forest Reserve** which also offers visitors one-day nature walks.

Port Elizabeth: "P.E.", as it is known among locals, developed from a small military outpost to guard the first British settlers arriving in the area in 1820, to its present status as one of the country' premier harbours. The then governor at the Cape, Sir Rufane Donkin, named it after his wife, Elizabeth.

Like the area leading up to it, P.E. is known for its long, hot summer days, golden beaches and balmy tropical nights. The oceanfront is bordered by a miniature railway, and children's play-ground. The museum complex landward of **Humewood Beach** is unique in the country in that it embraces both natural and cultural history exhibits.

The **Snake Park** has become famous for its more than 1,000 snakes and the performing dolphins at the **oceanarium** are firm favourites with visiting crowds. In the **Donkin Reserve** is an old lighthouse and museum featuring the shipping history of the city and port.

Port Elizabeth has in recent years developed into a major tourist destination. For the latest "in-places" for dinner and dancing ask the hotel porter or the Publicity Association.

Places to stay: Accommodation along the Garden Route ranges from campsites and bungalows, with a variety of low to medium-cost hotels, motels and guest houses in between. There are good hotels in George, Wilderness, Knysna, Plettenberg Bay and Port Elizabeth, with more modest accommodation at virtually every small settlement along the coast and at mountain resorts. The most interesting of these hotels is undoubtedly the Beacon Isle Hotel, standing like a gigantic mollusc on an island rock, in the embrace of Plettenberg Bay's long sweep of golden beach.

Parks Board camps at Storms River Mouth and on the Longvlei offer simple but attractive cottages and camping facilities. A very new hotel development in George is the Fancourt, the last word in modern sophistication and old-world charm. The hotel is named after Henry Fancourt White, who engineered the Montagu Pass. It is an outdoorsman's paradise with individual chalets, a world-class golf course, trout fishing facilities, horse riding and walking options.

With its temperate climate and year-round rainfall, only the mid-winter months of June and July tend to be cold and gloomy. Summer, here stretching from September through April, is a blissful time along the Garden Route. Since this area is one of the country's favourite holiday spots, it may be advisable to avoid visiting during the local school holidays – usually from early December to mid-January, and from late March through Easter.

Left, Port Elizabeth. **Right**, the Donkin Museum and lighthouse.

254

THE EASTERN CAPE AND THE WILD COAST

The Eastern Cape is frontier country. It was here that white settlers, in their ever-expanding quest for grazing land, made contact with large black communities for the first time. Eight frontier wars were waged over a period of nearly a century, ending in 1857 with whole communities either decimated or plunged into untold hardship.

It was to the border area that in 1820 an intrepid group of former British soldiers, who had fought in the Crimean war, were despatched to start a new life as settlers. It was a strange, unexplored and often dangerous country. They largely tamed the Eastern Cape, carving out a livelihood on farms and establishing small towns and hamlets that have survived to this day. They made an indelible impression on South African social and economic history, leaving a legacy that stretches from a commitment to press freedom to a system of jurisprudence; from literature and the arts to the establishment of a thriving wool industry.

And it is here that the cradle of latter-day black nationalism is also found. Major political organisations such as the African National Congress, the Pan-Africanist Congress and the Black Consciousness Movement took root here, and the region's widespread labour unrest in the late 1970s forced the white government to make major reforms.

The social turbulence that characterised the region echoes its natural history. The Eastern Cape is an ecological battleground, where an ever-changing pattern of vegetation is determined by a variable and capricious rainfall cycle. An area where savannah bushveld and thornveld alternate with lush grasslands; where the arid Karoo scrubland ebbs and flows like a floral tide across the plains and the Afro-montane forests and heathlands advance and retreat accordingly. Following a few rainy seasons, it can resemble a lush English countryside; but if extended periods of drought occur, they can turn the region into an extension of the arid Karoo interior.

Port Elizabeth to Grahamstown: On leaving the port city of Port Elizabeth in an easterly direction, the R335 leads the visitor to the **Addo Elephant Park**. In the period after World War I, the fledgling farming community at Addo was plagued by roaming elephant herds raiding croplands and then retreating to a safe sanctuary in the dense surrounding bush. The government was asked for assistance and the "last of the great white hunters", Major P. J. Pretorius, was despatched to relieve their plight. Within a year Pretorius hunted down 120 of the majestic beasts. Only 16 remained, many scarred by bullets, vengeful and cunning. They declared war on man and anyone who dared to enter Addo did so at his own peril.

This "hunter's hell", as the famous huntsman dubbed it, was declared a national park in 1931 to preserve its few remaining elephants. Today the population has grown to about 140 and is often seen from the road or at various watering-holes scattered around the 20,000-

Preceding pages: the Paddle-ski Race. Left, cliff-hanger on the Wild Coast. Right, Addo Elephant National Park.

acre (8,000-hectare) reserve. However, visitors are still cautioned not to try and feed the giants of the bush – in particular, not to bring any citrus fruit into the park, the scent of which is likely to stir the elephants into a frenzy. There is also a camp in the reserve offering excellent accommodation and meals.

Grahamstown, the centre of the border area, was established as a fortified military outpost to protect the British settlers. It was from here that the settlers spread their influence throughout the region and eventually into the rest of South Africa. On the historic fort on **Gunfire Hill**, an imposing monument marks this contribution. Today it is of-

ten referred to as "the City of Saints" because of the 40 churches from different denominations within its borders.

An observant visitor can spend many enjoyable hours in this charming town. Some important sights include the **1820 Settler Cultural History Museum** and the adjacent Albany museum of natural history; Grocott's Building in High Street, where the country's oldest surviving newspaper is published, and the renovated Observatory Museum, with its camera obscura, in Bathurst Street.

Dominating the centre of the town is the imposing Anglican **Cathedral of St Michael and St George**, used as an ammunition depot and a shelter for

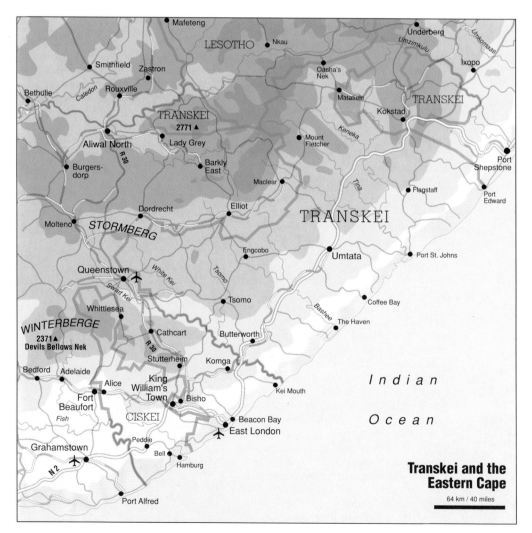

Transkei and the Eastern Cape

64 km / 40 miles

women and children during the frontier wars. The trading store owned by the famous Voortrekker leader, Piet Retief, has been restored and merits a visit for a glimpse into frontier life. Anyone interested in nature should enjoy a visit to the Wild Flower Garden in the Thomas Baines Nature Reserve or a drive into Andries Vosloo Kudu Reserve.

Each year in June the **Grahamstown Arts Festival**, a significant event on the South African arts calender, celebrates the wealth of artistic talent the country has produced. For one week, the normally sleepy town becomes a giant bustling stage with drama productions, music and dance performances, poetry reading and impromptu street shows taking place almost round the clock. Grahamstown is also renowned as a centre of learning, not least for **Rhodes University**, founded by the famous industrialist, Cecil John Rhodes. Its buildings were designed by the British Empire's most notable architect, Sir Herbert Baker at the turn of the century. The gateway to the old Grahamstown drostdy or magistrate's house now forms the entrance to the University.

South of Grahamstown a round-trip leads to Bathurst, Port Alfred and Salem. **Bathurst** is the centre of a prosperous agricultural region known for its pineapple crops. A recommended stopover is the Pig and Whistle Inn, a famous watering-hole. On a more sublime level, there is St John's Church, used as a refuge during the frontier wars and to-day the oldest unaltered Anglican church in South Africa.

Further on, at the mouth of the Kowie River, is the popular holiday spot of **Port Alfred** – or "Kowie" as it is called by the locals. Originally established by the settlers as a harbour, this tranquil town is popular with bathers, anglers, surfers and beachcombers. There are a few hotels of different categories as well as self-catering accommodation and camping facilities available. The marina is worth seeing. The luxurious Fishriver Sun Resort which has an excellent golf course and two hotels, is also within easy reach. The Kowie Canoe/Hiking

An unusual specimen: the devil fire fish.

Trail, the only self-guided combination trail of its kind in the country, starts here and takes one through a fascinating area of wetlands and low forest. Nearby is the well-preserved settlers' town of **Salem** where some of the descendants of the 1820 group still live.

The border region: To the east of Grahamstown lies the border area. In 1837 a group of German soldiers led by Baron Richard von Stutterheim, having aided the British during the sixth frontier war, disbanded and settled here, adding to the already cosmopolitan mix of the region. The names of hamlets, such as Berlin, Hamburg, Braunschweig, Potsdam and Stutterheim, reflect the influence of these new arrivals.

About 43 miles (70 km) east of Grahamstown the N2 crosses the **Great Fish River** which for many decades in the 19th century formed the border between the Cape Colony and Xhosa territory. The Great Fish was the scene – and most often the cause – of eight frontier wars that were fought in this area between 1781 and 1877. Three hills in the region have been named after prominent Xhosa leaders who fought against the colonial troops – **Makana's Kop**, for the man who led a full-frontal but futile assault on Grahamstown (1819); **Gaika's Kop** after the Xhosas' most celebrated chief, and **Sandile's Kop** to remember the most turbulent reign of the period (1840–77) which finally led to the defeat of the Xhosas.

The Great Fish River was formerly the border between South Africa and the independent state of the **Ciskei**, with its capital at **Bisho**. On its coastline, off the mouth of the Chalumna River, the world's first coelacanth was netted in 1938. Thought to be extinct for 80 million years, it was one of the scientific world's most notable discoveries. The amazing primitive fish, with fins resembling stumpy legs, was mounted and can be seen in the East London museum.

King William's Town ("King", as it is known to residents) is also steeped in settler history. This was the capital of the colony of British Kaffraria. A stopover should include visits to the South

Father, sun and daughter.

262

African Missionary Museum, Grey Hospital, and the King Nature Reserve. The **Kaffrarian Museum** has a section devoted to the early German settlers and a natural history section where the stuffed body of Huberta the hippo can be seen. Huberta captured the country's imagination in 1928 when she took off from Zululand on a 1,200-mile (2,000-km) journey southwards. On her way, she became the most feted hippo in history, pursued by photographers, journalists and adoring crowds. She popped up in cities and towns, wandering through the busy streets of Durban and gatecrashing plush parties. Finally, three years later, she was shot by hunters while bathing in the Keiskamma River. Her remains were recovered and today take pride of place in the King Museum.

To the north of King William's Town is the R30, which leads through the eastern reaches of the Karoo via Queenstown and Aliwal north to Bloemfontein.

To the west of King William's Town lies the town of **Alice**, named after the daughter of Queen Victoria. On the outskirts of the town is the **University of Fort Hare**, established in 1916 as the country's first tertiary educational institute for blacks. It attracts students from all over Africa and among its alumni are some of the continent's most influential political and intellectual leaders.

From Alice, a number of scenic drives can be undertaken into the **Amatola Mountains**. The Katberg escarpment is the highest point on the range and in winter its peaks are often capped with snow. But it is **Hogsback** that makes the Amatolas really memorable. Here, ferns and long strands of lichen cling to the trunks of ancient yellowwoods; brambles, wild berries and vines clamber over the forest flora tangle of flowers blooming beneath them; coloured fungi and soft carpets of moss coat the rocks and tree trunks along the streams.

It was in these spellbinding woods that the young J. R. R. Tolkien went exploring in his early boyhood. The landscape fired his imagination with the elfin kings, dwarf lords and dragons that were later to populate Middle Earth

Transkei coastline.

kingdom in *The Lord of the Rings*. When exploring the area, don't stick to the main road – Hogsback State Forest, Auckland Nature Reserve and the adjoining Zingcuka Forest in Ciskei offer some unforgettable day excursions.

A large number of nature walks and hiking trails can be undertaken in and around the Hogsback area, most notably the six-day Amatola Trail and visits to the Thirty-Nine Steps or the Madonna and Child waterfalls. Hogsback is a delightful place to visit all year round but it is at its most magical in winter, when frost and snow crackle underfoot and log fires warm the inns.

From King William's Town, the N2 leads to **East London**. Situated at the mouth of the Buffalo River, it is the largest city in the region and the only large river-port in the country. It is bordered by the sprawling dusty townships of **Mdantsane** and **Zwelithsa**, South Africa's second and third largest black residential areas. East London provides an array of leisure activities, the majority related to the ocean. The two most popular bathing spots in the area are Orient and Eastern beaches, both suitable for children, while Nahoon beach is considered an excellent surfing spot.

The **Urban Trail** takes visitors on a well-documented walk through the streets, stopping at various places of historical and natural interest: the City Hall; Gately House, a gracious national monument in the Victorian style; the Ann Bryant Art Gallery; the zoo on the banks of the Buffalo River; and the museum, where not only the coelacanth but also the world's only remaining egg of the extinct dodo-bird can be seen. Nature-lovers can visit the Amalinda Fisheries Station and the Bridle Drift or Fort Pato nature reserves.

A number of small coastal resorts have been established. between East London and the Transkei border at the Kei River mouth. Some, like Cintsa, Cefane and Double Mouth, are frequented mainly by local farmers, while Haga-Haga and Morgan Bay have grown into sizeable resorts with small hotels and holiday homes. Their common fac-

Mobile TB scanning unit; canning meat.

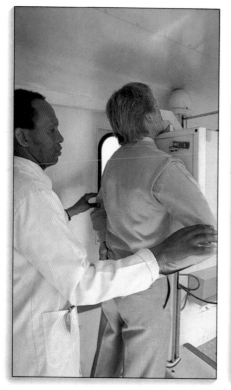

tors are their small size and situation off the highways. The locals like it this way: it frees some of the pristine lagoons, sun-drenched beaches, and abundant birdlife and fishing resources for their personal enjoyment.

Visitors who enjoy a strenuous hike can take the 58-mile (93-km) **Strandloper Trail** which meanders past these villages. Accommodation is mostly in the small resort hotels, well patronised by local fishermen, but hikers are free to camp anywhere along the coast.

Travelling northeastwards, one soon reaches the border of the **Transkei**. This area, together with the neighbouring Ciskei, was created as Xhosa homelands under the government's apartheid policy. In the late 1970s both were granted "independence" with their own capitals, national symbols and borders. However, this nominal independence was recognised only by South Africa, the rest of the world considering the territories integral parts of South Africa, which indeed, they are again since the end of the apartheid state in 1994.

The barbecue is known as braaivleis.

The Xhosas: The Xhosa clans that inhabit the Ciskei and Transkei are offshoots of the greater Nguni tribe. In the early 17th century, these clans moved southwards from Zululand with their stock. Here they intermingled with and eventually incorporated the indigenous Khoisan. Today, only the heavy click sounds of the Xhosa dialect is evidence of this Khoisan heritage.

One Xhosa (the *xh* is pronounced with a loud click of the tongue) custom that is still very much in evidence, is that of the *Abekwetha*. According to tribal custom, "a boy is merely a dog" and to attain manhood he must undergo a circumcision and initiation ceremony lasting two to three weeks. Teenage boys are taken to secluded areas where they are tutored by elders and circumcised.

They live in spartan conditions in grass huts until their wounds have healed. Returning to their villages, they daub their bodies and faces with white paint, wear grass skirts and face masks as disguises, and show off their skills in dances. To mark the end of the intitiation

period, the youths cleanse themselves in a river, and all their old possessions are burned. Finally they are presented with a new set of clothes in which they step forth into the world of men.

The rural areas of the Transkei and Ciskei are fascinating. The rolling grass hills are dotted with traditional mud and grass huts; women walk around with ochre-painted faces, smoking long-stemmed pipes; old men and children urge on teams of oxen to plough the hillside fields. Here the traditional way of life exists side by side with the trappings of modern civilisation such as cars, tractors, modern health clinics, commuter buses and transistor radios.

One seminal event of Xhosa history is the story of a self-proclaimed prophet-ess, Nongqawuse, who predicted how her people would rise against the British colonisers. The girl claimed to have seen a vision in a languid pool on the Gwara River of how the Xhosa dead would, on a certain day in 1857, rise up to drive the whites back into the sea from which they came. But to achieve this liberation they had first to offer an act of sacrifice – to kill all their cattle and burn their crops. Later, the prophet promised, their cattle and grain would return in abundant quantities.

On the appointed day, the sun rose to scenes of slaughter and waste, but nothing came of the prophecy. With all the food and wealth destroyed mass starvation ensued; tens of thousands of people died and the countryside was virtually laid bare. Nongqawuse was later arrested near Bashee, imprisoned on Robben Island, and then exiled to the Eastern Cape, where she died in 1898.

Southern Wild Coast: The southern coastal area of Transkei is relatively sparsely populated, and the resorts tend to be smaller and more intimate than those to the north. This area is a surf fisherman's paradise and hotels are geared to cater to their requirements. For seafood-lovers this is the area to visit, since fresh linefish and other marine delicacies are the staples on local menus. Often, the resorts consist of little more than a small hotel or bungalow

The untamed Wild Coast...

complex, and perhaps a few scattered fishermen's cottages surrounded by miles and miles of untamed Africa.

The first town encountered across the Transkei border is **Butterworth**, a market and industrial centre also serving as a tourist's gateway to the southern coastal resorts such as Qolora Mouth; Nxaxo Mouth with its mangrove swamps on a lovely lagoon and Ihem island situated at the confluence of the Naxao and Ngqusi Rivers.

Across the winding Cat's Pass are a number of charming resorts. **Mazeppa Bay** has groves of wild date palms on pure white beaches. **Qora Mouth** is just 4 miles (6 km) away on foot but 60 miles (100 km) by car via a looping, inland drive, and is renowned for its fishing and the homely Kob Inn resort.

On the N2 between the dusty town of Idutywa and Umtata, several turn-offs to the coast can be taken. Highly recommended is the one to **Coffee Bay**. However, before reaching the turn-off, one of the most enchanting spots on the southern African coastline can be ob-

…is a paradise for hikers.

served from up close: **Hole-in-the-Wall**. The entire area surrounding "holy-in-hol" (as the local children refer to it) is one of the most appealing natural features of the Wild Coast. It is a wave and river-bored tunnel through a large whaleback island lying in the inter-tidal zone directly in front of the Mpako River mouth.

Early Portuguese navigators called the dolerite chunk the Penido das Fontes, or "rock of fountains" for the way the surf thunders through the 65-ft (20-metre) portal and crashes up against the island's lofty cliffs. In Xhosa it is *esi-Khaleni* or the "place of sound" – for reasons obvious to anyone that has stood on the cobbled beach and listened to the booming echo funnelling through the hole. But vistors should be forewarned: these cliffs and the surrounding pounding seas are treacherous and many lives have been lost by the foolhardy.

Coffee Bay, the principal resort in the south, provides a measure of comfort. There are two hotels and a well-run camp-site, safe swimming, good surf-

ing, a windswept golf course, and boating of various kinds and, a rarity in this area, a well-stocked shop.

Shipwrecks: The Transkei coast is perhaps better known as the Wild Coast. But it was not the natural spectacles of dramatic sea cliffs and cathedral rock formations, nor its wave-pounded rocky points and desolate beaches that gave rise to this description. It was given by survivors of a number of shipwrecks – most notably the *Grosvenor*, but also the Portuguese vessels *Sao Jaoa* (1552) and *São Bento* (1554).

But it is the fascinating story of courage and intrigue surrounding the wrecking of the *Grosvenor* that has captured the imagination of fortune-seekers and romantics alike. The fully-laden treasure ship came to grief on a stormy night in 1782 off the Pondoland coast. The only hope for the 150 survivors was to set out on foot for Cape Town, 930 miles (1,500 km) away. After an arduous journey lasting several months, just 13 stragglers reached the port at Table Bay. Most of the shipwreck's survivors

died along the way, while others are believed to have joined black clans.

Among the survivors were two Scottish sisters named Campbell, who became the wives of a tribal chief in the south. A century later, a 5,000-strong Xhosa army faced the British garrison at Butterworth, during the ninth and final frontier war. Among the leaders of the Xhosa warriors was the young chief, Kreli, and among the senior British officers was a General Campbell. What the two men engaged in combat never realised was that they were distant cousins. Kreli was a descendent of one of the two Scottish sisters, who were relatives of the British officer.

About the same time, renewed interest in the wreck was sparked off by rumours that the cargo included the glorious Peacock Throne looted from the kings of Persia. In 1882 about 150 gold coins were recovered from Lambasi Bay, also known as Port Grosvenor. This led to a frantic flurry of activity to recover the "treasure". Spiritualists were employed, as were steam cranes, float-

The Cathedral Rocks; a web of intrigue.

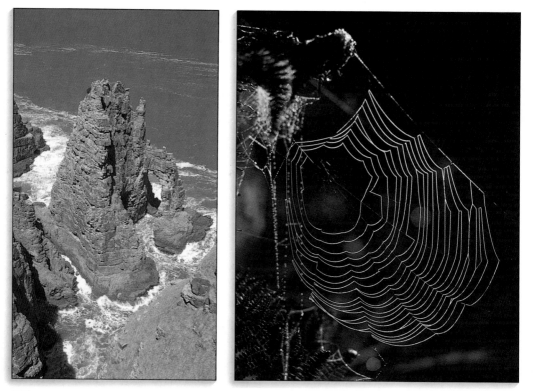

ing jetties and dredgers. There were bids to dig an undersea tunnel. All came to naught in the restless Wild Coast sea.

Many would-be salvagers lost their own fortunes in futile endeavours in "Grosvenor Gully". Ironically, apart from eight cannons salvaged in 1952, the richest haul taken from the ship was its iron ballast, recovered by the ship's blacksmith, who chose to remain on the coast and settle down in the area with two Mpondo wives.

Northern Wild Coast: The ultra-modern buildings of the University of the Transkei are a landmark at the southern entrance to the capital, **Umtata**. Established in 1882 on the banks of the Mtata River, the town seems to be in a continual state of development and disorder.

Umtata has plenty for the visitor to do, from a casino to an 18-hole golf course, a bowling green, the Izandla Pottery School, the Nduli Game Reserve, the Luchaba Nature Reserve, and boat rides on the Umtata Dam.

To the north of Umtata, the road cuts a diagonal line down into the wide and fertile **Mgazi River valley**. About 12 miles (20 km) further down the valley, where young boys craft extraordinarily accurate clay models of the motor-cars that pass, there is a turnoff to the **Mgazi resort** on the river mouth. This is another holiday resort with small cottages and chalets. Its hotel is well-known for its sumptuous seafood cuisine and the outdoor activities it arranges, including boat trips and hikes to the mangrove swamps at Mngazana where a "penny ferry" rowboat takes one across the river or to **Port St John's**.

Here the the twin promontories of Mount Sullivan and Mount Thessinger skirt the captivating harbour settlement. The mighty **Mzimvubu**, the only navigable river on the Wild Coast, has carved a most impressive portal for itself to the sea. Once a thriving colonial-type town, it saw an exodus of its white population after Transkei independence. Today the town survives in almost somnambulent idleness and indifference. Much of its present charm is to be found in its state of semi-decay – the grand old houses

Mangrove swamps are a typical Wild Coast feature.

having been abandoned or taken over by new tenants.

North of Port St John's, the coastline becomes very dramatic: high cliffs and rock formations have eroded into weird structures such as the **Cathedral Rocks**, and waterfalls plunge hundreds of feet into the angry breakers below. Few places here are easily accessible, but **Port Grosvenor** is an exception.

One place well worth exploring is **Mkambathi Nature Reserve**, north of **Flagstaff**, created on the site of an old leper colony. The reserve offers some of the best scenery the Wild Coast has to offer, all within a relatively small and walkable area. There are two fine estuaries for canoeing; rare species of palm tree growing in a ravine amphitheatre; long stretches of rocky beach; and accommodation in comfortable bungalows beneath tall shady trees, or in self-catering rondavels right on the sea shore.

A final stopover on the Wild Coast is **Mzamba**, a golden beach just south of the Mtamvuna River's impressive ravine-like mouth. The hotel and casino

here is called the Wild Coast Sun, a ultra-modern and very sophisticated resort representing "First World South Africa" rather than traditional life. The complex is a favourite weekend funspot for Durbanites, who come to gamble away their hard-earned money by night and to soak up the sun's rays by day.

The resort makes the most of its location between untamed river and frolicking surf, and many water sports are available. Upriver, a nature reserve offers scenic attractions such as the river gorge itself, an informal bird sanctuary with a large breeding colony of Cape vultures. The well-kept golf course – one of the best in southern Africa – provides both challenging shots over wide gorges and ravines and breathtaking views of the countryside.

Hiking trails: The rugged and lonely Wild Coast is ideally suited for experienced hikers who prefer to forge their way through flooded river mouths, across deep, forested ravines, and over high coastal cliffs. An informal hiking trail can be followed from the Mtamvuna River in the north, all the way to the Kei River in the south. Huts with only very basic facilities are provided at convenient daily walking distances along the coast, but hikers have the option of staying overnight in the resort and nature reserves along the way.

The 170-mile (280-km) trail is divided into five sections, each comprising three to six days of hiking. Walking steadily, hikers can cover the trail in about 25 days, but most people opt for a sub-section. Choosing which is hard because each section has unique charms: the northern part has the most dramatic scenery, but is also the most rugged and difficult; the central sections provide something of everything; the southern sections are milder in all respects.

Hikers should remember to carry ample supplies of fresh drinking water and to be on the lookout for thieves and beggars. If you're careful, it can be an experience of a lifetime. Bookings can be made through the Transkei Department of Agriculture and Forestry, Nature Conservation Section, Private bag X5002, Umtata, Transkei.

Left, Xhosa dwellings. **Right**, Xhosa women enjoy a good smoke.

THE KAROO AND THE NORTHERN CAPE

The Khoikhoi hunter-gatherers who roamed its vast expanse in search of game and water-holes called it **Karoo** – the thirsty land. For most visitors – and even for South Africans – the area comprising two-thirds of the country's total land surface is a "natural obstacle" one has to overcome en route to the lush green paradise of Cape Town or the bustling Witwatersrand metropolis.

In that sense it is almost unavoidable. But it is much more than a "necessary evil". For those who make the effort to explore the Karoo and the northern Cape, it can be a rewarding experience.

The origins of the Karoo system are still a mystery. What is known, is that 200–300 million years ago, layer upon layer of sediment were deposited in vast quantities. As the climate warmed the area was invaded by an ocean, trapping the remains of a temperate forest vegetation, thus creating the significant deposits of coal now being mined in the northern part of the system.

The entire sequence was capped by a massive volcanic outpouring of basalt lava 130 million years ago. The softer sandstone layers underneath gradually eroded while the hard volcanic dolorite remained, creating the characteristic flat-topped hills ("koppies") that punctuate the open plains of the Karoo.

It is ironic that what was once a gigantic freshwater swamp ruled by dinosaurs is today drought-stricken, almost devoid of surface water. The rainfall is unpredictable. When it does rain, it comes in short thunderstorms, often causing destruction and erosion as the water cascades into normally dry water-beds. But the spaciousness and solitude of the Karoo also accounts for its appeal. At dusk the sun departs in a symphony of bright orange and red colours. At night the cool, clear air tempts one outside to gaze at the brilliant stars of the Southern Hemisphere.

It is through this tantalising landscape that the country's major highway, the N1, winds its way after crossing the Hex River Mountains at De Doorns. The central Karoo can also be reached via the R29 or R57 from George and Oudtshoorn or from the eastern Cape along the R32 from Port Elizabeth. The Cape west coast and Namaqualand is best explored along the N7, the major route north, that connects Cape Town with the Orange River and Namibia.

The **Hex River Mountains** form a natural barrier between the western Cape and the rest of the country. One way to enjoy the beauty of the area is from the luxurious comfort of the Blue Train as it winds its way upwards for almost 15 miles (25 km) along a steep gradient. The renowned Blue Train travels two to three times a week in 24 hours between Pretoria and Cape Town, via Johannesburg, Kimberley and Matjesfontein. The railway pass is one of the most beautiful in the world and a major feat of engineering. If all the curves in the route are added together it would take the train through 16 complete circuits. The 6 million-plus vines of the Hex River Valley produce the bulk of the coun-

try's export grapes. In autumn the red-tinted leaves of the vineyards cover the whole valley in an ochre haze.

The Great Karoo: The delightful hamlet of **Matjiesfontein** was first developed as a refilling point for steam locomotives about to embark on the long haul through the arid Karoo. An enterprising Scotsman, James Logan, soon realised the commercial possibilities of this and built a beautiful Victorian-style hotel right on the edge of the railway line. Both the hotel and the quaint village retain much of their old-world charm; in 1975 the town was declared a national monument. Visitors flock to Matjiesfontein to spend a night at the hotel.

Continuing on the N1 from Matjiesfontein, one reaches **Laingsburg** – the scene of South Africa's major flood disaster of 1981 – and then **Beaufort West**, the hub of the rich farming district. The area is known for its merino sheep; the breed was brought to the country almost by accident but has become the mainstay of the wool industry.

In 1789 the Dutch royal family sent two rams and four ewes that they had earlier received as a gift from the Spanish monarch. The animals' offspring now number more than 35 million; they graze on a Karoo diet of shrubs, herbs and succulents, thus creating the distinctive taste of Karoo mutton.

Karoo and the Northern Cape

160 km / 100 miles

Bordering the town is the **Karoo National Park**, stretching up the slopes of the Nuweveld Mountains. Early hunters and explorers recounted tales of a land where thick swathes of grass stood shoulder-high and where the teeming herds of springbok were so huge that wagons had to be outspanned for two or three days to allow the herd to pass by. But "civilisation" brought with it hunters and guns and ploughs and fences and fires. Two animal species – the zebra-like quagga and the bluebok antelope – were shot to extinction, and other herds were decimated and driven into the remotest regions of the arid interior. Today, nature reserves like the Karoo National Park are trying their utmost to preserve some of that fauna and its typical Karoo habitat.

Visitors to the park are likely to see limited numbers of springbok, gemsbok, and hartebeest – reintroduced here by game rangers – as well as smaller predators such as lynx, black-backed jackal and wild cat. A unique feature is its great concentration of tortoises. Both the largest species – the leopard tortoise, weighing in at 100 lb (45 kg) , and the smallest, *homophus signatus*, at 3 inches (100 mm) long and weighing 5 oz (150 grams) – are found here.

From Beaufort West to Colesberg is a rather long drive whose main virtues are the empty road and wide-open countryside. The distinctive flat-topped shapes of three dolomite hills, "the Three Sisters", are clearly visible along the way. An even better example is Tooverberg just outside Colesberg. Another trademark of the Karoo is its creaking windpumps. This ingenious but simple device forms the backbone of the region's economic existence. Erected at a borehole and then left to its own devices the wind-pump continuously churns up water from deep underground to drinking troughs for livestock.

Colesberg is considered to be the halfway mark between Johannesburg and Cape Town and is often used as a stopover for people travelling between the major centres. Like the nearby town of De Aar, Colesberg was primarily

Time stands still in Naquamaland.

developed as a railway junction. South Africa was one of the last countries in the world to phase out steam locomotives on passenger routes although these graceful "iron horses" are still labouring on branch lines and in huge shuntyards like the one at De Aar, or by special request for tourists.

An alternative and very scenic way of reaching the central Karoo is to proceed along the Garden Route (N2) and then to cross the Swartberge through Meiringspoort (R29) or one of the other spectacular mountain passes. These routes were all designed and built by a father-son combination of genius: Andrew Geddes Bain and Thomas Bain. They left an indelible legacy in South Africa and some of the roads they built 150 years ago are still in daily use.

Between 1835 and 1870 they built at least 10 major passes across the Cape Folded Mountains – each a major feat of engineering. Moreover, the elder Bain also found fame as a writer of early Afrikaans poems and as a naturalist. His discovery of the skull of the "Blinkwater Monster" – one of the earliest animals known to have walked upright – made world headlines at the time.

The **Seweweekspoort Pass** is the least travelled of the three routes across the mountains but is the highest and probably most impressive. The better known, Swartberg Pass, winds its way through valleys of indigenous trees and flowers. Heavy snowfall in winter often forces the closure of this route. At the top of the Swartberge one looks down on the Gamkaskloof known among locals as Die Hel (the Hell) because of its deep ravines and gorges and impenetrable vegetation. The route most often taken is the Meiringspoort road following the Grootrivier through the mountain. It crosses the river no less than 26 times and passes a spectacular 180-ft (55-metre) waterfall.

The Eastern Karoo: From George the R57 leads through the Kammanassieberge to Uniondale, Willowmore and Graaff-Reinet. An alternative route to take is the R32, leading off the N2 north east of Port Elizabeth.

Graaff-Reinet, the "gem of the

Left, Kimberley Mining Museum. **Right**, the Big Hole, once the world's richest diamond mine.

Karoo", is the region's major town. Nestling in a bend in the Sundays River the town has retained much of its historical feel and character. Founded in 1786, it became the hub of political turbulence. Fed up with colonial rule and inspired by the example of the French Revolution, the inhabitants of Graaff-Reinet in 1795 chased the government representative from town and declared an independent – albeit, short-lived – republic.

The townsfolk have spent much time and effort preserving their heritage and take pride in the fact that more than 200 buildings have been declared national monuments, including an entire street, Stretch's Court, which has been restored to its 18th-century splendour. The Dutch Reformed Mission church and the old parsonage – once occupied by one of the country's most noted churchmen, Dr Andrew Murray – have both been converted into museums. In the gardens of the parsonage, now called Reinet House, grows the largest living grape vine in the world. With a girth of 8 ft (2.4

metres) and a height of 5 ft (1.5 metres) it covers an area of 1,335 sq. ft (124 sq. metres) – and still bears fruit.

Just outside town is a statue of Andries Pretorius, the great Voortrekker leader who lived in Graaff-Reinet and led his people to victory against the Zulus at the Battle of Blood River. West of the town lies the **Valley of Desolation**, part of the Karoo Nature Reserve and known for its bizarre dolorite formations with heights of more than 393 ft (120 metres).

Palaeontologists consider the Karoo basin and its unbroken fossil record one of earth's great natural wonders. A comprehensive exhibition of the area's geological development and the fossils it yielded can be seen the Museum of Natural History in Cape Town, and an extensive private collection is on display in the Graaff-Reinet Museum.

To the east of Graaff-Reinet, in the upper reaches of the Great Fish River, is the town of **Cradock**, built as a stronghold to defend the region against Xhosa attacks. Like most other rural towns in South Africa the impressive steeples of

Kimberley's old De Beers building.

Dutch Reformed church buildings are among its most notable features. Often they are imitations of European churches – in Cradock the model was St Martin-in-the-Fields in London.

Close to the town is the **Mountain Zebra National Park**, established in 1937, with the express purpose to save the zebra from extinction. At that time there were only a few of these graceful animals left and it was feared that they may go the way of the related quagga, which became extinct in the 19th century. Through a careful programme of conservation and breeding the park now accommodates about 200 zebras and smaller herds have been transferred to other parks in the province.

The Diamond Way: The distinctive Karoo hills at Three Sisters are an important junction for two roads that lead into the very heart of South Africa's mineral wealth. The N1 northwards via Colesberg, through the Orange Free State, is the Golden Route, taking one into the Witwatersrand mining area.

The R29 is the Diamond Way, leading to the "diamond capital of the world", Kimberley. Along this road, which later continues to diggings on the Vaal, such as Christiana and Bloemhof, many a fortune has been made and lost. The airport at Kimberley provides another gateway to the region.

There were few more apt placenames than that of the village of **Hopetown**. Here in 1866, a young boy found a shiny pebble on the banks of the Orange River and showed it to a neigbouring farmer, Schalk van Niekerk. It proved to be a 21.25-carat diamond, now known as the "Eureka" and kept at the Houses of Parliament in Cape Town. Three years later came a second discovery, and again van Niekerk was involved. A local Griqua traded a magnificent diamond of 83.5 carats for all of the farmer's earthly possessions. The polished gem is now one of the world's most famous diamonds, the "Star of South Africa".

At the confluence of three provinces, the Cape, the Free State and the Transvaal, lies a town synonymous with diamonds, **Kimberley**. How it happened to be part of the Cape rather than the Free State is in itself a tale of greed, political intrigue and gerrymandered boundaries. When, in 1871, the extent of the wealthy deposits trapped in the kimberlite pipe became known, the government at the Cape simply redrew the map and relocated Free State territory.

The discovery of diamonds in the Colesberg Hill sparked a rush that has never been equalled before or since. At one stage more than 30,000 men were digging frantically side by side. Within a few months the entire hill was worked away with picks and buckets and they started digging downwards, creating the Big Hole. A rough and raucous shantytown sprang up around the rim of the hole. Some semblance of order had to be brought to the diggings and individual miners were forced to form syndicates. Gradually these developed into large diamond companies.

Two men who emerged as the major figures of the diamond industry were Barney Barnato, a former boxer and actor who came to South Africa from London at the age of 20 and was a multi-

In the dry lands of the Karoo...

millionaire just five years later, and Cecil John Rhodes, the son of an English parson, who wheeled and dealed his way to the top and eventually, through his De Beers Consolidated Mines, monopolised the entire diamond market of the world. Steadily the Big Hole of Kimberley got bigger and bigger until it reached a depth of over 3,600 ft (1,100 metres). In the first 10 years of operations about 22½ million tonnes of diamond-bearing rock was hauled away as the miners dug their way downwards.

Then, almost as suddenly as it started, prospecting stopped. By 1914 the entire volcanic pipe and its "blue-ground" or kimberlite had been removed. The diggers left in search of other finds but not before an astonishing 14½ million carats (3 tonnes) of diamonds had been recovered. Today the vast, worked-out Big Hole, partly filled with water, is still the main attraction of the region. Its surface area of nearly 40 acres (16 hectares) forms the focal point of the reconstructed museum mining village.

...only the most hardy survive.

The open-air museum is the original tin shanty-town that existed during the great rush. It was carefully taken down and then reassembled with everything intact. Buildings such as Barney Barnato's boxing academy, the De Beers homestead, a blacksmith's workshop and a tobacconist can be seen. Visitors can buy licences to prospect and dig at the old mine, with diamonds as prizes.

In town, the **Alexander McGregor Museum** has a superb collection of natural history specimens as well as San artefacts. There are various Bushmen rock art sites in the area, such as that at Griekop Island and the petroglyphs (rock engravings) on the glacial pavements at Nooitgedacht, near Barkly West.

The discovery of diamonds triggered the industrialisation of the South African interior and Kimberley was the first town to have such luxuries as street lighting and a tram car (still in operation, offering a delightful way to reach the Hole from the centre of town). During the Anglo-Boer War the town was besieged for about four months by the Boer forces. Through a quirk of fate the

architect of the war, Rhodes, was among those trapped by the constant pounding of the Boer's Long Tom cannons.

Just outside the town is Magersfontein, site of one of the major battles of the war. Here, the Boer commandos, led by General Koos de la Rey, dug trenches at the foot of the hill, which enabled them to resist successfully a full-frontal British assault. A small museum and observation tower have been erected at the site of the battlefield.

The Northern Cape: From Warrenton, just north of Kimberley, the R27 leads along the edge of the Cape-Freestate border to Mafikeng. Next to the road are the lime qurries of **Taung**, where in 1924, an important palaeontological discovery was made – the skull of the Taung child or *Australopithecus africanus*. **Mafikeng** is another town steeped in war history. Known then as Mafeking, this town was also besieged for a lengthy period (seven months) by Boer forces, giving rise to harrowing accounts of hardship and suffering.

The British commander of the town

was Colonel Robert Baden-Powell, who later wrote that he conceived his ideas for the creation of the international Boy Scouts movement when he saw how young boys helped to perform vital tasks during the siege. Today Mafikeng – the original Tswana name, meaning "place of boulders" – is part of Mmbatho, capital of the Northwest province. Several sites of historical interest, dating to the siege, can still be seen, including the Brtitish fort on Canon Koppie.

The rest of the northern Cape can best be reached from Mafikeng on the R27 westwards. It goes past **Vryburg** – capital of the shortlived independent republic of Stellaland (1882–85) – to **Kuruman**. This is the major centre on the South African side of the **Kalahari**, the vast arid expanse that covers most of Botswana, and large parts of Zambia and eventually reaches up through Zaire to the Equator.

In 1824, Robert Moffat of the London Missionary Society established a mission station here that came to serve as fountainhead for the Christianisation of large parts of central Africa. It was from Kuruman that the famous explorer David Livingstone embarked on his expeditions into the heart of the continent. The trunk of an almond tree where Livingstone proposed to Moffat's daughter, Mary, can be seen in town.

The "eye" of the Kuruman River is one of the natural wonders of South Africa. Here, in the middle of one of the most arid parts of South Africa, crystal-clear water gushes out of the dolomite hills at an astonishing rate of 4½ million gallons (20 million litres) a day.

South of Kuruman the towns of **Kathu**, **Sishen** and **Postmasburg** lie in the middle of one of the richest mining areas in the country, producing significant amounts of iron, asbestos, copper and manganese. Every day, trains up to 1 mile (nearly 2 km) in length and powered by seven engines carry ore from Sishen across the Kalahari to Saldanha Harbour on the Cape west coast. **Upington** is the major town of what is known as **Bushmanland** and the small airport on the edge of town makes it easily accessible to visitors interested in ex-

An enduring survivor: the Kokerboom aloe.

ploring one of the most interesting but often overlooked parts of the country.

Dominating the entire region is the mighty Orange River, making its inexorable way to the Atlantic Ocean like a giant serpent. Carrying almost a quarter of the volume of South Africa's entire river system, the 1,240-mile (2,000-km) long Orange is the life-giving source of the entire region. Its lush, green banks, utilised extensively for the cultivation of cotton, deciduous fruit and grapes, are in stark contrast to the arid surroundings. At Upington, the river widens and is dotted with nearly 200 islands, the best known of which is the inhabited **Kanon-eiland**. At **Augrabies**, near Kakamas – 68 miles (110 km) west of Upington – the Orange thunders spectacularly over one of the six largest waterfalls of the world.

In times of drought, the flow is reduced but every so often flash floods upriver cause the river to burst its banks and the falls become a frightening torrent that gouges out a devastating swathe before it. Then, more than 80 million gallons (400 million litres) of water an hour can gush over the 185-ft (56-metre) fall into a deep gorge carved into the granite bedrock. Crashing down a further 115 ft (35 metres) over a series of secondary falls or cataracts, the water sends a vast column of spray into the air, enveloping the area in a heavy mist.

The falls and its 11-mile (18-km) gorge are part of the **Augrabies Falls National Park**. A few yards away from the falls there is little but sand and rock. The true beauty and force of the river and the might of the falls can best be observed from a suspension bridge.

Two large pools at the base of the falls are thought to be at least 425 ft (130 metres) deep and contain a great wealth in diamonds carried from the vicinity of Kimberley and washed over the edge.

The Kalahari Gemsbok National Park: The country's second most important park (next to the Kruger National Park) is situated about 125 miles (200 km) north of Upington and is best reached along the R360. Northwards the landscape becomes progressively more

Frolicking springbok.

sandy and arid. Defining the borders of the park are the Auob and Nossob rivers, in reality sand-chocked river beds that flow only once or twice a century. All that distinguishes the courses from the endless rows of oxide-reddened dunes of this bewildering, undulating expanse is the tall evergreen camelthorn trees growing in the riverbeds.

Although only half the size of the Kruger Park, the park merges unimpeded with Botswana's Gemsbok Game Reserve to form one of the largest conservation areas in Africa. Without this international co-operation it would not have been possible to manage a park here, where most water-dependent animals constantly have to migrate across great distances in order to survive.

The park has three rest camps with cottages and full facilities – **Nossob** in the east, **Mata Mata** in the west and **Twee Rivieren** at the southern entrance. After good rains, most animals abandon the over-trampled dry river-beds and move out into the dunes where sweet grasses burst forth, coating the shock-

ing red sand with a soft silver sheen, and where shallow pans of fresh water lie until the sun sucks them dry again.

At these times visitors will not see much of the varied game in the park, but in the more common periods of dryness most game converges on the river beds. The subterranean flow of these wadis ensure at least browsing food in the trees and thorn bushes, and artificial boreholes ensure regular drinking water.

It is not unusual to witness a cheetah running down a springbok along the Nossob's wide floor, or a large herd of handsome gemsbok with their rapier horns silhouetted against a sky bruised by thunder clouds. Black-maned Kalahari lions escape the midday heat beneath thorn bushes, while brilliantly-spotted leopards take refuge in the tall camelthorn trees.

But it is the park's 200-odd bird species, and most particularly its range of eagles and other raptors, that most impress visitors used to seeing the big mammals. The large camelthorn trees (*Acacia erioloba*) that define the river

Simple dwellings for contented people.

courses are the life-giving source of the region, providing nests for the sociable weavers and the colony of other birds that co-habitat there and offering shade to game and domestic stock.

The large crescent-shaped pods make for nutritious food when they fall. The gum is eaten by animals and used in traditional medicine by the area's people. Giraffes can wrap their long, prehensile tongues around the thorn-spiked branches and strip the leaves with seeming immunity to the cruel spines.

Namaqualand: A number of safari companies operating out of Cape Town and Johannesburg offer river-rafting and canoeing trips down the Orange River. Trips vary in duration from two days to a week, and include white-water options for the daring. This may be a novel way to explore the **Richtersveld** wilderness downstream from Augrabies. This rugged desert area bordering Namibia could be declared a National Park, thanks to the cooperation of the Namibian and South African governments and the indigenous inhabitants, and can also be reached along the R64 from Upington and Pofadder, or on the main highway (N7) leading northwards from Cape Town through Namaqualand and **Springbok**, the largest town in the region, to Steinkopf. From here the road through the Richtersveld is rough even for off-road vehicles, but the scenery is rewardingly dramatic.

The diversity of succulents is so rich that botanists are struggling to get them all classified and described. Some species are known from only one locality or even one specimen, never found again. Others, like the "halfmens" (*Pachypodium namaquanum*) are equally strange; Bushmen believed they were half-plant and half-human and anyone who has seen the single, thick tapering stem with its crowning rosette of tightly crinkled leaves will understand why.

Also characteristic are the stark tree aloes, or *kokerboom* (quiver trees) whose hollowed out limbs are used by the San to carry their arrows. The **Hester Malan Nature Reserve** near Springbok provides a chance to explore the area's fauna and flora at a leisurely pace.

The geometric tortoise of the Karoo.

In the belief that there are vast deposits of copper just waiting to be discovered in the interior one of the earliest governors at the Cape, Simon van der Stel, led an expedition to **Okiep** in 1685. Three shafts were sunk which did indeed reveal some copper ore, but because of the remoteness of the area no mining took place until almost two centuries later. The original shafts sunk by van der Stel and other mining memorabilia can be seen in town.

For most of the year the northwest coastal plain and stony Namaqualand floor cannot hide the wrinkles and cracks of its age-old skin, and the tattiness of its drab green-grey cover. But, come spring, fields burst forth in colours gay and dazzling. Nature favours these semi-arid scrublands with one youthful cosmetic flush of wild flowers that for a few days in September each year attracts people from all over the country. The Namaqualand daisies bloom vividly.

Coach tours from Cape Town take visitors either on day trips to the edge of the southwestern Cape – the Sandveld

area around Lambert's Bay – or deeper into the heart of Namaqualand to such delightful coastal spots as Tietiesbaai, Hondeklipbaai, Skulpfonteinput and Kleinsee. The Namaqualand wildflower extravaganza lasts for a very short time each year and never erupts in the same place all at once. While the Cape nature conservation department puts out boards to direct flower-lovers to the best spots as they come into bloom, a tourist's itinerary should take account of nature's fickleness.

The Diamond Coast: Following the Orange River once more in a westward direction, the arid savannah gives way to the semi-desert area of northern Namaqualand until it reaches the river's mouth at **Oranjemund**. Over aeons the river has changed its course many times and collected each of the northern Cape's major catchment basins. On its journey past Kimberley it gathered up the diamond-rich sediments and spewed its precious load up and down the northern Cape coastline, thus creating the world's richest deposits of alluvial diamonds.

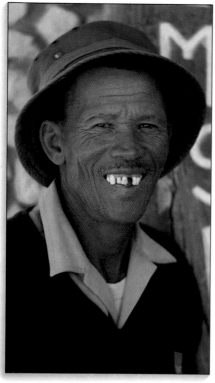

The diamonds were discovered almost by accident in 1926, by an officer in the British-Indian army, Captain Jack Carstens, who roamed the countryside while visiting his parents in Port Nolloth. The find proved much richer than could have been imagined. The geologist Hans Merensky claimed to have picked up 487 diamonds from under one stone alone and in a single month recovered 2,762 diamonds near Alexander Bay.

As news of the rich find spread across the world, fortune-seekers descended on the area in a mad rush, prompting the government to secure the area and ban private prospecting. The entire coast between Kleinsee and Oranjemund is controlled by the De Beers Consolidated Mining Company, and the public is not allowed off the main road.

This stretch of coast is worked by the world's largest armada of earth-moving equipment, constantly pushing the sea back with artificial dunes while the underlying sand is cleared down to the bedrock with shovels and hand-brooms. Every crack and crevice being methodically cleaned out. A vast wealth of diamonds is recovered here each year.

But, as the captains of fishing trawlers operating along the coast illustrate, you can't keep a determined prospector down. They have converted their vessels into giant "vacuum cleaners" from which divers dredge the sea-bed for the sparkling gems.

The desert-besieged fishing and diamond towns of the northwest coast are real frontier places, the men as rough as uncut diamonds and as raw as the cheap alcohol they consume in quantity. There are few women, plenty of stray dogs and the only acts considered punishable are illicit diamond dealing, murder and trying to take another man's woman.

The only "resorts" are to be found at **Strandfontein** near the Olifants River mouth, and at the **Port Nolloth** extension of McDougall's Bay. These are rudimentary places as resorts go, catering almost exclusively for fishermen and the rough-and-ready local sheep-farming communities. If there is such a place as "the end of the line", then Port Nolloth is surely that place.

Ranger in the Kalahari Gemsbok Park.

286

THE SOUTHERN SKY

South Africa stretches from the tropics down to about 35° south. Except for the metropolitan areas and some more heavily industrialised regions, the night skies are still dark and unpolluted. Moreover, a major part of the country is semi-desert, whose dry atmosphere aids the avid stargazer. The South Africa Astronomical Observatory at Sutherland in the heart of the Karoo is a well-known research facility for local and overseas astronomers.

To visitors from the Northern Hemisphere, the familiar constellations look upside-down and even the "Man in the Moon" seems to be standing on his head. All of the 20 brightest stars can easily be seen.

The most easily recognised constellation is Crusis or the Southern Cross. Viewed from South Africa, it is nearly circumpolar and is almost always up. It should be distinguished from the two other "crosses", the so-called "Diamond Cross" and "False Cross" lying slightly northeast of it in the Southern skies. Crucis is smaller, its stars are brighter and it is distinguished by the two bright "pointer" stars, Alpha and Beta Centauri, which lie on a line pointing to the short axis of the cross.

Alpha Centauri, the fourth brightest star in the heavens, is also – at 4.3 light years – the Sun's closest neighbour. In a small telescope, one is startled to see it resolve into two separate pinpoints of light; a larger telescope reveals a third, fainter, companion.

For direction-finding, the South does not have a convenient pole star as does the Northern Hemisphere, but the Cross fulfils this role. Mentally extend the Cross "downwards" 4œ times along its long axis. The spot on the horizon vertically below this position will be approximately due south. Alpha Crucis is the brightest "star" in the Cross (actually a double star). Conveniently, the five brightest stars of Crucis are arranged clockwise in order of apparent brightness: alpha, beta, gamma, delta and finally epsilon.

The Cross is also a convenient reference point for two very special objects: the two satellite galaxies of the Milky Way, the Large and Small Magellanic Clouds. Again extend the long axis of the Cross to about seven times. Either side

of this line one then sees what resembles two small clouds except that they do not move or change shape. At roughly 200,000 light years away, they are the Galaxy's closest neighbours, linked to it not only gravitationally, but via a tenous "bridge" of hydrogen gas.

The Large Magellanic Cloud (LMC) came into prominence in 1987 as a result of Supernova 1987A, whose massive explosion provided scientists with the first opportunity to test some of their hypotheses about the evolution of stars.

A very bright object, known as S Doradus, is prominent in the LMC and is associated with a gaseous nebula, known as the Tarantula Nebula, also a remnant of a much earlier Supernova event.

Near to the Small Magellanic Cloud a hazy white patch can be discerned with the naked eye. With binoculars it is more prominent and a small telescope resolves it into thousands of stars. This is one of the two great globular clusters, consisting of 100,000 stars or more and seen clearly only from the Southern Hemisphere. This one is called 47 Tucanae and its fellow globular cluster is Omega Centauri. ∎

ORANGE FREE STATE AND SE TRANSVAAL

The landscapes of the Orange Free State and the southeastern Transvaal are in many ways typical of the interior plateau of South Africa. Situated above the Great Escarpment, the region consists overwhelmingly of treeless, grassy plains. More rugged topography is present near South Africa's largest river, the Orange, where steep, flat-topped hills (*koppies*) dot the landscape. Flat-crested massifs are common in the eastern Free State in an arc bordering Lesotho and extending from Zastron in the south to Harrismith in the east. Some of these massifs reach altitudes of more than 1,200 ft (2,000 metres) and often carry sprinklings of snow in winter.

The Great Escarpment forms a giant step between the interior plateau and the low-lying hinterland of Natal. Here, west of Harrismith, the Wilge River, an important tributary of the Vaal, rises a few miles from the escarpment edge. These unusual circumstances have enabled the largely unused water resources of the Tugela River in Natal to be tapped to the benefit of the industrial areas of the Witwatersrand and northern Free State.

The Drakensberg Pump Storage Scheme involves the pumping of water across the escarpment into the Sterkfontein Dam from where it is used to produce power in a return journey through a huge underground generating complex. The ambitious **Lesotho Highlands Scheme**, presently under construction, will, in a similar transfer of water across a major divide, divert the headwaters of the Orange "backwards" into an upper tributary of the Vaal.

The region forms the core of the grassland region of South Africa. Because of the equable climate, flat land and good soils, most of the grassland has been ploughed under and turned into maize and wheat fields. The remainder is used for dairy and beef production and in the drier regions for sheep farming. Historically, indigenous trees were found only in river courses and on rocky outcrops. These, as well as grasslands, are con-

served at Golden Gate and other nature reserves. Elsewhere, they have been replaced by foreign species such as the bluegum and black wattle planted by white settlers for shelter and firewood.

The Free State and Southwestern Transvaal are often neglected by visitors and are generally seen only during an overflight between the Cape and the Witwatersrand or from the window of a speeding Blue Train. However, the region has much to offer in the way of scenic beauty and interesting historical sights. This is the heart of rural South Africa where major chapters of the country's turbulent history have unfolded.

Bloemfontein, the capital of the Free State, is an ideal vantage point from which the whole of the province can be explored. Situated near the centre of the N1 – the major thoroughfare that bisects the country from north to south – it can also be conveniently reached from Durban (along the N3 and R49) and Port Elizabeth (R32). Alternatively, motorists can enjoy the lush scenery of the Garden Route and then cut away at

George to traverse the Karoo on the R57 past Graaff-Reinet and Middelburg to Colesberg where it again joins the N1.

The region used to witness the migration of enormous herds of wildebeest, zebra, blesbok and springbok, species grossly depleted by hunting in the 19th century. Today their survival as well as that of other endemic species, such as the grey rhebok, is ensured within the boundaries of a number of smaller nature reserves. Species such as the sungazer lizard (*ouvolk*) are not as fortunate. The survival of the ouvolk, endemic to the eastern Free State, is under severe threat from farming activities, development and reptile collectors.

Back to the past: The region is renowned as one of the world's finest archaeological and paleontological treasure troves, the region preserves not only the secrets of prehistoric man, but also a rich heritage of more contemporary history which will delight visitors with a penchant for the past.

Following the sensational "missing link" discoveries at Taung and Sterk-fontein, paleontologists flocked to the country in search of more evidence on the cradle of mankind. At **Florisbad**, a mineral spring, northwest of Bloemfontein, the earliest find of modern man, *Homo sapiens,* was discovered, dating back 41,000 years. Of more recent origins but equally impressive are the excavated Stone Age settlements in the northern Free State and southeast of the North West province as well as the fabulous wealth of rock shelters with wall paintings done by San artists in the hilly country of the eastern Free State.

The spoor left by the region's more contemporary inhabitants is best picked up at Vegkop battlefield near **Heilbron** in the northern Free State, scene of a major military clash in 1836 between the north-moving Voortrekkers and the Ndebele. At **Vegkop**, now a national monument, the Voortrekker leader Hendrik Potgieter and 40 followers warded off an attack ordered by the mighty monarch, Mzilikazi, who had settled in the region to escape the wrath of Zulu king Shaka. The battle raged

Mealies in the Maize Triangle.

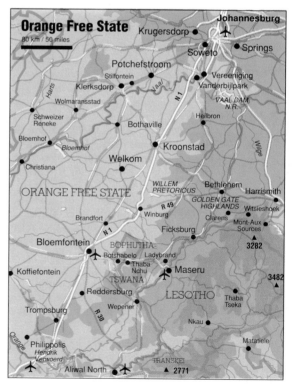

across the ancient ruins of Stone Age corbelled huts, mute reminders of a prehistoric African claim to the land.

Most white towns in the Free State and southwestern Transvaal conserve Voortrekker artefacts in local museums or libraries. **Winburg** and **Potchefstroom**, the oldest settler towns in the Free State and Transvaal respectively, are of special interest to the historically minded. Both served as capitals to early Voortekker states and Winburg, in particular, has preserved the period's architecture and atmosphere. The **Willem Pretorius Game Reserve** near Winburg is home to a vast variety of game and birds. A resort on the banks of the **Allemanskraal Dam** adjacent to the reserve offers somewhat rustic accommodation plus water sports facilties.

Potchefstroom, too, is steeped in Afrikaner history. It was here that the first shots of the Anglo-Transvaal War (1880–81) were fired when 500 Republicans rode into town, occupied the printing works and shot at the British soldiers who tried to disperse them. Today the charming town on the banks of the Mooi River is known more for its educational facilities – a university, teacher's training college and some of the country's top schools – and tree-lined streets. Potchefstroom can easily be visited on a day trip from Johannesburg (R29) or it can be a staging point for an "expedition" to the rural heart of the country and towns like **Christiana, Klerksdorp, Lichtenburg, Wolmaransstad** and **Zeerust**.

This is the centre of the "**Maize Triangle**" – formed by Christiana, Bothaville in the Free State and Bethal in southeast Transvaal. Maize and maize products such as the traditional *mieliepap* (porridge) is the staple food for the majority of South Africans and about 10 million tons of maize are produced in the country annually – the bulk coming from large, well-organised farms. Although hybrid species have been developed to suit the climate, the crop is very susceptible to the droughts that often predominate for lengthy periods.

No visit to the region would be com-

The Cape doesn't have the only table mountain.

plete without a taste of real Afrikaner culture. **Marico**, to the northwest of Potchefstroom, is in what is locally known as Mampoer Country. *Mampoer* is a potent, fiery brew distilled legally – but mostly illegally – from a variety of fruit. Even a very small tot is enough to inebriate. It takes decades of practice to enjoy it without ill-effect. As can be expected, the annual Marico *mampoer* festival is a jovial affair.

Bloemfontein: The modern capital of the Orange Free State, is regarded as one of the most diligent caretakers of early Afrikaner history. Its own history dates back to 1840 when a solitary Voortrekker, Johannes Nicolaas Brits, settled in his new *hartbeeshuisie* (a Voortrekker dwelling with thatched roof and dung floor) near a spring surrounded by clover. When other settlers arrived, the place became known as Bloemfontein (spring of flowers).

The town briefly served as capital of the Old Republic of the Free State before it was occupied by the British forces of Lord Roberts during the Anglo-Boer War (1899–1902). The occupation was a mixed blessing. The inomitable descendants of the Voortrekkers, who braved the dangers of the wild unknown to escape the British Empire, had nothing but contempt for the Union Jack hoisted over their town. But British occupation protected the town from the ravages of war, thus ensuring that to this day the city's well-preserved historical heritage and old-world charm are unequalled in the country.

A stroll down **President Brand Street** bears witness to this. Widely regarded as one of South Africa's most beautiful old streets, it has an architectural variety spanning more than a century.

Most of the buildings are open to the public. They include the **Old Presidency**, the **Fourth Raadzaal**, **City Hall**, **Court of Appeal** – Bloemfontein is the judicial capital of South Africa – and the **Afrikaans Literary Museum and Research Centre**. The city's oldest building, the **First Raadzaal**, is in St George's Street, as is a magnificent **Anglican cathedral** constructed in 1850. Even

Roadside tableau.

Bloemfontein's newest, most luxurious hotel, the Landdrost, had a historical name and great care has been taken to recreate the pioneer atmosphere, even though it was recently renamed "Holiday Inn Garden Court".

More contemporary buildings include the **Sand du Plessis Theatre** that has sparked a major controversy in town between those favouring rapid development and those arguing that its modern design would detract from the old-world charm of the city centre. Another well-known theatre is housed in the **Lamont-Hussey Observatory** on top of **Naval Hill**. The observatory was erected by the University of Michigan in 1928 but closed down in 1972. Still in operation is the Boyden Observatory, built by Harvard University and equipped with a 152-cm telescope.

The British side of Bloemfontein's character often surprises visitors to the capital of a province that is widely regarded as Afrikaner-dominated heartland. The city has a fairly large English-speaking community with roots in colonial and earlier times. A number of historical sites of a military nature, such as Naval Hill or **Queen's Fort** as well as the Ramblers cricket ground, which boasts a club house dating back almost a century, preserves this heritage. Moreover, the city is known for its educational facilities, with a major Afrikaans university and medical school as well as one of the country's premier schools, Grey College.

Other sections of the South African community, however, have equally deep emotional roots in Bloemfontein's soil – roots implanted by the two great freedom struggles fought on South African soil during the past century. On the one hand, the city is the keeper of the Afrikaner people's most treasured shrine to their struggle against the Empire during the Anglo-Boer War; on the other it is the cradle of black resistance against Afrikaner domination and apartheid.

To this day, many an Afrikaner pilgrimage is made to the **Military Museum** of the Boer republics, dedicated to the soldiers, women and children

The Raadhuis (town hall) in Bloemfontein.

involved in the war. The museum displays a vast collection of Boer War artefacts, among them the possessions of General Christiaan de Wet, the famous exponent of guerrilla warfare – at the time a new strategy which allowed the small, ragged Boer commandos to stage irregular forays against the British forces for an astounding three years. In the garden, an impressive obelisk and statue of two women, one with a dead child on the lap, commemorates the death of more than 28,000 Boer women and children in the British concentration camps.

Similar pilgrimages to the birthplace of the South African Native Congress – known as the African National Congress (ANC) since 1923 – will take place in future. No monument commemorates the birth of Africa's most celebrated freedom movement, founded in Bloemfontein in 1912, and – since 1994 – majority party in parliament and the Government of National Unity, but street names in the neighbouring, sprawling black town of **Botshabelo** say it all. The township's 230,000 black inhabitants, mostly poverty-stricken squatters displaced by apartheid legislation, named one of their mud-and-corrugated-iron-shack suburbs Freedom City. Children play soccer on a dusty, empty plot known as Freedom Square.

The same dreams of freedom are expressed in similar street names at **Sharpeville** near Vereeniging in the southern Transvaal, the scene where 67 black protestors were shot by policemen during a mass anti-pass law demonstration in 1960. This event marked the start of the armed struggle against the government by guerrillas of the ANC and other black resistance groups, and also the beginning of South Africa's isolation in the international community.

Hiking through heaven: The magnificent mountain ranges and undulating veld of the eastern Free State offer some of the most spectacular tours in South Africa. A network of roads provide easy and scenic access to the region's towns, villages and tourist facilities. Linking Harrismith in the north to Ladybrand in

Skateboard skills; a remnant of the colonial past.

the south, these roads either hug the magnificent slopes of the Drakensberg, the Maluti's and other mountain ranges, or cut through undulating veld and cultivated land with breathtaking views of hazy blue peaks in the distance.

They offer the motorist the choice of making a complete round trip or a series of shorter excursions starting from the much wider ring of main roads made up by the R49, the N1 and the R30. The whole area is interlinked with the high reaches of the Lesotho mountain kingdom, an independent state which offers some magnificent scenery.

The region is also renowned for its hiking trails which take the backpacker deep in to the heart of untrammelled wilderness where no season is out of season. Supper served next to a cosy log fire in one of the local restaurants is the perfect end to a winter hike to the misty snow-clad peaks of the Drakensberg. So is a typical South African *braai* under clear, starry skies in summer.

A relic of the present day. The trails not only cut through country blessed with a breathtaking wealth of scenery, indigenous vegetation, wild and birdlife, but also pass numerous examples of rock art and various other historical sights.

One of the most spectacular hikes starts at the **Witsieshoek Mountain Resort** situated high in the foothills of the Drakensberg in the tiny black homeland of **Qwaqwa**. This strenuous three-hour walk from a car park behind the resort to a steep chain ladder deep in the heart of the mountain, takes the hiker to the summit of the country's highest peak, **Mont-aux-Sources**.

A short walk across the "Roof of South Africa" leads to the point where the mighty Tugela plunges thousands of feet down to Natal. The resort's comfortable accommodation, which includes electric blankets for freezing winter temperatures, also serves as a convenient base for tackling other scenic trails in Qwaqwa. Trout fishermen frequent the **Meti Matso Dam**, stocked with rainbow trout and black carp. Traditional artefacts, ceramics and handwoven rugs are among the bargains on offer at the

industrial centre adjacent to Qwaqwa's capital, Phuthaditjhaba.

Another very romantic hideaway is the **Maluti Mountain Lodge**, situated near **Clarens**, a beautiful, small mountain village with typical eastern Free State sandstone architecture. This sophisticated establishment provides good accommodation in a main building as well as in fully-equipped chalets with a stunning view of the mountains. Clarens, a popular retirement village, is also home to a colony of artists.

The town of **Bethlehem**, named after the birthplace of Christ by the devout Voortrekkers who settled there in the previous century, serves as the region's capital as well as tourist headquarters. It has excellent facilities, including hotels, restaurants and shops for camping and hiking supplies. Several short hiking trails in the vicinity take one through the town's bird sanctuary, the holiday resort on the banks of the Jordan River and the local game reserve.

The **Golden Gate Highlands National Park** is one of South Africa's most beautiful nature reserves. Situated in the foothills of the **Maluti Mountains**, this 15,000 acres (6,000 hectares) of spectacular scenery, inhabited only by game and bird species indigenous to the region, derives its name from the blazing shades of gold cast by the sun on its huge sandstone cliffs. The main rest camp, **Brandwag**, accommodates guests in comfortable hotel rooms and chalets. Rondavels, caravan and camping sites provide somewhat more rustic accommodation at a second rest camp, **Glen Reenen**. Guests have access to a wide variety of sporting facilities, horses, ponies and a natural rock pool used for bathing. Golden Gate can be explored by car or on foot. The **Rhebok Hiking Trail** follows a two-day route through valleys, ravines and streams to the summit of the mountain.

Near Fouriesburg, the **Brandwater Hiking Trail** offers a strenuous but rewarding five-day trek through river valleys, ravines and an amazing diversity of indigenous vegetation. The trail passes many a panoramic view of the

The Free State has a smattering of secondary industries.

Maluti, Rooi and Witteberg Mountains as well as sandstone farmsteads, historic places of interest dating back to the Anglo-Boer War, rock art, game camps and **Salpeterkrans**, reputedly the largest sandstone cave in the Southern Hemisphere. Hikers spend three nights in caves and a fourth in an old farmstead.

Ficksburg, the agricultural centre of the eastern Free State, has a wealth of old sandstone architecture. Its cherry orchards, covered by blossoms in the spring, are famous. So is its annual cherry festival in November. **The Imperani Hiking Trail** near town follows a circular route across the Imperani Mountain, passing rock art, sandstone caves and vantage points with spectacular views of the Malutis.

Ladybrand provides access to **Maseru**, capital of Lesotho. The towns are at opposite ends of the Caledon Bridge, the main border post between South Africa and Lesotho. When gambling was not allowed in South Africa, many a Free State farmer is reputed to have acquired excellent skills at

The Golden Gate Highlands National Park.

Maseru's gambling tables. Things have changed since a place in the centre of the Free State decided to deprive Maseru's casinos of some of its most faithful South African clientele.

Yes, there is indeed a place deep in the heart of Free State farm country where slot machines cough up jingles and coins and croupiers call for bets. The **Thaba 'Nchu Sun**, situated on the R64 between Ladybrand and Bloemfontein, offers an entertaining night out to locals and tourists alike. Designed and built in traditional African style, it accommodates guests in sophisticated luxury. The casino's square pyramids with patterned walls face **Thaba 'Nchu** – the "black mountain" – and the **Maria Moroka National Park**, situated in a natural amphitheatre formed by the mountain and a number of smaller hills. Facilities at the complex include a spa, pool, gym, sauna, tennis courts, a golf course, games rooms for children and cinemas. Game rangers accompany tourists on game-spotting drives and two hiking trails leading through the park.

River side: The life styles on the banks of the two mighty rivers tracing the Free State's northern and southern borders are as different as can be. The banks of the **Vaal River** is a fun-seeker's paradise in the heart of South Africa's most frenetic urban society. The banks of the Orange River, some 280 miles (450 km) southwest, as the crow flies, provides tranquil oases for man and beast in a hard, dry region where creaking windmills and dust kicked up by whirlwinds are often the only visible signs of life.

The Vaal River, the natural border between the Free State and the Gauteng, originates from the confluence of small streams and rivulets on the plains of Swaziland and flows in a westerly direction to the Harts River. The **Vaal Dam** near **Vereeniging** supplies water to the Witwatersrand, the industrial pulse of South Africa. The vast expanse of water also caters to the recreational needs of the millions of people who live and work in the Witwatersrand.

The Vaal Dam and the river banks between Vereeniging and **Vanderbijl-park** house weekend retreats, exclusive yacht clubs and other playgrounds, resorts, camp-sites, picnic and angling spots. During weekends, yachts, power boats, waterskiers and sailboards occupy the water while a riot of colourful bikinis, umbrellas and picnic blankets covers its banks, but the water also draws those seeking tranquil spots far from the madding crowd.

Anglers love the barrage at **Loch Vaal** and the grassy riverbanks at **Parys**, where flat rock bed divides the river into numerous little streams and islands. One of these islands has a beautiful golf course linked to Parys by a suspension bridge. The popular ice-rink adjacent to Sasolburg's riverside resort is reputedly the biggest in the Southern Hemisphere.

Sasolburg is better known as the headquarters of the South African Coal, Oil and Gas Corporation (Sasol), which perfected a unique method of extracting liquid fuels from coal. Today Sasol I and Sasol II (at Secunda in the eastern Transvaal) provide a large percentage of the country's fuel requirements.

The hardships...

The **Orange River** forms the border between the Free State and the Cape. South Africa's mightiest river rises in the well-watered Lesotho Highlands and flows through progressively more arid landscape to the Atlantic Ocean. The river carries almost a quarter of the country's total water run-off – up to 2.4 million gallons (9 million litres) a second during a flood.

In the semi-arid regions of the southern Free State its water is a precious source for agricultutral development and this has lead to the construction of the Jariep Dam and Van der Kloof Dam, which regulate the water flow and eventually irrigate 370,000 acres (150,000 hectares). These dams as well as a number of game reserves in the area are veritable oases in this inhospitable and dry region.

The **Jariep Dam** is also popular with anglers and water sports enthusiasts. Comfortable rondavels at the dam's resort offer a wonderful view of water islands and distant hills. The nearby nature reserve is home to the largest herd of springbok in the country as well as other game species.

The beautiful **Doornkloof** and **Rolfontein** nature reserves, situated on the shores of the Van der Kloof Dam, preserve large tracts of indigenous vegetation as well as local game and bird species. Rolfontein can be explored on foot. An expedition through the reserve is a one- or two-day hike, accompanied by guides, and includes overnight accommodation in rustic huts and a canoe trip on the dam.

Dreams of El Dorado: Both the Free State and southwestern Transvaal have important mines which explore the gold-bearing reefs of the Witwatersrand supergroup. In the Free State these reefs are buried beneath thousands of feet of Karoo strata in the southwestern Transvaal they are covered by dolomite.

The discovery of gold in the Free State in 1947 was a momentous event. It lead to the development of a series of mines that currently produce more than a third of the country's total gold output and it also put South Africa's first "state

...of subsistence farming.

of the art town" decisively on the map.

Welkom was designed and built primarily to accommodate the thousands of employees required by the new mines. The town has little history but is had the highest per capita income in the country. It is also the only major town in South Africa without traffic lights. Traffic is regulated by 23 traffic circles.

Smaller mining neighbours, **Virginia** and **Odendaalsrus**, share Welkom's abundance of facilities which include an airport, hotels, restaurants, a sophisticated car racing track, sports facilities a theatre complex and even a local radio station. Tourists who visit the mines are entertained with traditional mine dances.

The gold mines in the southwestern Transvaal are the deepest in the world, exceeding 13,000 ft (4,000 metres) in some cases. Gold mining in the area between **Klerksdorp** and **Stilfontein** dates back almost a century but has lately fallen on difficult times, forcing operations at the oldest gold mine at Stilfontein to be shut down.

Fortunes in the region have not only been found and lost on gold mines. Empty dreams of El Dorado still echo in the wind blowing over the tiny towns of **Koffiefontein** and **Jagersfontein** in the southern Free State, where the discovery of diamonds late in the 19th century lead to a mighty diamond rush. A huge open diamond mine adjacent to Koffiefontein was closed a few years ago when the price of diamonds on the world market suddenly plummeted.

A few solitary members of a dying breed of diggers still work the gravel terraces of Christiana, Wolmaransstad and Lichtenburg in the Northwest province where the discovery of diamond deposits in the 1920s was followed by a series of diamond rushes which at one stage produced such a volume as to threaten the collapse of the world's diamond markets. Visions of the amazing riches once contained in the potholes and gravel runs continue to haunt the dying breed of diggers searching for that single stone which would allow its fortunate finder to exchange a shack for a mansion.

Harnessing the wind.

STEAM LOCOMOTIVES

The parts for Blackie, South Africa's first steam locomotive, were brought ashore in Cape Town in September 1859 by Edward Pickering, a British contractor introduced to build a 44-mile (72-km) railway line from Cape Town to Wellington for the Cape Town Railway and Dock Company. The venture was ridden by constant enmity between company and contractor and ultimately by a fearful drunken brawl between their respective labourers.

These "railway disturbances" allowed Durban to gain "line-honours" with the opening in June 1860 of South Africa's first completed railway. The original engine, the Natal, puffed away smartly on its 2-mile (3.2-km) track between the harbour and the market square until it was bought in 1875 by a Port St John's saw-mill owner as a stationary engine to drive his machinery. Instead it terrified the local Xhosa, forcing the owner to bury it to allay their fears. It was later disinterred, restored and is currently on display at Durban station.

The discovery of the Kimberley diamond fields and the need for rapid and cheap transportation of goods and people to the interior led to the construction of railway trunk routes throughout South Africa. Cape Town was linked to Kimberley in 1885 by the Cape Government Railways (CGR). Port Elizabeth and East London soon followed suit. After the discovery of gold the CGR extended the line across the Orange Free State to the Transvaal border. Also the line from Durban was advanced to the Transvaal. In 1887, however, President Paul Kruger, seeking independence from the British-controlled railway system, formed the Nederlandsche Zuid-Afrikaansche Spoorwegmaatschappij (NZASM), linking Pretoria to Delagoa Bay in Portuguese East Africa, present day Mozambique. Sleeping sickness and malaria took their toll: on some stretches, as many as 10 men perished for every mile of track built.

But economic pressure forced a connection of the separate systems. By 1896 Pretoria, Kimberley and Bloemfontein were all linked to the harbours of Cape Town, Durban, Port Elizabeth and East London.

During the Anglo-Boer War the captured lines of the Boer Republics were incorporated into the Imperial Military Railways. When the war ended in 1902, the network became known as the Central South African Railways. South African Railways (SAR) came into being with the formation of the Union of South Africa in 1910, consolidating the separate systems into a single service.

By the early 1960s, SAR was operating a record number of 2,682 steam locomotives. But even then it was clear that the puffing behemoths would not survive the 20th century. By the beginning of the 1980s, only 1,702 remained, thanks to the official policy of replacing steam with electrical and diesel locomotives. The end came in June 1991, when Transnet, the privatised SAR, officially announced the end of main-line steam traction in South Africa.

But all is not lost. Transnet, which still has 493 steam engines on its books, has established the Transnet Preservation Board and the Transnet Museum which is to become custodian of South Africa's steam heritage. In the future steam will be seen on the museum's steam safaris, the museum's spectacular line between George and Knysna and on a variety of day trips. ∎

THE NEXT-DOOR NEIGHBOURS

Southern Africa's interdependence is not merely economic. With the exception of the former Portuguese colonies Mozambique and Angola and 31 years of German rule in Namibia, the whole region has British colonial origins. Nearly everywhere, English is the official language. British administration, telecommunications and customs such as "early morning tea" still prevail in one form or another. With its high standard of tourist infrastructure, southern Africa can with some justification be described as "the other Africa".

NAMIBIA: (formerly South West Africa , the German colony and later the UN protectorate). Life under Namibia's sun has always been tough. This is a region of stark landscapes, parched savannahs and dry river-beds. Over millions of years, the forces of nature sculpted fascinating formations while plants and animals evolved life-forms like nothing else on earth.

The capital, **Windhoek**, has an international airport and is well-placed as a starting point to explore the rest of the country. Those preferring to enter Namibia by four-wheel drive from Botswana or tarred road from South Africa. The country's 1 ¼ million people depend for their livelihood on mining, fisheries, tourism and farming. Most hotels are simple but well-run, with a few first-class establishments and a clutch of delightful guest farms. Most of the more popular tourist destinations are easily accessible by tarred or gravel roads.

One of the world's great game sanctuaries, the 8,600 sq. mile (22,270 sq. km) **Etoscha National Park**, lies in the north of the country. Characteristic of the park is a central salt pan with peripheral water-holes to which big game teems. A new series of game reserves has more recently been proclaimed in Caprivi, an area with waterways and wildlife-filled islands reminiscent of the Okavango Delta in Botswana.

Two major natural phenomena lie in the south: the **Fishriver Canyon**, the world's second largest, and **Sossusvlei**, with 1,000-ft (300-metre) sand dunes, the world's highest. The latter is part of the **Namib Desert** which runs along the Atlantic coast for the length of the country. The Namib is a world of dunes, gravel plains and mountain ranges.

Also worth visiting are the coastal towns of **Lüderitz** and **Swakopmund**, with a strong German colonial influence, a 100,000-strong seal colony, the Welwitschia flats, the Waterberg Plateau and Lake Otjikoto. Popular routes lead from Windhoek via the **Gamsberg Pass** through the Namib to **Swakopmund**, and from Swakopmund via rock formations and Bushman paintings to **Etoscha National Park**. Another classic run leading from Winghoek is due north to Etoscha.

BOTSWANA: The Kalahari Desert, a thornbush savannah with a few sand dunes, covers almost the entire surface area of this land-locked country. Flowing into its northern reaches, a number of rivers bring waters from afar. The most important, the **Okavango**, expends itself in a world of glimmering water surfaces and thousands of palm-fringed islands. The lesser rivers, **Linyanti** and **Chobe**, plus waterholes, supply enough water to facilitate a string of game sanctuaries between the Okavango Delta in the northwest and the Victoria Falls on the other side of the Zimbabwe border in the north-east. This is the main safari region.

Further south lie the **Makgadikgadi Pans**, one of the world's largest salt pan systems, and – for daring visitors – the extremely harsh central **Kalahari Game Reserve**, its neighbour **Kutse** and **Mabuasehube** in the southwestern reaches of the country.

Botswana's total population is 1 million, mainly Tswanas. The most colourful minority are the Bushmen, who can be spotted with certainty at **Tsodilo Hills**, or with great luck in the central Kalahari. With the exception of four larger towns, all settlements are better described as sprawling villages. The country's main exports are diamonds, nickel, copper and beef.

The secret of the safari magic in Botswana lies in the very size of the game areas and the comparative difficulty experienced in exploring them by road. A four-wheel-drive vehicle is essential for any worthwhile encounter. Several safari companies offer excellent overnight camping tours with various standards of comfort. Alternatively, tourists can fly with regular charter flights to far-flung lodges inaccessible by road but with first-class standards of hygiene and comfort. These lodges rarely have more than 16 beds. No matter where one chooses to stay, an authentic African experience is almost guaranteed.

ZIMBABWE: The country has much to attract the visitor. However, one out-standing feature matches natural phe-nomena anywhere else on earth: the Zambezi River system. A breathtaking sequence of powerfully flowing water-ways, the awe-inspiring **Victoria Falls**, one of the largest man-made lakes at **Kariba**, and the **Zambezi Gorge**.

Formerly the British colony of Rhodesia,, Zimbabwe acquired its inde-pendence in 1980 after a 10-year bushwar. The country has a good road network and a wide selection of hotels, many first-class. Common points of entry by air are Harare, Victoria Falls and Bulawayo, and by road from South Africa, Beitbridge. Zimbabwe's 9.7 million inhabitants, made up of Shona,

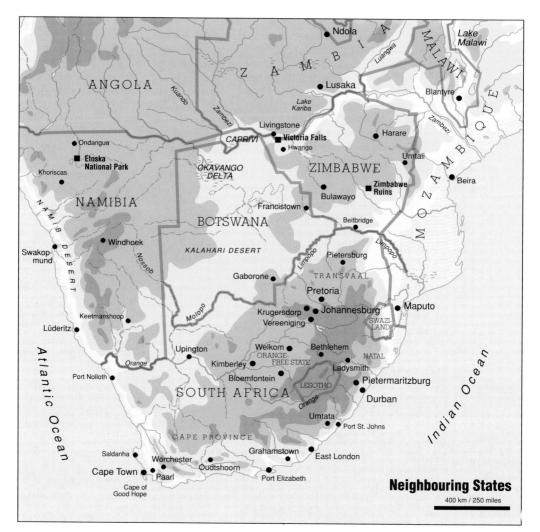

Neighbouring States

400 km / 250 miles

Matabele and a white minority of some 100,000, live off mining and farming, with some industry and tourism.

Most visitors only spend one or two nights at Victoria Falls en route to South Africa or Botswana. Popular extensions by air from Victoria Falls lead to Lake Kariba which also has a number of romantic islands, or **Hwange National Park**. Those with more time to spare can take a lovely self-drive trip via the eastern highlands to **Masvingo** and the **Zimbabwe ruins**, which gave the country its name. An eerie, mystic atmosphere envelops the ruins in which some 11,000 people once lived.

Next in line is **Bulawayo** and the famous **Matopas National Park**. At "World's View", one of the highest points amidst the weird granite bolders of the Matopas, Cecil John Rhodes, founder of Rhodesia, lies buried. The self-drive portion of the trip then continues along the Zambezi River system from Victoria Falls via the Mana Pools to the capital **Harare**.

Alternatively, there are good camp-ing safaris which lead along the Zambezi River system from Victoria Falls via Kariba to Mana Pools and Harare. Another feature is white-water rafting at Victoria Falls or canoe safaris on the Zambezi River below Kariba.

ANGOLA and MOZAMBIQUE: These two immediate neighbours of South Africa – former Portuguese colonies – will only appeal to a minority of tourists because of the effects of recent wars. An exception is a group of small idyllic Indian Ocean islands just off the Mozambique coast. Facilities include good accommodation and cuisine, classic watersports and private air strips.

SWAZILAND: Huddled between Mozambique and the Republic of South Africa is Africa's second smallest country, the kingdom of Swaziland. It straddles the break-off point of the great southern African Escarpment between the 4,000-ft (1,200-metre) high **highveld** and the 800-ft (250-metre) high **lowveld**. This makes for some striking scenery, and motorists wishing to travel from the Eastern Transvaal into Kwazulu/Natal

Namibia's Sossusvlei, the highest sand dunes in the world.

will find it well worth their while to take at least an extra day for a Swaziland detour. The country has a rich tribal tradition, colourful Swazi homesteads are scattered across the countryside, and there are picturesque scenic walks.

The most impressive route would be via **Piggs Peak**, **Mbabane** and **Manzini**. The main roads are tarred, and fine hotels, some with nightclub and casino facilities, welcome tourists.

LESOTHO: Another immediate neighbour of South Africa which is also ruled by a royal family, is the mountain kingdom of **Lesotho** (formerly Basutoland), an enclave within the Republic of South Africa. No point in the country has an altitude less than 3,000 feet (1,000 metres), while some of the undulating mountain ranges climax in dramatic 10,000-ft (3,300-metre) snowclad peaks, the highest in southern Africa. Fourteen border posts give access to the kingdom. Roads are being continuously upgraded, with tarred roads connecting the main centres, particularly in the western side of the country around the capital, **Maseru**.

An excellent mode of travel which presents itself amidst the rugged terrain is by Basotho pony. Trekking centres organise tours for riders who seldom tire of the changing mountain scenery. Visitors are made to feel welcome and busy markets selling handicrafts, pottery, woven grasswork and even attractive handwoven mohair tapestries add colour along the roadside. Accommodation varies from sophisticated hotels with their own casinos and nightclubs to fairly basic self-catering alpine lodges, many of which are pleasantly rustic.

ZAMBIA: Moving further afield, Zambia (former British colony of Northern Rhodesia), named after the mighty Zambezi River, presents an attractive alternative to the adventurous safari-goer. Although not well-developed touristically, it offers a number of excellent national parks, amongst the best on the continent. The most accessible of these is **South Luangwa**, just off the tarred road connecting the Zambian capital Lusaka to Lilongwe in Malawi. Another highlight is the Zambian side

of Victoria Falls; white-water rafting and canoeing operators along the river are among the best. Specialised operators offer fly-in safaris and mobile camping safaris to the national parks.

MALAWI: This country (the former British colony of Nyasaland) is well-suited as a fly-in extension from Johannesburg or as a safari combination with Zambia or Zimbabwe. The country's number one feature is the 355-mile (570-km) **Lake Malawi**, an unspoiled part of Africa with translucent waters, shimmering sands, primeval rocky outcrops and verdant tumbling hills. A network of tarred and gravel roads allows visitors to explore the lake shore or venture into highlands and plateaus affording breathtaking views across the lake or on to shimmering savannahs. Game reserves offer wonderful sojourns amidst prolific birdlife.

The standard of hotels is often good; two first-class beach resorts on the southwestern lakeshores offer a variety of water sports and snorkling amidst the lake's famous tropical fish (which include many species common in domestic aquariums abroad). Fishing villages line the shore, presenting almost biblical scenes of fishermen going out for the daily catch in canoes, carved from single large tree trunks, and using self-manufactured nets.

INDIAN OCEAN ISLANDS: Within easy reach of South Africa by regular air service are the Indian Ocean islands of the **Comores**, **Reunion**, **Mauritius** and the **Seychelles**. Each has its own unique character, but all share the attractions of spectacular coral reefs and palm-fringed, powder-soft white beaches. Some of the hotels are amongst the best beach hotels to be found anywhere.

Some 250 miles (400 km) off Mozambique lies **Madagascar**, separated from the mainland 140 million years ago. The island's long isolation has led to unique plant and animal forms evolving, such as the lemur, many species of chameleon and butterfly as well as a great diversity of orchids and succulents. The coastline, although often very beautiful, is poorly developed, with the exception of the island of **Nosy Be**.

Right, Kung Bushman woman.

310

INSIGHT GUIDES
TRAVEL TIPS

FOR THOSE
WITH MORE THAN
A PASSING INTEREST
IN TIME...

Before you put your name down for a Patek Philippe watch *fig. 1*, there are a few basic things you might like to know, without knowing exactly whom to ask. In addressing such issues as accuracy, reliability and value for money, we would like to demonstrate why the watch we will make for you will be quite unlike any other watch currently produced.

"Punctuality", Louis XVIII was fond of saying, "is the politeness of kings."

We believe that in the matter of punctuality, we can rise to the occasion by making you a mechanical timepiece that will keep its rendezvous with the Gregorian calendar at the end of every century, omitting the leap-years in 2100, 2200 and 2300 and recording them in 2000 and 2400 *fig. 2*. Nevertheless, such a watch does need the occasional adjustment. Every 3333 years and 122 days you should remember to set it forward one day to the true time of the celestial clock. We suspect, however, that you are simply content to observe the politeness of kings. Be assured, therefore, that when you order your watch, we will be exploring for you the physical—if not the metaphysical—limits of precision.

Does everything have to depend on how much?

Consider, if you will, the motives of collectors who set record prices at auction to acquire a Patek Philippe. They may be paying for rarity, for looks or for micromechanical ingenuity. But we believe that behind each $500,000-plus

bid is the conviction that a Patek Philippe, even if 50 years old or older, can be expected to work perfectly for future generations.
In case your ambitions to own a Patek Philippe are somewhat discouraged by the scale of the sacrifice involved, may we hasten to point out that the watch we will make for you today will certainly be a technical improvement on the Pateks bought at auction? In keeping with our tradition of inventing new mechanical solutions for greater reliability and better time-keeping, we will bring to your watch innovations *fig. 3* inconceivable to our watchmakers who created the supreme wristwatches of 50 years ago *fig. 4*. At the same time, we will of course do our utmost to avoid placing undue strain on your financial resources.

Can it really be mine?

May we turn your thoughts to the day you take delivery of your watch? Sealed within its case is your watchmaker's tribute to the mysterious process of time. He has decorated each wheel with a chamfer carved into its hub and polished into a shining circle. Delicate ribbing flows over the plates and bridges of gold and rare alloys. Millimetric surfaces are bevelled and burnished to exactitudes measured in microns. Rubies are transformed into jewels that triumph over friction. And after many months—or even years—of work, your watchmaker stamps a small badge into the mainbridge of your watch. The Geneva Seal—the highest possible attestation of fine watchmaking *fig. 5*.

Looks that speak of inner grace *fig. 6*.

When you order your watch, you will no doubt like its outward appearance to reflect the harmony and elegance of the movement within. You may therefore find it helpful to know that we are uniquely able to cater for any special decorative needs you might like to express. For example, our engravers will delight in conjuring a subtle play of light and shadow on the gold case-back of one of our rare pocket-watches *fig. 7*. If you bring us your favourite picture, our enamellers will reproduce it in a brilliant miniature of hair-breadth detail *fig. 8*. The perfect execution of a double hobnail pattern on the bezel of a wristwatch is the pride of our casemakers and the satisfaction of our designers, while our chainsmiths will weave for you a rich brocade in gold *figs. 9 & 10*. May we also recommend the artistry of our goldsmiths and the experience of our lapidaries in the selection and setting of the finest gemstones? *figs. 11 & 12*.

How to enjoy your watch before you own it.

As you will appreciate, the very nature of our watches imposes a limit on the number we can make available. (The four Calibre 89 time-pieces we are now making will take up to nine years to complete). We cannot therefore promise instant gratification, but while you look forward to the day on which you take delivery of your Patek Philippe *fig. 13*, you will have the pleasure of reflecting that time is a universal and everlasting commodity, freely available to be enjoyed by all.

Should you require information on any particular Patek Philippe watch, or even on watchmaking in general, we would be delighted to reply to your letter of enquiry. And if you send us

fig. 1: The classic face of Patek Philippe.

fig. 4: Complicated wristwatches circa 1930 (left) and 1990. The golden age of watchmaking will always be with us.

fig. 6: Your pleasure in owning a Patek Philippe is the purpose of those who made it for you.

fig. 9: Harmony of design is executed in a work of simplicity and perfection in a lady's Calatrava wristwatch.

fig. 2: One of the 33 complications of the Calibre 89 astronomical clock-watch is a satellite wheel that completes one revolution every 400 years.

fig. 5: The Geneva Seal is awarded only to watches which achieve the standards of horological purity laid down in the laws of Geneva. These rules define the supreme quality of watchmaking.

fig. 7: Arabesques come to life on a gold case-back.

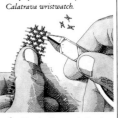

fig. 10: The chainsmith's hands impart strength and delicacy to a tracery of gold.

fig. 11: Circles in gold: symbols of perfection in the making.

fig. 3: Recognized as the most advanced mechanical regulating device to date, Patek Philippe's Gyromax balance wheel demonstrates the equivalence of simplicity and precision.

fig. 8: An artist working six hours a day takes about four months to complete a miniature in enamel on the case of a pocket-watch.

fig. 12: The test of a master lapidary is his ability to express the splendour of precious gemstones.

PATEK PHILIPPE
GENEVE
fig. 13: The discreet sign of those who value their time.

your card marked "book catalogue" we shall post you a catalogue of our publications. Patek Philippe, 41 rue du Rhône, 1204 Geneva, Switzerland, Tel. +41 22/310 03 66.

THOMAS COOK MASTERCARD TRAVELLERS CHEQUES...

...HOLIDAY ESSENTIALS

Travel money from the travel experts

THOMAS COOK MASTERCARD TRAVELLERS CHEQUES ARE
WIDELY AVAILABLE THROUGHOUT THE WORLD.

Getting Acquainted

The Place

South Africa is located between the latitudes of 22° and 35° South, and extends from Limpopo in the north 1,200 miles (2,000 km) down to the Cape Peninsula in the southwest, and 930 miles (1,500 km) from the semi-desert of Namaqualand in the west to the subtropical north coast of Natal.

Including its four "independent" states (Bophuthatswana, Ciskei, Transkei, and Venda), the country has an area of 471,442 sq. miles (1,224,500 sq. km), five times larger than Britain.

The country is divided into four provinces: Cape Province, in the west and south, is more than twice as big as all the other provinces combined (Transvaal in the north, Orange Free State in the middle, and Natal in the east). To the north, South Africa borders on Namibia, Botswana, Zimbabwe; to the northeast, on Mozambique. Wholly surrounded by South Africa are the countries of Lesotho and Swaziland; these, however, have never belonged to South Africa, remaining British protectorates until their independence in the mid-1960s.

With its great diversity of scenery, South Africa can be divided naturally into 21 regions:

The Lesotho Highlands: This, the highest part of southern Africa, straddles the boundary between South Africa and Lesotho and reaches an elevation in excess of 11,000 ft (3,400 metres). Much of the area is a mountain tundra which receives regular winter snows.

The Highveld: This gently undulating, high-lying area of the interior plateau consists chiefly of grassland and coincides with the largest remaining portion of an ancient plain formed by erosion (the African Surface). It is home to the Witwatersrand urban complex and most of South Africa's gold, coal and maize are produced here.

The Northern Transvaal: Of considerable scenic diversity, this area encompasses the rugged Soutpansberg Mountains and Waterberg Plateau, and the intervening Pietersburg Plain. The Soutpansberg is well watered and is a centre of timber production. Most of the rest of the area is given over to cattle ranching.

The Ghaap Plateau: This flat, featureless plain with its semi-arid climate is devoted almost exclusively to cattle ranching. A number of powerful springs, such as the Eye of Kuruman, emerge from its dolomite rocks.

The Bushmanland Plain: The flat, arid expanse of this portion of the interior plateau is sparsely covered by low scrub. Dotted by innumerable seasonal lakes (pans), it is suited to little else but extensive sheep ranching.

The Bushveld Basin: The world's largest body of basic and ultra-basic rocks occupies the flat central part of this basin and is a rich treasure-house of minerals including platinum, chrome, iron and vanadium. Its clayey black turf soils favour the production of cotton, tobacco and other cash crops and citrus is grown on its margins. The encircling Bankenveld ridges flank the city of Pretoria. The ancient volcanic plug of the Pilanesberg, in the western part of the basin, is the setting for the Sun City resort complex.

The Kalahari Basin: Now a semi-arid Acacia savannah, this flat sand-covered area was once a sea of desert dunes. The red dune ridges now support a sparse grass/woodland mosaic which is home to a wide variety of grazing antelopes in the Kalahari Gemsbok National Park.

The Lower Vaal and Orange Valleys: Occupied by the major westward-flowing rivers of South Africa these broad valleys, although at best semi-arid, have attracted much of the development in the northern Cape. The valley of a major tributary, the Harts River, contains the largest irrigation scheme in the southern hemisphere (the Vaalharts). Kimberley, located between the two valleys, is South Africa's centre of diamond production. Below Upington the Orange River enters a deep gorge through the imposing Aughrabies Falls. Further towards the coast its valley becomes barren and rugged in the extreme.

The Karoo: A vast expanse of semi-arid plains dotted with flat-topped hills (koppies), the Karoo is covered by sparse scrub and grass which are well suited to the rearing of sheep.

The Transvaal Drakensberg: This section of the Great Escarpment receives ample rain brought by winds from the Indian Ocean and supports impressive stands of mountainous forest as well as the world's largest plantation of exotic timber in the Sabie area. An early centre of gold production, it boasts spectacular mountain scenery with numerous resorts and hiking trails.

The Natal Drakensberg: Many peaks along this stretch of the Great Escarpment exceed 9,800 ft (3,000 metres) and make it the premier mountaineering centre of South Africa.

The Cape Fold Mountains: Scarcely less spectacular than the Natal Drakensberg, this series of ranges is home to the unique *fynbos* (macchia) vegetation in the winter rainfall area of the southwestern Cape. Rugged sandstone peaks offer good hiking and rock-climbing, while intervening valleys are the centre of South African wine and fruit production. The scenery of the coastal zone, with its numerous deep bays and sandy beaches backed by majestic mountain chains, is amongst the world's finest.

The Namaqua Highlands: Consisting of arid, rocky mountains, the valleys of this rather forbidding area are decked by an immense carpet of spring flowers in years of good winter rains. Its remote northern extremity, adjacent to Namibia, is known as the Richtersveld.

The Limpopo Valley: The Limpopo River forms the boundary between South Africa and Zimbabwe. An area of dry savannah woodland, it has numerous game farms and several nature reserves, although large tracts remain devoted to cattle ranching.

The Lowveld: This zone of low, undulating plains separates the foot of the Great Escarpment from the Lebombo Mountains in the eastern parts of the Transvaal, Swaziland and northern Natal. With its hot, humid summer climate the Lowveld is a major producer of tropical fruit and sugar. A significant area of natural woodland has, however, been protected in a number of reserves, the largest of which is the Kruger National Park.

The Southeastern Coastal Hinterland: Stretching from Swaziland in the north to the Ciskei in the south, this is an area of rolling hills crossed by deep river valleys. Its ample rainfall produces a run-off which exceeds, in aggregate, that of the Orange River. The warm Mozambique current ensures that year-round swimming is possible along the Natal-Zululand coast.

The Lebombo Mountains: This range marks the eastern border of South Africa with Mozambique throughout much of its length. Eastward flowing rivers en route to the Indian Ocean traverse it in a series of spectacular gorges.

The Zululand Coastal Plain: These bush-covered, sandy flats have numerous lakes and estuaries around which several nature reserves have been established. Browsing herbivores dominate the dense woodland, and frequent stretches of water support a diverse population of birds and aquatic creatures.

The Southern Coastal Platform: Stretching from the southernmost tip of the continent to Port Elizabeth, this raised marine platform offers picturesque forests and lagoons along the most typical stretch of the Garden Route lying between George and Humansdorp.

The Swartland: This gently undulating plain between the Cape Fold Mountains and the Atlantic coast has a semi-arid climate and is a major producer of wheat.

The Namib: Like the Swartland, this coastal desert is lapped by the Benguela Current whose cold waters support most of South Africa's fishing industry. Barren in the extreme, its sparse scrubland becomes a carpet of flowers after winter rains.

Time Zone

Time in South Africa is Greenwich Mean Time plus two hours. An attentive visitor will notice that the sun in Durban rises and sets significantly earlier than in Cape Town. The explanation for this is simple: the distance between the two cities is roughly equivalent to that between Birmingham, England and Berlin, Germany. You'll also notice that it gets dark almost immediately – it's pitch-black a mere half-hour after sunset.

The sun rises in the east, even on the Cape: but it's easy to lose your orientation in the first few days, until you've got used to the sun being in the north. Then, east and west will fall into place for you.

Climate

The Cape peninsula has a typically Mediterranean climate, while the weather in the interior, on the high veld, is moderate. Only the Kruger Park and the North of Transvaal could really be described as subtropical.

As the seasons are exactly opposite to those in the Northern hemisphere, Christmas comes right in the middle of the hottest season when it is 30°C (86°F) in the shade.

Thanks to the **sunshine** which graces the Cape's coastal resort areas with 300 more hours of sun each year than the Canary Islands, any time of year is the right time to travel. Particularly ideal are autumn (March–April) and spring (September–October).

Rainfall is an uncertain quantity on the Cape. South Africa is characterised as an arid region (the rate of evaporation is higher than that of precipitation). Two-thirds of the country receives less than 19 inches (500mm) of rainfall a year. In the interior, precious rain falls mostly in the summer months (October–March), generally in brief but violent showers. The Western Cape receives its precipitation in winter (May–September); along the country's southern coast it could rain at any time of year (and the high humidity in Natal can make for some truly muggy days).

Snow falls nearly every year in the high mountains, but seldom results in more than a powdery dusting along the ground. The reason for this is lack of humidity rather than the temperature.

People

South Africa has a total population of some 37.5 million, of whom over 28 million (around 75 percent) are black.

The "blacks" on the Cape are divided into nine major peoples, of whom the cultures, traditions and customs differ significantly. Each group is further divided into several tribes: the Zulus, for instance, have over 200 different tribes.

Some of the black languages have certain similarities. The largest, the Nguni language family, includes those peoples who moved down the coast from East Africa some 300–400 years ago and ran into the white settlers in the area of Port Elizabeth at the end of the 18th century. The Zulus, Swazis, Xhosa, and several smaller groups belong to this linguistic family.

A majority of the native peoples dwell in the homelands. Four of the ten so-called TBVC states – Transkei, Bophuthatswana, Venda, and Ciskei – are considered by the South African state as being independent. However, they're still tied to the larger country's apron strings, not only economically; internationally, they are not recognised as being independent.

A scant 10 percent of the population are Coloureds. Descendants of early settlers and Hottentots or slaves from the east, these people live almost exclusively in the west, and speak Afrikaans.

Asians, who came to work on the sugar cane plantations in the second half of the last century, and who still live for the most part in Natal, make up about 3 percent of the total population. They live in accordance with their own traditions, maintaining their music, language and their culture. 60 percent of Asians are Hindu and 20 percent are Muslim.

Whites, are as mixed a lot as the black population. In the course of the last 350 years, white people have poured into the country from around the world: Dutch and German, British and French, Jews, Portuguese, Greeks, Italians, Poles and others.

Today, Afrikaaners – white, Afrikaans-speaking South Africans, also known as Boers – form the majority of the white population with 57 percent. These people are descendants of the Dutch, who were the first to arrive on the Cape. English-speaking South Africans comprise some 37 percent of the white population. Of other European nations, Portugal and Germany are the best-represented.

Economy

There is probably nowhere else in the world where there are such contrasts between rich and poor as in South Africa. On the one hand the country displays all the typical third world characteristics of other African countries: explosive population growth (2.3 percent per annum), low productivity, low level of education and training (5 million black youths without any qualification), unemployment, desperate housing shortages, and increasing malnutrition. The other side of South Africa belongs firmly in the first world, with its highly-developed industry, various export technology products, modern telecommunications and an advanced infrastructure.

Industrial growth took off in the 19th century as a result of gold and diamond discoveries, taking advantage of cheap African labour which continues to be widely exploited for new products and technologies. Major industries include motor vehicles, machinery, chemicals, fertilisers, textiles, electronics, computers and tourism. Gold provides over half the country's export income, which is further bolstered by diamonds, uranium and metallic ores.

As far as agriculture is concerned, natural conditions in South Africa are not exactly favourable. Only 11 percent of the land area is suitable for the growing of crops, and in these areas the requisite precipitation is not always guaranteed, a fact clearly demonstrated by the disastrous drought in southern Africa in 1991–2. Nevertheless, in normal conditions, South Africa is one of the few net exporters of food in the world. Much more of the land is given over to livestock than arable farming.

Government

Nelson Mandela, leader of the African National Congress (ANC), was elected the first black president of the Republic of South Africa. His rise to power followed years of political struggle to end the oppressive apartheid regime, which resulted in his imprisonment for over two decades. Mandela replaced Frederik Willem de Klerk, leader of the National Party, who became one of two vice-presidents in the government of national unity set up after the country's first free elections. The move towards black majority rule and a democratic constitution brought the previously outlawed ANC into the political arena and ended more than 300 years of political disenfranchisement of the black Africans.

F.W. de Klerk was originally installed as president in 1989 and bowing to internal and external pressure he instituted reforms that brought South Africa more in line with the rest of the world. By pulling down the pillars of apartheid he set the country on the road towards a just society, freeing it from international isolation.

Planning the Trip

What to Bring

Clothing

As in any warm climate, you'll be most comfortable in light cotton clothing. Most hotels offer a next-day laundry and pressing service, and big cities also have coin-operated laundromats. Holiday centres require only casual dress, although for dinner in a hotel or restaurant one generally dresses more formally.

In winter (June–August), it's generally still comfortably warm in Natal (Durban). The rest of the country tends to be around 20°C (68°F) in the day's sun; however, at night and in the early morning, it can be cold, even extremely cold. Warm clothing is therefore a "must".

On the **Cape** and the high veld (Johannesburg) it can become quite cool, especially in the evenings. Always take a jacket or anorak with you.

When **hiking** in the game preserves, wear camouflage colours: beige, brown, khaki, or olive green. This isn't only to keep you from being too noticeable to the animals; it seems to be true that flies and insects are more attracted to white or colourful clothing. Long-sleeved shirts are also a protection against insect bites.

Rain is termed "lovely weather" in South Africa – an indication that the country's citizens would like to see more of it. When it does rain, however, it pours, and one is quickly soaked through to the skin. It's wise to take a raincoat or umbrella with you.

Topless bathing is taboo on the beaches or at hotel pools; but bikinis are perfectly okay.

In addition, don't forget to pack comfortable **shoes, sun-tan oil** and a **sun hat** – not only for beach wear, but also for hiking, particularly in the interior where the sun can be fierce.

Electricity

The standard current throughout the country is 220/230 volts. Only sockets with three-pronged plugs are used, which means that to use European or American applicances you'll have to get an adaptor (which you can find in any electrical appliance shop on the Cape). Some of the larger hotels will loan adaptors to you on request.

Entry Regulations

Visas & Passports

All visitors, of course, need a valid passport. Holiday-makers from Germany, Great Britain, the Republic of Ireland, Lichtenstein and Switzerland can travel to South Africa without a visa. Visitors from America or Australia are required to have a visa. However, if any visitors, regardless of passport, travel through Transkei or Swaziland, a visa is required, which you can get at the border. Lesotho's visa requirement has recently been abolished. Visitors from other countries can receive a South African visa free of charge, but must apply at least four weeks before their date of departure.

Transit visas are issued to travellers who plan to go through South Africa to neighbouring countries, whether by airplane, train, or car. Applicants must be able to show a return ticket and a visa for their final destination.

Multiple-entry visas are recommended for all visitors who want a South African visa and also plan to visit Lesotho, Swaziland, Transkei or other surrounding countries, returning afterwards to South Africa (for their return flight, for example). If you don't decide on such an excursion until you actually get to the Cape, you'll need to apply for a **re-entry visa** before leaving South Africa. This takes at least a week, and can be obtained from the

Swatch. The others just watch.

seahorse/fall winter 94-95

shockproof
splashproof
priceproof
boreproof
swiss made

swatch✛
SCUBA 200

American Express offers Travelers Cheques built for two.

Cheques *for Two*[SM] from American Express are the Travelers Cheques that allow either of you to use them because both of you have signed them. And only one of you needs to be present to purchase them.

Cheques *for Two* are accepted anywhere regular American Express Travelers Cheques are, which is just about everywhere. So stop by your bank, AAA* or any American Express Travel Service Office and ask for Cheques *for Two*.

Department of Home Affairs in Pretoria, tel: (012) 314 8911, or its regional offices in every major city.

A **temporary residence permit** is issued at arrival when you give your reason for and length of stay. If you should want to stay for longer than three months, you'll have to have this permit renewed at the Department of Home Affairs, one of its offices, or a police station; try to do this between 10 and 14 days before the previous permit expires.

Customs

Items for personal use, such as clothes, jewellery, sports equipment, film, used cameras and video cameras, binoculars, etc. are duty-free. Beyond this, an incoming visitor may bring new or used goods (such as presents) of up to 500 Rand in value into the country, as well as 2 litres of wine, 1 litre of alcohol, 50 ml of perfume, 250 ml eau de toilette, 400 cigarettes, 50 cigars, or 250 grams of tobacco. Any spirits or tobacco products which exceed these limits are subject to duty, and can't be written off as part of the 500 Rand limit.

A permit is required for **weapons**; this can be obtained from the customs official upon entry, and is valid for 180 days. The visitor must be able to prove that he legally owns the weapon.

For **animals**, you'll need an import permit from the Director of Veterinary Services in Pretoria, tel: (012) 206 9112. This should be arranged at least two months before your trip. Pets, incidentally, aren't allowed into game preserves.

If you're bringing **cars** or **motorcycles** into the country, make sure you obtain the necessary documentation from an internationally recognised automobile club.

A special permit is required to bring **plants and animal products** (for example seeds or hunting trophies) into or out of the country. The CITES convention maintains strict control over trade in endangered species of plants and animals.

Generally forbidden: drugs, medication (excepting that for personal use), pornography.

Health

Cholera and smallpox vaccinations are no longer required. Yellow fever inoculations are only necessary for those travelling out of a yellow fever zone in Africa or South America.

Malaria tablets are highly recommended to all visitors to the Transvaal, the Kruger National Park and Zululand in Natal. Another sensible precaution is a good insect repellent, particularly in the evening. It's also wise to wear long-sleeved shirts, and to use mosquito coils, which you can buy in any supermarket.

Ticks are found in long grass and can carry tick bite fever (if it should be an infected one that bites you). When walking in long grass it is advisable to wear trousers tucked into boots or long socks.

Snake bites are not very common, because snakes are sensitive creatures and generally try and slither away from "visitors" as fast as they can. Before you take a needle and serum and do yourself any undue damage, you should first look for a doctor or clinic. Wherever you are in South Africa, medical aid is generally no further than two hours away. The best serum is vigilance: don't sit on any fallen tree or stone without first checking that there are no snakes underneath; walk firmly and look where you're going. If you get bitten then check what kind of snake the culprit was – you can recognise a snake bite by the two adjacent pricks. Don't panic, but calm the patient, lie him down and be reassuring – a snake bite is not a death sentence! Try and suck out the poison, but there is no point in doing this after more than about five minutes. Make a tourniquet.

Scorpion bites are very painful. Put cooking salt on the wound; an icepack reduces the pain.

Bilharzia is found in virtually every inland body of water in the Transvaal, Natal and Eastern Cape (except in rapidly flowing water or lakes at high altitudes). Don't wade or swim in ponds or brooks. When in doubt, ask about specific local conditions.

AIDS hasn't yet become as major a problem in South Africa as on the rest of the continent; nonetheless, the disease is spreading quickly.

You don't have to worry about **food**

and beverages – you won't suffer ill effects from consuming fruit, vegetables, lettuce, fruit juices, ice cream, and water from the tap in South Africa.

Currency

Rand is the currency in South Africa, Namibia, Bophuthatswana, Ciskei, Transkei and Venda. 1 Rand=100 cents. In Lesotho, Swaziland, and Botswana, the Rand is generally accepted as payment, in addition to the local currency.

Visitors can bring 500 Rand each in or out of the country; there's no limit on foreign currencies or traveller's cheques. You can exchange extra Rand into other currencies at the end of your trip, but you have to prove that you brought the money in with you: don't forget to save your exchange receipts.

Traveller's cheques are the safest form of currency. Cheques in German marks and US dollars will yield the highest rate of exchange.

Banks are the best place to exchange cheques or cash; you can take care of this directly at the airport upon arrival. Major hotels also exchange money.

Most hotels, shops, restaurants and travel agencies accept **international credit cards**: Visa, MasterCard (Eurocard), Diners Club and American Express.

Krugerrand can only be taken out of the country by visitors. If you buy these in the international departure hall of the Jan Smuts Airport in Johannesburg, you won't have to pay sales tax.

Tax returns: You won't have to pay tax if you have your purchases sent directly to your home address. When purchasing diamond jewellery or precious metals from a shop which is a member of the Jewellery Council of South Africa, Johannesburg, tel: (011) 29 6441, the tax is recorded on a separate receipt and credit card slip. When leaving the country, have your departure confirmed at the Jewellery Council counter; the Council will then send a form back to the shop, which will destroy the credit card slip. This practice, however, is only possible with a shop which is a Council member.

New Year's Day	1 January
Good Friday	varies
Easter Monday	varies
Founders' Day	6 April
Labour Day	1 May
Ascension Thursday	varies
Republic Day	31 May
Kruger Day	10 October
Vow	16 December
Christmas Day	25 December
Boxing Day	26 December

Getting There

The advent of the new generation of Boeing 747s means that most flights to and from Europe are non-stop. It's best, however, to ask when you book – a stopover can make the flight up to 1½ hours longer. South African Airways (SAA) fly to South Africa from Bangkok, Hong Kong, Miami, New York, London, Perth, Rio de Janeiro, Sao Paulo, Singapore and Taipei.

Since the liberalising of air routes in 1992, 47 other airlines began again competing for the profitable South African international routes.

Johannesburg is southern Africa's transportation hub. From here, you can fly to Botswana, the Ivory Coast, Kenya, Malawi, Namibia, Zaire, Zambia and Zimbabwe, as well as Mauritius, the Comoro Islands, Madagascar and Reunion. Some international flights also operate directly to Cape Town and Durban.

Cheaper flights are available from carriers such as Aeroflot, Balkan Air, LTU on their direct flights between Europe and South Africa, in addition to transfer connections by Air Zimbabwe via Harare, Air Namibia via Windhoek and others. New carriers come on-line continuously.

A regular bus service operates between the international airports and the cities. In addition, a shuttle service is available to or from the major hotels; this can be booked in advance and costs around R45. A taxi from Jan Smuts Airport to Johannesburg will cost you around R80.

By Sea

The days when you could take one of the weekly mail boats from Cape Town to Southampton, England, for far less than the price of a plane flight are no more. However, there are still a considerable number of shipping companies offering passage to the Cape.

Various cruise liners call at South African ports, detailed information is available from travel agents.

Medite Travel places from 4 to 12 passengers on Italian freighters. The passengers enjoy comfortable cabins with private bath, lounge, and meals with the Captain and officers. Routes: Cape Town to Livorno, Italy; Antwerp, Holland; or Felixstowe, Great Britain. The voyage lasts some two weeks. Information: Medite Shipping Co., Antwerp, tel: (032) 3234 0360 or Medite Travel, Durban, South Africa, tel: (031) 301 6061.

It's also possible to travel by ship from America. Both the **Royal Viking Lines**, 95 Merrick Way, Coral Gables, Florida, tel: (305) 460 4777 and **Lykes Line**, Lykes Center, 300 Poydras St, New Orleans, Louisiana, tel: (504) 523 6611 can accommodate passengers and cargo.

By Rail

It is possible to enter South Africa by train from Namibia, Zimbabwe and Botswana (see also *Getting Around, page 322*).

Namibia: Windhoek to Johannesburg. Travel time about 45 hours. Departs Wednesday (6.45pm), Saturday (midnight), and Sunday (6.45pm). Change in De Aar to the Trans-Karoo from Cape Town to Johannesburg. The connection is best on the Saturday run. There's only a dining car after De Aar; before that, you can only get snacks.

Botswana: Francistown–Gaberone–Johannesburg. Travel time about 19 hours.

Zimbabwe: Bulawayo–Johannesburg. Travel time about 24 hours. Departs Thursday mornings.

By Bus

This is faster and cheaper than the train, but you should be ready for lengthy, if comfortable, periods sitting down.

Namibia: The Inter-Cape Mainline goes from Windhoek to Cape Town and Johannesburg. Windhoek–Cape Town Monday and Thursday, 6pm (18 hours); Windhoek–Johannesburg Monday and Thursday, 6pm (21 hours).

Zimbabwe: Trans Lux Harare–Bulawayo–Johannesburg, daily except Thursday and Sunday (21 hours).

By Car

For reasons of insurance and security, you can't go to or from South Africa by way of Zimbabwe and Mozambique in a rented car. In Botswana, you can only drive rented cars on paved roads (with the exception of rented four-wheel drive vehicles). If you want to go to Namibia, Botswana, Lesotho or Swaziland (or are coming from one of these countries), you'll need a written statement from the rental company that you're authorised to take the car over the border.

BORDER CROSSINGS

Most border crossings are not open for 24 hours every day, check what time they close before you depart.

Namibia: Vioolsdrift (from Cape Town): 24 hours; Ariamsvlei (from Johannesburg): 24 hours; Onseepkans (from the Aughrabies Falls): 6am–10pm; Rietfontein (from the Kalahari chamois park): 6am–10pm. From Mata-Mata, there's no access to Kalahari-Rietfontein or Twee Rivieren.

Botswana: Ramatlabama (near Mmabatho): 7am–8pm; Skilpadhek (near Lobatse): 7am–5pm; Kopfontein (near Gaberone): 7am–10pm; Stokpoort (from Johannesburg): 8am–4pm; Grobbelersbrug (from Johannesburg): 8am–6pm.

Zimbabwe: Beitbridge: 6am–8pm.

Mozambique: Lebombo (near Komatiepoort): 8am–5pm.

Swaziland: Oshoek (near Mbabane): 7am–10pm; Golela (in the South): 7am–10pm; Mahamba (from Piet Retief): 7am–10pm.

Lesotho: Fickburg Bridge: Monday–Thursday 6am–8pm, Friday–Sunday 6am–10pm; Maseru Bridge: 6am–10pm; Van Rooyens Nek (near Wepener): 7am–8pm.

Transkei: Both border crossings: 24 hours.

Further information on border crossings is available from the Department of Home Affairs (Pretoria), tel: (012) 314 8911, ext. 520. Information about Botswana's Eastern border crossings – controlled by Bophuthatswana – can be obtained from the South African Consulate (Mmbatho), tel: (0140) 3 2521.

Disabled

A disabled person with a measure of patience and a sense of humour would enjoy touring South Africa, though facilities are sadly not always readily available. However, the National Parks Boards offer accommodation for disabled people in every one of their camps all over the country. Also, the Independence Living Centre offers reliable advice about transportation, tourist attractions and accommodation. They have branches in Johannesburg, Cape Town and Durban. Another tourist organisation, SATOUR, can also assist with information. They offer a concise booklet on where to stay for the disabled tourist.

The Disabled People of South Africa (DPSA) have an information centre in Durban.

National Parks Board, PO Box 787, Pretoria 0001. Tel: (012) 343 1991; fax: 343 0905.

Independence Living Centre in Johannesburg, PO Box 32099; Braamfontein 2017, tel: (011) 720 6546; Cape Town, 11 Barkeley Road, Mowbray 7700, tel: (021) 685 4100.

Disabled People of South Africa, DPSA Information Centre, PO Box 1059, Pinetown 3600. Tel: (031) 72 6523.

SATOUR, PO Box 1094, Johannesburg, 2000. Tel: (011) 331 5420; fax: 331 5241.

Useful Addresses

South African Tourism Board (SATOUR)

Austria: Stephennusweg Platz II, A1170 Vienna. Tel: (0222) 4704 5110; fax: (0222) 4704 5114.

Germany: Alemania Haus, An der Hauptwache 11, PO Box 101940, 6000 Frankfurt. Tel: (069) 20656; fax: (069) 28 0950.

Israel: 14 Floor, Century Towers, 124 Ibu Givirol St, Tel Aviv. Tel: (03) 527 2950; fax: (03) 527 1958.

Japan: 2 Floor Akasaka Lions Building, 112 Moto Akasaka, Minatoku, Tokyo. Tel: (03) 3478 7601; fax: (03) 3478 7605.

Netherlands: Parnassustoren Te Locatellikade, 1076 AZ Amsterdam. Tel: (020) 664 6201; fax: (020) 662 9761.

Switzerland: Leestrabe 42, 8802 Kilchberg, Switzerland. Tel: (01) 715 1815; fax: (01) 715 1889.

United Kingdom: 6 Old Grove, London SW19 4DZ. Tel: (0181) 944 6646; fax: (0181) 944 6705.

United States: 747 3rd Ave 20th Floor, New York 10017. Tel: (212) 838 8841; fax: (212) 826 6928.

South African Embassies

Australia: Canberra ACT, 2600 Rhodes Place, Yarralima. Tel: (062) 73 2424/5/6/7; fax: (062) 73 2669.

Austria: A-1190 Vienna, Sandgasse 13. Tel: (0222) 32 6493; fax: (0222) 32 7584.

Canada: Ottawa KIM IMB, 15 Sussex Drive. Tel: (0613) 744 0330; fax: (0613) 744 8287.

Germany: Auf der Hostert 3, Bonn 5300. Tel: (0228) 82010; fax: (0228) 352579.

Israel: Yaklisu House, 2 Kaplan St, PO Box 7138, Tel Aviv 61071. Tel: (03) 25 6147; fax: (03) 26 5532.

Netherlands: Wassensaarseweg 40, PO Box 90638, 2509 LP The Hague. Tel: (070) 392 4501/2/3/4; fax: (070) 345 8226.

Switzerland: 1 Timgfranstraße, Berne. Tel: (031) 44 2011; fax: (031) 44 2064.

United Kingdom: South Africa House, Trafalgar Square, London WC2N 5DP. Tel: (0171) 930 4488; fax: (0171) 839 1419.

Consulate, 135 Edmund St, Birmingham B3 2HS. Tel: (0121) 236 7471. 69 West George St, Stock Exchange House, Glasgow 92 1BX. Tel: (0141) 221 3114; fax: (0141) 221 7413.

United States: 3051 Massachusetts Ave, Washington DC 20008. Tel: (0202) 232 4400; fax: (202) 651607. Consulate, 326 East 48 St, New York NY 10017. Tel: (212) 371 7997; fax: (212) 371 7577.

Consulate, 50 North, 2a Cienega BLVD, Suite 300, Beverly Hills, California 90211. Tel: (213) 657 9200/8; fax: (213) 657 9215.

Practical Tips

Emergencies

During the last few years there has been an increase in crime in the large cities. Nevertheless, South Africa is still a comparatively "safe" country, and provided you take all the usual precautions regarding your personal belongings, then you should be OK. As is the case in most other countries, walking the streets, particularly alone, at night and showing off your jewellery is not to be recommended.

Any **loss of valuables** should be immediately reported to the police. The number to ring in all large cities is 10111.

Medical Services

The standard of medical aid in South Africa is very high and compares favourably with that of Europe and America. Doctors are listed under Medical/Mediese in all telephone directories. One finds All-Night-Chemists in all major cities.

You can get their telephone numbers from INFO:

Johannesburg, tel: (011) 402 5000.

Cape Town, tel: (021) 418 5000.

Durban, tel: (031) 305 5000.

Dentists are listed under Dentists/Tandaartse in all the local telephone directories.

There are both private and government hospitals. The government hospital telephone numbers are listed under *Emergency Services* at the front of the telephone directory.

There is no National Health Agreement between South Africa and overseas countries, so you will have to pay directly for the service you receive. Travel medical insurance is therefore recommended. Be sure to keep the receipt to submit to your own medical insurance company at home.

Business Hours

Like so much else in South Africa, regulations governing business hours have loosened up considerably.

Shops are generally open Monday–Friday 9am–5pm, Saturdays 8.30am–1pm. In smaller towns, they are often closed for lunch 1–2pm. Some of the larger shopping malls (with up to 200 shops) don't close until 6pm on Saturday. Supermarkets, too, tend to keep their doors open longer (usually from 8am until 6pm), and recently it has become possible to shop in certain supermarkets and bookstores on Sunday,

Another important element in the Cape in particular, are the so-called "cafés" in every little village. These don't, as you might think, purvey cake and coffee, but rather newspapers, cigarettes, sweets and some groceries; they are often open 7am–8pm, seven days a week.

Public offices are open Monday–Friday 8am–3.30pm.

Although **banks** don't all observe the same hours of business, they generally only vary by half an hour: Monday–Friday 9am–3.30pm, Saturday 8.30–11am. In the countryside most banks close for lunch 12.45–2pm.

Opening times for **airport banks**:

Jan Smuts, Johannesburg: open 24 hours.

D F Malan, Cape Town: the bank is open during normal office hours and the exchange office opens two hours before international flights.

Louis Botha, Durban: open regular hours, Tuesday, Wednesday, Friday, and Saturday 4–6pm, Sunday 9am–1pm and 8.30–10.30pm.

Religious Services

There has been religious freedom in South Africa since the beginning of the last century. According to surveys carried out in the 1980s, 77 percent of the population counts itself as Christian, with 1.7 percent Hindus and 1.1 percent Muslims. Those of the Jewish faith represent 0.4 percent.

A total of 22 churches belong to the South African Council of Churches (SACC), the South African arm of the World Council of Churches. The largest traditional Christian church is the Nederduits Gereformeerde Kerk (NG-Kerk) with 3.5 million adherents. Then come the Roman Catholics with 2.4 million and the Methodists with 1.1 million. Paradoxically, as long ago as 1980 the Dutch Reformed churches, which were considered to be ardent supporters of apartheid, had more black members than white.

The independent South African churches, involving some 3,000–4,000 institutions, are almost entirely composed of black congregations. Sometimes one of these churches may simply be a community; churches come and go, and some are not even registered.

Large numbers of churches are to be found in the large cities, although religious life is also very colourful and varied in the countryside.

Media

South Africa has had television since 1976. SABC, the South African Broadcasting Corporation, provides four channels with entertainment and information programmes. Channel 1 alternates between English and Afrikaans: on Mondays, the language is English until 8pm (news at 5.45pm) and after the 8 o'clock news; on Tuesdays, it's just the reverse. Channels 2 and 3 broadcast in various tribal languages; after 9pm, you can receive Channel 4 on either of these channels. Channel 4 presents entertainment shows and films in both official languages.

Bophuthatswana also has its own station, which can only be seen in certain areas (such as Soweto). The advent of satellite and extra-terrestial television has increased the choice for viewers who can afford it. A private channel (M-Net) broadcasts almost exclusively sports events and entertainment programmes, but you can only pick it up with the help of a decoder. Many hotels have these, as well as video channels).

RADIO

As well as English and Afrikaans programmes offering radio plays, classical music and the like, there are nine "black" channels: each of the main native languages has its own station.

PRINT

Newspapers are sold mornings and afternoons on the street corners. European papers and magazines can be found at the booksellers' CNA, at quite high prices; these are often several days old.

Postal Services

You can only buy stamps at the post office. Experience shows that it's wise to lay in a supply when you arrive, as post offices are either few and far between, or are closed for lunch when you arrive at their doors.

Post office opening times: Monday–Friday 8.30am–4.30pm, Saturday 8.30am–midnight. Smaller, rural branches close for lunch 1–2pm.

Telecoms

You can send faxes from most hotels, but not from post offices, which only provide telegrams.

Using the telephone is fairly cheap. Telephone boxes only accept 10 and 20 cent coins. Take note: the busy signal sounds something like the ringing of many European – rather than American – telephones.

You can make international calls from some pay telephones, but you'll need a pile of 50 cent and 1 Rand coins. It will take about 20 seconds to establish a working connection.

International calls can be made from any major post office, but you have to pay for a minimum of three minutes; plus each additional minute. At the front of every telephone book there's a list of countries which you can direct-dial.

Hotels generally charge two to three times more than the official rate.

DIALLING CODES

Britain: 09 44 followed by area code plus subscriber's number; **US:** 09 1; **Canada:** 09 1; **Australia:** 09 61; **New Zealand:** 09 64.

Tourist Information

Most of the larger towns and cities have a Tourist Information Bureau which can be identified by a large white "I" on a green background. They provide city maps, information on current events, museums and other points of interest.

In other areas and city centres the Publicity Association fulfils this func-

Don't be overcharged for overseas calls.

Save up to 70% on calls back to the U.S. with WorldPhone.®*

While traveling abroad, the last thing you need to worry about is being overcharged for international phone calls. Plan ahead and look into WorldPhone – the easy and affordable way for you to call the U.S. and country to country from a growing list of international locations.

Just dial 1-800-955-0925 to receive your free, handy, wallet-size WorldPhone Access Guide – your guide to saving as much as 70% on phone calls home.

When calling internationally, your WorldPhone Access Guide will allow you to:
- Avoid hotel surcharges and currency confusion
- Choose from four convenient billing options
- Talk with operators who speak your language
- Call from more than 90 countries
- Just dial and save – regardless of your long distance carrier back home

WorldPhone is easy. And there's nothing to join. So avoid overcharges when you're traveling overseas. Call for your free WorldPhone Access Guide today – before you travel.

Call 1-800-955-0925.

THE TOP 25 WORLDPHONE COUNTRY CODES.			
COUNTRY	WORLDPHONE TOLL-FREE ACCESS #	COUNTRY	WORLDPHONE TOLL-FREE ACCESS #
Australia (CC)♦		**Japan** (cont'd.)	
To call using		To call anywhere other	
OPTUS ■	008-5511-11	than the U.S.	0055
To call using		**Korea** (CC)	
TELSTRA ■	1-800-881-100	To call using KT ■	009-14
Belgium (CC)♦	0800-10012	To call using DACOM ■	0039-12
China (CC)	108-12	Phone Booths+	Red button 03,
(Available from most major cities)			then press*
For a Mandarin-speaking		Military Bases	550-2255
Operator	108-17	**Mexico** ▲	95-800-674-7000
Dominican Republic	1-800-	**Netherlands** (CC)♦	06-022-
	751-6624		91-22
El Salvador♦	195	**Panama**	108
France (CC)♦	19▼-00-19	Military Bases	2810-108
Germany (CC)	0130-0012	**Philippines** (CC)♦	
(Limited availability in eastern		To call using PLDT ■	105-14
Germany.)		To call PHILCOM ■	1026-12
Greece (CC)♦	00-800-1211	For a Tagalog-speaking	
Guatemala♦	189	Operator	108-15
Haiti (CC)+	001-800-444-1234	**Saudi Arabia** (CC)+	1-800-11
Hong Kong (CC)	800-1121	**Singapore**	8000-112-112
India (CC)	000-127	**Spain** (CC)	900-99-0014
(Available from most major cities)		**Switzerland** (CC)♦	155-0222
Israel (CC)	177-150-2727	**United Kingdom** (CC)	
Italy (CC)♦	172-1022	To call using BT ■	0800-89-0222
Japan♦		To call using	
To call to the U.S.		MERCURY ■	0500-89-0222
using KDD ■	0039-121		
To call to the U.S.			
using IDC ■	0066-55-121		

(CC) Country-to-country calling available. May not be available to/from all international locations. Certain restrictions apply.	+ Limited availability.	■ International communications carrier.
	▼ Wait for second dial tone.	♦ Public phones may require deposit of coin or phone card for dial tone.
	▲ Rate depends on call origin in Mexico.	

WORLD**P**HONE℠

From MCI

Let it take you around the world.

* Savings are based on typical hotel charges for calls back to the U.S. Your savings may vary depending upon originating country and hotel, time of day and length of call. All rates effective 7/94.

A Wise Man Never Thinks How Far He's Come. He Thinks How Far He Can Still Travel.

REMY XO BECAUSE LIFE IS WHAT YOU MAKE IT

tion, while Municipality provides information in smaller towns. You will find numbers listed in the telephone book under XYZ **Publicity Association** or **Municipality**.

Here are the telephone numbers of some of them:

Bloemfontein Publicity Tel: (051) 405-8490 (OFS).

Captour Tel: (021) 462-2040 Cape (C).

Durban Publicity Tel: (031) 304-4934 (N).

East London Publicity Tel: (0431) 2-6015 (C)

George Publicity Tel: (0491) 2-4248 (C).

Grahamstown Publicity Tel: (0283) 2-2629 (C).

Johannesburg Publicity Tel: (011) 29-4961 (TVL).

Kimberley Information Office Tel: (0531) 80-6265 (C).

Knysna Publicity Tel: (0445) 2-1610 (C).

Natal South Coast Publicity Tel: (03931) 2-2322 (N).

Nelspruit Publicity Tel: (01311)59-2033 (TVL).

Pietermaritzburg Publicity Tel: (0331) 45-1348 (N).

Pretoria Information Bureau Tel: (012) 313-7980 (TVL).

Port Elizabeth Publicity. Assoc.Tel: (041) 52 1315 (C).

South African Board of Tourism: local offices

SATOUR (South African Tourism Board) has offices in a number of cities where maps and information on the whole of South Africa can be obtained (including accommodation guides).

Bloemfontein: Shop 9, Sanlam Parkade, Charles St, PO Box 3515, Bloemfontein 9300. Tel: (051) 47 1362; fax: (051) 47 0862.

Cape Town: Shop 16, Plaza Level 3, Golden Acre, Adderley St, Private Bag X9108, Cape Town 8000. Tel: (021) 21 6274; fax: (021) 419 4875.

Durban: Shop 104, 320 West St, PO Box 2516, Durban 4000. Tel: (031) 304 7144;.fax: (031) 305 6693.

East London: 4th Floor, NBS Building, Terminus St, PO Box 1794, East London 5200. Tel: (0431) 43 5571/2; fax: (0431) 43 5242.

Johannesburg: Suite 4611, Carlton Centre, PO Box 1094, Johannesburg

2000. Tel: (011) 331 5241; fax: (011) 3315420.

Jan Smuts Airport, tel: (011) 970-1669; Fax: 394-150.

Kimberley: Ground Floor, Louverdis Building, 2 Market Square, Private Bag X5017, Kimberley 8300. Tel: (0531) 3 1434; fax: (0531) 81 2937.

Pietersburg: Cnr Voster and Landelros Maine St, PO Box 2814, Pietersburg 0700. Tel: (01521) 3025; fax: (01521) 91 2654.

Port Elizabeth: PO Box 1161, Port Elizabeth 6001. Tel: (041) 551761; fax: (041) 55 4975.

Embassies

Australia: Embassy, Fourth Floor, Mutual and Federal Centre, 220 Vermeulen St, Private Bag X150, Pretoria 0001. Tel: (012) 325 4315/24; fax: (012) 323 0557.

Consulate, BP Centre, Thibault Square, Long St, PO Box 4749, Cape Town 8000. Tel: (021) 419 5425/9; fax: (021) 419 7345.

Belgium: 275 Pomana St, Msickleneik. Tel: (012) 44 3201/2.

Canada: Nebank Plaza, corner Church and Beatrix St, Arcadia, Pretoria, PO Box 26006, Arcadia 0007. Tel: (012) 324 3970; fax: (012) 323 1564.

China: 1147 Schoemann St, Hatfield, PO Box 649, Pretoria 0001. Tel: (012) 43 6071/2/3.

Germany: 180 Blackwood St, Arcadia, PO Box 2023, Pretoria 0001. Tel: (012) 344 3854; fax: (012) 343 9401.

Ireland: Consulate, 8/9/10 London House, 21 Loveday St, Johannesburg 2001. Tel: (011) 836 5869.

Israel: Dashing Centre, 339 Hilda St, Hatfield, PO Box 3726, Pretoria 0001. Tel: (012) 421 2222.

Japan: Consulate, Standard Plaza, 440 Hilda St, Hatfield, Pretoria, PO Box 11434, Brooklyn 0011. Tel: (012) 342 21005/5; fax: (012) 43 3922.

Netherlands: 825 Arcadia St, Arcadia, Box 117, Pretoria 0001. Tel: (012) 344 3910/5; fax: (012) 343 9950..

Switzerland: 818 George Ave, Arcadia, PO Box 2289, Pretoria 0001. Tel: (012) 43 7788/9; fax: (012) 342 1819.

United Kingdom: Embassy, Greystoke, 225 Hill St, Arcadia, Pretoria 0001. Tel: (012) 43 3121; fax: (012) 43 3207.

Consulate, Southern Life Centre, 8 Riebeeck St, PO Box 500, Cape Town 8000. Tel: (021) 25 3670; fax: (021) 25 1427.

Consulate, 10th Floor Federated Insurance House, 320 Smith St, PO Box 1401, Durban 4000. Tel: (031) 305 3041; fax: (031) 307 4661.

United States: Embassy, Seventh Floor Thibault House, 225 Pretorius St, Pretoria 0001. Tel: (012) 28 4266.

Consulate, 4th Floor Broadway Industries Centre Foreshore, Cape Town 8001. Tel: (021) 21 4283; fax: (021) 21 4283

Consulate, 29th Floor Durban Bay House, 33 Smith St, Durban 4001. Tel: (031) 304 3734.

Parks Board

National Parks Board, Central Bookings, PO Box 787, Pretoria 0001. Tel: (012) 343 1991; fax: (012) 343 0905.

Regional Offices can be contacted at the following addresses:

PO Box 7400, Roggebaai, Cape Town 8012. Tel: (021) 419 5365.

PO Box 774, George 6530. Tel: (0441) 74 6924.

KwaZulu/Natal Parks Board, PO Box 662, Pietermaritzburg 3200. Tel: (0331) 47 1981; fax: (0331) 47 1980.

Ciskei Department of Wildlife Resources, PO Box 186, Bisho, Ciskei. Tel: (041) 95 2115.

KwaZulu Department of Natural Resources, 367 Loop St, Pietermaritzburg 3201. Tel: (0331) 94 6698; fax: (0331) 42 1948.

Transkei Nature Conservation, Private Bag X5002, Umtata, Transkei. Tel: (0471) 2 4322 or 24 9309.

Venda Department of Environmental Affairs, Private Bag X2503, Sibasa, Venda. Tel: (015581) 31001.

Automobile Association (AA)

The AA services are offered free to members of other Automobile Associations world wide. These services are also available to members of the public, but a fee is charged to non-members. Their services include car hire (Avis), international motoring advice, route maps, road travel and weather information.

Cape Town: Martinhammeschlag Way,

PO Box 70, Cape Town 8000. Tel: (021) 21 1550; fax: (021) 419 6032.

Durban: 33 St George St, Durban 4000. Tel: (031) 30 1034; fax: (031) 301 7673.

East London: 27 Fleet St, East London 5201. Tel: (0431) 2 1271/2; fax: (0431) 43 5781.

Johannesburg: AA House, 66 De Korte St, Braamfontein, 2001. Tel: (011) 407 1000; fax: (011) 339 2058.

Kimberley: 13 New Main St, Kimberley 8301. Tel: (0531) 2 5207; fax: (0531) 3 2882.

Pietersburg: Library Garden, 1st Floor, Pietersburg 0700. Tel: (01521) 7 5145; fax: (01521) 91 4303.

Port Elizabeth: 2 Granville Rd, PO Box 27468, Greenacres 6001. Tel: (041) 34 1319 Fax: (041) 33 1413.

Pretoria: Gezina 370 Vorhoekkers Rd, Gezina 0084. Tel: (012) 704287; fax: (012) 330 0162.

Getting Around

By Air

Reduced fares are available for SAA flights. There are midnight flights serving Johannesburg, Cape Town, Durban and Port Elizabeth at a 40 percent reduction on the usual fare. These are very popular so it is essential to make a booking. Payment is required within 24 hours of booking. These flights operate weekdays.

Confirmation should be obtained regarding weekend flights.

"See South Africa" is a special package which can be purchased in Europe from SAA or from the National Airline of your home country, as wel as in South Africa.

Senior Citizens (over 60) receive a 30 percent reduction on airfares.

Family Fares on SAA operate as follows:

1 Adult (eg father) paying full fare; 1 Adult (eg mother) paying 60 percent of fare; Children 12 and over pay 60 percent of fare; Children 2 and under pay 10 percent of fare.

SAA OFFICES

Bloemfontein, corner of Andrew and Kerk Sts. Tel: (051) 48 1812/47 3611.

Cape Town, Southern Life Building, corner of Lower Burg St and Thibault Square. Tel: (021) 25 4610.

Durban, Shell House, corner of Smith and Aliwal Sts. Tel: (031) 305 6491.

Johannesburg, Shop 137 Upper Level, Carlton Centre. Tel: (011) 773 9590; for reservations tel. (011) 333 6504.

Port Elizabeth, Greenacres Shopping Centre, Shop 69. Tel: (041) 34 4444.

Pretoria, De Bruyn Park Building, corner of Vermeulen and Andries Sts. Tel: (012) 26 7028/315 2942.

SPECIALISED CHARTER AIR SERVICES

Fly In Safaris from Zululand operate from Hluhluwe, PO Box 79, Hluhluwe 3960. Tel: (03562) 144; Fax: (03562) 144.

Aviacon Charter operate from Lanseria (near Johannesburg). Tel: (011) 659 1707; Fax: (011) 659 1798.

Speed Air (Pty) Ltd operate from Lanseria (Johannesburg). Tel: (011) 659 2870; Fax: (011) 659 2991.

National Airways operate from Lanseria (near Johannesburg). Tel: (011) 659 2500; Fax: (011) 659 1120.

Foster Webb Charter operate from Lanseria (near Johannesburg) and offer catering facilities. Tel: (011) 659 1731 or 678 6349; Fax: (011) 659-1440.

Air 2000 Charter operate from Lanseria (near Johannesburg) to destinations throughout Africa. Tel: (011) 659 2649; Fax: (011) 659 2931.

Further enquiries regarding charter companies can be made to:

Welco Air Services, PO Box 2020, Honeydew 2040. Tel: (011) 659 1040; Fax: (011) 659 1040.

By Rail

Long distance trains have sleeping berths. The use of the berth is included in the train fare, but a bedding ticket must be purchased. This can be done when making a reservation, or on the train. First Class coupes and compartments carry two and four passengers, while Second Class coupes and compartments carry three and six passengers. Most long distance trains

have a dining salon and catering trolleys provide a catering service. It is possible to rent a compartment/coupe at a special price which is about 80 percent of the price of a fully occupied one (some families, for example, do this if they want a compartment to themselves).

Discount fares apply to children under 6 who travel free, and children of the age 7–11 pay half price. Senior citizens (over 60) are entitled to a 40 percent discount.

Overseas tourists are entitled to a 25 percent discount on first class fares provided their visit does not exceed 3 months.

Platform boards can be found on the departure platform on which coach and compartment numbers are listed against the names of the passengers. The train conductor is also available to assist you.

The distinguished **Blue Train** is a luxury express which transports its passengers in ultimate comfort with excellent service from Pretoria and Johannesburg to Cape Town and back. Accommodation is in compartments for two people, some with their own bathroom. Three meals (included in the price) are served in the dining car and in the lounge car one can enjoy a drink and meet people.

Booking opens a year in advance and it is advisable to make use of this. The trains leave every Monday, Wednesday and Friday in both directions at 10am (Pretoria) and 10.50am (Cape Town) and arrive 25 hours later.

Other trains on the main routes are the **Orange Express** which operates once a week between Cape Town and Durban via Kimberley and Bloemfontein, leaving Cape Town Monday 6.30pm, leaving Durban Thursday 5.30pm, arriving 37 hours later.

The **Trans-Natal Night Express** operates daily between Durban and Johannesburg, leaving in both directions at 6.30pm arriving at 8am the next morning.

The **Trans-Karoo Express** operates daily between Cape Town and Johannesburg. It leaves Johannesburg every day at 12.30pm and Cape Town at 9.20am, arriving 24 hours later.

Impala Rand, Johannesburg, tel: (011) 868 2915, offer a "Hotel on Wheels" to the Eastern Transvaal by SAR train with a stop over at Graskop where luxury buses will take you sight-seeing.

Connex Travel, the travel bureau of the South African Railways, will handle all your reservations for the Blue Train and all other trains:

Johannesburg, tel: (011) 773 8796; Fax: 337 1776.

Cape Town, tel: (021) 218 2672; Fax: 25 1519.

Durban, tel: (031) 302 3363; Fax: 307 3773.

By Bus

Inter-city coach services are offered by **Greyhound Citiliner**, contact Central Reservations: Greyhound Citiliner, PO Box 11229, Johannesburg 2000; fax: (011) 339 8372. Reservations can also be made through offices in:

Johannesburg, tel: (011) 403 6463.

Durban, tel: (031) 37 6478.

Cape Town, tel: (021) 45 4125.

Citiliner operates frequent luxury coach services to various destinations including:

Johannesburg to Durban; 4 times daily, 6–8 hours.

Johannesburg to Port Elizabeth; daily except Saturday in both directions, 15 hours.

Cape Town; daily, 16 hours.

Kimberley (semi-luxury); daily, 7 hours.

Nelspruit; daily, 5 hours.

Translux operates a luxury coach service from Pretoria to Vereeniging, Pietermaritzburg, Durban; daily, 9 hours.

From Johannesburg to Umtata, East London, Port Elizabeth; daily, 13 hours.

From Johannesburg to Kroonstad, Welkom, Bloemfontein; 2 times daily, 7 hours.

From Johannesburg to Cape Town; Sunday, Monday, Wednesday, Friday, return Sunday, Tuesday, Thursday, Friday, 18 hours.

From Cape Town (Garden Route) to Port Elizabeth; daily, 13 hours.

Reservations can be made through:

Johannesburg, tel: (011) 773 2944/52.

Translux Durban, tel: (031) 310 3365.

Port Elizabeth, tel: (041) 520 2400.

Cape Town, tel: (021) 218 3871.

Central Reservations: Translux, PO Box 19, Johannesburg 2000. Fax (011) 774 3871.

Transcity is an economical service from Pretoria via Johannesburg to Durban, operating daily except Saturday in both directions, 9 hours. To Cape Town; daily except Tuesday in both directions, 18 hours.

Cape Town to Port Elizabeth; daily, 13 hours.

Cape Town to Upington; Sunday, Tuesday, Thursday, Friday, return Sunday, Monday, Wednesday, Friday.

Durban to Port Elizabeth; Sunday, Tuesday, Wednesday, Thursday, return Monday, Tuesday, Wednesday, Friday, 14 hours.

Central Reservations: Transcity PO Box 19, Johannesburg 2000. Fax: (011) 774 3871.

Johannesburg, tel: (011) 773 2944 (to 52).

Port Elizabeth, tel: (041) 520 2400.

Cape Town, tel: (021) 218 3871.

Prestige Travels offer a daily service between White River (Eastern Transvaal), Pretoria and Johannesburg. Reservations: White River, tel: (01311) 3 1228.

Turnkey Travel operates a service between Phalaborwa (Eastern Transvaal) and Johannesburg and Pretoria, daily except Saturday. Reservations: Phalaborwa, tel: (01524) 4492/8.

Inter Cape Ferreira Express operates 2 times daily between Cape Town and Port Elizabeth serving towns along the N2. Reservations: Cape Town, tel: (021) 934 4400; Port Elizabeth, tel: (041) 53 3184.

Copper Rose operates between Port Elizabeth and East London twice a day. Reservations: East London, tel: (0431) 47 5055.

Leopard Express operates between Port Elizabeth and Grahamstown, daily. Reservations: Grahamstown, tel: (0461) 2 4589.

Garden Line Transport operates from Mossel Bay to Middelburg (Cape), Fridays, return Sundays; from Mossel Bay to Queenstown, Fridays, return Sundays. Reservations: George 6530, tel: (0441) 74 2823.

Margate Mini Coach operates between Durban and Margate, daily. Reservations: Margate, tel: (03931) 2 1600.

By Car

South Africa has a very good network of roads, some 52,000 miles (84,000 km) of tarred roads, and even the untarred roads are usually in good condition. Travelling overland, visitors will enjoy the lack of traffic.

In South Africa you drive on the left-hand side of the road. Traffic laws are strictly enforced.

When driving through any of the homelands be careful of cattle or goats using the road. You will recognise homeland areas by the huts which are scattered very picturesquely all over the countryside.

Speed limits are generally well signposted. The maximum speeds on freeways are: 120 kmh (74 mph), rural roads: 100 kmh (62 mph), in built up areas: 60 kmh (37 mph).

Seat belts must be worn at all times by the driver and passengers.

Car rental firms offer a wide variety of cars from a Volkswagen Golf to an air-conditioned Mercedes 280 SE, at three times the rate. Mileage charges are usually extra. Check with your car hire firm for details.

It is often cheaper to arrange your car hire from home. The following companies have offices and representatives within South Africa.

Avis Rent-A-Car, PO Box 221, Isando, 1600. Head Office: Johannesburg, tel: (011) 08000 34444 (toll free); fax: (011) 974 1030. Cape Town, tel: (021) 934 0808. Durban, tel: (031) 424 977.

Budget Rent-A-Car, PO Box 1777, Kempton Park, 1620. Head Office: Johannesburg, tel: (011) 392 3907; fax: 392 3015. Cape Town, tel: (021) 934 0216. Durban, tel: (031) 423 809.

Imperial Car Rental, 185 Commissioner St, Johannesburg, 2001. Head Office: Johannesburg, tel: (011) 337 2300; fax: 337 2300. Cape Town, tel: (021) 934 0213 ext. 308. Durban, tel: (031) 42 4648.

Other vehicles available, range from four-wheel-drive jeeps to caravans, campers and camper-mobiles. For further information contact The SA Vehicle Rental Association (Johannesburg), PO Box 2940, Randburg, 2125. Johannesburg, tel: (011) 789 2591; fax: 789 4525.

Where to Stay

How to Choose

When it comes to sleep, the guest has the power of choice: from the most exclusive luxury hotels to modest pensions; motels along the main motorways; small country inns; rustic rondavels accommodation (straw-thatched huts) in the game reserves; rooms to let in private farmhouses; and a whole range of camping and caravan sites, as well as several youth hostels and the YMCA and YWCA which one encounters in every English-speaking country.

The European luxury standard is seldom matched on the Cape. But most hotels are modern and large, more roomy, in general, than those in Europe. Food is varied and good, service often warm and personable.

Bed and Breakfast facilities are on the increase. In these private homes, the proprietor's first concern is the guest's well-being. You can reserve through a central booking agency, and an internal code indicates the type of accommodation available:

Code A: in the main house
Code B: private entrance
Code C: apartment

Some hotel chains have branches throughout the country. Travel and booking agencies take advantage of such facilities. Large chains advertise special passes which give cheaper rates for single overnights.

The Southern Sun Group has the most hotels on the Cape and there's one in every big city, generally with four or five stars. Because of the modern furnishings, some critics maintain that these hotels are lacking in culture.

A step toward luxury and appearance, then, is represented by Sun International Hotels. Most of these 26 luxury establishments contain casinos where entertainment is the first priority.

Holiday Inn, which belongs to the Southern Sun Group, is a chain of fam-ily-oriented hotels (children, for example, only have to pay for meals if they sleep in their parents' room). In South Africa, these are good, middle-class hotels, not comparable to the establishments of the same name in other countries.

Protea Hotels can be categorised as good, middle-class establishments (except for a couple of four- and five-star hotels). One advantage is that the chain has nearly 60 hotels, which means that even in small towns you're likely to find a decent room.

Also members of a chain are the hotels of the Karos Group; each branch has a distinctive, individual character.

City Lodge Hotels are set up for the business market, providing functional, reasonably-priced accommodation.

Relais du Cape and Portfolio of Country Places are more like country clubs than hotels; their members are selected. Generally owner-operated, these country hotels offer first-class service and exemplary cuisine; location and furnishings are wonderful. In the following list, they're categorised as private hotels, as are those of the 12 hotels recognised by Fedhasa, the parent hotel organisation, as the best in the country.

INTERNATIONAL BOOKING OFFICES

Holiday Inn: for Germany, Austria and Switzerland: Martin-Luther-Strasse 43, 6 Frankfurt/Main. Tel: 0130/5678; fax: (069) 609 00 332.

For Britain and the rest of Europe: 15 Park St, Windsor, Berkshire, SL4. Tel: (0171) 722 7755; fax: (0171) 722 5483.

For the USA and Canada: Professional Representatives Incorporated, 1000 East Broadway, Glendale, California, 91205. Tel: (800) 465 4329 (toll free), (800) 421 8905; fax: (818) 507 5802.

Sun International: for Germany and Europe: Feldbergstrasse 8b, 6370 Oberursel. Tel: (06171) 57071/2; fax: 54149.

For Britain: Badgemore House, Gravelhill, Henley-on-Thames, Oxfordshire, RG9 4NR. Tel: (01491) 57 4546; fax: (01491) 57 6194.

Protea Hotels: for Germany and Europe: Gistlstrasse 76, 8023 Pullach. Tel: (089) 793 2615; fax: (089) 793 4225.

For Great Britain: Reservations Africa, 2 Ely St, Stratford-upon-Avon, Warwickshire, CV37 6LW. Tel: (0789) 41 4200; fax: 41 4420.

LOCAL BOOKING OFFICES

Booking offices for hotel and accommodation chains in South Africa are listed below. Only a selection of their hotels are printed here.

Bed & Breakfast (Pty) Ltd, PO Box 91309, Auckland Park, 2006. Tel: (011) 482 2206; fax: 726 6915.

City Lodge has no central bookings. Main offices for information: PO Box 782 630, Sandton, 2146. Tel: (011) 884 5327; fax: 883 3640.

Holiday Inn,and **Southern Sun** PO Box 4280, Johannesburg, 2000. Tel: (011) 482 3500; fax: 726 3019. Toll free: (0800) 117711

Karos Hotels, PO Box 87534, Houghton, 2041. Tel: (011) 643 8052; fax: 643 4343.

Protea Hotels, PO Box 17299, Hillbrow, 2038. Tel: (021) 484 1717. Toll free: (0800) 119000.

Search Africa takes reservations for all Hotels, Country Lodges & National Parks: PO Box 5321, Rivonia, 2128; Johannesburg, tel: (011) 803 8669; fax: 803 3229; Cape Town, tel: (021) 419 0120; fax: 21 1743.

SA Farm Holidays Assoc., PO Box 247, Durbanville 7550. Cape Town, tel: (021) 96 8621; fax: 96 1667; Pretoria, tel: (012) 73 8021; fax: 73 6572; Pietermaritzburg, tel: (0331) 6 7171; fax: 6 7171.

Sun International, PO Box 784 487, Sandton, 2146. Tel: (011) 780 7800; fax: 780 7457.

Travel Africa, PO Box 781 329, Sandton, 2146. Tel: (011) 883 4345; fax: 883 2556.

Classification of hotels is based on the five-star principle listed below:

☆☆☆☆☆ = Deluxe
☆☆☆☆ = Luxury
☆☆☆ = Excellent
☆☆ = Very good
☆ = Comfortable

Stars can only be an approximate measure: many first-rate country hotels don't have any, but you may find them better than some five-star establishments. So you can also sleep well without stars.

Reservations: During high season (generally school holidays) hotels will be busy. Advance booking at these times is esssential.

The following list of hotels is divided into eight regions. Within one region the hotels in the major cities (Johannesburg, Cape Town, Port Elizabeth, etc.) are mentioned first, followed by the hotels in other towns. The towns are arranged by the smaller regions and in alphabetical order. The order of accommodation is as follows:

 a) Hotel chains
 b) Private hotels with addresses
 c) Non hotels
 d) Youth hostels and YMCA

Johannesburg Pretoria & Sun City

Hotel Chains

JOHANNESBURG

Sandton Sun ☆☆☆☆☆ Alice and 5th Streets, PO Box 784902, Sandton 2146.Tel: (011) 780 5000; fax: (011) 780 5002; telex: 430 338. A luxurious five-star hotel in the heart of Johannesburg's most exclusive business and residential suburb. Air conditioning, telephone, non-smoking bedrooms available, À la carte restaurant, facilities for the disabled, sauna, fitness centre and swimming pool.

Karos Indaba ☆☆☆☆ Hartebeespoort Dam Rd, Witkoppen, Fourways, PO Box 67129, Bryanston 2021. Tel: (011) 465 1400; fax: (011) 705 1709; telex: 43 1161. Air conditioning, telephone, non-smoking bedrooms , facilities for disabled guests, restaurant. Swimming pool, fitness centre , sauna, squash and tennis courts.

Balalaika Hotel ☆☆☆ 20 Maud St, Sandown, PO Box 783372, Sandton 2146. Tel: (011) 884 1400; fax: 884 1463; telex: 42 4962. Tranquil setting in the centre of the exclusive Sandton suburb. Air conditioning, telephone, non-smoking bedrooms, facilities for disabled guests, restaurant. Swimming pool.

Holiday Inn Garden Court Johannesburg Airport ☆☆☆ 6 Hulley Road Isando Private Bag 5, Jan Smuts Airport, Kempton Park 1627. Tel: (011) 392 1062; fax: (011) 974 8097; telex: 74 5503. Half a mile (1km) from the airport. Air conditioning, telephone, non-smoking bedrooms available, facilities for the disabled.

Swimming pool. Pets accommodated.
Holiday Inn Garden Court Sandton ☆☆☆ Corner of Katherine & Rivonia Roads, PO Box 783394, Sandton 2146. Tel: (011) 884 5660; fax: (011) 783 2004; telex: 43 0801. Close to the city. Air conditioning, telephone, non-smoking bedrooms , facilities for the disabled. Swimming pool.

Jan Smuts Holiday Inn ☆☆☆ Jan Smuts International Airport.Tel: (011) 975 1121; fax: (011) 975 5846; telex: 74 9534. Convenient for the airport. Air conditioning, telephone, non-smoking bedrooms available, facilities for the disabled. Swimming pool.

Karos Johannesburger ☆☆☆ On the cornrner of Twist & Wolmerans St, PO Box 23566, Joubert Park 2044. Tel: (011) 725 3753; fax: (011) 725 6309; telex: 42 2314. Located in the centre of Johannesburg, suitable for businessmen and vacationers. Air conditioning, telephone. Swimming pool.

Protea Gardens Hotel ☆☆☆ 35 O'Reilyy Road, Berea, PO Box 688, Houghton 2041. Tel: (011) 643 6610/1; fax: (011) 484 2622; telex: 42 2297. Set in lush green gardens. Air conditioning, telephone, non-smoking bedrooms available, restaurant. Swimming pool, fitness centre and sauna.

Sandton Holiday Inn ☆☆☆ Graystone Drive & Rivonia Road, PO Box 781743, Sandton 2146. Tel: (011) 783 5262; fax: (011) 783 5289; telex: 42 7002. The hotel is set in beautiful gardens. Air conditioning, telephone, non-smoking bedrooms available, À la carte restaurant, facilities for the disabled. Swimming pool.

Sunnyside Park Hotel ☆☆☆ 2 York Road, PO Box 31256, Braamfontein 2017. Tel: (011) 643 7226; fax: 642 0019. Near the city, but offering the peace and quiet of the country. Air conditioning, telephone, non-smoking bedrooms available. Swimming pool.

Jan Smuts Airport City Lodge ☆☆ Sandvale Rd, Edenvale, PO Box 448, Isando 1600. Tel: (011) 392 1750; fax: (011) 392 2644. Warm and friendly inexpensive hotel close to the international airport. Air conditioning, telephone, non-smoking bedrooms available, and facilities for disabled guests. Swimming pool.

Randburg City Lodge ☆☆ On the corner of Main Rd & Peter Place, Bryanston West, Sandton, PO Box 423, Cramerview 2060. Tel: (011) 706

7800; fax: (011) 706 7819. Clean and comfortable accommodation conveniently located for the Sandton and Randburg business centres. Air conditioning, telephone, non-smoking bedrooms available, facilities for disabled guests, restaurant. Swimming pool, fitness centre, sauna, squash and tennis courts.

Sandton Katherine Street ☆☆ Katherine St & Graystone Drive, PO Box 781643, Sandton 2146. Tel: (011) 444 5300; fax: (011) 444 5315. Value for money hotel in upmarket Sandton. Air conditioning, telephone, non-smoking bedrooms, facilities for disabled guests. Swimming pool.

PRETORIA

Riviera International Hotel and Country Club ☆☆☆☆ Mario Milani Dr, PO Box 64, Vereeniging 1930. Tel: (016) 22 2861; fax: (016) 21 2908; telex: 74 3217. Exclusive hotel with 18-hole golf course and conference facilities. 45 minutes drive from Johannesburg. Air conditioning, telephone, facilities for disabled guests, restaurant. Golf course, swimming pool, bowling green, fishing, squash and tennis courts.

Holiday Inn Garden Court ☆☆☆ Corner of Van Der Walt & Minnaar St, PO Box 2301, Pretoria 0001. Tel: (012) 322 7500; fax: (011) 322 9429; telex: 32 2525. Located in central Pretoria with comfortable rooms. Air conditioning, telephone, non-smoking bedrooms available, facilities for disabled guests. Swimming pool.

Karos Manhattan ☆☆☆ 247 Scheiding St, PO Box 26212, Arcadia 0007. Tel: (012) 322 7635; fax: (012) 320 1252. Close to the shopping centre. Air conditioning, telephone, sauna, squash court, swimming pool.

Pretoria Holiday Inn ☆☆☆ Corner of Church & Beatrix St, PO Box 40694, Arcadia, Pretoria 0007. Tel: (012) 341 1571; fax: (012) 44 7534; telex: 32 1755. In the centre of Pretoria, good base for businessmen. Air conditioning, telephone, non-smoking bedrooms available, facilities for disabled guests, restaurant. Swimming pool.

Private Hotels

JOHANNESBURG

The Carlton Court ☆☆☆☆☆ Main St, PO Box 7709, Johannesburg 2000. Tel: (011) 311 8911; fax: (011) 331

3555; telex: 48 6130. A warm and friendly hotel in the city centre. Air conditioning, telephone, restaurant and non-smoking bedrooms available.

Sunnyside Park ☆☆☆☆ 2 York Rd, Parktown, PO Box 31256, Braamfontein 2017. Tel: (011) 643 7226; fax: (011) 642 0019; telex: 42 2441. Set in the countryside but convenient for the city Air conditioning, telephone, non-smoking bedrooms available, restaurant and swimming pool.

The Rosebank ☆☆☆☆ Corner of Tyrwhitt & Sturdee Ave, PO Box 52025, Saxonwold 2132. Tel: (011) 447 2700; fax: (011) 447 3276; telex: 42 2268. Friendly suburban hotel with three restaurants, conference facilities and bar.

Capri ☆☆☆ 27 Aintree Ave, Savoy Estates, PO Box 39605, Bramley 2018. Tel: (011) 786 2250/1; fax: (011) 887 2286. Comfortable hotel near the M1 motorway. Air conditioning, telephone, non-smoking bedrooms available, À la carte restaurant .

Mariston ☆☆☆ Corner of Claim & Koch St, PO Box 23013, Joubert Park 2044. Tel: (011) 725 4130; fax: 725 2921. Aparthotel style rooms with telephone, restaurant and swimming pool.

The Devonshire ☆☆☆ On the corner of Jorissen & Melle Street, PO Box 31197, Braamfontein 2017. Tel: (011) 339 5611; fax: (011) 403 2495. Luxury accommodation close to the business centre and motorways. Air conditioning, telephone, non-smoking bedrooms , restaurant and sauna.

JOHANNESBURG ENVIRONS

Aloe Ridge Hotel ☆☆☆ Swartkop Muldersdrift, PO Box 3040, Honeydew 2040. Tel/Fax: (011) 957 2070. Luxury hotel set in a game reserve with authentic Zulu village, 40 km from Johannesburg. Air conditioning, telephone, restaurant. Fishing, swimming pool, squash and tennis courts.

Heia Safari Ranch ☆☆☆ Swartkop Muldersdrift, PO Box 1387, Honeydew 2040. Tel: (011) 659 0605; fax: (011) 659 0709. Luxurious hotel set in a nature reserve, 40 km from Johannesburg. Telephone, restaurant., fishing, swimming pool, tennis court.

PRETORIA & RUSTENBURG

The Farm Inn ☆☆☆ Lynwood Road East, next to Silverlakes Golf Estate,

Pretoria, PO Box 71702, Die Wilgers 0041. Tel: (012) 807 0081; fax: (012) 807 0088. Unusual accommodation in an African stone and thatch palace in a private game sanctuary. Telephone, restaurant. Hiking trails, fishing, horse riding and swimming pool.

Westwinds Country House ☆☆☆ Westwinds Farm Zuurplaat, Rustenburg District, PO Box 56, Kroondal 0350. Tel: (0 142) 75 0560; fax: (0 142) 75 0032. Sometimes called the jewel of the Western Transvaal. Air conditioning, telephone, restaurant. Hiking trails, horse riding and swimming pool.

Olifantsnek ☆☆ 184 Machol Street, Olifantsnek, PO Box 545, Rustenburg 0300. Tel: (0 142) 9 2208; fax: (0 142) 9 2100. A family-run country hotel. Telephone, restaurant. Tennis court, sauna and swimming pool.

Bed & Breakfast Apartments & Resorts

PRETORIA RUSTENBURG BOSHOEK

La Maison ☆☆☆ 235 Hilda St, Hatfield, Pretoria 0083. Tel: (012) 43 4341; fax: (012) 342 1531. This hotel has an excellent reputation for its cuisine and is just 30 minutes drive from Johannesburg. Telephone, restaurant and swimming pool.

Sundown Ranch ☆☆☆ Rustenburg/ Boshoek Road, PO Box 139, Boshoek 0301. Tel: (0 142) 73 3121; fax: (0 142) 73 3114. Country-style hotel with Air conditioning, telephone, restaurant. Horse riding, swimming pool, squash and tennis courts.

Youth Hostels

Fairview Youth Hostel, 4 Collage St, Johannesburg, Box 33774, Jeppestown 2043. Tel: (011) 618 2048.

Kew Youth Hostel, 5 Johannesburg Rd, Kew 2091. Tel: (011) 887 9072.

YMCA, 104 Rissik St, Braamfontein, PO Box 23222, Joubert Park 2044. Tel: (011) 403 3426.

YWCA (only women up to 35 years old), 311 Dunwell Rd, Braamfontein 2001. Tel: (011) 339 8212.

Hotel Chains

Karos Lodge at the Kruger Gate ☆☆☆☆ Sabie River, Kruger Gate, PO Box 54, Skukuza 1350, Hazyview, Eastern Transvaal. Tel: (01 311) 6 5671; fax: (01 311) 6 5676. By the Sabie River at the entrance to Kruger Park. Air conditioning, telephone, non-smoking rooms available, facilities for the disabled, restaurant, hiking trail, tennis court and swimming pool.

Pine Lake Sun ☆☆☆☆ Main Hazyview Rd, PO Box 94, White River 1240. Tel: (01 311) 3 1186; fax: (01 311) 3 3874; telex: 33 5690. Air conditioning, telephone, non-smoking rooms available, restaurant. Fishing, golf course, swimming pool, fishing, hiking trails, horse riding, bowling green, squash and tennis courts.

Sabi River Sun ☆☆☆☆ Main Sabi Rd, PO Box 13 Hazyview 1242. Tel: (01 317) 6 7311; fax: (01 317) 6 7314. Luxury hotel located close to the Kruger National Park, Eastern Transvaal. Air conditioning, telephone, non-smoking rooms available, restaurant. Fishing, swimming pool, bowling green, squash and tennis courts.

Hazyview Protea otel ☆☆☆ Burgers Hall, PO Box 105, Hazyview 1242, Eastern Transvaal. Tel: (01 317) 6 7332; fax: (01 317) 6 7335; telex: 33 5737. Luxury hotel 10 miles (15 km) from the Kruger National Park. Air conditioning, telephone, non-smoking rooms available, restaurant. Swimming pool, sauna and tennis court.

Highveld Protea Inn ☆☆☆ Corner of Rotterdam & Stanford St, PO Box 611, Evander 2280, Eastern Transvaal. Tel: (0 136) 2 4611; fax: (0 136) 62 4005; telex: 74 9147. Located 15 km from one of the country's largest petrochemical sites. Air conditioning, telephone, non-smoking rooms available, restaurant and swimming pool.

Karos Tzaneen Hotel ☆☆☆ 1 Danie Joubert St, PO Box 1, Tzaneen 0850, Northern Transvaal. Tel/Fax: (0 1523) 307 3140. Peaceful hotel in the Drakensberg foothills. Air conditioning, telephone, restaurant and swimming pool.

Mabula Game Lodge ☆☆☆ Private Bag X1665, Warmbaths 0480, Northern Transvaal. Tel: (01 533) 616/717; fax: (01 533) 733. Set in 20,00 acres 8,000 ha of a private game reserve two hours from Johannesburg. Offers game drives, walking trails, horse riding, swimming pool, sauna, fitness centre, tennis and squash courts. Air conditioning, telephone and non-smoking rooms are available.

Protea Park Hotel ☆☆☆ 1 Beitel Street, PO Box 1551, Potgietersrus 0600, Northern Transvaal. Tel: (0 154) 3101/2; fax: (0 154) 6842. Set in peaceful parklands. Air conditioning, telephone, non-smoking rooms available, restaurant and swimming pool.

Private Hotels

Magoebaskloof Hotel ☆☆☆, PO Magoebaskloof 0731. Tel: (0152 76) 4276; fax: (0152 76) 4280. Friendly hotel. Telephone, restaurant, facilities for disabled guests and sports facilities including a swimming pool.

Park Hotel ☆☆☆, 1 Beitel St, Box 1551, Potgietersrus 0600. Tel: (0154) 3101/2; fax: (0154) 6842. Set in peaceful parklands. Air conditioning, telephone, non-smoking rooms available, restaurant and swimming pool.

Shangri-La Country Lodge ☆☆☆ Eersbewoond Rd, Box 262, Nylstroom 0510. Tel/Fax: (01 470) 2381/2371. Telephone, restaurant,swimming pool.

Bergwater Hotel ☆☆, Box 503, Louis Trichard 0920. Tel: (0155) 226 2/3/4; fax: 5 1202. Top class service. Air conditioning, telephone, non-smoking rooms available, restaurant, facilities for disabled guests,swimming pool.

Bed & Breakfast Apartments & Resorts

Regional office, tel: (01311) 3 2997.
Bohms Zeederberg Guest House PPP District Hazyview, Box 94, Sabie 1260. Tel: (01317) 6 8101; fax: (01317) 6 8193. Set in the Sabie Valley, near Kruger Park. Air conditioning, telephone, restaurant and swimming pool.

Magoebaskloof Holiday Resort PPP Road R71 PO Magoebaskloof 0731. Tel: (015 276) 4276; fax: (015 276) 4280.

Youth Hostels

Hazyview Youth Hostel, Box 214, Hazyview 1242. Tel: (01317) 6 7465.

KwaZulu/Natal

Hotel Chains

Beverley Hills Sun ☆☆☆☆☆ 54 Lighthouse Road, PO Box 71, Umhlanga Rocks 4320. Tel: (031) 561 2211; fax: (031) 561 3711; telex: 62 2073. Ten minutes drive from Durban. Air conditioning, telephone, non-smoking rooms available, restaurant and swimming pool.

Drakensberg Sun ☆☆☆☆ Cathkin Park, PO Box 335, Winterton 3340. Tel: (036) 468 1000; fax: (036) 468 1224; telex: 64 6106

Elangeni Strand ☆☆☆☆ 63 Shell Parade, PO Box 4094, Durban 4000. Tel: (031) 37 1321; fax: (031) 32 5527; telex: 62 0133. Located opposite Durban's North Beach. Excellent restaurant and luxury hotel facilities.

Karos Richards Hotel ☆☆☆ Hibberd Dr, PO Box 242, Richards Bay 3900. Tel: (0351) 3 1301; fax: (0351) 3 2334; telex: 63 1169. The only luxury hotel in the heart of Zululand. Air conditioning, telephone, restaurant and swimming pool.

Karridene Protea Hotel ☆☆☆ Old Main South Coast Rd, PO Box 20 Illovo Beach 4155. Tel: (031) 96 3332; fax: (031) 96 4093. A modern hotel with good sports facilities. Air conditioning, telephone, restaurant, facilities for disabled, swimming pool.

Marine Parade Hotel ☆☆☆ 167 Marine Parade, PO Box 10809, Marine Parade, Durban4056. Tel: (031) 37 3341; fax: (031) 32 9885; telex: 62 1448. Sea facing bedrooms in a hotel just 400 metres from the beach. Also close to the central business district.

Mont-aux Sources ☆☆☆ Mont-aux-Sources, Private Bag X1, Mont-aux-Sources 3353. Tel/Fax: (036) 438 6230.Quiet hotel away from the city centre. Telephone,sports facilities and swimming pool.

Karos Bayshore Inn ☆☆ The Gulley, PO Box 51, Richards Bay 3900. Tel: (0351) 3 1246; fax: (0351) 3 2335; telex: 63 1277. Hotel close to the sea. Air conditioning, telephone, restaurant and swimming pool.

Stilwater Protea Hotel ☆☆ Dundee Rd, Private Bag X9332, Vryheid 3100. Tel: (0381) 6181; fax: (0381) 80 8846. Good base from which to tour Northern Natal. Air conditioning, telephone, restaurant and swimming pool.

Private Hotels

Royal Hotel ☆☆☆☆☆ 267 Smith St, Box 1041, Durban 4000. Tel: (031) 304 0331; fax: (031) 307 6884. Voted the best city hotel in South Africa for five consecutive years. Includes seven restaurants, 14 function rooms. Air conditioning, telephone, fitness centre and swimming pool.

Brackenmoor Estate Hotel ☆☆☆ Lot 2013, PO Box 518, St Michael's on Sea, Uvongo 4265. Tel: (03 931) 50065/7 5165; fax: (03 931) 75109. Sixteen bedroom country hotel with telephone, fitness centre and swimming pool.

Hilton Hotel ☆☆☆ Hilton Road, PO Box 35, Hilton 3245. Tel: (0 331) 3 3311; fax: (0 331) 3 3722. Private hotel with country atmosphere. Restaurant, telephone, non-smoking rooms available and swimming pool.

Oyster Box Hotel ☆☆☆ 2 Lighthouse Road, PO Box 22, Umhlanga Rocks 4320. Tel: (031) 561 2233; fax: (031) 561 4072. Hotel with a beachfront location. Air conditioning, telephone and swimming pool.

Sani Pass Hotel & Leisure Resort ☆☆☆ Sani Pass Road, PO Box 44, Himeville 4585. Tel/Fax: (033) 701 1435/6.This hotel is set in Natal's Drakensberg Mountains. Great for sports and activity holidays, facilities include sauna, swimming pool, golf course, horse riding, tennis and sqaush courts

Beach Lodge Hotel ☆☆ Marine Dr, PO Box 109 Margate 4275. Tel: (03 931) 2 1483/4; fax: (03 931) 7 1232. Comfortable rooms with traditional German cuisine swimming pool and close to the beach.

Bed & Breakfast Apartments & Resorts

Central bookings: PO Box 800, Durban 4000. Tel: (031) 306 3755; in the evening, tel: (031) 787 3169; fax: (031) 304 6915.
Regional office: (031) 306 3755; fax: (031) 306 6415.

Youth Hostels

Durban Beach, 13 Smith St, Durban.167 9th Ave, Morningside, Durban. Tel: (031) 23 1695.

Eastern Cape Ciskei & Transkei

Hotel Chains

Kennaway Protea Hotel ☆☆☆ Esplanade PO Box 583, East London 5200. Tel: (0 431) 2 5531; fax: (0 431) 2 1326; telex: 25 0254. Convenient for both East London's city centre and its beaches. Air conditioning, telephone and non-smoking rooms available.

Kei Mouth Beach Hotel ☆☆ Beach Road, PO Box 8, Kei Mouth 5260. Tel: (0 438) 88 0088; fax: (0 438) 88 0088. Luxury hotel close to the beach. Good restaurant, watersports and golf.

Private Hotels

Grosvenor Lodge ☆☆☆ 48 Taylor street, PO Box 61, King William's Town 5600. Tel: (0 433) 2 1440; fax: (0 433) 2 4772. Warm and friendly hotel with air conditioning, telephone and restaurant.

Esplanade Hotel ☆☆ Beachfront, East london, PO Box 18041, Quigney, East London 5211. Tel: (0 431) 2 2518; fax: (0 431) 2 3679. Affordable and comfortable.

Jeantel Hotel ☆☆ 2 Shepston St, PO Box 116, Queenstown 5320. Tel: (0 451) 3016; fax: (0 451) 8 1428. Basic facilities including restaurant, telephone and bar

Bed & Breakfast Apartments & Resorts

Regional office, tel: (0432) 81 1575.

Youth Hostels

Youth Hostel, 128 Moore St, Eastern Beach, East London 5021. Tel: (0431) 2 3423.

Fugitives' Drift Lodge, Dundee, PO Rorke's Drift 3016. Tel: (03425) ask for 843.

Game Valley Lodge, Pietermaritzburg, Box 1301. Tel: (03393) 800; fax: (31193) 30 32.

Hartford Country House☆☆☆, Box 31, Mooi River 3300. Tel: (0333) 3 1081.

Western Cape

Hotel Chains

Far Hills Protea Hotel ☆☆☆ N2 National Road, PO Box 10, George 6530. Tel: (0 441) 71 1295; fax: (0 441) 71 1951. Hotel in the countryside. Non-smoking rooms available, telephone in rooms, restaurant and swimming pool.

Kango Protea Hotel☆☆☆, Oudtshorn. Tel: (0443) 22 6161; fax: 22 6772.

Karos Wilderness Hotel ☆☆☆ N2 National Rd, PO Box 6, Wilderness 6560. Tel: (0 441) 9 1110; fax: (0 441) 9 0600. Holiday resort-type accommodation with air conditioning, telephone in rooms, restaurant and sports facilities including a swimming pool.

Knysna Protea Hotel ☆☆☆ 51 Main St, PO Box 33, Knysna 6570. Tel: (0 445) 2 2127; fax: (0 445) 2 3568. Hotel considered by some to be the pearl of the Garden Route. Air conditioning, telephone in rooms, facilities for disabled guests, swimming pool and restaurant.

Wilderness Holiday Inn ☆☆☆ Located near miles of unspoilt beaches. Air conditioning, telephone in rooms, non-smoking rooms available, facilities for disabled guests, restaurant and swimming pool. Tel: (0 441) 9 1104; fax: (0 441) 9 1134; telex: 24 8409.

Country Protea Inn ☆☆ Corner of Meintjies and Loop St, PO Box 8, Middleburg Cape Tel: (04 924) 2 1126/2 1187; fax: (04 924) 2 1681. Country hotel in the Karoo district. Air conditioning, telephone in rooms and restaurant.

Port Elizabeth City Lodge ☆☆ Corner of Beach and Lodge Rds, Summerstrand PO Box 13352, Humewood 6013. Tel: (041) 56 3322; fax: (041) 56 3374. Value-for-money accommodation by Humewood Beach. Air conditioning, telephone in rooms, facilities available for disabled guests, restaurant and swimming pool.

Port Elizabeth Holiday Inn ☆☆ Marine Dr, Summerstrand, PO Box 204, Port Elizabeth 6000. Tel: (041) 53 3131; fax: (041) 53 2505; telex: 24 3126. Comfortable hotel overlooking the Indian Ocean. Air conditioning, telephone in rooms and restaurant.

Private Hotels

Eight Bells Mountain Inn ☆☆☆ Ruitersbosch District, PO Box 436, Mossel Bay 6500. Tel: (0 444) 95 1544/5; fax: (0 444) 95 1544/5; telex: 24 8187. Country inn on the Garden Route. Telephone in rooms, restaurant and a wide variety of sports facilities available.

Formosa Inn ☆☆☆ N2 National Rd, PO Box 121, Plettenberg Bay 6600. Tel: (04 457) 3 2060; fax: (04 457) 3 3343. Chalet accommodation in parkland gardens all with TV and ensuite facilities. Good restaurant, cellar and swimming pool.

Fairy Knowe Hotel ☆☆ Dumbleton Rd, PO Box 28, Wilderness 6560. Tel: (0 441) 9 1100; fax: (0 441) 9 0364. Resort hotel on the banks of the Touw River, with telephone in rooms, a bar and restaurant.

Bed & Breakfast Apartments & Resorts

Tsitsikama Lodge ☆☆ N2 National Rd, Tsitsikamma, PO Box 10, Storms River 6308. Tel: (04 230) 802; fax: (04 230) 702. Luxury log cabins in forest setting. River walks and special honymoon suites available.

Youth Hostels

George Youth Hostel 29 York St, George 6530. Tel: (0441) 74 7807.

YMCA 31 Havelock St, Box 1200, Port Elizabeth 6006. Tel: (0441) 55 9792.

Cape Town & Southwestern Cape

Hotel Chains

Cape Sun ☆☆☆☆☆ Strand St, PO Box 4532, Cape Town 8000. Tel: (021) 23 8844; fax: (021) 23 8875; telex: 52 2453. Luxury hotel in the centre of Cape Town. Air conditioning, telephone in rooms, non-smoking rooms available, facilities for disabled guests, restaurant, fitness centre and swimming pool.

Capetonian Protea Hotel ☆☆☆☆ Pier Place, Heerengracht, PO Box 6856, Roggebaai, Cape Town 8012. Tel: (021) 21 1150; fax: (021) 25 2215; telex: 52 0000. Friendly hotel with air conditioning, telephone in rooms, non-smoking rooms available, and swimming pool.

Cape Town Holiday Inn ☆☆☆ Mill St Gardens, PO Box 2793, Cape Town 8000. Tel: (021) 45 1311; fax: (021) 461 6648; telex: 52 0653 Hotel at the foot of Table Mountain. Air conditioning, telephone in rooms, non-smoking rooms available, facilities for disabled guests, restaurant and swimming pool.

Karos Arthur's Seat Hotel ☆☆☆ Arthur's Rd, Sea Point, Cape Town 8001. Tel: (021) 434 1187; fax: (021) 434 9798; telex: 52 7310. Mediterranean-style hotel neat Table Mountain and Devil's Peak. Air conditioning, telephone in rooms, facilities for disabled guests and swimming pool.

Marine Protea Hotel ☆☆☆ Voortrekker St, PO Box 249, Lambert's Bay 8130. Tel: (027) 432 1126; fax: (027) 432 1036. Hotel in quaint village with reputation for its seafood.

Bellville City Lodge ☆☆ Corner of Wille van Schoor Ave and Mispel Rd, PO Box 3587, Tygerpark 7536. Tel: (021) 948 7990; fax: (021) 948 8805. Value-for-money accommodation close to the airport. Air conditioning, telephone in rooms, non-smoking rooms , facilities for disabled guests, restaurant and swimming pool.

Devon Valley Protea Hotel ☆☆ Devon Valley Rd, PO Box 68, Stellenbosch 7600. Tel: (021) 882 2012; fax: (021) 882 2610; telex: 52 2558. Hotel set in the wine region. Air conditioning, telephone in rooms, non-smoking rooms , facilities for disabled guests, restaurant and swimming pool.

Private Hotels

Ambassador by the Sea ☆☆☆☆ 34 Victoria Rd, PO Box 83, Sea Point 8060. Tel: (021) 439 6170; fax: (021) 439 6336. Luxury hotel with rooms with views. Telephone in rooms, restaurant and swimming pool. .

Cedarberg Hotel ☆☆ Voortrekker St, PO Box 37, Citrusdal 7340. Tel: (022) 921 2221; fax: (022) 921 2704. Comfortable accommodation in the Olifants River Valley with air conditioning, telephone in rooms, restaurant and swimming pool. .

Helmsley Hotel ☆☆ 16 Hof St Gardens, Cape Town 8001. Tel: (021) 23 7200; fax: (021) 23 1533. Comforta-

ble accommodation includes telephone in rooms and swimming pool.

Metropole Hotel ☆☆ 38 Long St, PO Box 3086, Cape Town 8000. Tel: (021) 23 6363; fax: (021) 23 6370. City centre hotel with air conditioning and telephone in rooms.

Shrimpton Manor ☆ 19 Alexander Rd, Muizenberg 7945. Tel: (021) 788 1128/9; fax: (021) 788 5225. Excellent cuisine in the manor house with basic rooms and swimming pool.

Bed & Breakfast Apartments & Resorts

Regional office: (021) 61 6543; fax: (021) 683 5159.

Youth Hostels

YMCA 60 Queen Victoria St, Gardens 8001. Tel: (021) 24 1247.

YWCA 20 Bellevue St, Gardens 8001. Tel: (021) 23 3711.

Orange Free State & Western Transvaal

Hotel Chains

Bloemfontein Holiday Inn - Naval Hill ☆☆☆ 1 Union Ave, PO Box 1851, Bloemfontein 9300. Tel: (051) 30 1111; fax: (051) 30 4141; telex: 267 645. City centre hotel with air conditioning, telephone in rooms, non-smoking rooms available, facilities for disabled, restaurant and swimming pool.

Welkom Inn ☆☆☆.corner of Tempest & Stateway Rds, PO Box 887, Welkom 9460. Tel: (057) 357 3361; fax: (057) 352 1458; telex: 26 3024.Located 5 km from the airport. Air conditioning, telephone in rooms, non-smoking rooms available, facilities forguests, restaurant and swimming pool.

Bloemfontein City Lodge ☆☆ corner of Voortrekker St & Parfitt Ave, PO Box 3552, Bloemfontein 9300. Tel: (051) 47 9888; fax: (051) 47 5669. Close to Bloemfontein business centre. Air conditioning, telephone in rooms, non-smoking rooms available, facilities for disabled guests and swimming pool.

Private Hotels

Eldorado Motel ☆☆☆ Main St, PO Box 313, Kuruman 8460. Tel: (05

373) 2 2191/2/3; fax: (05 373) 2 2191. This motel has comfortable rooms with air conditioning, telephone, and a swimming pool.

Indaba Hotel ☆☆ 47 Fichardt St, PO Box 103, Sasolburg 9570. Tel: (016) 76 0600; fax: (016) 76 1938. Central hotel with carvery, bar, function room and swimming pool.

Park Hotel ☆☆, 23 Muller St, PO Box 8, Bethlehem 9700. Tel: (058) 303 5191; fax: (058) 303 5191. Friendly hotel Air conditioning, telephone in rooms, non-smoking rooms available, facilities for disabled guests, restaurant and swimming pool. .

Bed & Breakfast Apartments & Resorts

Regional office: (021) 61 6543; fax: 683 5159.

Nebo Holiday Farm Nebo Farm, PO Box 178, Ficksburg 9730. Tel: (05192) 3947/3281. Accommodation on a 1,200-acre (486-ha) estate. Telephone in rooms, restaurant, sports facilities and swimming pool.

Cape Province

Hotel Chains

Waterwiel Protea ☆☆☆ Voortrekker St, PO Box 250, Kakamas 8870. Tel: (054) 431 0838; fax: (054) 431 0836. Small hotel with air conditioning, telephone in rooms and swimming pool.

Diamond Lodge ☆☆ 124 Du Toitspan Rd, PO Box 2068, Kimberley 8300. Tel/Fax: (0 531) 81 1281. Good standard of accommodation with air conditioning, telephone in rooms, non-smoking rooms available, facilities for disabled guestsand bar.

Private Hotels

Drostdy Hotel ☆☆☆ 30 Church St, PO Box 400, Graaff-Reinet 6280. Tel: (0 491) 2 2161; fax: (0 491) 2 4582. An elegant award-winning hotel. Air conditioning, telephone in rooms, restaurant and swimming pool.

Kamieskroon Hotel ☆☆ Old National Rd, PO Box 19, Kamieskroon 8241. Tel: (0 257) 614; fax: (0 257) 675. Family-owned hotel in Namaqualand. Specialises in eco-tourism and photographic workshops.

Kokerboom Motel ☆☆ PO Box 340, Springbok 8240. Tel: (0 251) 2 2685; fax: (0 251) 2 2257. Spacious hotel in Namaqualand. Air conditioning and telephone in rooms.

New Masonic Hotel ☆☆ Stockenstroom St, PO Box 44, Cradock 5880. Tel: (0 481) 3115/2114; fax: (0 481) 4402. Friendly hotel with basic accommodation.

Bed & Breakfast Apartments & Resorts

Regional bookings, tel: (011) 482 1206; 787 3169 (evening); fax: 726 6915.

Youth Hostels

Kimberley Youth Hostel, Bloemfontein Rd, Kimberley 8300. Tel: (0531) 2 8577.

Campsites & Motorhome Parks

The Holiday Resort groups Club Caraville (CC) and Overvaal (OV) have their initials placed after the name of the sites. Bookings can be made through a central booking office or directly with the site concerned.

Overvaal Resorts (OV), central bookings, Box 3046, Pretoria 0001. Tel: (012) 346 2277; fax: 346 2276.

Eating Out

What to Eat

Many South African specialties are derived from Malaysian cuisine: Malaysian slaves were often used as cooks in white households. In and around Cape Town particularly, southeast Asian dishes have established a firm foothold on the menus of restaurants and hotels.

Bobotie is a sweet-and-spicy dish of ground meat. *Bredie* is traditionally a casserole of mutton and vegetables.

Sosaties are skewers of mutton or pork with small onions. *Chutney* is a sweet-and-sour fruit conserve which is served as a condiment with curries. *Koeksusters* are only advised for those with a very sweet tooth: small cakes fried in fat, then immersed in syrup.

In Durban and the surrounding area, the cuisine has a distinctively Indian flavour. Workers and traders who were brought in from India to work in the sugar-cane trade imported their wonderful *curries*: various casseroles made of vegetables, legumes, lamb, chicken or beef on saffron rice, accompanied by such condiments as bananas, tomatoes, chutneys, and particularly grated coconut, which is supposed to take away some of the bite of especially hot curries. Catering to timid foreign tastes, curries are also served mild and medium-hot.

Biltong delights the hearts of South Africans living abroad (particularly young ones). Resembling dry sticks of wood, these strips of beef are salted, spiced and air-dried until they're completely dried out. A special delicacy is *venison biltong*: when a game farmer produces his own, this leaves commercially prepared beef biltong in the dust.

Braaivleis (outdoor grilling) is as much a part of the South African way of life as sunshine and rugby. There's hardly a picnic spot, campsite or bungalow in the national parks that hasn't got a barbecue and grill. Many hotels also offer *braais* in their gardens on weekends. An important ingredient of braaivleis is *boerewors*, a large sausage made of mutton and beef. The best specimens can be purchased at small rural butchers in the Orange Free State or Transvaal, who make them with the same recipes used by their grandmothers.

Thanks to the country's various climatic and soil conditions, all kinds of fruit are grown in South Africa. On the Cape, there are marvellous grapes, apples and pears; while East Transvaal and Natal produce tropical fruits such as paw-paws, avocados, mangos, lichees, pineapples, bananas, and many others. You can get fruit fresh, as juice, or as delicious fruit rolls, fruit pulp dried in thin layers and rolled up, ideal snacks for long car trips.

As for *beverages*: the local beers are good, with Windhoek beer, from Namibia, perhaps the best in flavour

and purity. Fruit juices and mediocre wine are sold in 3 or 5 litre containers, which have a little tap on the side so that the contents are not exposed to air, and remain fresh. *Liquifruit* and *Monis* juices are produced without the addition of sugar.

Rooibos tea lies, in flavour, somewhere between the better-known herbal teas and black tea. It's made from the fine twigs of the local red bush, and is quite refreshing when chilled. You can get it in most hotels and restaurants, or in any local supermarket.

Except in the major hotels and cities, mineral water is still largely unknown. The local mineral water *Skoonspruit* (clean spring) is cheaper than the imported product. If there isn't any mineral water, you can always order soda.

If you're fond of liqueurs, make sure you sample *Amarula*. This mandarin-flavoured liqueur, made from the yellow fruit of the marula tree, is the local equivalent of Cointreau and it's extremely sweet. There is also *Van der Hum*, a golden-coloured mandarin liqueur which is very sweet.

Where to Eat

Restaurants

Restaurants on the Cape are generally good to very good and tend not to be too expensive. Every year, 54 judges select the best restaurants (previous winners are marked with an asterisk in the following list).

JOHANNESBURG & PRETORIA

Baytree, Hans Strydom Drive, Linden. Tel: (011) 782 7219.

Bougainvillea*, 1 Standard Bank Building, Cradock Ave, Rosebank. Tel: (011) 788 4883. French cuisine.

Chapters, 5th St, Sandton. Tel: (011) 783 8701.

Chardonnay's, Joshua Doore Centre, Louis Botha Ave, Wynberg. Tel: (011) 786 1618. French cuisine.

Chez Patrice* 5 Riviera, 97 Soutpansberg Rd, Sunnyside, Pretoria. Tel: (012) 70 8916.

Frog, 376a Jan Smuts Ave, Craighall. Tel: (011) 787 2304.

Harridan's*, Market Theatre, Bree St, Johannesburg. Tel: (011) 476 6084.

Hertford, Pelindaba Rd, Bryanston.

Tel: (011) 659 0467. A country restaurant feel.

Ile de France, Dunkeld West Shopping Centre, 281 Jan Smuts Ave, Dunkeld West. Tel: (011) 442 8216. French cuisine.

Leipold's, 94 Jutta St, Braamfontein (city centre). Tel: (011) 339 2765. South African cuisine.

Le Marquis*, 12 Fredman Drive, Sandown. Tel: (011) 783 8947. French cuisine.

La Madelaine*, Esselen St, Sunnyside, Pretoria. Tel: (012) 44 6076 258. French cuisine.

Linger Longer*, Juta St, Braamfontein (city centre). Tel: (011) 339 7814 94.

Lupo, Dunkeld West Shopping Centre, 281 Jan Smuts Ave, Dunkeld West. Tel: (011) 880 4850. Italian cuisine.

Ma Cuisine, 40 7th Ave, Parktown North. Tel: (011) 880 1946.

Pearl Garden*, 24 9th Ave, Rivonia. Tel: (011) 803 1781. Oriental cuisine

Saint James*, Johannesburg Sun Hotel, 84 Smal Streets. Tel: (011) 29 7011. French cuisine.

The Three Ships*, Carlton Hotel, Main St (city centre). Tel: (011) 331 8911.

Zoo Lake, Zoolake Gardens, Parkview. Tel: (011) 646 8807.

DURBAN & ENVIRONS

British Middle East Indian Sporting & Dining Club, 16 Stamford Hill Road, Durban. Tel: (031) 309 4017. Indian cuisine.

Chatters, 32 Hermitage St, Durban (city centre). Tel: (031) 306 1896.

La Dolce Vita, Durdoc Centre, 460 Smith St. Tel: (031) 301 8161. North Italian cuisine.

Le St Geran*, 31 Aliwal St, Marine Parade. Tel: (031) 304 7509. French cuisine.

Les Saisons, Maharani Hotel, Marine Parade (beach). Tel: (031) 32 7361

Le Troquet, Cowie's Hill, 860 Old Main Rd, Cowie's Hill. Tel: (031) 86 5388. French cuisine.

Michael's Cuisine*, Waterfall Shopping Centre, Inanda Rd, Waterfall. Tel: (031) 763 3429.

Panchinello's, Elangeni Hotel, Marine Parade (beach). Tel: (031) 37 1321.

Razzmatazz, 21 Beach Rd, Amanzimtoti (south coast). Tel: (031) 903 4131.

Scalini, Marine Sands, 237 Marine Parade (beach). Tel: (031) 32 2804. Italian cuisine.

Seasons*, St Helens Rd, Gillitts. Tel: (031) 75 1518.

Sir Benjamin's, Holiday Inn Hotel, Marine Parade (beach). Tel: (031) 37 3341.

The Colony, Oceanic Centre, Harris Crescent. Tel: (031) 368 2789.

The Royal Grill*, Royal Hotel, 267 Smith St, Durban (city centre). Tel: (031) 304 0331.

Wolfgang's, 136 Florida Rd, Morningside. Tel: (031) 232 861.

THE CAPE PENINSULA

Alibi, Waterkant St (city centre). Tel: (021) 25 2497. Italian cuisine.

Blues, Victoria Rd, Campsbay (beach). Tel: (021) 438 2040.

Boschendal Wine Estate, Groot Drakenstein. Tel: (02211) 4 1252. South African cuisine.

Buitenverwachting*, Husseysvlei, Klein Constantiaweg, Constantia. Tel: (021) 794 3522.

Burgundy, Market Square, Hermanus. Tel: (0283) 2 2800.

Champers, Deer Park Drive, Highlands. Tel: (021) 45 4335. French cuisine.

Fisherman's Cottage*, 3 Gray Rd, Plumsted. Tel: (021) 797 6341. Seafood.

Floris Smit Huijs*, 55 Church St (city centre). Tel: (021) 23 3414.

Freda's, 110 Kloof St, Gardens. Tel: (021) 23 8653.

Jonkershuis Restaurant, on the Groot Constantia vineyard, Constantia Road. Tel: (021) 794 6255. South African cuisine.

Kaapse Tafel, 90 Queen Victoria St (near Museum). Tel: (021) 23 1651. South African cuisine.

Laborie Restaurant, Taillefert St, Paarl. Tel: (02211) 63 2034. South African cuisine.

Le Petit Ferme, Pass Rd, Franschhoek. Tel: (02212) 3016. Midday meals and coffee and cakes.

Le Quartier Francais*, 16 Huguenot St, Franschhoek. Tel: (02212) 3113. French cuisine.

Mamma Roma, Stelmarket Centre, Merriman Ave, Stellenbosch. Tel: (02231) 6064. Italian cuisine.

Rozenhof, 18 Kloof St, Gardens. Tel: (021) 24 1968.

Spier Wine Estate, Lynedoch, Stellenbosch. Tel: (02231) 9 3812. South African cuisine.

The Bressay Bank, Hout Bay Harbour.

Tel: (021) 790 5460. Seafood, Cape Town's only swimming restaurant. Closed July and August.

Truffles*, Main Road, Hatfield. Tel: (021) 72 6161.

Drinking Notes

Wine

Groot Constantia, Constantia Road, Wynberg. Open daily 10am–5pm; hourly guided tours of the cellar. Groot Constantia belonged to Governor Simon van der Stel, who brought both viticulture and oaks to the Cape. The wines of this most famous Cape vineyard were popular with Napoleon, Bismarck and the European aristocracy, and are still excellent. The manor house is a fine example of Cape Dutch architecture and is open to the public, as is the Wine Museum in the old wine cellar (which isn't a cellar at all). Tel: (021) 794 5067.

Stellenbosch is the second-oldest city in South Africa, founded in 1679 by Simon van der Stel. Today, it's an enchanting university town and wine-growing area. Stellenbosch is particularly well-known for its numerous well-preserved historical buildings in the Cape Dutch style. Stellenbosch is a good town to explore on foot; begin in Dorp Street.

You can get information and brochures from the Stellenbosch Publicity Association, 30 Plein St, Stellenbosch. Tel: (02231) 3584

The Stellenbosch Wine Route, a 7.5-mile (12-km), well-marked route around Stellenbosch, brings you to many private vineyards, most of which offer guided tours of their cellars and wine-tastings.

The Paarl Wine Route also leads to several vineyards; most famous among these is Nederburg, whose wines have taken many international gold medals in the last 20 years.

Franschhoek: The French settled here in 1688 and laid the cornerstone for the South African wine industry. Nine of the pioneer farms still exist today, but most of them are closed to visitors; however, you can visit Boschendal. Take note of Le Quartier Francais: it was once named one of the 10 best restaurants in South Africa.

Attractions

Cultural

The country's many different peoples set the tone: cultures from around the world make themselves felt in South Africa. The western world is represented with the traditional opera, ballet and classical music, while Africa is present in, for example, song festivals and the visual arts.

Computicket is an extremely practical and time-saving innovation: a computerised reservation office in every major shopping centre for tickets to concerts, operas and the cinema. In Johannesburg and Pretoria, you can also buy tickets there for the bus ride to Sun City and for the bus lines Inter Cape Mainliner and Greyhound. Information about sales offices:

Johannesburg, tel: (011) 331 9991.
Cape Town, tel: (021) 21 4715.
Durban, tel: (031) 304 2753.

The metropolises enjoy an active, varied cultural life. Each of the four provinces has its own opera house and symphony orchestra, which perform at an extremely high artistic level.

A number of South African singers perform on European stages (including Barry Coleman, Sharon Rostorf, Deon van den Walt); and John Cranko, the choreographer of the Stuttgart Ballet, who was originally from Cape Town.

Johannesburg & Pretoria

Proud of its international reputation is the **Johannesburg Market Theatre**: three stages in a former market hall with a notorious past. Old signs ("No spitting"; "Only vaccinated chickens") still ornament the old white bricks; the spotlights are concealed in the massive pillars holding up the dome; and the audience is seated on cast-iron seats covered with plush. Information: Market Theatre, Johannesburg, tel: (011) 832 1641. The restaurant next door, Harridan's, tel: (011) 838 6960,

is also popular. Throughout the country, the Market is a symbol for political protest theatre. Several anti-apartheid shows left from here on tours to Europe and New York (*Woza Albert, Township Fever, Serafina* and others).

Other stages in Johannesburg include the Andre Huguenot Theatre, the Alhambra, Windybrow and Alexander Theatre. Concerts are also held in the Town Hall or in the Pedagogical High School's Linder Auditorium.

Some small stages have also attracted attention. In Roodepoort, not far from Johannesburg, the bi-annual **Roodepoort Eisteddfod** in October has been a hot topic of conversation since 1981. It's one of the largest international music competitions for orchestras, solo instrumentalists, singers, choruses, folk music and dance. Some 2,500 participants come from 30 to 35 foreign countries – a tribute to international understanding. Information: Eisteddfod-Johannesburg, tel: (011) 472 2820; fax: (011) 472 1014.

An evening in the **Pretoria State Theatre** is enough to make you forget you're in Africa. Whether the show is *My Fair Lady* or *Lohengrin*, performances are up to European standards, which surprises not a few visitors. Completed in 1981, the theatre in the capital city has five stages and 3,000 seats; the stages range from the large opera house, with 1,300 seats, to the intimate studio, which seats 150.

PACT (Performing Arts Council of Transvaal) keeps cultural life going: there are 2,700 performances a year, ranging from grand opera to concerts, including events arranged for the native populations. Information: State Theatre, Pretoria, tel: (012) 322 1665, ext. 381.

Further details can be found in the "Entertainment" listings of the daily papers.

Cape Town & Environs

Cape Town's **Nico Malan Opera House** presents performances of opera, ballet and theatre. Tel: (021) 21 7839. In the **Baxter Theatre** of Cape Town University, on Main Road in Rondebosch, you can see classical and contemporary theatre, as well as works by South African authors. Tel: (021) 689 8918. **The Arena** or **Little Theatre** on Orange Street in Gardens offers works for

those interested in experimental theatre. Tel: (021) 24 0034. The **Theatre on the Bay** in Camps Bay presents light dramas and comedies. Tel: (021) 438 3301.

Symphony concerts are held in the Town Hall or in the smaller rooms of the Old Townhouse on Greenmarket Square, or at St Georges' Cathedral on Wale Street (city centre). Tel: (021) 415 1250.

In Athlone, the Joseph Stone Theatre presents predominantly protest theatre, as well as films with a political twist; but jazz and pop concerts are also held here. Tel: (021) 415 1250.

For decades, the summer performances of Shakespeare plays under the oak trees of **Maynardville Park** in Wineberg have been immensely popular. Enquire at Computicket. Tel: (021) 21 4715.

Summer months see outdoor Sunday afternoon concerts in the **Oude Libertas Open-Air Amphitheatre** in Stellenbosch.

Held in June and July, the **National Arts Festival** in Grahamtown (80 miles/130 km northeast of Port Elizabeth), a high point of the South African cultural calendar, includes events ranging from classical music to dance and theatre (from Shakespeare to contemporary authors) to exhibitions, lectures and an international film festival. Information: 1820 Foundation, Box 304, Grahamstown, 6140. Tel: (0461) 2 7115; fax: 2 4457.

Durban & Environs

South Africa's newest opera house is the **Natal Playhouse** in Durban, which opened its doors in 1985. Re-opened, that is to say, for the attractive Tudor timberwork facade has fronted a building for entertaining the masses for ages. Two cinemas, which also did service as theatres, were located here at the beginning of the century. Even the constellations painted on the ceiling have been preserved in the renovated building. The Playhouse contains four theatres: from the large opera house (which presents quite good ballet and musical performances, as well as symphony concerts) through classical and experimental theatre to the intimate Cellar, offering cabaret and musical revues. Also popular are the lunchtime concerts in the foyer. Box office, tel: (031) 304 3631, or Computicket, tel: (031) 304 2753.

At the University, the **Elisabeth Snedden Theatre** often presents quite good plays, usually modern. Small classical concerts in the art gallery of the complex in the impressive Durban Town Hall also meet with widespread approval. Sitting on the steps on Wednesdays at noon, you can hear concerts of African musicians.

A hopeful theatre group has established itself in Durban. **Theatre for Africa** deals with ecological subjects, accompanied by African music.

For details and programme information, see the daily paper.

Museums

Johannesburg

The Africana Museum, Public Library, Market Square, Market St. Tel: (011) 836 3787 and 836 8482. Open Monday–Saturday 9am–5.30pm, Sunday 2–5pm. The collection has been moving to Old Newtown Market, Bree Street, (next to the Market Theatre), a substantially enlarged venue. It tells the story of life in South Africa from the Stone Age to the present (including a collection of African musical instruments).

The **Geological Museum** showing South Africa's mineral wealth remains part of the Africana Museum, as does the **Bensusan Museum of Photography**, Empire Road 17, tel: (011) 403 1067, which features a collection of old cameras (including a camera obscura) and photos about the history of Johannesburg and South Africa.

National Museum of Military History, Earlswoldway (behind the zoo). Tel: (011) 646 5513. Open daily 9am–4.30pm. It covers all the major wars fought on South African soil or in which South Africa participated, particularly the Boer War (1899–1902) and the two World Wars.

James Hall Transport Museum, Rosettenville Road, Wemmer Pan. Tel: (011) 435 9718. Open Monday–Saturday 9am–5.30pm, Sunday 2–5pm. It exhibits vintage cars, trains, carriages, steam tractors, fire engines and other historical vehicles.

Johannesburg Art Gallery, Joubert Park. Tel: (011) 725 3180. Open October–April, Tuesday–Sunday 9am–5pm,

Wednesday–Sunday 7–9pm. It houses works of South African and European artists including Monet, Pissaro, van Gogh, Degas, Renoir.

Gold Reef City, tel: (011) 494 4100. Open 8.30am–5pm, closed Mondays. Located 4 miles (6 km) from the Johannesburg city centre, Crown Mines is a replica of historical Johannesburg during the gold rush. Tourist attractions include its many historic buildings as well as the chance to visit the now-defunct gold mines. In the adjacent gold forge, you can see how molten gold is formed into bars. Visits here are entertaining for children and adults alike. Many companies offer guided tours from Johannesburg.

Planetarium, Yale Road, Braamfontein. Tel: (011) 716 3799. Demonstrations Friday 8pm, Saturday 3pm and 8pm, Sunday 4pm. A fascinating introduction to astronomy from the perspective of the spaceships Voyager, Mariner, Viking Magellan and Galileo.

Santarama, Pioneer Park, Rosettenville Road. Open daily 10am–5pm. An area with miniature replicas of many of South Africa's most important buildings, as well as a model train and a life-sized replica of Jan van Riebeeck's *Dromedary*.

Pretoria

Transvaal Museum, Paul Kruger St (opposite new City Hall). Tel: (012) 322 7632. Open Sunday 11am–5pm, Monday–Saturday 9am–5pm. This natural history museum was founded in 1893 and contains collections of insects, reptiles, amphibians and mammals. The "Genesis of Life" exhibition shows the story of life throughout the animal kingdom. Prehistoric animals and Austin Roberts Bird Hall with a display of all bird species found in South Africa. Facility for identifying bird calls.

SA Museum of Science and Technology, 2nd Floor, Didacta Building, Skinner St. Tel: (012) 2 0035 (for appointments). Open Monday–Friday 8am–1pm, 2–4pm. The only museum of its kind in South Africa. Displays on water research, forestry, atoms, nuclear physics and space travel.

National Cultural History Museum, Boom St. Tel: (012) 341 1320. Open Monday–Saturday 8am–4.30pm, Sunday 11am–4pm. Prehistoric rock art,

archaeological displays, ethnological section on tribes of South Africa, collection of materials from the ZAR period (19th century).

Kruger House Museum, Church St. Tel: (012) 26 9172. Open Monday–Sunday 10am–4pm. The house in which Paul Kruger lived 1884–1900; some of his personal belongings and gifts of admirers.

Melrose House Museum, Jacob Mare St (opposite Burghers Park). Tel: (012) 26 7893. Open Tuesday–Saturday 10am–5pm, Sunday noon–5pm. Built in 1886 by one of the transport riders with materials imported from Britain; lovely Victorian homestead of wealthy family. The peace treaty ending the Boer War was signed here in 1902.

Voortrekker Monument Museum, opposite the Voortrekker Monument. Tel: (012) 26 6770. Open Monday–Saturday 9am–4.45pm, Sunday 11am–4.45pm. Houses the tapestries depicting the Great Trek and its hardships; exhibits illustrate the life of the Voortrekkers (pioneers) from an actual wagon to what they used from the environment to survive.

Pretoria Art Museum, at the corner of Arcadia Park and Wessel St. Tel: (012) 44 4271. Open Tuesday–Saturday 10am–5pm, Wednesday 7.30–10pm, Sunday 1–6pm. Collections of South African artists and old Netherlands and Flemish paintings.

Northern Transvaal

Barberton Museum's theme is "From the Valley of Death to the Valley of Gold" illustrating the turbulent early history of Barberton. Open Monday–Friday 10am–5pm and Saturday 10am–1pm.

The **Lydenburg Museum** has been re-located in this nature reserve and has exhibits on the archaeological, ethnographic and cultural history of this area. Open Monday–Friday 9am–noon, 2–4pm and Saturday 9am–noon.

Phalaborwa on the R71 68 miles (110 km) from Tzaneen, just outside Kruger Park, is the centre of a rich mining area and an open cast copper mine which can be visited after prior arrangements on Friday afternoons. Tel: (01524) 2211. There is also a museum which shows the archaeological, ethnological and mining history of the region.

The **Masorini Open Air Museum** in the Kruger Park (7 miles/12 km from Phalaborwa) is the reconstruction of an iron age village.

Bakone Malapa Open Air Museum, Pietersburg, lies 5 miles (9 km) south of the town on the R37 to Burgersfort. A traditional kraal of the north Sotho where tribesmen demonstrate their crafts such as weaving, pottery and carving. Archaeological remains and rock paintings can also be seen and long walks are possible. Open Wednesday–Monday 8.15–11am and 12.30–3.15pm. Tours at 8.30am, 10am, 12.30pm and 13.30pm.

The **Diggings Museum,** less than a mile before getting to Pilgrim's Rest, is certainly worth a visit. You can even try your hand at swirling a digger's pan around. Tours and demonstrations Monday–Friday 10am, 11am, noon, 2pm, Sunday 10.30am.

At **The Reduction Works**, tel: (0131532, then ask for 25 or 50), you can see how the gold was extracted from the rock. Demonstrations Monday–Saturday 10.30am, and 2pm, Sunday 10.30am.

Eastern Transvaal

Sabi: this laid-back little town, dwarfed by the mountains around it, is the centre of the forestry industry in the Eastern Transvaal. The **Forestry Museum**, Fords St, takes one into the world of trees and the industry that grew around them. Contains exhibits from ancient wooden tools to the use of wood in the Polaris project. Open Monday–Friday 9am–1pm, 2–4pm and Saturday 9–11am.

Schoemansdal 9 miles (15 km) west on the R522 was a ghost town which has been rebuilt into a living museum with demonstrations of the crafts and tasks of the pioneers (candle making, curing of hides, ironwork and others).

KwaZulu/Natal

Pietermaritzburg: Natal's capital city contains a number of buildings dating from the days of British colonial rule.

Fort Napier, near the train station. Open Wednesday 2.30–4pm. Erected in 1843 as headquarters of the British Army, the building today houses a small military museum as well as St George's Garrison Church.

Macrorie House Museum, corner of Pine and Loop Streets. Open Tuesday–Thursday 9am–1pm, Sunday 9am–4pm. This museum depicts the lifestyles of British settlers in Natal during the Victorian age.

Natal Museum, Loop and Club St. Museum is -open Monday–Saturday 10am–4.30pm, Sunday 2–5pm. Exhibits devoted to African wildlife, geology, paleontology, and tools used by various African tribes in Natal in the Victorian age.

Tatham Art Gallery, 2nd floor of the city hall. Open Monday–Friday 10am–5pm. Paintings of the 19th and 20th centuries, with drawings by Picasso, Braque, Chagall, Moore and South African artists.

Voortrekker House, Boom Street. Open Monday–Friday 9am–5pm, Saturday 9am–12.30pm. The oldest house in Pietermaritzburg offers a glimpse into the lifestyle of the Voortrekkers.

Voortrekker Museum, Church St (in the same building complex as City Hall). Open Monday–Friday 9am–1pm, 2–4.30pm, Saturday 8am–midnight. This museum covers the history and lifestyle of the Voortrekkers in Natal. One of its most valuable objects is the chair of Dingaan, carved from ironwood. The same complex of buildings includes the Covenant Church and the house of Andries Pretorius, leader of the Voortrekkers at the Battle of Blood River, after whom Pretoria was named.

Vryheid: located 162 miles (262 km) north of Pietermaritzburg, Vryheid can be reached by taking the R33 to Dundee and then continuing along the same road. From 1884–88, the city was the capital of the New Republic. The museum in the former Council Room is open Monday, Wednesday, Thursday 10am–midnight and 3–4pm, Saturday 10am–midnight. On Lancaster Hill, you can see the remains of British fortifications erected during the Boer War. Along the road to Paulpietersburg, the battlefield of Kambula is testimony to the attack of 22,000 Zulus on the camp.

Transkei, Eastern Cape & Ciskei

King Williamstown: the **Kaffaria Museum** contains one of the largest collections of African mammals. The hippopotamus Huberta, for example, wandered from Zululand to East London, covering 992 miles (1,600 km) in three years, resting in swimming pools, frolicking in gardens, and even taking a night-time stroll through the main street of the city. The whole country mourned when Huberta was shot, supposedly by accident, in 1931. The ethnological, anthropological and historical sections are interesting as well. There's an old Trading Store next to the main building. Open Monday–Saturday 9am–12.45pm, Monday–Friday 2–5pm, Sunday 1–5pm.

The **Mission Museum**, the only one of its kind in South Africa, is devoted to the missionary work in southern Africa. Open Monday–Friday 9am–12.45pm, 2–5pm.

East London: the East London Museum is famous for containing the first coelacanth to be captured, caught near the city in 1938. This fish, with its leg-like feelers, has been in existence for 300 million years, but it was believed to have died out 50 million years ago. Since 1938, nearly 100 specimens have been caught, mostly around the Comoros Islands. Other highlights of the museum include the only dodo's egg in existence; the dodo was a heavy flightless bird which died out in the 17th century. The museum's ethnological exhibits are also of interest. Open Monday–Friday 9.30am–5pm, and on Saturday and Sunday 9.30am–12.30pm, 2.30–4pm.

Alice: the **F. S. Malan Museum** houses an exhibition of tools and artifacts of the Xhosa. Other points of interest include Fort Hare University, opened in 1916, the Loveday Mission Station and Fort Thompson.

Dimbaza: 3.5 miles (6 km) west of Dimbaza on the road to Middeldrift, there's the **Earthworm Reservation**, a wildlife preserve for earthworms. And these are truly remarkable specimens: almost 10 feet (3 m) long, and up to 3 inches (8cm) thick. Because of the small hollows which the earth-moving work of these giant creatures leaves behind, the area has been nicknamed *Kommetjievlakte* (Saucer Plain).

The Garden Route

Mossel Bay: the **Bartholomew Diaz Museum** is devoted to historical exhibits: the old mill contains a faithful replica of the *Caravelle* (which sailed to Mossel Bay in 1988, on the 500th anniversary of the Diaz voyage from Portugal). Open Monday–Friday 9am–12.30pm, 2–3.45pm. A few miles to the north, in Hartenbos, a **Voortrekker Museum** includes objects from the Great Trek of 1838.

On the Post Office Tree, sailors used to hang messages for passing ships in an old boot. The tree is near the fresh-water spring which Diaz and other sailors used to top up their water supply.

Oudtshoorn: the **Jewish Gallery** pays tribute to the role Jews played in the building of Oudtshoorn. Next to the museum, the Dorpshuis is a typical example of a "feather palace", furnished in the appropriate style. Also in Oudtshoorn is the "Need-work" house of the poet C.J. Langenhoven, whose poem *The Star of South Africa* became the country's national anthem.

Port Alfred: the **Kowie Museum** contains exhibitions pertaining to the settlers of the 1820s. The Settler Express train travels through lovely Trappes Valley to Grahamstown and back. Even more exciting is the Kowie Canoe Trail, which leads 15 miles (24 km) down the Kowie River, with one overnight stop.

Cradock is located on the R32, 143 miles (230 km) north of Port Elizabeth. **The Great Fish River Museum** on Hoog Street is devoted to the lives of the Voortrekkers and British settlers in the 19th century. Open Tuesday–Saturday 9am–midnight, 2–3pm.

Eastern & Northern Cape Province

Port Elizabeth: in the **Cultural History Museum** there are exhibitions of furniture and tools from pioneer days, as well as an interesting collection of dolls. Open Tuesday–Saturday 10am–1pm, 2–5pm, Sunday and Monday 2–5pm.

The **Port Elizabeth Museum** allows the visitor to look at the sea life of Algea Bay and the bird life of the Eastern Cape. Open daily 9am–1pm, 2–5pm, Monday–Saturday 8.30am–5pm,

Sunday 2–5pm. In the **Children's Museum**, children are permitted to touch the animals on display. The **King George IV Art Gallery** focuses on the works of British artists of the 19th and 20th centuries, but also contains South African works.

Grahamstown: the **Albany Museum** presents the history of primitive man. Open Tuesday–Friday 9.30am–1pm, Tuesday–Sunday 2–5pm. In the **1820 Settlers Museum**, original English jewellery, porcelain and silver are displayed, but there are also South African objects such as furniture and farm tools. Open Tuesday–Friday 9.30am–1pm, Tuesday–Sunday 2–5pm.

One of the few extant camera obscuras, the toy of the rich in the Victorian Age, can be seen in the **Observatory Museum**. Open Tuesday–Friday 9.30am–1pm, Tuesday–Sunday 2–5pm.

Fort Beaufort: the **Historical Museum** in Durban Street displays, in addition to a collection of weapons and tools, many documents. Particularly impressive is the collection of pictures by Thomas Baines, a traveller from the last century whose pencil sketches captured every facet of life. Open Monday–Friday 8am–12.30pm, 2–5pm, Saturday 8.30am–12.45pm. Housed in a former military barracks in Bell Street is the **Military Museum**. Open Monday–Saturday 10am–4pm, Sunday 1–4pm. Next door, the Martello Tower was once part of an unusual Corsican system of defence.

Kimberley: noteworthy sights are the **Big Hole** and the **Mine Museum** (follow the signs with the diamond-miners). Kimberley Street and other sections of this diamond city, which boomed in the days of the diamond rush, have been rebuilt and restored. In **De Beers Hall**, tel: (0531) 31557/8/9, you can follow the life cycle of a diamond, all the way up to the mognificent 616, the largest uncut diamond in the world. Open daily 8am–6pm. **McGregor Museum** in Atlas Street, tel: (0531) 32645, is a natural-history museum specialising in the peoples, animals and plants of arid regions. Open Monday–Friday 9am–5pm, Saturday 9am–1pm, Sunday 2–5pm. The **Old Museum**, 10 Chapel St, is a geological museum containing minerals and stone samples from around the world.

The **Duggin-Cronin Gallery**, next to McGregor Museum, presents a unique collection of ethnological photographs, artifacts and stone paintings, illustrating the culture and lifestyle of the native peoples of South Africa. Photos dating from the period 1919–39 bear witness to the fact that many traditions and customs are rapidly dying out.

William Humphreys Art Gallery, in the City Administration Building, contains one of the best collections of the works of South African artists, as well as works of the Flemish, Dutch, English and French schools. Open Monday–Saturday 10am–1pm, 2–5pm, Sunday 2–5pm.

The **Magersfontein Battlefield** and **Museum**, tel: (0531) 22029, are located on the R29 South, 19 miles (31 km) from Kimberley. During the Boer War, the British Army suffered one of three defeats here in the same "Black Week". The museum includes a relief battle map. Open daily 8am–5pm.

Central Cape Province

Beaufort West: three historic buildings form the museum complex: the *Stadhuis* (Town Hall), which houses, among other things, an exhibit honouring native son Christiaan Barnard, who was the focus of international attention in 1967 when he performed the first heart transplant; the Sending Church, containing objects relating to church history; and the Sending Vicarage, where Barnard was born.

Graaff Reinett: the museum complex consists of three houses: the Old Residency, containing a collection of firearms; the Reinett House, with a noteworthy collection of furniture from the 18th and 19th centuries; and the Reinett Museum, which exhibits such things as Karoo fossils and reproductions of Bushman drawings.

Cape Town

The **Josephine Mill** on Boundary Road, Newlands is Cape Town's only extant water mill still in operation, and dates from 1818. Open Monday–Friday 10am–6pm. Guided tours daily at 10.30am and 2.30pm.

The **Bo-Kaap Museum**, 71 Wale St, tel: (021) 43 1552, depicts the Moslem way of life of the Cape Malays.

Open Tuesday–Thursday and Saturday and Sunday 10am–4.30pm,

Cultural History Museum, 49 Adderley St. Tel: (021) 41 1051. Open Monday–Saturday 10am–5pm. The old parts of the building dating from 1679 were used as slave quarters and later as the High Court before the museum was housed here. It contains exhibits from ancient Egypt, Greece, Rome and the Far East as well as collections of coins, stamps and weapons, Cape silver, glassware and furniture.

Koopmans de Wet House, 35 Strand St. Tel: (021) 41 2068. Open Monday–Saturday 10am–5pm. Displays a priceless collection of Cape-Dutch furniture, Delft porcelain and other antiques.

South African Museum, Government Ave, Gardens. Tel: (021) 24 3330. Open Monday–Sunday 10am–5pm. Founded in 1825 it is South Africa's oldest natural sciences museum; it covers paleontology, archaeology and ethnology as well as entomology, ornithology and marine biology (with particular emphasis on whales).

South African National Gallery, off Government Ave, Gardens. Tel: (021) 45 1628. Open Monday 1–5.30pm, Tuesday–Saturday 10am–5.30pm. At first the Gallery aimed at collecting art from the mother countries of the Netherlands, Germany, Britain, France and Belgium. Now it gives equal emphasis to South African art of which it has the largest collection in the country.

Cape Peninsula

Stellenbosch: at the **Oude Meester Brandy Museum** in Old Strand Street, you can learn about the history and development of brandy in the Cape region, and admire the wine presses from Baden. Open Monday–Friday 9am–12.45pm and 2–5pm, Saturday 10am–1pm and 2–5pm, Sunday 2.30–5.30pm.

The six historic houses of the **Village Museum**, at 18 Ryneveld St, were built between 1709 and 1929. They have since been lovingly restored and furnished with contemporary furniture. Open Monday–Saturday 9.30am–5pm, Sunday 2–5pm.

Paarl: set at the foot of the Paarl Mountain, and easily visible from afar, the **Afrikaanse Taal Monument** com-

memorates the genesis of the language – a genesis in which the Paarlers played a significant role. A brochure available at the site is the best guide to the monument's symbolism. Daily 8am–5pm.

Swellendam, located at the foot of the Langeberg Mountains, is the third-oldest city in South Africa. The **Drostdy Museum**, Drosdty St displays workshops of nearly-forgotten crafts – a smithy, a cobbler, charcoal-burner, engraver and cooper – and is worth a visit. Open Monday–Friday 9am–12.45pm and 2–4.45pm, Saturday 10am–midnight and 2.30–4.30pm. Swellendam Publicity Association, Voortrekker St, tel: (0291) 42770.

The **Boland Open-Air Farm Museum** offers insight into the lives of farmers 200 years ago. Here, daily demonstrations include the production of leather thongs, rolling tobacco, baking and other household activities; they also cover seasonal occupations such as drying grapes, shearing sheep, spinning, weaving and distilling liquor. Open Monday–Saturday 9am–4.30pm.

Orange Free State

Bloemfontein: there are a whole series of museums in Bloemfontein, with an emphasis on the military. **The Boer Republic's Military Museum** is mainly devoted to the Boer War and life in the prison camps. The Military Museum in **Queen's Fort** is dedicated to the soldiers who died in the Basuto War. Near the Women's Memorial, south of Bloemfontein, a **War Museum** depicts the Boer War and life in the concentration camps where more than 26,000 women and children died. Adjacent to the **Afrikaans Literary Museum,** a music and theatre museum houses exhibits pertaining to Afrikaans music and theatre history. **The National Museum** displays one of the largest collections of fossils in South Africa, including the famous Florisbad Skull; in 1930, when it was discovered north of Bloemfontein, it was the oldest *homo sapiens* find so far recorded, some 40,000 years old. Built in 1848, the first Raadzaal (Council Hall) is still standing: a simple straw-thatched building with a single room, floored with dung and clay, like all buildings of the time. Called the Jewel of the Free State, **Clarens** can be found by taking the

711 from Bethlehem toward the mountains. Also well-known is Cinderella Castle, built of 50,000 beer bottles. A collection of semi-precious stones and unusual stone-carvings, guarded by knights, is on display here.

In **Ladybrand** (43 miles/70 km south of Ficksburg), the Catharina Brand Museum displays a collection of stone paintings, stone tools and fossils, including replicas of some particularly important specimens.

Western Transvaal

Klerksdorp: the **Klerksdorp Museum** contains interesting exhibits of cultural history, as well as collections of geology and archaeology. Open Monday–Friday 10am–1pm, 2–5pm, Saturday 9.30am–12.30pm, Sunday 2–5pm.

Potchefstroom: the **Potchefstroom Museum** displays weapons and household objects from the Voortrekker period, as well as one of the original ox-carts from the Battle of Blood River. Open Monday–Friday 10am–1pm, Saturday 9am–12.45pm, Sunday 2–5pm. Two other museums are devoted to the poet Totius and the first president of South Africa.

Oudedorp (the old village) contains buildings, canals and fruit gardens from the original settlement of 1848. (The museum will give you directions as to how to get there.)

The museum in **Rustenburg**, open Tuesday–Saturday 8am–1pm, 2–5pm, Sunday 11am–5pm, contains exhibits of cultural history and archaeology.

Monuments

KwaZulu/Natal

Durban: in Stanger (on the N2, 68 miles/110 km north of Durban) you can see *Dukusa*, the main kraal of the famous Zulu king Shaka, and a monument commemorating the king, who was murdered by his half brother Dingaan.

Fort Pearson (on the road to the Tugela Delta, branching off about 3 miles/5 km before the John Ross Bridge over the Tugela River) was built by the British before their invasion of Zululand in 1878.

Ultimatum Tree is a wild fig tree about 1 mile (1.5 km) from the fort. It was here that King Ceteswayo's delegation presented the ultimatum that led to the 1879 Zulu War.

Colenso: this history-filled city lies 87 miles (140 km) northwest of Pietermaritzburg on the N3. Shortly after the Winterton exit, there is a wayside memorial to Winston Churchill's capture by the Boers in 1899. About 1 mile (1.5 km) further on, the Blaauwkrantz Monument commemorates the Voortrekkers who fell in the Battle of Dingaan on 16 February 1838.

Dundee: the centre of Natal's coal-mining industry, Dundee is located 109 miles (176 km) north of Pietermaritzburg on the R33. The museum in Talane and the Boer War Memorial are testimony to the past. South of Dundee, Rorke's Drift and Isandhlwana were battlefields in the war between the British and the Zulus in 1879. Today, the arts and crafts museum is open weekdays 8am–4.30pm, Saturday 9am–1pm.

Blood River, located 146 miles (235 km) north of Pietermaritzburg, can be reached by following the R33 past Dundee toward Vreyheid. The bronze statue of 64 wagons stands as a monument to the victory of 464 Voortrekkers over 12,000 Zulus in 1838; the battle was to avenge Dingaan's murder of Retief and 72 of his men, after which they killed hundreds of women and children.

Ulundi: the capital of KwaZulu was the site of a battle between the British and the Zulus in 1879. Battlefield Monument marks the location of Ceteswayo's kraal until his final defeat. In Oudini, you can see the Royal Residence and a small museum.

Cape Town

The Castle of Good Hope in Buitenkant Street (Monday–Saturday 10am–4pm, guided tours hourly except 1pm) is the oldest building in South Africa, dating from 1666, and was the residence of the first Cape governors. The State Apartments contain the William Fehr Collection of paintings, antique furniture and porcelain.

Northern Cape

Kuruman: this was the mission station of the missionary Moffat, whose daughter married Dr Livingstone. For years, the church, dating from 1838, was the largest building north of the Orange; it provided seating for 800 people, although Moffat had initially converted only nine Tswanas. The Kuruman Eye is a remarkable spring that it produces 5 million gallons (18 million litres) of water a day. The spring is surrounded by a lake clear as glass, bordered by an attractive park.

Diary of Regular Events

January: Cape Minstrels Carnival of the Malays and coloureds in Cape Town: a boisterous musical happening with a unique flavour.

February: Art and Antiques Fair in Cape Town.

March: Mussel Festival in Jeffreys Bay (Eastern Cape). Parades at universities to collect money for charities are held throughout the country.

March/April: Johannesburg, Rand Easter Show (two weeks around Easter), the largest exposition in South Africa.

April: dance competition of native tribes held in Johannesburg.

June: Grahamstown Art Festival (Eastern Cape) over two weeks with music, theatre, arts and crafts, etc.

End of July: Shembe Festival in Durban. An authentic Zulu dance festival near Inanda, originally started by a missionary. Only Zulu dancers can take part; visiting spectators sometimes allowed.

September: The Great Railway Contest with steam train races in Port Elizabeth.

October: Roodeport Eisteddfod, the largest music/dance festival in the Southern Hemisphere, with participants from all around the world. The event is held every two years in Roodepoort, Johannesburg.

Stellenbosch Food and Wine Festival: a chance to sample the marvellous wines and culinary specialties of South Africa.

The Durban Tattoo is a folk fair on the Scottish model, with military tattoos, sports events and fireworks.

The Cape Craft Exhibition with arts and crafts is held in Cape Town (Alphen Park, Constantia).

A **Medieval Craft Fair** with a medieval crafts exhibition is held several times a year in the Groot Constantia Park in Cape Town.

Festivals

Festivals, exhibitions and international fairs, national sporting events and championships: the Cape offers something for every taste. If you're interested in a particular event, ask at SATOUR for the brochure *Calendar of Events*, which appears twice a year, and also lists contact addresses. SATOUR Johannesburg, tel: (011) 331 5241; Fax: (011) 331 5241 ext. 29.

Arts & Crafts

South Africa, with its numerous peoples of different cultures, has an abundance of artists and craftsmen who are creative in the most diverse ways imaginable: painters, of whom especially some wild life artists are internationally acclaimed; graphic artists, sculptors, who work not only in wood and bronze, but also some who create very unusual metal works of art depicting creatures from insects to eagles; South African potters who produce work of individualistic nature and high artistic quality and craftsmanship; artists who work with leather, who make jewellery, porcelain sculptors, glassblowers and artists who create glass windows, lamps etc.; woodwork from sculpture to handmade furniture; then there are weavers and spinners producing hand-knitted garments and individually styled designer clothes.

There are various Arts and Crafts Routes that enable the visitor to see the artists and their work in their studios, to meet them over a cup of tea and to experience the environment they live in; perhaps even to buy a piece of art.

Johannesburg & Environs

For Johannesburg and environs one can get an excellent Arts and Crafts Map which takes one through the busy streets and suburbs, from galleries to curio shops, from museums to markets, where arts and crafts can be viewed and bought. Obtainable from Arts and Crafts Map, 6 Routville Road, Vall Bay, 7975, tel: (021) 64 2839 or Johannesburg Publicity Association, tel: (011) 29 4961

The **Black Art Galleries**, unique to South Africa for their portrayal of township and homeland life, must not be missed. The Fuba Gallery downstairs from the Market Theatre in Newtown, tel: (011) 836 0561/2/3, exhibits well known Black South African artists. The Katlehong Art Centre in Katlehong, tel: (011) 905 4501, the Funda Academy in Germiston in Fordsburg, tel: (011) 825 3235 ext. 342, and the Alex Art Centre in Fordsburg, tel: (011) 838 3034, are but a few of the excellent black art galleries worthwhile visiting. These galleries are also found on the Arts and Crafts Map.

Artists under the Sun is a Sunday art exhibition that takes place in the park around the Zoo Lake (opposite the Zoo, off Jan Smuts Ave). Every first Sunday of the month. For further information tel. (011) 616 6907.

The **Johannesburg Art Gallery** in Klein Street, Joubert Park, exhibits Monet, Picasso, Van Gogh, Degas and Renoir, as well as contemporary South African artists.

Magnolia Dell, at the junction of Queen Wilhelmina and University Streets in Pretoria. Every first and last Saturday in the month, there is an exhibition called Art in the Park.

Transvaal

The **Crocodile Ramble**, the best known of the Arts and Craft Routes, meanders along the Crocodile River and includes some of the top artists and craftsmen in South Africa. Studios are open to the public on the first weekend of every month 9am–5pm. Information and map, tel: (011) 957 2580/2793; fax: 957 2376.

The **Wag'n Bietjie Route** can be found just east of Pretoria in the Bushveld, offering a variety of arts and crafts. Information and map, tel: (012) 802 0637.

White River in the Eastern Transvaal just north of Nelspruit is home to various well known South African wild life artists and sculptors, as well as numerous black woodcutters, weavers and clay potters. Information and map, tel: (01311) 3 1176 or SATOUR, tel: (01311) 4 4406.

KwaZulu/Natal

For a scenically beautiful Arts and Craft Route visit Port Shepston, where the Natal Route starts. It winds its way along the coast right down to the Wild Coast where it ends. The Midland Route has five artists that can be visited, nevertheless it is of interest since it starts in Pietermaritzburg, goes through Dargle, as far up as Fort Nottingham, and then returns to Pietermaritzburg. It takes you through a lovely part of the Natal Midlands. Information and maps for both routes are available from the Arts Association in Durban, tel: (031) 29 4934.

The **Rorke's Drift Workshop** near Dundee is one of the biggest black art centres in the country, training artists in spinning, weaving, printing materials and pottery, tel: (03425) 627 or The Arts Association in Durban, tel: (031) 29 4934.

Pietermaritzburg: "Art in the Park" offers an interesting exhibition, where artists meet for a week in the Alexandra Park during May and June to sell and show their work. For further information tel. (0331) 45 1348.

Durban: the African Arts Centre in the Guildhall Arcade is a showcase of African arts and crafts. Various Zulu products are sold, including woodcarvings, basketwork, ceramics, stone sculptures and embroidery.

The **Durban Art Gallery** has a collection of European artists including Rodin, Constable, Utrillo, Carol and others. Contemporary South African artists are also exhibited. Open Monday–Wednesday and Friday 8.30am–5pm, Thursday 8.30am–7pm, Sunday 11am–5pm. For further information tel. (031) 29 4934.

Eshowe: Zulu tribal customs can be seen at close quarters in Eshowe. There is the **Museum of Zulu History** in the Nonquai Fort as well as three inhabited Kraals near the town, where the visitor can admire the local handicraft, watch tribal dances and see the medicine man at work. Accommodation is in Zulu round huts. For information contact Shakaland, PO Box 103, Eshowe, 3815. Tel: (03546) 648 or 655; fax: 824.

The Garden Route

Mossel Bay: the Arts and Craft Centre is located in the Munro houses next to the museum complex.

Grahamstown: every year at the end of June/beginning of July, there is the **National Arts Festival** that attracts tourists and artists from the whole country. There are theatre, music and dance performances, street theatre and displays of handicraft.

Orange Free State: the attractions of Qwaqwa's capital Phutaditjaba are firstly its wonderful location and then its handicraft centre, whose products include weaving from mohair and Karakul wool, hand-painted porcelain, bronze work and basketwork.

The Cape

There are three Arts and Crafts Routes in the Western Cape, for all of whom you can obtain information and maps from Captour, tel: (021) 25 3320/1; fax: 21 7615. The Treasure Coast Art Route runs from Marina da Gama near Muizenberg to Seaforth near Simonstown and includes 21 artists and galleries – every first Sunday of the month 10am–5pm. The Noordhoek Art Route near Houtbay includes four artists and is open every first Sunday of the month 10am–5pm. The Akkedis Art Route near Villiersdorp includes 15 artists and is open every last Sunday of the month 11am–5pm.

An excellent Arts and Crafts Map, similar to that of Johannesburg, clearly maps out the quaint craft and curio shops, the beautiful galleries, the jewellers, the African artifact shops and the museums of Cape Town. Obtainable from Arts and Crafts Map, 6 Routville Road, Vall Bay 7975, tel: (021) 64 2839 or Captour, tel: (021) 25 3320/1; fax: 21 7615.

The **Cape Crafters Market** has some 500 craftsmen and 10 markets, where art can be bought directly from the artists. Of special interest are the Cape Crafts Exhibition in October and the Medieval Crafts Fair in December. The venue is at Alphen Park, Constantia. For further information contact Lorain Bester, tel: (021) 510 1695 or 531 6500.

The Cape also has the largest and most active branch of the Association of Potters in South Africa. For details tel. (021) 88 7030.

At **Grahamstown Festival** artists and craftsmen from all over the country meet in this small university town in June to exhibit and sell their work. Information from The 1820 Foundation, Box 304, Grahamstown 6140, tel: (0461) 2 7-115; fax: 2 4457.

Transkei

Umtata: The Xhosa are famous for the high quality of their handicraft. Pottery, leather, jewellery and other items are produced by disabled people in the Ikhwesi Lokusa Workshop. The best pottery in the region emanates from the Izandla pottery a few miles outside the town, where it is also possible to see the potters at work. Next door is Hilmond Weavers, one of the largest hand-weaving shops, producing wall carpets and pillowcases from the pure mohair spun by the pupils of a local school for the blind.

The Wank' Handicraft Centre lies some 3 miles (5km) from town on the N2 to East London. Here you can purchase typical Xhosa handicrafts from all parts of the region. The Xhosa are especially well known for their work with pearls, which were not originally intended for jewellery but for symbolising life.

East London: every Sunday there is a handicraft market selling Xhosa products in the Marina Glen Park on the eastern promenade. The Ann Bryant Art Gallery is located in an elegant old Victorian house and displays the works of South African artists and British 19th-century painters.

Ciskei

Dimbaza: a number of handicraft workshops have been established and are located 12 miles (19 km) west of King Williamstown. The carpets are woven in typical African patterns from Karakul wool. They are extremely robust and long-lasting.

Wesley lies on the R72 from Port Alfred where the coast road turns inland. This is the location of the Kei Carpets factory which produces fine hand-knotted carpets. Guided tours are possible.

Venda

This smallest of the independent republics (former homelands) lies tucked away in the northeastern corner of South Africa and has a lot to offer: scenic beauty wherever you go, a people who are still connected to legends and spirits, skilled and varied crafts and interesting archaeological sites. The **Ditike Craft Centre** in Thohoyandu sells clay pots, carvings, basket ware and articles woven out of grass or reed of high craftsmanship for which the Vha-Venda are known.

White River in the Eastern Transvaal, north of Nelspruit, is the home of many natural painters and sculptors as well as woodcarvers, weavers and potters. For further information tel. (01311) 31176 or SATOUR, tel: (01311) 44406.

Tours

As well as natural wonders and African experiences in the game reserves, South Africa offers virtually unlimited possibilities for holiday activities of all kinds. If your particular area of interest isn't discussed here, enquire at SATOUR.

A variety of operators offer tours to all parts of the country lasting between one and ten days:

Connex Travel (the travel bureau of the South African Railways), PO Box 1113, Johannesburg 2000. Tel: (011) 774 4504; fax: 337 1776.

Grosvenor Tours, PO Box 3845, Honeydew 2040. Tel: (011) 708 1777; fax: 708 1237.

Impala Tours, PO Box 1900, Kempton Park 1620. Tel: (011) 339 1658; fax: 974 1346.

Rand Coach Tours, PO Box 81240, Parkhurst 2120. Tel: (011) 339 1658; fax: 403 1383.

Springbok Atlas, PO Box 10902, Johannesburg 2000. Tel: (011) 493 3780; fax: 493 3770.

Welcome Tours, PO Box 997, Johannesburg 2000. Tel: (011) 833 7030; fax: 834 4971.

Safaris & Adventure Tours

The following companies are specialists in safaris and adventure tours in South Africa, Namibia, Botswana, Zimbabwe and Malawi:

Bonaventure Tour Operators, PO Box 84540, Greenside 2034. Johannesburg, tel: (011) 646 6120 or (0800) 111 007 (toll free); fax: (011) 486 1050.

Drifters Adventours, PO Box 48434, Roosevelt Park, 2129. Tel: (011) 486 1224; fax: 486 1237.

Holidays for Africa, PO Box 40802, Arcadia, Pretoria 0001. Pretoria, tel: (012) 325 8127; fax: 323 7279. Specialises in individual tours.

Prestige Travel, PO Box 2630, White River 1240. Tel: (01311) 3 1228; fax: 5 0802. Trips into the Lowveld (with Krugerpark).

Reservations Africa, PO Box 650762, Benmore 2010. Johannesburg, tel: (011) 883 4832; fax: 883 4302. Individual planning of tours with accommodation in small guest houses and hotels.

Safari Escape Tour, Ronday, Chanteclair Lane, Constantia 7800. Cape Town, tel: (021) 794 4832; fax: 794 4833. Day tours in the southwestern Cape region.

Safari Lodge (Tours), PO Box 79, Hazyview 1242. Tel: (01317) 6 7113; fax: 6 7258. A variety of tours into the Eastern Transvaal, Swaziland, Northern Natal and Cape Province.

Specialised Tours, PO Box 14049, Cape Town 7000. Tel: (021) 25 3259; fax: 25 3329. A large choice of tours for up to eight people.

Swan Tours, PO Box 1044, Germiston 1400. Johannesburg, tel: (011) 873 4033; fax: 51 4223. Tours along the Garden Route.

TWS Travel, PO Box 781121, Sandton 2146. Tel: (011) 783 6022.

Wild Adventure Expeditions, PO Box 94, Sarnia 3615. Durban, tel: (031) 82 1409. Tours for small groups with emphasis on animal life, nature and history. Qualified guides.

Zululand Safaris, PO Box 79, Hluhluwe 3960. Tel: (03562) 144 761. Tours through Zululand.

Helicopter Tours

A novel way of sightseeing is from a helicopter, and some operators now offer special helicopter tours.

Court Helicopters, PO Box 18115, Rand Airport 1419. Johannesburg, tel: (011) 827 8907; fax: (011) 824 1660; Cape Town, tel: (021) 934 0560. Court Helicopters operate from Johannesburg and Cape Town. Tours can vary from a lunch time flip to a two day tour.

Dragonfly Helicopter Adventures, PO Box 346, White River 1240. Tel: (01311) 5 0565; fax: (01311) 3 2839. "Mountain Magic" is a trip over the highlights of the Eastern Transvaal; "Winged Safari" is a safari at a private game reserve.

Gold Reef City Helicopters, tel: (011) 4961400. Tours over Johannesburg and Soweto from Gold Reef City.

Game and Nature Reserves

Long gone are the days when the plains of Southern Africa were teeming with herds of wildebeest, springbok, zebra and buffalo, as far as the eye could see. The blue bock, a kind of antelope, was hunted to extinction as long ago as 1800; only a few decades later it was the turn of the qagga, a relative of the zebra, that used to live in large herds in the interior. Many of the animals that have survived are on the list of endangered species. Even in the late 1970s, when a ban was placed on the trading of their horns, the black rhino population still numbered around 15,000; today barely 3,000 remain. In the past 15 years, trophy-hunting has become an established pastime on the Cape; there is an official count and quota for all game which can be hunted. South Africa is the only African country which allows you to hunt the "big five": elephants, rhinoceroses, buffalo, lions and leopard. An expensive hobby.

The national parks and game reserves provide a last refuge for Southern Africa's threatened wildlife. The first game reserve was established by Paul Kruger in 1898, and now there are a total of 17 national parks dotted around South Africa, including the Richtersveld Park on the Orange River bordering Namibia, which was established in 1991. Most of the parks are equipped with accommodation provided specially for visitors, including guest houses, rondavels and simple huts.

In addition to the national parks, each province has its own provincial parks: 118 in all, of which 50 percent are located in Natal. While most of these parks offer overnight accommodation, some are geared solely to the day tripper and for hikers. There is also an increasing number of private nature and game reserves (more than 500 in Transvaal alone) whose services and accommodation vary from the extremely basic to the lavishly luxurious. The best known private lodges can be found on the western fringes of the

Kruger Park. In contrast to the Kruger Park, here one can travel around in open vehicles, accompanied by one or two game wardens. Night-time safaris are often part of the programme. As far as animal spotting is concerned, these parks cannot hope to compete with their big brother; after all, the Kruger Park has the largest variety of game in all of Africa.

It is advisable to book accommodation in the parks well in advance and to try and avoid the school holidays. Guided trails in the parks must also be booked, and often there is more demand than places. Campers and holiday makers in caravans should book directly with the reserve concerned. Park opening times in all national and provincial parks vary according to the sunrise and sunset.

The speed limits within the parks vary from 15 mph (25 kmh) to 30 mph (50 kmh) and are strictly enforced. Because of stops for photography and suchlike, you should reckon on an average speed on the asphalt roads of 18–21 mph (30–35 kmh) and 15–18 mph (25–30 kmh) on sand. Maps showing the distances from point to point can be bought at the entrance gates.

Find out beforehand whether the park has restaurant facilities, because many of the smaller ones are only geared to self-caterers. If you're going to be on the road the whole day, its a good idea to take along your own supply of cold drinks, food, nuts and dried fruit. Note that in the game reserves it is forbidden to get out of the vehicle except in the designated areas. Feeding the animals is not only forbidden, but also highly irresponsible; an animal might like your titbits too much and end up having to be shot.

Johannesburg, Pretoria, Witwatersrand, Sun City

Even though this area is the centre of administration and industry, it has ample opportunities to get back to nature. Game farms, hiking trails, picnic spots, lakes, rivers, dams and a magnificent mountain range, the Magaliesberg, are within easy reach.

Pilansberg Nature Reserve: this reserve lies in Bophuthatswana, only 2–3 hours' drive from Johannesburg on the R565 from Rustenburg.

Bounded by volcanic hills, this reserve is home to some 8,000 head of game that roam freely through the 193 sq. miles (500 sq. km). Open daily.

Facilities at Kwa Maritane: luxury time share and hotel; Tshukudu: luxury chalets; Mankwe: safari tents. Trails of varying duration; tented trail camps. Tel: (014651) 2 1286.

Reservations: Pilansberg National Park, Box 1201, Mogwase 0302, Bophuthatswana. Tel: (01465) 2 4405.

Mabula Game Reserve: northwest of Warmbath, 1 hour from Pretoria. This reserve is a rich wilderness area supporting the "Big Five" as well as 250 species of birds. Drives in open Land-Rovers offer excellent viewing. Open daily.

Hotel and time-share chalets; tennis, swimming and golf; self-guided walks. Reservations: The Director, Mabula Lodge, Private Bag X 16651, Warmbaths 0480. Tel: (015334) 616/717.

Krugersdorp Game Reserve: this reserve, on the R24 to Magaliesberg, 40 minutes from Johannesburg, covers some 5 sq. miles (14 sq. km) of indigenous Transvaal fauna and flora and is home to eland, zebra, blesbok, gemsbok, antelope, lion and white rhino. Open daily 8am–5pm.

Chalets and rondavels; caravanning and camping; tea-room and swimming pool. Trails: guided 4 hour-tours on Saturdays and Sundays. Reservations: The Tourist Officer, Department of Parks and Recreation, PO Box 94, Krugersdorp 1740. Tel: (011) 660 1058/1076.

Suikerbosrand Nature Reserve: this lies 12 miles (20 km) from Heidelberg on the Nigel/Klipivier Road 1 hour from Johannesburg. Typical highveld vegetation; numerous birds and various wildlife species abide on this reserve. Open daily: 7am–6pm.

Caravanning and camping; picnic sites; educational centre with film shows; farm-museum with the oldest farm in the Transvaal. Trails: 2.5 miles (4 km) self-guided trail; 6 miles (10 km) and 10 miles (17 km) day hike; 6-day, 41-mile (66-km) hike. Reservations: Suikerbosrand Nature Reserve, Private Bag X 616, Heidelberg 2400. Tel: (0151) 2181.

De Wildt Cheetah Breeding Station: on the R566 from Pretoria to

Brits. Until the late 1960s it was thought that cheetahs did not breed in captivity but at De Wildt this was proven wrong. From work done here it was also found that the very rare king cheetah (where the spots melt together to form stripes) was not a separate species, but the result of recessive genes in both parents. Wild dog, caracal and brown hyena can also be seen. Open Saturdays and Sundays.

Two-hour tours in open Land-Rovers are conducted on Saturdays at 8.30am–2pm and on Sundays at 9am–2pm for which one has to book. Reservations and information: Box 16, De Wildt 0251. Tel: (01204) 4 1921.

Northern & Eastern Transvaal

This area is rich in diverse landscapes and vegetation. Much of the Eastern Transvaal is subtropical lowveld (tablets against malaria must be taken), a scenic area of woodland and savannah. The Northern Transvaal is characterised by wide open plains, majestic mountains and primeval indigenous forests. Thus the area is renowned for the presence of some of the country's finest game reserves.

For more information contact National Parks Board, PO Box 787, Pretoria 0001. Tel: (012) 343 1991; fax: 343 0905.

Kruger National Park: this internationally renowned nature and game reserve of nearly 7,700 sq. miles (20,000 sq. km) is home to the largest variety of wildlife species to be found on the African continent. The flora and fauna of the vast landscapes supports 137 mammal species, 112 reptiles and 493 bird species; hundreds of birds ranging from the great African Fiseagle to the little glossy sunbird. Eight entrance gates provide access; four gates can be reached from Nelspruit (Malelane, Crocodile Bridge, Numbi, Paul Kruger) the latter two via White River. Orpen and Phalaborwa gates are entrances to the centre of the Park. The northernmost area is accessible via Punda Maria and Pa Furi Gates. An airstrip at Skukuza Rest Camp links the Park to Johannesburg and Phalaborwa daily.

Accommodation in the park caters for most needs. Family rondavels, self-contained rondavels and huts with communal washing facilities are offered. A limited number of camps serve group needs. All rest camps offer restaurants, shops, cooking and barbecue facilities.

The main camps are at Punda Maria, Shingwedzi, Letaba, Olifants, Satara, Skukuza, Pretoriuskop, Lower Sabi, Bergen-Dal and Crocodile Bridge. Skukuza is the largest facility with 207 rondavels and 107 places for tents and caravans. Crocodile Bridge offers 20 rondavels and only 12 camping lots. There is also a number of smaller wilderness camps where facilities are much more basic. These include: Nwanetzi, Roodewal, Nwqnedzi (near Satara), Malelane (near Bergen-Dal), Balule (near Olifant), Maroela and Jock of the Bushveld. They offer accommodation for between 12 and 18 people and can only be booked en bloc.

Trails: The Kruger National Park also offers six specific guided Wilderness Trails. These are the Wolhuter Trail and the Bushman Trail (between Pretoriuskop and Malelane), the Olifants Trails (in the vicinity of Letaba), the Nyalaland (near Punda Maria), the Metzi Trail (northeast of Skukuza) and the recently introduced Sweni Trail (east of Satara) and each one includes two days walking in the bush, viewing game, discovering bushman paintings and sighting birds, and three nights in tents, with everything supplied and transported by the National Parks Board. A maximum of eight people may undertake the trails.

For more information contact National Parks Board, PO Box 787, Pretoria 0001. For reservations tel. (012) 343 1991; fax: 343 0905.

Honnet Nature Reserve: 55 miles (90 km) from Louis Trichardt adjacent to a mineral spa, this reserve offers large numbers of game that roam between the ancient baobab trees and the bush. Bus tours and hiking trails can be undertaken, but no private cars may be taken into the reserve.

Facilities are at the spa only: hotel; caravan parks; rondavels; shop; sporting amenities. Trails: 6 miles (10 km) Baobab Trail. Reservations: Tshipise Mineral Baths, PO Box 4, Tshipise 0901. Tel: (015539) 4 or (01553) 2210 or 2209. Hunting and Safaris, tel: (015539) 719.

Lesheba Wilderness Area: this is halfway between Louis Trichardt and Vivo, in an area unique for its high cliffs, deep gorges, curiously weathered rocks, its numerous game and the colony of vultures that nest on the cliffs. Two self-catering camps. Reservations: PO Box 795, Louis Trichardt 0920. Tel: (015562) ask for 3004.

Ben Lavin Nature Reserve: this peaceful reserve is at the foot of the Soutpansberg 7 miles (12 km) southeast of Louis Trichardt. It is home to rare species such as pangolin, antbear, aardwort, brown hyena, as well as other game. Two hides overlooking waterholes provide fascinating game viewing. Open daily 6am–6pm.

Caravan and camping. Trails: Tabajwane trail, circular 5-mile (8-km) route; Fountain trail; circular 2.5-mile (4-km) route. Reservations: PO Box 782, Louis Trichardt 0920. Tel: (01551) 3834.

Hans Merensky Nature Reserve: 43 miles (70 km) east of Tzaneen, situated on the southern banks of the Great Letaba River, this reserve of some 20 sq. miles (52 sq. km) has plentiful game including leopard and hippo. Other predators such as lion and hyena move through the reserve. Of interest is the Tsonga Kraal Open Air Museum that displays the Tsonga way of life and where craftsmen demonstrate their arts.

Facilities: at the spa adjacent to the reserve: rondavels, swimming pool and indoor heated spa, tennis and riding. There are bus tours in the reserve as well as overnight accommodation. Trails: Giraffe trails, circular 21-mile (35-km) route (3 days); Mopanie Interpretative Trail, less than 1 mile (1 km); Letaba Nature Trail, 3 miles/5 km (2 hours); Waterbuck Nature Trails, 9 miles/15 km (4 hours). Reservations: Private Bag X502, Letsitele 0885. Tel: (015238) 632/3/4/5. Spa, tel: (015238) 667.

Blyde River Canyon Nature Reserve: this reserve lies in the most magnificent scenery, where the Highveld drops approximately 2,600 ft (800 metres) into the Lowveld (with viewpoints such as God's Window); where the Treur and the Blyde meet at right angles and have carved the most bizarre potholes out of the ancient rock at Bourke's Luck Potholes (with bridges and footpaths to view them); and where the Kadishi Stream is one of only very few active tufa forming streams in the world.

There are two resorts: **Blydepoort Resort** on the R532 from Graskop to Tzaneen. 75 chalets; caravanning and camping; two restaurants and shop; sport facilities. Trails: short trails and long hikes possible. Reservations: Overvaal Blydepoort, Private Bag X368, Ohrigstadt 1122. Tel: (013231) 901/902.

Sybrand van Niekerk Resort on the Lowveld side off the R531 from Acornhoek to Hoedspruit. Chalets and huts; caravanning and camping; restaurant and shop; sporting facilities. Trails: short trails and long hikes possible. Reservations: Sybrand van Niekerk Resort, Box 281, Hoedspruit 1380. Tel: (0020) ask for Bydedam 2.

Tshukudu Game Lodge and Nature Reserve on the R40 between Hoedspruit and Mica. This family-owned and run establishment only accommodates a maximum of eight people and is thus ideal to get away from the hustle and bustle of everyday life, driving through the reserve in open-top Land-Rovers. Thatched rondavels. Reservations: PO Box 289, Hoedspruit 1380. Tel: (015282) ask for 6313.

Timbervati Private Nature Reserve: this wild life area, situated north of the Sabi Sand resorts and bordering the western boundary of the Kruger Park between Phalaborwa and Orpen Gates, covers 290 sq. miles (750 sq. km) of unspoilt bushveld abounding in wild animals and birds. It is also the birthplace and home of the magnificent white lion. Within the reserve Motswari, M'bali, Tanda Tula and Ngala game lodges offer excellent opportunities for the enjoyment of wildlife experiences, be it on game drives in open safari cars or on walking trails.

The Motswari Game Lodge, 60 miles (97 km) from the Kruger Park (Orpen Gate) in the Timbavati Complex, offers safari drives by day or by night to view game as small as the chubby antbear to as big as the great African elephant. 18 rondavels and huts; meals included; shop; petrol station; sporting facilities. Trails: guided day hikes. Reservations: Box 67865, Bryanstone 2021. Tel: (011) 463 1990.

M'bali Game Lodge: 5 miles (9 km) from Motswari in the Timbavati Complex, M'bali offers peace and quiet for up to 14 guests in "habitents" situated high above the ground on wooden platforms overlooking a dam on the Sharalumi River. Trails: guided day hikes. Reservations: Box 67865, Bryanston 2021. Tel: (011) 463 1990/1.

Tanda Tula Game Lodge: this lodge lies in the north of the Timbavati Reserve, bordering on the Kruger Park. Tanda Tula, shangaan for "love of quietness", is home to the Big Five, as well as numerous birds and indigenous vegetation. Visitors enjoy the informality and flexibility of the lodge. 16-bedded game lodge; bar and swimming pool; shop. Reservations: Tanda Tula Game Lodge, PO Hoedspruit 1380. Tel: (0131732) 2322 or (011) 886 1810 4.

Nyala Game Lodge: this lies not far from the other camps in the Timbavati Complex and offers comfort while you enjoy the wilderness experience. 20 rooms (en suite); "sleep-out" bomas; meals available. Reservations: PO Box 110, Hoedspruit 1380. Tel: (0131732) ask for 5123.

Matumi Game Lodge: this beautiful lodge lies 26 miles (43 km) west of the Kruger Park, just off the main road which leads to the Orpen Gate. 16 chalets; meals available. Reservations: Box 57, Klaserie 1381. Tel: (0131732) ask for 4313.

Manyeleti Game Reserve is situated in Gazankulu between the Timbavati and Sabi Sand on the eastern boundary of the Kruger Park. The 88-sq. miles (230-sq. km) reserve is administered by the Gazankulu Department of Nature Conversation. Khoka Moya Trails operate two camps in the reserve:

Khoka Moya Camp is 12 miles (20 km) from the Kruger Park (Orpen Gate), and offers open-car safari drives by day and night and hiking trails to view the abundance of game in this area. Four huts; meals available; swimming pool and bar. Trails: hiking trails with armed rangers. Reservations: Safariplan, Box 4245, Randburg 2125. Tel: (011) 886 1810.

Honeyquide Safari Camp, 12 miles (20 km) from the Kruger Park (Orpen Gate), is the first traditional luxury safari styled tented camp. Hiking trails and night drives are included. Luxury tents; dining room; canvas bar; pool. Trails: hiking trails with armed rangers.

Reservations: as Khoka Moya, above.

Sabie Sand Private Nature Reserve: this great reservation of 230 sq. miles (600 sq. km) lies south of the Timbavati, bordering on the Kruger Park at the Paul Kruger Gate. The beautiful game reserves and lodges of Inyati, Londolozi and Sabie Sabie can be found in this reserve. In addition this great area also encompasses the 115-sq. miles (300-sq. km) Ratray Reserves which are divided into three camps: the renowned Mala Mala, Harry's Camp and Kirkman's Kamp. Information available from Sabie Sands, Exeter Ranch Safaris, Box 2060, Nelspruit 1200. Tel: (01311) 27 572 or (0131252) 604.

The **Inyati Game Lodge** on the Sand River in the Sabie Sand Reserve offers accommodation for up to 18 guests and dinner is served in "bush bomas" while tribal dancers accompanied by drums perform traditional ceremonies. Cottages; meals available. Reservations: Box 784365, Sandton, 2146. Tel: (0131252) ask for 630.

Londolozi Game Reserve: situated on the Sand River, bordering on the Kruger Park at the Paul Kruger Gate, this reserve is renowned for its top-of-the-range quality, comfort and service, amid the wild African bush and its unique wild life. Facilities at Tree Camp (eight guests), Bush Camp (rock cabins, max. eight guests) and Main Camp (en-suite, luxury chalets, max. 24 guests). Reservations: PO Box 1211, Sunning Hill Park 2157. Tel: (011) 803 8421.

The **Sabie Sabie Private Game Lodge** in the Sabie Sand Reserve, on the perennial Sabie River, has a reputation of friendly hospitality and high standards. The rich wild life area can be experienced on safari drives, and even from the camp itself. Facilities at Bush Lodge (25 chalets) and River Lodge (20 chalets). Reservations: Box 16, Skukuza 1350. Tel: (0131252) 116 or 232.

Mala Mala: this internationally renowned Game Lodge situated 6 miles (10 km) from the Kruger Park (Paul Kruger Gate) in the Ratray Reserves, within the Sabie Sand Private Nature Reserve, offers safari drives to view the Big Five, walks and comfort of luxury camps and a personal guide who looks after the guests from waking calls to after-dinner drinks. 26 cottages with 24-hour room service; restaurant and bar; swimming pool and laundry service. Reservations: Box 2575, Randburg 2125. Tel: (011) 789 2677.

Harry's Camp in the Ratray Reserves in the Sabie Sand Complex is beautiful and different with Ndebele-styled bungalows and emphasis on outdoor living. The bush experience is thus that much more unique at Harry's Camp. Three cottages; seven rooms. Reservations: as above.

Close to the other two camps, **Kirkman's Kamp** is perched high up above the bushveld, offering a spectacular view of the river and the surrounding bush and wild life. Five cottages en-suite; 10 rooms en-suite. Reservations: as above.

Wolkberg Wilderness Area: this is accessible along a signposted road off the R71 some 24 miles (40 km) from Pietersburg. This wilderness hiking area covers 65 sq. miles (170 sq. km) of high mountains and deep valleys of the Transvaal Drakensberg and a section of the Strydpoort Range. Lush forests, great mountain waterfalls and the Mohlapitse River Potholes make this a perfect sanctuary for nature lovers. Camping (permits necessary); no restaurant. Reservations: State Forester, Serala State Forest, Private Bag, Haenertsburg 0730. Tel: (0152222) ask for 1303.

Percy Fyfe Nature Reserve: lying 16 miles (26 km) northeast of Potgietersrus, this reserve specialises in the breeding of Tsessebe, roan and salbe antelopes. Basic accommodation; no restaurant. Reservations: Private Bag X2585, Potgietersrus 0660. Tel: (01541) 5678.

Potgietersrus Nature Reserve and Game Breeding Centre: on the northern outskirts of Potgietersrus on the road to Pietersburg this reserve and breeding centre is administered by the National Zoological Gardens of SA. It specialises in rare, endangered African species such as pygmy hippo and scimitar-horned oryx and addax from North Africa. But one can also see animals from South America and Asia. It takes aboutless than a mile before getting to Pilgrim's Rest two hours to drive through the reserve.

Lapala Wilderness Area: this area, which lies in the Waterberg Mountains, about 77 miles (125 km) northwest of Nylstroom, is rich in game and birds as it incorporates a 30-mile (50-km) riverfrontage. Self-contained chalets; camping; canoeing and fishing. Trails: guided wilderness trails. Reservations: PO Box 645, Bedfordview 2008. Tel: (011) 53 1814 or 53 8411.

Emaweni Game Lodge: some 60 miles (100 km) north of Nystroom, in the Tafelkop Nature Reserve, this lodge is 2 hours' drive from Pretoria. Game-viewing drives are offered to view the wildlife the reserve supports. Luxury chalets; meals available and bar; swimming and fishing. Reservations: PO Box 823, Pretoria 0001. Tel: (012) 21 1778 or 325 3601.

Mabula Game Reserve: this reserve lies half an hour's drive northwest of Warmbaths (two hours from Johannesburg) at the foot of the Waterberg Mountains. The varied habitat supports the Big Five and much of the smaller game. Walks and Land-Rover drives are offered. Lodge; swimming, tennis, horse rides. Trails: self-guided and guided walks. Reservations: Mabula Lodge, Private Bag X16651, Warmbaths 0480. Tel: (015334) 616 or 717.

Loskop Dam Game Reserve: 32 miles (53 km) north of Middelburg, the reserve supports white rhino, giraffe, zebra, buffalo, kudu and more than 200 bird species and is of particular interest to biologists as it encompasses the transition from lowveld to highveld. Caravanning and camping; fishing; adjoining reserve offers accommodation. Reservations: Private Bag X 1525, Middelburg 1050. Tel: (01202) 3075/6/7.

KwaZulu/Natal

Natal has a subtropical coastline in the east, the majestic Drakensberg in the west and sweeping savannah and rolling hills down the middle. It offers a wide variety of habitat for all kinds of wildlife. The Natal Parks Board administers 64 game and nature reserves which you find in many of the beautiful spots all over Natal, but concentrated mainly along the north Coast and in the Drakensberg foothills. The Drakensberg has 11 peaks on the Natal side which top 9,800 ft (3,000 metres), the highest being Injasuti with 11,184 ft (3,409 metres) which is in the Giants Castle Game Reserve.

In many of the game reserves one can participate in Wilderness Trails (from half-day to 4 days) under the guidance of armed game guards. This is an unsurpassable way of experiencing the bush and its animals – and yourself. Pony-trails are offered on the same basis; in some instances you sleep in caves or under overhangs. The Natal Parks Board offer various types of accommodation from chalets – where everything from linen to pots and pans and often a cook to prepare your meals is provided – to rustic huts where you have to bring your own linen and cooking utensils. Food and drinks must be brought along in all parks. Reservations for all Natal Parks Board Reserves and all trails is done through their Central Reservations Office in Pietermaritzburg at The Natal Parks Board, PO Box 662, Pietermaritzburg 3200. Tel: (0331) 47 1981; Fax: 47 1980.

Reservations for the caravan and camping sites at the five St Lucia camps is done through St Lucia Publicity Association, PO Box 106, St Lucia 3936. Tel: (03592) 225 or 143.

The reserves of Ndumu, Kosi Bay and Baya Camp are administered by the KwaZulu Department of Natural Resources, 367 Loop St, Pietermaritzburg, 3201. Tel: (0331) 94 6698; fax: 42 1948.

Sodwana Bay National Park: lying some 248 miles (400 km) from Durban and 55 miles (90 km) east of Ubombo, Sodwana is in the first place an angler's paradise (deep sea and shore) as well as the meeting point for divers from all over South Africa. From Cape Vidal (north of St Lucia) to the Mozambique border and three sea miles out to sea, a Marine Reserve has been proclaimed and this, plus the fact that you find the most southern coral reefs here, makes this an ideal area for diving. They even have a resident moraine eel here named Monty who is so used to divers that he just about shakes hands with them. But the park is also a haven for a great variety of birds that nest in the great fig trees growing in the swampy marshes close to the tidal pools and you can come across a number of antelope and smaller animals. Facilities: 20 huts; very large camping and caravan site; shop; petrol; deep-sea fishing; diving.

Mkuzi Game Reserve: lying some 208 miles (335 km) from Durban on the main North Coast road, this reserve with its four hides overlooking waterholes and its numerous hiking trails through low-lying thornveld, past lakes and through fig tree forests has much to offer. It has an abundance of game including the elegant and rare leopard, black and white rhino, hippos, crocodiles and of course giraffe and all the antelopes. 21 cottages; huts; camping and caravanning.

Trails: 3-day Wilderness Trail; three-hour walking trails; 2-miles (3-km) Fig Forest Walk and River View Trail.

Lake St Lucia Complex: on the central Zululand coast the St Lucia Lake extends for 37 miles (60 km) northwards from St Lucia Estuary which lies 15 miles (25 km) east of Mtuba-tuba. This "lake" is actually an estuary opening to the sea at the southern end and running parallel to the sea only separated from it by some of the highest forested dunes in the world – a unique ecological system. In the north the lake widens considerably and the three interlinked nature reserves encompassing the whole area are an intriguing mosaic of lakes, rivers, pans, swamp forests, open grasslands, dune forests and wide open deserted beaches. The estuary mouth is said to be the only place in the world where you can at times see sharks, hippos and crocodiles sharing the same habitat. But then hippos and crocodiles had to get used to a salinity which periodically was higher than that of the sea due to the severe drought so that the five rivers feeding the lake did not bring nearly enough fresh water – causing great concern to nature conservation bodies.

Though the area is most popular for angling and ski-boat fishing it has a lot to offer for the nature lover. The trails – from a 2-mile (3-km) self-guided trail to 4-day trails with a guide – have a charm of their own not found in any of the other reserves. Numerous crocodiles and hippos inhabit the lake and the pans but you also come across reedbuck, bushbuck and the beautiful, elegant nyala and other small game. For bird lovers it is a paradise: 360 species frequent the lake and its environs. In the northern part of Lake St Lucia flocks of 20,000 flamingoes have been seen and here is also the only breeding colony of pink-backed pelicans in southern Africa. Thousands of fish-hunting birds and other water foul have found a sanctuary here: the giant goliath heron, saddle-beaked storks, spoonbills, dabchicks (who carry their young on their backs) and scores of others; but the thick bush and reeds are also inhabited by rare birds like the Woodwards batis. The two trails from False Bay Park are particularly suited for bird watching. The Crocodile Centre of St Lucia has interesting displays and information about this largest of the Earth's reptiles. Six separate camps are part of the St Lucia Complex: Mapelane, St Lucia Estuary, Charter's Greek, Fanie's Island, Cape Vidal and False Bay Resort on the northwestern shore of the lake. Huts and Cottages: Mapelane (9); St Lucia Village (none in the Park, but plenty of private accommodation and hotels); Charter's Creek (16); Fanie's Island (13); Cape Vidal and Eastern Shores Nature Reserve (23); False Bay Resort (4). Caravan sites: Mapelane, St Lucia, Fanie's Island, False Bay.

Camping: in all six resorts book well in advance for holiday periods through the St Lucia Publicity Association (see previous page). Restaurants and shops: only in St Lucia village.

Trails: some are only done April–September as the summer months are extremely hot and humid. Some of the self-guided trails must also be booked in advance. Always be aware of hippos even though they are seldom away from the water during the day. The guided trails start from St Lucia, Cape Vidal, Charters Creek, Fanie's Island and False Bay Park.

Hluhluwe Game Reserve: located about 230 miles (370 km) north of Durban, 10 miles (17 km) west of Hluhluwe village where you find a hotel, a few shops and a service station. Hluhluwe is quite hilly and because it lies at a higher altitude, 2,130 ft (650 metres), it is cooler in summer than Umfolozi. The diverse vegetation of forest, woodland, savannah and grassland makes this reserve scenically different and you find all the main wildlife species, including black and white rhino, wildebeest, giraffe, buffalo, lion and leopard amongst many others and elephants have recently been re-introduced. Bird life is abundant. 25 cottages; huts; Zulu cultural museum; petrol. Trails: self-guided trail and half-day guided walks.

Umfolozi Game Reserve: located 31 miles (50 km) west of Mtubatuba on the R618, 170 miles (270 km) north of Durban. Resting between the White and the Black Umfolozi Rivers, with rugged savannah vegetation, the reserve is famous for its Operation White Rhino in the 1960s which helped to save that animal from extinction, by drug-darting them and breeding them. All the major animals are found here as well as many lesser known ones, but you are virtually certain to see white rhino of which there are 900 in the park. Two heated camps; nine cottages; huts; two bush camps, which have to be booked en bloc. Trails: 3-day wilderness trails (April–September); primitive trails (combining Wilderness Trails and backpacking); guided half day walks.

Umlalazi Nature Reserve: located about 80 miles (128 km) north of Durban, 1 mile (2 km) from Mtunzini. The clear blue waters of the coast can be seen from the quaint log cabins in this lagoon and coastal reserve with mangrove swamps and dune forests, that attracts a wide variety of bird species in addition to bush pig, reedbuck and bushbuck. 13 log cabins; camping site; picnic spots. The Mtunzini Lagoon resort offers water-skiing and boats for hire; shops, petrol.

Trails: two self-guided trails (mangrove and dune forest).

Vernon Cooke's Nature Reserve: located 9 miles (15 km) west of Scottburgh. Two dams in the reserve attract many birds and game including eland, zebra, blue wildebeest, bushbuck and porcupine. During September/October the reserve is ablaze with wild flowers, almost rivalling Namaqualand.

Oribi Gorge Nature Reserve: located 13 miles (21 km) west of Port Shepston; 80 miles (128 km) south of Durban. The reserve includes a 1,300-ft (400-metres) deep spectacular gorge which attracts numerous birds. The gorge is covered in the once widespread indigenous forest, home to leopard, samango monkeys and water monitor and 200 species of birds including seven eagles. Seven cottages; huts; picnic site; Oribi Gorge Hotel at Fairacres not far away. Trails: 21 miles

(35 km) of day walks and trails have been established.

Coleford Nature Reserve: located 13 miles (22 km) south of Underberg. Underberg is one of South Africa's premier trout-fishing areas and there are excellent trout fishing opportunities in the two rivers that meander through the reserve. There is also some game. 14 cottages; huts; picnic sites; tennis, riding, croquet; trout fishing (permits from camp office). Trails: day walks.

Vergelegen Nature Reserve: from Nottingham Road (all gravel) or on tar via Bulwer and Himeville and then 21 miles (35 km) gravel. To get away from it all, this reserve provides a secluded sanctuary in amongst the deep valleys, pine plantations and green countryside. Two cottages; trout fishing (get permits beforehand). Trails: mapped out day walks.

Loteni Nature Reserve: 47 miles (76 km) west of Nottingham Road. A rugged reserve with a ravine coming down from the 10,800-ft (3,300-metres) high Drakensberg. An abundance of birds and a variety of buck live here. 15 cottages; huts; camping site; trout fishing (permits available from camp office). Trails: Eagle Trail (7.5-mile/12-km trail).

Kamberg Nature Reserve: 26 miles (42 km) west of Rosetta in the foothills of the Drakensberg. With the Mooi River flowing through it, this peaceful reserve offers excellent trout fishing, interesting trails and wildlife observation. Seven cottages; huts; trout fishing (permit available from office). Trails: Mooi River self-guided trail (2.5 miles/4 km) (designed for visitors in wheelchairs); six other walks and climbs.

Giant's Castle Game Reserve: 43 miles (69 km) southwest of Estcourt. The 15-mile (25-km) long and 9,840-ft (3000-metre) high wall known as the Giant's Castle is a rugged but majestic part of the Drakensberg, in which bushmen lived until the end of last century. Close to the main camp is a bushmen museum and also a cave with bushmen paintings. Twelve different antelope are at home here as well as the very rare lammergeyer (bearded vulture) which, together with other vultures and birds of prey, can be viewed from a hide.

Facilities at Main Camp (21 cottages/huts), Hillside-Camp (one hut,

camping site) and Injasuti Camp (19 huts, camping site); trout fishing. Trails: 31 miles (50 km) of trails lead through reserve; four guided trails; walks and hikes; mountain climbing; 2–3 day guided mountain rides (accommodation in huts and caves).

Royal Natal National Park lies 26 miles (42 km) west of Bergville. This park looks upon the majestic Amphitheatre, one of the most magnificent mountain landscapes in Southern Africa: 5-miles (8-km) wide and cast in one piece of solid rock, it embraces the Tendele Valley below like a Greek Amphitheatre. The Tugela, one of five major rivers that have their source on top of the 10,777-ft (3285-metre) high Mont-aux-Sources falls in a series of waterfalls 4,900 ft (1,500 metres) down the face of the Amphitheatre, the one fall being 700 ft (213 metres). The best way to explore this wonderful world is on foot or on horseback on one of the 31 trails, climbs or bridle paths. A 28-mile (45-km) hike leads up to the top of the Sentinel via two chain ladders.

The area also displays a variety of plants: more than a thousand species occur here, and in the adjoining Rugged Glen Nature Reserve you come across yellow-wood and Cape chestnut, erica and proteas. The rugged cliffs and kloofs are ideal for all sort of birds of prey and vultures and of course one finds various antelope in the park.

Facilities at the Royal Natal National Park Hotel (just outside the park) and Tendele Hutted Camp (with 16 cottages); lodge; camping at Mahai and Rugged Glen; shop; trout fishing and riding (permits from the camp office); picnic sites. Trails: 31 walking routes ranging from 2 miles (3 km) to 28 miles (45 km); guided walks.

Ndumu Game Reserve: located 290 miles (470 km) from Durban in northern Zululand on the Mozambique border. This secluded reserve of lush vegetation, fever tree forests, numerous lakes and pans is the perfect haven for fish, aquatic birds, colonies of crocodiles and hippos, the robust rhino, the sly striped polecat and many more. Land-Rover drives around the pans can be undertaken as well as guided walks through this reserve with its very special atmosphere. It is a paradise for bird-lovers as nearly as

many bird species have been recorded here as in the Kruger National Park which is 190 times larger. Open daily 9am–3.30pm. Seven huts. Trails: guided hiking trails.

Kosi Bay Nature Reserve: a few miles south of the Mozambique border in the northeastern corner of Zululand. Four crystal-clear lakes are surrounded by the 42 sq. mile-reserve (110 sq. km) of mangrove swamps, marshes, swamp forests with umdoni and fig canopy trees and raphia palms. The rare leather back and loggerhead turtles breed on the stretch of coast south of Kosi Bay and flufftail, palmnut vultures and other interesting birds inhabit this reserve. Four-wheel drive vehicles are essential for sandy roads and river crossings and swimming in the lakes is not recommended because of bilharzia, crocodiles and hippos. Three cottages; camping; fishing and boats for hire. Trails: walks with rangers; overnight trails.

Baya Camp: on the shores of Lake Sibaya, accessible via Jozini and Mbazwana. Two hides overlooking dune forests and coastal plains provide excellent bird-watching opportunities. Hut camp; no swimming in the lake due to bilharzia, crocodiles and hippos; fishing (licences obtainable); boat for hire. Trails: guided trails; walking routes. A four-wheel drive vehicle is recommended but not essential.

Natal Inland Midmar Public Resort and Nature Reserve: located 15 miles (24 km) from Pietermaritzburg on the N3. The 11 sq.-mile (28 sq.-km) reserve surrounds the dam and the resort gives a very colonial impression with tea served on the manicured lawns, as you watch the yachts on the dam. Wildlife can be viewed by taking a boat ride along the shore line. Adjacent to the resort is the Midmar Historical Village displaying Natal's pioneering past. 63 cottages/huts; camping and caravan sites; restaurant and bar; swimming (no bilharzia); fishing, sailing, water-skiing, tennis, squash, bowls and riding.

Albert Falls Public Resort and Nature Reserve: 11 miles (18 km) from Pietermaritzburg. This small reserve is one of the most beautiful spots in the Natal Midlands. Walks or rides take you around the scenic Albert Falls Dam, across the Umgeni River, to the Gold-Panning Falls, while viewing zebra, impala, blesbok, reedbuck and other small buck. 28 cottages and huts; two camping and caravan sites; swimming; squash, tennis, sailing, riding and canoeing. Trails: several day walks.

Spioenkop Public Resort and Nature Reserve: 22 miles (35 km) southwest of Ladysmith. At Spioenkop one of the important battles of the Anglo-Boer-War (1900) was fought. Today the dammed Tugela and the game reserve offer pursuits like horse-riding, yachting, walks and trails in the game reserve and guided tours of the battle fields and a Boer War Museum. 34 cottages/huts; one bush camp; camping and caravan site; pool; boat rides; tennis, riding. Trails: walking trails with game rangers; History Trail (leads to the Spioenkop Battlefield).

Chelmsford Public Resort Nature Reserve: 12 miles (20 km) south of Newcastle, on the Ladysmith road. The resort, dominated by the Leokop Mountain, boasts Egyptian and spurwinged geese, spoonbill, yellow-billed duck, darter and dabchick. The dam attracts game including rhino and zebra. 12 cottages; camping and caravan sites; fishing and boat trips.

Itala Game Reserve: located in the Pongola Valley, north of Louwsburg, 37 miles (60 km) northeast of Vryheid. This scenically beautiful combination of bushveld, deep valleys, cliff faces, granite outcrops, grassed hilltops and six rivers is home to a large variety of game, including Natal's only herd of tsesseby and many birds of prey. 40 chalets/huts; two bush camps; camping; swimming in rock pools; picnic sites. Trails: 3-day Wilderness Trails (March–October); 1-day guided trails.

Mala Chite Camp: a Ratray reserve 5 miles (8 km) southeast of Mkuze village. Named after the malachite kingfisher, this reserve combines outdoor adventure and five-star comfort and lives up to its name with the nearly 400 species of birds that have been seen there. Fishing in the nearby Jozini Dam and game viewing in open Land-Rovers. Four thatched double rondavels; meals provided (but unlicensed – so bring your own drinks); fishing (20 minutes away). Trails: walking safaris with ranger. Reservations: Ratray Reserves, PO Box 2575, Randburg 2125. Tel: (011) 789 2677.

Tamboti Bush Camp: 18 miles (30 km) northeast of the village of Hluhluwe. It lies in the 15 sq. miles (40 sq. km) of Punata Game Ranch that border on the Mkuzi Game Reserve and is known for its superb opportunities of viewing game, including rhino, giraffe and leopard on day and night game drives in open Land-Rovers. Four thatched huts; meals provided (but unlicensed); swimming. Trails: walking safaris with ranger. Reservations: Tamboti Bush Camp, 11 Surrey Lane, Kloof. Tel: (031) 764 0137.

Zulu Nyala Safaris: off the N2 between Hluhluwe and Mkuze, Zulu Nyala is the largest privately owned safari ranch in Natal encompassing at least five different ecological systems. For bird watchers and photographers, enjoy the sunset river cruises. Three exclusive camps with thatched huts for max. 20 people; meals available (or self catering). Reservation, tel: SATOUR (011) 331 5241.

Ubizane Game Ranch: 5 miles (8 km) from Hluhluwe village on Hluhluwe Game Reserve road. This private ranch overlooks a fever tree forest. Game drives in open four-wheel-drives and walking trails allow guests to see white rhinos (bred on the ranch), giraffe and many other animals. Night drives allow for the viewing of nocturnal animals. Three luxury timber bungalows on stilts; meals available (unlicensed, but hotel on same property). Trails: walking trails with ranger. Reservations: PO Box 102, Hluhluwe 3960. Tel: (03562) ask for 3602.

Bona Manzi Game Park and Bushlands Game Lodge: 6 miles (10 km) south of Hluhluwe village, these two private reserves offer accommodation in tree houses and excellent game viewing areas. Facilities at Bona Manzi (three tree houses and a tree lodge) and 10 huts; swimming pool; meals available (unlicensed). Bushlands: eight luxury tree houses; meals provided; swimming pool and bar. Trails: walking trails. Reservations: Bona Manzi, PO Box 48, Hluhluwe 3960, tel: (03562) ask for 3530, or through Bushlands, PO Box 79, Hluhluwe 3960. Tel: (03562) ask for 144.

Harold Johnson Nature Reserve: 15 miles (24 km) north of Stanger. This reserve overlooks the Tugela river mouth and Indian ocean and here one can walk through some of Natal's most beautiful vegetation. Camping and caravanning. Trails: self-guided trails; educational trails by arrangement. Reservations: PO Box 148, Darnall 4480. Tel: (0324) 6 1574.

Natal Inland Zulu Bush Safaris: On the R612 between Nongoma and Hlobane. Ideal for bird-watching and game-viewing. Accommodation overlooks the beautiful Msihlengeni waterfall and the river. One lodge (four people); bush camp; swimming pool; self catering. Reservations: SATOUR, tel: (011) 331 5241.

Transkei, Eastern Cape & Ciskei

This region of varying beauty – from the weather beaten coastline with sandy beaches, silent lagoons and wide river mouths to the lush inland vegetation of enchanting gorges, beautiful mountains, tumbling rivers and dry grassland plains – is as yet fairly unknown. The area from the mouth of the Kei River to the Umtamvuna River, known as the wild coast of the Transkei, is rugged and unspoilt. The 150 miles (250 km) of green thick indigenous forest, hilly grassland and sheer cliffs that fall to the white deserted beaches, is one of the most beautiful coasts of the African continent. Hotels are situated in remote villages along the coast.

The Wild Coast Hiking Trails explore this magnificent coast. The route follows the coast line with hiking stopovers in huts along the way. The trail is divided into five sections: Umtamvuna–Msikaba (3 days); Msikaba–Aqate Terrace (7 days); Silaka–Coffee Bay (6 days); Coffee Bay–Mbashe (5 days); Ngabara–Kei River (6 days). The trail is not for the faint-hearted and a challenge for anyone with a lust for adventure.

Reservations: Transkei Nature Conservation Division, Department of Agriculture and Forestry, Private Bag X5002, Umtata, Transkei. Tel: (0471) 2 4322 or 24 9309.

For information on parks and trails in the region contact The National Parks Board or SATOUR.

Malekgonyane Nature Reserve lies in the Drakensberg on the Lesotho border and is beautiful in spring when the sweeping montainous grassland is covered in fire-lilies, gladioli, red-hot pokers and other wild flowers. There are numerous walks, sparkling streams and waterfalls. Enquiries and booking: Transkei Nature Conservation, Private Bag X 5002, Umtata, Transkei. Tel: (0471) 2 4322 or 24 9309.

Mkambati Game Reserve lies halfway between Port Edward and Port St Johns in one of the most beautiful parts of the beautiful Transkei coast; isolated beaches, mysterious forested ravines, swamp forests and awe-inspiring cliffs make this reserve ideal for those who look for solitude. A lodge and cottages/rondavels at four different camps; self-catering except for guests of the lodge; shop; ideal for angling; canoes for hire. Trails: short walks to long hikes; guided horse trails. Reservations: Transkei Department of Finance, Box 574, Kokstad, 4700. Tel: (0372) 3101.

Dwesa Nature Reserve lies halfway between Coffee Bay and the Kei River. The fact that it was the Transkei's first nature reserve (1893) says something about the scenic beauty of this part of the coast. The mode of transport in the reserve is by foot and many walks can be undertaken from the camp which only consists of five huts. Fishing is very good, but it is not permitted to collect bait. Bungalows. Trails: walks. Reservations: Transkei Nature Conservation, Private Bag X 5002, Umtata, Transkei. Tel: (0471) 2 4322 or 24 9309.

Bosbokstrand Private Nature Reserve: located 35 miles (60 km) north of East London. The beach has rocky as well as sandy stretches and fishing is regarded as excellent. Clearly marked trails take one through the game area. A-frame chalets; caravan park; shop. Trails: marked walking trails. Reservations: Bosbokstrand Nature Reserve, Box 302, Randfontein 1760. Tel: (011) 696 1442.

Mpongo Game Reserve lies 18 miles (30 km) north west of East London. It has many of the large animals like rhino, giraffe and even lion (in an enclosure) but is particularly rich in its bird life. There are guided trails of 3–12 miles (5–20 km) length and of particular appeal are the night safaris and the horseback trails. Caravanning and camping; restaurant and shop; Natural History Museum. Trails: guided trails;

night hikes; horse trails. Reservations: Officer in Charge, Mpongo Game Reserve, Box 3300, Cambridge. Tel: (04326) 669.

L.L. Sebe Game Reserve: the reserve is situated 12 miles (20 km) from Peddie in the Ciskei and lies between the Fish and the Keiskamma rivers. It offers fresh water angling, game viewing and limited hunting. An enchanting hiking trail meanders along the Great Fish River. Two lodges (one for hikers). Trails: 2-day hike and a few shorter ones.

The Garden Route

180 miles (300 km) of coastline from Riversdale in the west to Storms River in the east, bounded by Indian Ocean in the south and the Tsitsikamma mountain range in the north, make up the renowned Garden Route. The mountains, the lush indigenous flora, the forests, the many lakes and the meandering rivers make this area a uniquely beautiful haven for all nature lovers.

Wilderness National Park: this park, which stretches along the coast from Wilderness village to the Goukamma Nature Reserve, encompasses several beautiful lakes and vleis (afrikaans for wet-lands) including the Knysna Lake and the Swartvlei, the largest natural saltwater lake in SA. The rare Cape clawless otter and the exotic Knysna Loerie make this wetlands area their home. This park is an ornithologists' dream, particularly because of the abundance of aquatic birds. Two camps with self-catering chalets and huts; caravanning and camping; launderette and shop; watersports, fishing, hiring of canoes. Trails: walking trails. Reservations: National Parks Board, tel: (021) 343 1991; fax: 343 0905.

Tsitsikamma Forest Park: situated some 60 miles (100 km) east of Knysna, this park with its ancient trees, its lush indigenous forests and gentle streams supports bushbuck, bush pig, blue duiker and numerous bird species. Caravanning and camping. Trails: trails of varying duration (1 hour–5 days). Reservations: The Regional Director, Tsitsikamma Forest Region, Private Bag X 537, Humansdorp 6300. Tel: (0423) 5 1180.

Tsitsikamma Coastal National Park: extending from Plettenberg Bay and the Groot River mouth, near Hurmansdorp, this park is home to the well known and challenging Otter Trail. The trail leads through the evergreen forests, the rocky outcrops and the beaches of the Indian Ocean. Small animals and numerous birds accompany the hiker. The park stretches 3 miles (5 km) out to sea and was the first marine national park. The meeting of the warm Agulhas and cold Benguela currents has resulted in an interesting mingling of tropical and cold water marine life. A snorkelling and a scuba-diving trail have been laid out, the latter only for divers with a valid certificate. Cottages and holiday apartments; caravanning and camping; shop, restaurant; fishing and diving. Trails of varying duration (1 hour–5 days); underwater trail. Reservations: National Parks Board, tel: (012) 343 1991; fax: 343 0905.

Addo Elephant National Park lies 4 miles (7 km) north of Port Elizabeth near the Zuurberg Range in the Sundays River Valley. It was established as a refuge for the last 11 remaining coastal elephants – today there are 165 of them. The park, overgrown by a tangle of creepers and small trees, supports also a number of black rhino, buffalo and numerous antelope. Porcupine, antbear and bush pig are some of the nocturnal animals. No citrus fruits of any kind may be taken into the park (because the elephants may become aggressive to get at them). Chalets and rondavels; camping and caravanning; restaurant, shop, petrol. Reservations: as above.

Zuurberg National Park lies 7 miles (12 km) north of Addo Elephant National Park in the Winterhoek mountains. The park shelters some unique plants in its ravines and rolling hills, like the Zuurberg Cycad, which is found nowhere else but in this park. It is known for its richness in vegetation and bird life. Accommodation in a nearby hotel. Trails: two short trails. Information from Port Elizabeth Publicity Association, tel: (041) 52 1315.

Cape Town & Southwestern Cape

Valleys, coastal plains and rugged mountains characterise the region in which the beautiful city of Cape Town rests. Just north lies Namaqualand, a semi-desert of rocky outcrops, Spartan vegetation, space and silence which in spring is transformed into a carpet of brilliant colours, when millions of wild flowers open their fragile petals – as if to make up for the drabness of the rest of the year.

Bontebok National Park: lying 4 miles (7 km) south of Swellendam, this park was established to save the bontebok from extinction. Today it has some 200 bontebok and several other antelope; the park is also renowned for its abundant flora. Late winter and early spring sees this botanical area carpeted with brilliant colour. Four fully equipped caravans for hire; camping; shop. Trails: three short hiking trails. Reservations: National Parks Board, Pretoria (see above) or Regional Office, Cape Town, tel: (021) 419 5365.

Cape of Good Hope Nature Reserve: although this reserve at the tip of the Cape peninsula appears rather barren and uninteresting, one finds more than half the plant species of the peninsula here, of which 10 only occur in this reserve. It is also one of the world's largest breeding grounds for tortoises. It also offers beautiful sea landscapes, particularly the one from Cape Point. Restaurant; curio shop and information centre. Information from Regional office of the National Parks Board, SATOUR or Captour, Cape Town. Tel: (021) 419 536.

De Hoop Nature Reserve: located 37 miles (60 km) east of Bredasdorp, this reserve covers 154 sq. miles (400 sq. km) of very varied habitats. This part of the coast is one of the most important mating and calving areas in the world for the Southern Right Whale, as well as the southern-most vulture breeding area in Africa. Open daily 8am–4.30pm. Two basic chalets; camping. Trails: guided coastal walk (24 miles/40 km); day walks. Reservations: Private Bag X16, Bredasdorp 7280. Tel: (02922) 782.

Helderberg Nature Reserve: the Helderberg mountain stands guard over Somerset West, and this small but picturesque reserve reaches halfway up its rocky side. Many paths run through the reserve through mountainsides of erica and proteas, but best known is Disa Gorge where January–March one can see the exquisite

"flower-of-the-gods", the red Disa orchid growing on inaccessible rock faces. A remarkable variety of birds is also encountered here. Open daily 9.30am–6pm. Picnic site; herbarium. Trails: seven trails, 15 minutes–3 hours. Information from the Regional Office of the National Parks Board Cape Town or SATOUR, tel: (021) 419 5365.

Salmonsdam Nature Reserve: lying 28 miles (45 km) west of Hermanus, this mountainous area, with its deep kloofs, forests and its beautiful waterfall, is coloured by the many species of protea and erica. Bontebok, klipspringer, other small mammals and numerous birds live here. Open 7am–6pm. Basic hut accommodation; caravanning and camping. Trails: 3 trails (2–3miles/3–5 km). Reservations: PO Box 5, Stanford 7210. Tel: (0283) 789.

West Coast National Park Langebaan: situated about 60 miles (100 km) north of Cape Town. Encompassing one of the great wetlands of the world – the Langebaan Lagoon. The park is internationally renowned as the world's fourth most important bird sanctuary. For up to 55,000 birds this lagoon and the islands in the vicinity are the final destination after a flight from Greenland and the Arctic regions during our summer. But there are also quite a number of antelope. In spring the Postman Nature Reserve (incorporated into the West Coast Park) is ablaze with wild flowers. Lagebaan village with lodge and cottages; caravanning and camping; educational boat trips, canoes for hire, water-sports. Trails: various hiking routes and horseback trails. Information from the Regional Office of National Parks Board or SATOUR or Captour, Cape Town, tel: (021) 419 5365.

Western Transvaal & Orange Free State

This area encompasses the highveld of grassy plateaus, largely covered by the farmlands of the Orange Free State, the magnificent Drakensberg mountain range in the east, snow-capped in winter, and the varying habitats along the Orange and Vaal Rivers.

Western Transvaal Krugersdorp Game Reserve: on the R24 a mere 40

minutes from Johannesburg. A reserve with a great variety of game including giraffes, white rhino, eland, roan, sable, buffalo and many others as well as a lion camp. Beware of cheeky baboons. Various educational trails (4–6 miles/7–10 km) are conducted by the Wildlife Society. Open daily 8am–5pm. Chalets and huts (bring cooking, caravanning and camping utensils); shop. Trails: guided half-day trails. Reservations: The Tourist Officer, Department of Parks, PO Box 94, Krugersdorp 1740. Tel: (011) 660 1076.

Rob Ferreira Game Reserve: on the R29 northeast of Christiana. The Vaal River forms the southern border of Rob Ferreira, attracting birds in abundance. The reserve is well stocked with animals, including white rhino and many of the antelopes. Open daily 7am–5pm. Chalets; flats; caravanning and camping; restaurant, supermarket; two swimming pools; mineral bath. Trails: 5-mile (8-km) trail. Reservations: Overvaal Resorts, PO Box 3046, Pretoria 0001. Tel: (012) 346 2288.

Rustenburg Nature Reserve: situated 60 miles (95 km) northwest of Johannesburg on the R24, the reserve lies in the beautiful Magaliesberg mountains, taking in part of the plateau on top as well as the northern mountain slopes with their picturesque gorges, waterfalls, sheer cliffs and many an inviting rock pool. The best manner of exploring it is on foot, but you can also drive through it and you might come across a number of antelope, even sable. Caravanning and camping; visitors' centre. Trails: 3-hour trail and a two-day trail. Reservations: PO Box 511, Rustenburg 0300. Tel: (0142) 3 1050.

Golden Gate Highlands National Park: situated to the southwest of Harrismith in the foothills of the Maluti mountains near the Lesotho border, the park is known for its strange and fantastic rock formations. In autumn and spring red hot pokers, fire lilies and watsonias colour the park magnificently. Although Golden Gate is first and foremost known for its scenic beauty, birds and game can be seen as well. It is an ideal area for hiking and a number of trails go to particularly beautiful spots. Lodge, chalets, huts; caravanning and camping; restaurant and shop; swimming pool, tennis, golf, bowling. Trails: a 2-day trail and half a dozen short to 1-day trails; horses can be hired. Reservations: National Parks Board, tel: (012) 343 1991; fax: 343 0905.

Tussen-die-Riviere Game Farm: 10 miles (17 km) east of Bethulie. This reserve supports more game than any other reserve in the Orange Free State, including white rhino. During the summer months the reserve is open for the public, (1 November–30 April). 1 May–31 October hunters help with the necessary culling. As they receive 20 times as many applications as they need hunters, lots are drawn. Self-catering accommodation. Trails: two nature trails. Information from the Director of Nature Conservation, Box 517, Bloemfontein 9300. Tel: (051) 405 5243.

Willem Pretorius Game Reserve: located between Kroonstad and Winburg on the N1, this reserve boasts the largest herd of wildebeest (some 600) and giraffe; buffalo and white rhino have also been introduced. A large dam is part of the reserve and many of the 200 bird species that have been recorded here are seen in the vicinity of the dam. Boat trips are organised and fishing is good. Flats, rondavels, huts; caravanning and camping; restaurant and shop; golf, tennis, bowls. Reservations: Willem Pretorius Game Reserve, PO Box, Ventersburg 9451. Tel: (01734) 4229.

Namaqualand & The Karoo

The Great Karoo, an endless thirsty land with singular farms, and the Namaqualand of semi-desert vegetation and springtime floral magnificence, makes up this beautiful region.

Akkerendam Nature Reserve: less than 1 mile from Calvinia. Although Calvinia lies in Bushmanland, its flower carpet in spring-time is as magnificent as that of Namaqualand. The black springbok and the bat-eared fox are amongst the mammals found on this beautiful stretch of land with its three dams. The shorter of its two trails was designed for senior citizens. You need permission to do either of the trails. Trails: two trails (1–2 hours and 6–7 hours). Information from The Town Clerk, PO Box 28, Calvinia 8190. Tel: (02772) ask for 11 or 241.

Augrabies Falls National Park: situated 75 miles (120 km) west of Upington on the Orange River. The central feature of this park is the magnificient Augrabies Falls of the Orange River. Although the main falls are 183-ft (56-metre) high, the cataracts before that drop the river another 300 ft (90 metres) and the sheer granite walls of the gorge are up to 820-ft (250-metre) high – an awe-inspiring sight. And the area along the Orange with its *kokerbooms* (quiver trees) aloes and black basalt rocks gives this reserve a stark charm all of its own. It can be explored by car, but you experience this barren yet beautiful landscape much more by walking. April–October is the most pleasant time (it can get very hot in December and January), but the falls are at their best November–January. Chalets; caravanning and camping; shop, restaurant, petrol. Trails: Klipspringer Hiking Trail (3 days, April–October) – but you can walk to various view points. Reservations: National Parks Board, tel: (012) 343 1991; fax: 343 0905.

Hester Malan Nature Reserve: in spring this reserve, which is 10 miles (16 km) southeast of Springbok, is carpeted by colourful wild flowers and well worth a visit. During the rest of the year visitors enjoy the beauty of the landscape, a variety of arid region mammals and birds and the collection of Namaqualand succulents. Open daily 8am–4pm. Trails: three short trails. Information from Private Bag X1, Springbok 8240. Tel: (0251) 2 1880.

Kalahari Gemsbok National Park: very different from the coastal and Transvaal reserves, this park of semi-desert lies between the dry river beds of the Nossob and Auob in the northwest corner of South Africa, between Namibia and Botswana. Large herds of wildebeest, springbok and gemsbok move through the sandy and rocky terrain. The Kalahari lions and cheetah also make this dry area their home. There are three camps at Twee Rivieren, Mata-Mata and Nossob. Huts and chalets (self-catering); caravanning and camping; shop, petrol; restaurant at Twee Rivieren; swimming pool at Twee Rivieren. Reservations: National Parks Board, tel: (012) 343 1991; fax: 343 0905.

Karoo National Park: situated just north of Beaufort West on the N1, the Karoo makes an ideal stop-over on the way to Johannesburg. More than 115 sq. miles (300 sq. km) in size, it covers mountains and the surrounding plains with animals like the mountain zebra, caracal and bat-eared fox. However, the other end of the animal kingdom is not neglected here: there is a very interesting collection of Karoo insects at the information centre. In addition to living animals, this park also deals with those that inhabited the area millions of years ago; a very interesting Fossil Walk takes visitors to half excavated reptiles which are of particular interest because they were a link between reptiles and mammals. Chalets; restaurant and shop. Trails: Springbok Hiking Trail (3-day fitness required). Reservations: National Parks Board, Box 787, Pretoria 0001. Tel: (012) 343 1991; fax: 343 0905.

Karoo Nature Reserve: this must be the most unusually shaped of any nature reserve as it encircles the town of Graaf-Reinett. The Vanrhyneveld Pass Dam falls within the reserve and the Valley of Desolation, which is actually more a gorge, is regarded as one of the most beautiful scenic spots in South Africa. No accommodation but facilities in Graaf Reinett. Trails: four trails (1–12 miles/2–20 km). Information from PO Box 349, Graaf-Reinett 6280. Tel: (0491) 2 3453.

Mountain Zebra National Park: located 16 miles (27 km) west of Cradock in the Eastern Cape. The park is home to a breeding population of black eagle and affords very good game viewing: if you are lucky, even wildcat and Cape fox. Chalets, old farmhouse; caravanning and camping; restaurant, shop, petrol. Trails: Mountain Zebra Hiking Trail (3 days); short and half-day hikes. Reservations: National Parks Board, Box 787, Pretoria 0001. Tel: (012) 343 1991; fax: 343 0905.

Vaalbos National Park: on the way from Kimberley to Barkley West, this is the youngest of South Africa's National Parks and is still being developed. However, it lies in a very interesting region where Kalahari, Karoo and grassveld mingle. Buffalo and black rhino have already been re-introduced. At present no accommodation. Information is available from SATOUR in Kimberley, tel: (0531) 3 1434.

South Africa has a coastline of some 1,860 miles (3,000 km) and all along it there are beaches of all shapes and characters. In northern Natal you find beautiful and practically deserted beaches stretching for miles; isolated beaches can also be found along the Transkei or Wild Coast. At the other end of the scale are the main tourist beaches with restaurants, entertainment, life savers – and thousands of sun worshippers during the holiday seasons.

Swimmers should beware of the following hazards:

– backwashes or sidewashes can move you along or out without you noticing it at first;

– a smooth patch amongst an otherwise foaming sea indicates a strong current at that point;

– be particularly careful and never go swimming if you are on your own;

– Bluebottles and sharks are an unlikely but not impossible hazard: sharks like murky water – therefore do not swim near river mouths or after heavy rains and do not swim at night as sharks feed at night. Forty-two of the Natal coast beaches are protected by shark nets. Bluebottle stings can be painful – their blue tentacles wrap around your arm or leg and cause an intense burning sensation.

The Natal Coast

Kosi Bay to Durban: there are wonderful beaches along the coast from Kosi Bay, near the Mozambique border, down to the Tugela delta. Many of them, unfortunately, aren't equipped with shark-nets, and some of them can only be reached with a four-wheel drive vehicle. Nonetheless, daring swimmers entrust themselves to the calm waters of the Kosi Bay Delta, Sodwana Bay, Mapelane, St Lucia, Cape Vidal and Richard's Bay. Under no circumstances should you swim in the lakes or lagoons, especially St Lucia Lake: there's danger from crocodiles and hippos. Campground swimming pools are a safer alternative.

From Zinkwazi Beach to Transkei, the larger beaches are effectively protected from sharks. The nets are only lifted during heavy rainfall and during the sardine runs in July.

North of Durban: Umhlanga Rocks, Umhlote Beach and Ballito Bay are the most beautiful stretches of coast. In the holiday season, Durban's beaches are popular resorts; if you insist, nonetheless, on bathing here, keep a watchful eye on your possessions.

The numerous tidal pools are also very popular: at high tide, the hollows in the rocks fill with water. A popular favourite among these is the one at Thompson's Bay (north of Ballito Bay).

South Coast: in the rock pools along the marvellous beaches of the south coast, you can see sea urchins, anemones and other sea creatures close at hand. A particularly lovely one is on Treasure Beach.

Dune forests often reach all the way down to the beach in the northern region of the South Coast, providing shady trails for hours of beach walks.

Between Port Shepstone and Port Edward, on the border of Transkei, there are 11 large beaches which are protected against sharks.

Transkei, Ciskei, Eastern Cape

Port Edward to **Port Alfred**: there are reasons why the Ciskei and Transkei coast is called the Romantic Coast: its many bays; inviting, not-too-populous sandy beaches; shallow lagoons; and rivers where you can sail, canoe, or water-ski. But swim with care in this area: there aren't any shark-nets and sharks are particularly fond of river deltas, especially after heavy rainfall, when the water is muddy.

There is an excellent swimming site between Mzamba and the Umngazi Delta and the beach near Port St Johns is also very beautiful. East London offers three large beaches and a tidal pool near Fullar's Bay. Between Kidds Beach and the Great Fish River, there are several good places to swim, and Kidds Rock has another lovely tidal pool. Also between the deltas of the Boesmans River and the Kariega, there is over a mile of small beaches of various sizes where you can swim safely and enjoyably. Kenton-on-Sea is one of the loveliest bathing spots in South Africa.

Kei Mouth is at the end of the Kei River, which forms the Transkei border. This broad delta is perfect for swimming and all sorts of water sports; it's also popular with deep-sea or coastal fishermen. The tropical coastal forest is ideal for long walks while those in the mood for adventure can take one of the old ferries over to Transkei (don't forget your passport). Just south of Kei Mouth, Morgan's Bay lies in a particularly impressive stretch of coastal landscape with high cliffs; spray from the breaking waves is thrown up to a height of almost 100 ft (30 metres). The forests and coastal regions are home to a wide variety of birds and from Haga-Haga, you can embark on interesting coastal walks or an excursion to one of the many tidal pools.

The Garden Route

Kings Beach, Humewood and McArthur Pool are the safest places to swim, overseen by lifeguards. The stretch of coastline north of St Francis Bay, notably Jeffrey's Bay, is especially good for swimming. This is also a popular area for surfing: St Francis Bay is a particular favourite.

Mossel Bay has many sheltered lagoons, such as Hartenbos, Little and Great Brak Rivers, and beaches down to Victoria Bay, with calm waters.

Mossel Bay to **Plettenberg Bay**: Great Brak River is a little village on the coast, 12 miles (20 km) east of Mossel Bay, with a lagoon and sandy beach surrounded by wooded hills.

Herold's Bay is located on the N2 National Road, some 15 miles (25 km) southwest of George. A small, sheltered holiday village, it offers a sandy beach and large tidal pools for safe sea bathing.

At Sedgefield, on Swartvlei, you can bathe either in sheltered lagoons or on magnificent sand beaches.

Buffels Bay, near Knysna, is known for its picturesque beaches, which extend to Brenton-on-Sea.

The beach at Noetzie, east of Knysna, can only be reached on foot or with a four-wheel-drive vehicle (the lagoon, too, is safe for swimming).

Oyster Bay to **Port Alfred**: Oyster Bay is a holiday village with broad sandy beaches, 16 miles (26 km) southwest of Humandorp. In the nature preserve between Oyster Bay and Cape St Francis, you can observe the antics of the sea otters.

St Francis Bay is a magnificent spot

on the coast of the Indian Ocean, with broad sandy beaches and excellent facilities for swimming and water sports. The lagoon on the Seekoei and Swart Rivers is known for its extensive bird life, including flamingoes and swans by the hundreds. The old, 91-ft (28-metre) lighthouse on Seal Point, dating from 1876, is still operational.

Jeffrey's Bay lies a few miles to the north. Its "Super Tube" is on a par with "Bruce" – surf you can rely on the year round.

But Jeffrey's Bay is also a paradise for more contemplative souls. Every tide casts a treasure trove of shellfish upon the beautiful beaches; you can even find the chambered Nautilus and Pansies (other shellfish are displayed in the library). Jeffrey's Bay is also known for its variety of arts and crafts.

Kenton-on-Sea is 35 miles (56 km) south of Grahamstown, between the Bushman River and Kariega, which flow into the river at a distance of over a mile from each other. The beach between these two deltas has sandy beaches, tidal pools and bizarre rock formations. Six miles (10 km) to the west, near Kwaaihoek, there's a replica of the Diaz Cross.

Southwestern Cape

West of Mossel Bay are popular beaches near Infanta, Witsand and Stilbaai. You can take spectacular walks along the cliffs of Cape Hangklipat Hermanus. Between June and November you can spot whales in Walker Bay and other bays in the area.

The western coast near False Bay has several lovely beaches especially south of Simonstown. Dandy Bay is the secret nudist beach (although nude bathing is officially not allowed).

Atlantic Coast: Camps Bay has long, sandy beaches, grassy lawns and a salt-water swimming pool, located at the feet of the Twelve Apostles.

Clifton can offer four long, magnificent sandy beaches, separated from each other with huge blocks of granite.

Sandy Bay is, unofficially, a nudist beach.

Sea Point is a popular, and thickly-populated, suburb of Cape Town, with a lovely beach promenade almost 2 miles (3 km) long and a large salt-water pool. It's also known for its numerous gourmet restaurants.

Western coastal regions: the beaches of Strandfontein (at the level of Vanrhynsdorp) are the most popular in the area among swimmers. The coast before McDougall's Bay, near Port Nolloth, is protected by shallow reefs, and is ideal for swimming.

Spas

Northern Transvaal

Warmbaths: 62 miles (100 km) from Pretoria on the N1. This is a renowned mineral resort with an ultra-modern health complex with various pools and hydro-therapy facilities. Accommodation is in chalets, flats and caravan park and camping sites. A nature reserve with a variety of game is part of the complex where you can take lovely walks. Warmbaths Tourist Information, tel: (015331) 2111.

Waterfalls: this whole region is rich in waterfalls of varying height: near Sabie is the Bridal Veil falls, plus Horseshoe, Lone Creek and Sabie falls; near Graskop is the Mac falls, plus Lisbon and Berlin falls. All of them are worth a detour.

Garden Route

Cradock: to get to the Karoo Sulphur Springs, take the R32 toward Middelburg. Lovely trails and paths lead through this area.

Cape Peninsula

Montagu: these mineral springs have been touted for their curative powers for more than 200 years. Montagu Springs are located almost 2 miles (3 km) north of Montagu, in the Cogmans Kloof (Gorge) Nature Preserve. There are many hiking trails. Information: Montagu Tourist Information Bureau, Bath St, Montagu. Tel: (0234) 42471.

Central Cape Province

Aliwal North lies on the R30 between Bloemfontein and East London. The Aliwal Spa has mineral springs and thermal baths; facilities include four open-air and two indoor pools, a bio-kinetic centre and a children's water playground. Bus tours take visitors to see nearby Bushman drawings. For information tel. (0551) 2123.

Boat Trips

On the Cape Peninsular boat trips can be undertaken from the harbour in Cape Town or from Hout Bay. Tours range from "Sunset Cruises" to deep sea fishing. You can visit Duiker Island in False Bay, a refuge for seals and birds, including the rare bank cormorant that only inhabits the coast of South Africa and Namibia.

Circe-Launches, tel: (021) 790 1040.

Crest-Cruises, tel: (021) 43 6359.

Bertie Reed Yacht Charter, tel: (021) 419 7746.

Falkon Charters, tel: (021) 97 5624.

Houtbay Boat Yard, tel: (021) 790 3619.

Ocean Star Yacht Charters, tel: (021) 25 4292.

Sealing Tours, tel: (021) 25 4480.

Hot Air Ballooning

For this "Sport of Gods" – floating effortlessly above the earth and enjoying the unhindered view – two companies in Johannesburg offer their services. Both operate from the Magaliesberg valley northwest of Johannesburg, which is regarded worldwide as an area ideally suited to ballooning. Flights take place soon after dawn as weather conditions are ideal then. Passengers are picked up from their hotels very early, or you can make it a 1½ day trip by staying overnight in one of two lovely country hotels.

The Zulu Lifestyle and Balloon Safari is a two-day safari which includes a stay at a traditional Zulu kraal (village) at the Aloe Ridge Hotel north of Johannesburg. Accommodation is in Zulu huts which have been furnished to provide all the comfort desirable for a good night's rest. Watch game from above as you fly over a small game reserve. The Natal Midlands Balloon Safari lasts three or four days, with accommodation in a luxurious country hotel.

Bill Harrops Original Balloon Safaris, Box 67, Randburg 2125. Tel: (011) 705 3203.

Hot Air Ballooning Company, PO Box 32, Broederstroom 02400. Tel: (01205) 5 1021 or 5 1138; fax: 5 1277. They also organise flights in the Pilanesberg Nature Reserve and the

Eastern Transvaal.

The Lindbergh Lodge Safari lasts for four days on a private ranch in Western Transvaal. It includes watching the animals from above and day and night drives in open Land-Rovers. The journey from and back to Johannesburg is included in the price.

Wineland Ballooning, tel: (02211) 41685, offers trips through the Berg River Valley near Paarl.

Steam Trains Journeys

South Africa is one of the few countries where the steam locomotive is still used, and why steam enthusiasts come here from all over the world. The Transnet Museum organises three or four steam train safaris per annum to different parts of the country to enable visitors to see steam locomotive yards and depots. They last 14 days and the price includes meals and bus tours to places of interest en route. Photo stops are held at the most scenic places.

Transnet Museum, PO Box 3753, Johannesburg 2000. Tel: (011) 773 9238; fax: 773 9125. Apart from those tours there are regular steam train excursions in various parts of the country:

The **Magalies Valley Steamer** (Transvaal) leaves on the first Sunday of each month from Johannesburg to Hekpoort, more frequently during holidays. Catering car and lounge car; and fires lit for barbeque at Hekpoort; meat and salads for sale. For information tel. (011) 773 9238.

The **Preservation Group**, PO Box 1419, Roosevelt Park 2129, tel: (011) 888 1154/5/6; fax: 782 9194, runs the next two excursions: Magaliesberg Express (Transvaal) departs from Johannesburg Station at 9.30am twice a month on Sunday mornings. There is a lounge car with full bar services and souvenir shop. On arrival braai fires are lit and meat and salads are on sale. Eating utensils and folding chairs must be brought by the passengers.

Jacaranda Express (Transvaal) runs from Johannesburg to Cullinan via Pretoria on the first Sunday in November when the jacaranda trees are in flower. During lunch break, organised the same way as for the Magaliesberg Express, the museum and historic village of Cullinan can be visited.

Since 1906 the **Apple Express** has been chugging between Port Elizabeth and Avontuur in the fruit-growing area of the Langkloof. Every first Saturday of the month it takes tourists the 44 miles (71 km) to Loerie and back. For booking and further information tel. (041) 520 2360.

The **Outeniqua Choo-Choo** (Cape) travels between George and Knysna daily Monday–Friday taking 4 hours each way and winding through the most breathtaking mountain scenery. Tickets can be bought at the stations in George and Knysna. For booking and information tel. (041) 520 2662.

The **Chugging Pug** in Cape Town does shorter trips every second Sunday from Paarden Eiland every hour between 10.30am and 3.30pm. For information tel. (021) 25 3320; fax: 462 2040.

The **Strelitzia Steam Train** (Natal) travels between Durban and Kelso, every Sunday at 9am, returning at about 3pm. Barbeque fires are lit at Kelso. For information tel. (031) 361 8095.

The **Banana Express** (Natal) travels between Port Shepstone (on the South Coast) and Harding every second Sunday, leaving Port Shepstone at 10am and returning at about 3.30pm after a barbeque at Harding. For information tel. (031) 361 8095.

Rovos Rail, PO Box 2837, Pretoria 0001, tel: (012) 323 6052; fax: 323 0843, is a private organisation operating a luxury steam train, called *Pride of Africa* that prides itself being the most luxurious in the world. It carries a maximum of 40 passengers on a four-day steam safari through the Eastern Transvaal departing from Pretoria Station every Saturday. This safari includes sightseeing by luxury coach and a stop-over at an exclusive private game reserve. The tour price includes accommodation, meals, alcoholic beverages, tours, transport and insurance. A Flexi Safari is also available (doing just part of the trip). They also offer, once a month, a one-day trip to or from Durban and a two-day trip to Cape Town, which includes sight-seeing excursions en route e.g. in Kimberley.

Waterval Boven and Waterval Onder on the N4 to Nelspruit. One village is above the Elandsriver Waterfall, the other below it. At Waterval Boven you

can see the old **NZASM** railway tunnel next to the road tunnel which was built for the Eastern Railway from Pretoria to Lorenco Marques (1894). You can walk through the 1,300-ft (400-metre) long tunnel but you need either a torch or a very good sense of touch (as the tunnel is curved it is pitch dark in there.) You can also follow a footpath to the side of the tunnel which takes you to a view point over the **Elands River Falls**.

At Waterval Onder is a hotel which dates from 1879 when it was built as a stage coach stop-over. Krugerhof, which stands on the same property, is the house where President Kruger spent his last weeks in South Africa during the Anglo-Boer War.

Steam trains are in daily use in the Kimberley region in the Northern Cape. There are daily departures to De Aar (155 miles/250 km) or to Kraankuil at the halfway point.

Geological Sites

The classical geological formations of South Africa are of interest to scientists throughout the world. Geological strata which in other parts of the world are hidden way down below, are often visible on the surface, especially the very old rocks; a sort of hands-on geological history book.

The major geological areas include:

Barberton Mountain Land in the Eastern Transvaal – microscopic fossils of the earliest known forms of life found in the chert rocks.

Witwatersrand Basin around Johannesburg – the richest goldfield in the world.

Bushveld Complex north of Pretoria – volcanic layers containing the world's largest reserves of platinum, chrome and iron ore.

Pilanesberg near Sun City – one of the largest extinct volcanoes on earth.

Cape Supergroup in the southern margin – spectacular sandstone mountain ranges including the most famous landmark of all, Table Mountain.

The Karoo stratae, covering nearly half of South Africa – a massive layered cake of sandstones and rocks with a capping of basalt representing the widespread lava flows that accompanied the break-up of Gondwanaland. The picturesque mountain landscapes that characterise the **Drakensberg** and the **Lesotho Highlands** are carved wholly within the basalt capping.

Preserved within the sandstones and rocks of the Karoo basin is an unbroken record of vertebrate evolution, from fishes through amphibians and reptiles, including the dinosaurs.

In the Eastern Transvaal a geological route has been developed which can be hiked by hobby geologists: the Kaapse Hoop Hiking Trail in the Barberton/Nelspruit area has boards with geological explanations en route. More of these popular trails are in preparation. For further information contact:

Professor Viljoen, Department of Geology, Wits University, PO Wits, 2050. Tel: (011) 716 2608.

The Geological Society of South Africa, PO Box 44283, Linden 2104. Tel: (011) 888 2288; fax: 888 2181. The Society also publishes two journals: *The South African Journal of Geology* and *The Geo-Bulletin Quarterly*.

Geological museums:
Geological Museum, Johannesburg, tel: (011) 836 3787.
Geological Survey Collection, Transvaal Museum, Pretoria, tel: (012) 322 7632.
Alexander McGregor Museum, Kimberley, tel: (0531) 32645.
South African Museum, Cape Town, tel: (021) 24 3330.

Minerals & Precious Stones

You can find minerals and semi-precious stones of every shape and size in serious shops in South Africa.

The Hout Bay Mining Rock Shop (Cape), Beach Crescent, Hout Bay, tel: (021) 790 5637, offers a wide selection of jewellery made of semi-precious stones, as well as minerals and various gift items. Open Monday–Sunday 9am–5.30pm.

Mineral World and The Scratch Patch (Cape), Valley Road, Simonstown, tel: (021) 862020; fax: 862502, is one of the largest factories which process semi-precious stones.

Botswana Game Industries and Yardley's Gem and Rock Shop (Johannesburg), 60 Juta St, Braamfontein. Tel: (011) 403 2820; fax: 335 3536.

Driving along the R64 from Kimberley to Upington, you pass through Griquastadt (the first mission station

north of the Orange). Here, Earth's Treasure, a stone-polishing and cutting workshop, processes semi-precious stones of the northern Cape region.

If you want to embark on a treasure hunt yourself, contact the Federation of South African Gem and Mineralogical Societies, PO Box 17273, Groenkloof 0027, Pretoria, tel: (012) 467562 (Horst Windisch), or the Gemmological Society of South Africa, PO Box 650 818, Benmore 2010 (Arthur Thomas). Tel: (011) 783 3687 or 334 5383/4; fax: 334 5605.

Mines

Diamonds are without a doubt the most exciting precious stones, and the purest, for they're made of pure carbon. Under enormous pressure, at high temperatures, the stones are formed in the earth's interior over millions of years, and forced up toward the surface by volcanic eruptions.

Kimberley, with its Big Hole, is South Africa's most famous diamond mine. Dug in 1871, the world's largest man-made hole is 1,308 ft (400 metres) deep and 1,635 ft (500 metres) in diameter. Up to 30,000 adventurers dig for the shining stones as if possessed. The Kimberley Mine Museum brings pioneer days again to life, as does the small restored city dating from the mine's foundation. The Diamond Museum will make even hardened hearts beat faster. Open daily 8am–6pm (closed on Good Friday and Christmas). For information contact Johannesburg, tel: (011) 638 5126 or Kimberley, tel: (0531) 3 1557.

The world-champion diamond was found in 1905 in the Premier Mine, East of Pretoria. The *Cullinan* weighed 3,106 carats (about 1.3 pounds/600 grams) and was as large as a child's fist. Four of the nine diamonds cut from this stone ornament the English Crown Jewels, among them the 530-carat *Great Star of Africa*, the largest-ever cut diamond. Guided tours of the Cullinan Premier Mine are held Monday–Friday at 9am and 10.30am. For information contact Premier Diamond Mine, tel: (01213) 9 2911.

The beryl is the most varied precious mineral: its family includes the emerald, the aquamarine, the morganite and the yellow beryl.

Some of the best-known tourma-

lines are found in Namibia and the Northwest Cape. No other precious stone exists in such a variety of colours.

The Rustenburg Platinum Mine, tel: (01421) 9 1011, in the Western Transvaal is the largest in the world. It is possible to visit the mine but necessary to book in advance.

The Blue Mine to the west of Springbok in Namaqualand was expanded up until the end of the 19th century. It can be reached on foot.

Archaeology & Palaeontology

The Karoo is one of the world's largest fossil graveyards from the age of reptiles. It is regarded by scientists as one of the natural wonders of the world. In the Karoo National Park near Beaufort West on the N1 between Cape Town and Bloemfontein there is a fossil trail, which takes the visitor back 250 million years of geological history. This 440-yard (400-metre) long trail is suitable for wheelchairs and visually impaired. Information is available from the Park Warden, Karoo National Park, PO Box 316, Beaufort West 6970. Tel: (0201) 5 2828/9.

The Rubidge fossil collection on the farm Wellwood in the Graaf Reinet area is in all probability the finest private collection in the country.

The SA Archaeological Society will assist with information on archaeological sites that can be visited by the public. Visitors are welcome to attend the monthly evening lectures and monthly outings. Further information is available from the South African Archaeological Society, PO Box 15700, Vlaeberg, 8018.

Archaeological Sites

Transvaal: In a park right in the heart of Johannesburg are the Melville Koppies, believed to have been occupied by man for 100,000 years. An ancient iron-smelting furnace can be seen on top of the hill. 80 percent of all plant species in the Witwatersrand region can be found in this park, including medicinal and also poisonous varieties. The reserve is open on the fourth Sunday of each month when guided tours are offered. Information and a guidebook are available from the Johannesburg Parks & Recreation Department, PO Box 6428, Johannesburg 2000. Tel: (011) 41 3612.

Suikerboschrand Nature Reserve is close to Heidelberg. There are ruins of stone walled Iron Age villages in the reserve of Sotho/Tswana origin.

The **Sterkfontein Caves** not far from Krugersdorp, tel: (011) 956 6342, are limestone caves where archaeological history was made with the discovery of the so-called missing link. Guided tours take place Thursday–Sunday 9am–5pm. The caves are closed every year from the second week of January to the first week of February.

The **Museum of Man** on the turn-off to the Echo Caves in the eastern Transvaal (off the Ohrigstad–Tzaneen Road) is an archaeological excavation site with interesting reaching back well in excess of 100,000 years. This Iron Age site of Phalaborwa origin is situated in the Kruger National Park on the road between Phalaborwa Gate and Letaba Rest Camp. It is well signposted and guided tours are available. A kiosk on the site provides information on the history and archaeology of the site.

Kruger National Park: there are many sites with rock paintings in the Stolznek area in the south of the Park. People who have booked the trails in that area will be able to visit some of these sites

The **Sudwala Caves** in the Eastern Transvaaal near Waterval Boven are a network of interconnected chambers. There are daily tours from 8.30am–4.30pm. In the Dinosaur Park you can see replicas of the dinosaurs that lived in these caves 100 million years ago. The park is open daily from 8.30am–5pm.

Ermelo lies 75 miles (120 km) from Waterval Boven on the R36. There are a number of interesting archaeological sites in the vicinity: e.g. the corbelled stone houses of a tribe that is now extinct; the Goliath Foot Print is a footprint of 4 ft (1,24 metres) and can be seen on a rock in a beautifully wooded area on the farm called Arthur's Seat near Lothair; and on the farm Welgelegen there are many Bushman drawings. Since all these lie on private property permission to view them must be obtained beforehand. For information tel. (01341) 2112.

Cape Province

Cape Town: in the lower levels of the Golden Acre shopping complex are the remains of Wagenaar's Dam, built in the 17th century after the Dutch East India Co. established a settlement at the Cape.

Wonderwerk Cave: This important solution cavity is situated on the road between Kuruman and Danielskuil in the Kuruman hills, in the Northwestern Cape. The site is signposted, but the cave itself is protected by a gate and fence. The key can be obtained from the custodian who lives on the farm. The site has been intermittently inhabited for over half a million years and has provided valuable information on Early, Middle and Later Stone Age ways of life.

Postmasburg (Northwestern Cape): just to the northwest of the town, within its municipal boundaries, lies Blinkklipkop, an ironstone outcrop with an ancient specularite mine. It has been mined for probably a few thousand years by the indigenous people of the area.

Barkley West: Canteen Koppie on the Vaal River, approximately 1 mile (1.3 km) southeast of the town. This site contains a vast amount of stone age implements of all ages. It is worth a visit if you are interested in stone implements.

Driekopseiland: This site is situated in the bed of the Riet River in the northwestern Cape. It consists of large sheets of glacial striated bedrock on which over 3,000 rock engravings are visible.

KwaZulu/Natal & Drakensberg Area

Umgungundlovu (secret plot of the elephant), situated in northern Natal between Melmoth and Babanango at a mission station, was the military headquarters of the Zulu king Dingane. It was built around 1828 and destroyed by fire in 1838 on the orders of the king. The archaeological excavations have exposed numerous hut floors. Part of the site is being reconstructed.

Ulundi (the high place) is close to and southwest of the modern town Ulundi. It was king Cetshwayo's capital and was destroyed by the British army during the Zulu wars of the late 19th

century. It has been partially restored and also doubles as a holiday resort where visitors can rent a traditional Zulu hut.

The Drakensberg in Natal, the Orange Free State and Lesotho has numerous caves and shelters with exquisite rock paintings. There are many nature reserves and hiking trails in this area and sites can be visited by hikers. Directions and permits can be obtained from the officials of these various parks and resorts. Information: Natal Parks Board.

Orange Free State

Willem Prinsloo Game Reserve: This reserve near Winburg contains many ruins of early Tswana Iron Age settlers. The ruins are easily accessible and are on and next to the road that meanders along the low range of hills on the reserve.

Florisbad: This famous site is situated near Bloemfontein and is a recreation facility. Appointments to visit the archaeological or palaeontological part of the site can be made via the National Museum of Bloemfontein.

Bophuthatswana

Norlim: The famous limeworks where the Taung skull (Australopithecus africanus) was found are situated at this town. The site is open to the public and the position where the skull was found is marked with a little monument.

Caves

Caves which are on state-owned land require permits for entering. The caves are generally dry and the average temperature is 16°C (60°F), but visitors are advised of a possible occurrence of histoplasmosis (cave disease). It is best to arrange itineraries and access through clubs, who gladly welcome overseas visitors. The following societies will be able to help:

South African Speleological Association, PO Box 6166, Johannesburg 2000.

Cave Research Organisation of South Africa, PO Box 7322, Johannesburg 2000. Tel: (011) 640 4394.

The **Cango Caves** near Oudshorn are the best known South African limestone caves. A small section of the subterranean cave complex is open to the general public on guided tours. The main attractions are the imposing sculptures formed by stalactites and stalagmites. The caves are open December–February and April 8am–5pm, tours every hour; May–November and March 9am–3pm, tours every two hours. There is a museum on site, featuring plants, animals and rock formations from the caves.

The **Sudwala Caves** in the Eastern Transvaal near Waterval Boven are a network of large interlocking chambers, one of which is used for musical recordings, because of the incredible acoustics in this chamber 220 ft (67 metres) diameter and 120 ft (37 metres) height. Within the caves the temperature remains a constant 17°C all year round. Guided tours take place daily 8.30am–4.30pm. On the first Saturday of each month a six-hour tour is available to the more remote chambers like the fairy tale Crystal Room. Outside the caves is a world famous Dinosaur Park. The first of Sudwala's dinosaurs was commissioned to illustrate the age of the caves (100 million years). Now there are many dinosaurs representing species drawn from around the world; life-size, they inhabit the hillside to the side of the caves and are well worth a visit. The Dinosaur Park is open every day from 8.30am–5pm.

The **Echo Caves** on the road from Ohrigstad to Tzaneen are the least well known of the limestone caves, which does have the advantage that fewer people visit them and you can be lucky and enjoy this underworld on your own just with the guide. They derive their name from the fact that the local people used one of the flowstones as a drum to warn of approaching Swazis. Because these caves extend for some 24 miles (40 km), the sound travelled for surprisingly long distances and the people could take refuge in the caves.

From an archaeological point of view the caves are fascinating as finds corroborated legends that long ago strangers in long white robes came to look for gold and to barter with them. Some of these finds are exhibited at the Museum of Man on the turn-off from the tar road to the Echo Caves. Both the Echo Caves and the Museum of Man are open daily from 8am–5pm.

Botanical Excursions

Seen in relation to its land mass, South Africa's wealth of flora is remarkable: there are 24,000 flora species, as compared to 10,000 in Europe. The Botanic Institute issues computer printouts which list every species according to family, together with common synonyms; there are also a great many books containing extensive information about most plant families.

The Botanical Society organises regular excursions with foreign visitors. Information is available from the Botanical Society of South Africa, Kirstenbosch, Claremont 7735. Tel: (021) 797 2090.

South Africa contains both state and private nature preserves. Richtersveld, the country's 17th national park, was opened in July, 1991; the park ranges across 625 sq. miles (1,620 sq. km) of land south of Namibia, bordered, for the most part, by the Orange river. This area is richer in succulents than anywhere else in the world. Half of the species are endemic, and therefore unique to the area.

The Dendrological Society is one of the largest arboreal organisations in the world. Keep copies of their national lists of native (green) and imported (yellow) trees on hand, as all of the number and name-plates in nature preserves, botanic gardens and the like accord with this information. Further information is available from the Dendrological Society of South Africa, PO Box 104, Pretoria 0001. Tel: (012) 57 4009.

Here is a list of botanic gardens worth visiting arranged by regions (*those with exclusively native plants are indicated with an asterisk*).

Cape Region

Caledon*: Caledon Wildflower Garden; Namaqualand wildflowers.

Cape Town*: Kirstenbosch Botanic Garden, Rhodes Drive, Constantia. Open daily April–August 8am–6pm, September–March 8am–7pm; guided tours Tuesday and Saturday 11am. Measuring 2 sq. miles (5 sq. km), Kirstenbosch is one of the most important botanic gardens in the world: here, you can see most of the 22,000 plant varieties native to South Africa, notably the entire Fynbos family, of which the Protea are members. A bus runs from the city centre three times a day.

Kleinmond*: The Harold Porter National Botanic Garden contains plants of the winter rainfall region.

Stellenbosch: Hortens Botanicus, Neethling St, is a botanic garden with a rare collection of local succulents and orchids. Open Monday–Friday 9am–5pm, Saturday 9am–11am.

Swellendam*: Karoo Botanic Garden is located on Roux Road on the N2 motorway, 2 miles (3 km) north of Worcester. This garden specialises in the plants of the country's dry regions. In spring, it's a veritable sea of flowers. Among botanists, the garden is internationally renowned for its extensive collection of succulents.

Transvaal

Johannesburg: Johannesburg Botanic Garden includes an herb garden. The Wilds, Houghton Drive, Houghton, is a conservation area devoted to local flora, containing numerous sorts of wildflowers from Namaqualand.

Nelspruit*: Nelspruit Botanic Garden contains African trees. Open in summer Monday–Friday 7.30am–6pm, in winter Monday–Friday 8am–5pm.

Pretoria*: Pretoria National Botanic Garden has various biomes, particularly those of the drier regions of southern Africa (Madagascar, Namibia).

Roodepoort*: Transvaal National Botanic Garden contains flora of the high velds (Bankenveld).

Sun City: the Botanic Garden is devoted to "the dramatic and bizarre elements of the plant world".

KwaZulu/Natal

Durban: Durban Botanic Gardens, between Syndenham Road and Botanic Gardens Road, Lower Berea, are open daily from 9am on. A special feature is the world-famous orchid house, containing 3,000 species from around the world.

Pietermaritzburg: the Natal National Botanic Gardens contains exotic trees and flora of Natal.

Orange Free State

Bloemfontein: the Botanic Garden is mainly given over to plants native to the Free State, but it's also known for a fossilised tree-trunk said to be at least 150 million years old.

With its sliding roof and computerised air-conditioning system, the orchid house in Hamilton Park is worth a visit. 3,000 orchids are arranged in a fairy-tale landscape complete with waterfalls, footbridges, and ponds.

Harrismith: Drakensberg Botanic Garden on Platberg presents a cross-section of flora from the Drakensberg Mountains, as well as several lovely walking trails.

Flower Shows

Every province has a flower festival or show which shouldn't be missed. Even non-gardeners will be glad they went.

February: Johannesburg (Botanical Gardens); autumn flower show.

April: Durban Exotica, international flower show.

August: Northwestern Cape Namaqualand in bloom. A show put on by Nature and therefore dependent upon the weather.

September: Johannesburg (Botanical Gardens); spring flower show.

Cape Town; wildflower show.

October: Durban International Orchid Exhibition.

Pretoria Jacaranda Carnival (with parade and Carnival Queen).

November: Johannesburg Botanical Gardens, Succulent and Cactus Show.

Parks, Gardens & Zoos

Johannesburg & Pretoria

Aquarium and **Reptile Park**, corner Paul Kruger St and Boom St, contains a large assortment of fresh- and salt-water fish, reptiles, and snakes. Open daily 9am–4.30pm.

Pretoria Zoo, Boom Street, is one of the largest zoos in the world, with more than 3,500 species. Visitors can travel up to an observation tower over the cages via cable car. A street market in front of the entrance sells woodcarvings, basketry and stone sculptures. Open daily 8.30am–5pm.

De Wildt Cheetah Research Centre is located at Silkaatsnek on the R53, some 1.5 hours by car north of Johannesburg. This is a breeding station for cheetahs, wild dogs and hyenas. Guided tours are conducted Saturday 8.30am and 2pm, Sunday 9am and 2pm; advance reservations recommended.

Johannesburg Zoo, Jan Smuts Ave, Parkview, contains more than 3,000 species of mammal, bird and reptile. Night tours are conducted on Wednesdays and Fridays, 6.30–9.30pm. Tel: (011) 646 2000. Open daily 8.30am–5.30pm.

KwaZulu/Natal

Aquarium/Delphinarium, Durban, corner West St and Marine. Parades held daily. In the main tank, fish are fed by a diver twice a day (11am and 3pm); daily tours of the delphinarium are held at 10am, 11.30am, 2pm, 3pm and 5pm. The aquarium contains some 1,000 species of fish, including sharks, rays and giant sea turtles, as well as a notable collection of shellfish.

Transkei, Eastern Cape & Ciskei

East London: the Aquarium (feeding times 10.30am and 3pm; shows at 11.30am and 3.30pm) is located on the Esplanade, halfway between Orient and Eastern Beaches. Here, you can observe more than 400 kinds of sea creature and fresh-water fish close at hand. It isn't only brightly-coloured, intricately-patterned subtropical fish which are displayed here; you can also see sea anemones, squid, sharks, sea turtles, penguins and seals to entertain the public.

Queens Park Botanic Garden and Zoo (open daily 9am–5pm) lies on a hill between the city centre and the Buffalo River. In the middle of the beautifully laid-out garden with native plants and trees, the zoo attracts young visitors with its special children's section. At 2pm, you can accompany the zoo-keepers on their feeding rounds.

The Garden Route

Port Elizabeth: the main attraction in the Oceanarium is the twice-daily dolphin show (11am and 3pm). Seals and penguins are on display as well.

In the Snake Park you can see exotic and native snakes, vipers, crocodiles and other reptiles. Visitors to the Tropical House wander through a tropical landscape with waterfalls, rock cliffs and lush vegetation, watching the colourful birds all the while. Also interesting is the Night House, where you can observe nocturnal birds and animals by artificial light. Open daily 9am–1pm, demonstrations at 10am, 12.15pm, 2.30pm and 4.15pm.

In Sea View, tel: (041) 524138, 15 miles (25 km) west of Port Elizabeth, there's a zoo with lions, leopards and rhinos. Fishing trips Saturday and Sunday. For information about diving excursions contact the Publicity Association, tel: (041) 521315.

Cape Peninsula

Cape Town: South Africa's oldest garden, The Gardens, at the upper end of Adderly Street, was laid out by Jan van Riebeck in 1652 to provide passing ships with fresh vegetables. Today, it's a parkland with rose gardens, birdcages and a sundial dating from 1787. During the legislative period in Cape Town, this is the location of the Parliament and the Presidential residence Tuynhuis.

Mariner's Wharf: World of Birds, Valley Rd, Hout Bay, tel: (021) 790 2730, is Africa's largest bird park, containing 3,000 species. It's paradise, especially for bird-watchers and photographers. Open daily 9am–6pm.

Orange Free State

Bloemfontein: the Zoo contains more different species of ape than any other zoo in South Africa. Most famous, however, is the "Liger" – a cross between a lion and a tiger. Night tours are especially popular. Open daily 8am–5pm.

Namaqualand

Clanwilliam: located 172 miles (277 km) from Cape Town on the N7, this is the centre of a fertile agricultural region which produces fruit, grain, vegetables and *Rooibos* tea. Tours available, tel. (02682) 64.

At the Wildflower Garden in Clanwilliam Damm, you can see the profusion of spring wildflowers from the footpaths. Bidouw Valley, on the way to Wuppertal, is considered a microcosm of Namaqualand because of the variety of its wildflowers.

Ornithology

Southern Africa is a paradise for bird-lovers; 22 of the 27 living orders are found in this country and some 718 species. One of the reasons for the astounding diversity in bird life is the great variety of vegetation zones.

Below are listed the major vegetation zones with the nature reserves which are best suited to observing the birds of that particular region.

The Eastern Woodlands (or Bushveld) have the richest avifaunas: the Kruger Park and the Natal Reserves of Ndumu, Mkuze, Hluhluwe and Umfolozi, of which Ndumu is regarded as a bird watchers' paradise. For further information contact:

Kruger Park, National Parks Board, tel: (012) 343 1991.

Natal Reserves, National Parks Board, tel: (0331) 47 1981.

Birds of the Eastern Mistbelt forests can be seen in **Game Valley** (Safari World) near Cramond, tel: (03393) 787, and in the Karkloof Nature Reserve, tel: (0331) 47 1981.

Another interesting area is the **Magoebaskloof** between Pietersburg and Tzaneen, further north in the mistbelt forests of the Transvaal. For information contact the Directorate of Forestry, Northern Transvaal, Private Bag 2413, Louis Trichard 0920. Tel: (01551) 2201.

The birds of the coastal evergreen forests of the southern Cape can be seen in the **Tsitsikama Forest National Park** near Port Elizabeth. Information is available from the National Parks Board, tel: (012) 343 1991.

Birds of the Highveld can be seen anywhere along the road but a stay at **Barberspan** near Delareyville in the western Transvaal should be very rewarding; it is the largest waterfowl sanctuary in the Transvaal. Information is available from the Barberspan Nature Reserve, PO Barberspan 2765. Tel: (0144322) 1202.

Another worthwhile game reserve for the ornithologist is the **Willem Pretorius Game Reserve** between Winburg and Kroonstad in the central Orange Free State. For more information contact the Willem Pretorius Game Reserve, Ventersburg 9451. Tel: (01734) 4229.

Mountain birds are most accessible in the **Golden Gate Highlands National Park** near Bethlehem, in the eastern Orange Free State – National Parks Board, tel: (012) 343 1991, as well as in the beautiful reserves of the Natal Drakensberg – Natal Parks Board, tel: (0331) 47 1981.

The arid regions have an extremely interesting bird life. **The Karoo National Park** near Beaufort West in the Cape and the Kalahari Gemsbok National Park in the northern Cape on the Namibia/Botswana border are among the most convenient reserves to find the birds adapted to the harsh conditions. For information contact National Parks Board, tel: (012) 343 1991.

Namaqualand on the Cape West Coast is not just a botanist's but also a bird watchers' paradise in September when the otherwise arid plains resemble carpets of flowers. The **Hester Malan Nature Reserve** near Springbok is well worth a visit (day-time only).

The Fynbos of the southwestern Cape has several endemic species of birds which can be seen in the **Cape of Good Hope Nature Reserve** and the **Helderberg Nature Reserve** near Somerset West (both day visitors only).

The various branches of the Southern African Ornithological Society (SAOS) arrange regular outdoor meetings in the bird-rich areas, which are led by experienced members. The bird clubs in Johannesburg, Pretoria, Cape Town, Port Elizabeth and Durban can be contacted through the local museum or South African Ornithological Society, PO Box 87234, Houghton 2041, R.S.A. Tel: (011) 888 4147.

Tailor-made and group safaris for bird lovers are offered by Lawson's, PO Box 507, Nelspruit 1200, tel: (01311) 4 2257; fax: 2 7482, and by Wilderness Safaris, PO Box 651171, Benmore 2010, tel: (011) 884 1458; fax: (011) 883 6255.

The bible of ornithologists in this part of the world is *Roberts Birds of Southern Africa*.

Hiking

The best way to discover South Africa's lofty mountains, sun-drenched beaches, virgin indigenous forests and pine-scented plantations is on foot. Opportunities ranging from short rambles suitable for families with young children to week-long expeditions and guided wilderness trails in big game country abound. A network of self-catering overnight hiking trails traverses the country from the Augrabies Falls National Park in the Northern Cape to the Western Cape mountains and the Soutpansberg in the Northern Transvaal. While some trails follow the coastline, others meander past challenging peaks which are often covered in snow during the winter. Others yet again wind through the aromatic Fynbos vegetation of the Western Cape or the grasslands of the Orange Free State. Hiking trails vary in length from two to eight days, although shorter alternatives are usually available on long routes.

Heading the list of South Africa's most popular trails is the **Otter Hiking Trail** along the Southern Cape Coast, while the **Blyderivierspoort** and **Fanie Botha** hiking trails in the Eastern Transvaal are other perennial favourites. Of the several wilderness areas available to outdoor enthusiasts seeking solitude and tranquility, those in the Drakensberg need little introduction. Although footpaths are available, backpackers are not obliged to stick to a particular route, nor are any facilities provided.

Backpacking requires a greater degree of experience and self-reliance and, depending on weather conditions, nights are spent either under the stars, in caves or in many instances in a small backpacking tent. Other wilderness areas include the Cedarberg, Groot-Winterhoek and Boesmanbos (Western Cape), the Baviaanskloof and Groendal (Eastern Cape), Ntendeka in Natal and the Wolkeberg in Transvaal. For many hikers, however, the ultimate outdoor experience is a guided Wilderness Trail such as those conducted in several game reserves of the Natal Parks Board and the Kruger National Park (information under *Game and Nature Reserves*).

If you are keen on hiking in South Africa, advance planning is essential since it is almost impossible to get a booking at short notice for popular hiking trails. Contact your nearest South African Tourism Board (SATOUR) office for a copy of *Follow the Footprints* which lists trailing opportunities, as well as information regarding duration, capacity, cost, facilities and reservation addresses.

On full payment of a reservation, which is usually a year in advance, a map is issued which serves as a confirmation of the booking besides giving useful information on climate, geography, flora and fauna of the trails. Keep it in a safe. as you may need it again.

Useful addresses for information and booking:

National Parks Board, Pretoria. Tel: (012) 343 1991; fax: 343 0905.

Natal Parks Board, PO Box 662, Pietermaritzburg 3200. Tel: (0331) 47 1981; fax: 47 1980.

Drifters Adventours offer hiking tours in the spectacular Cedarberg mountains on the Cape West Coast, along the Garden Route and Eastern Cape, Transkei Wild Coast, the Drakensberg, Eastern Transvaal and the Fish River Canyon in Namibia. The price for 3–8 day hikes includes transport from Johannesburg, a professional guide, accommodation and most meals. For the very detailed brochure and information write to Drifters Adventours, PO Box 48434, Roosevelt Park 2129. Tel: (011) 486 1224; fax: 486 1237.

The most useful periodical is the *SA Hiker*, PO Box 28459, Kensington 2101. Tel: (011) 29 1842; fax: 337 8061.

Mountaineering & Climbing

South Africa's mountains and marvellous cliff formations are particularly inviting to mountain climbers, whatever the season. Rock-climbers incline toward northern Transvaal, or the Cedar or du Toits Kloof Mountains in the Cape. Often, the best mountains for climbing are privately owned (especially in Transvaal). Climbing clubs have applied for permits for these from the farmers who own them, and it's a good idea to contact these clubs.

Transvaal's **Magalies Mountains** lie only two hours by car from Johannesburg. On the mountains' north side, the rock faces have been eroded in places into picturesque gorges, lined with clear mountain brooks and giant trees (difficulty rating up to 8b on the French scale). But North Transvaal also offers tempting and difficult faces with walls up to 1,300 ft (400 metres) high. Information and application: Mountain Club of South Africa, Transvaal Section. Tel: (011) 803 3716.

Natal's **Drakensberg Mountains** have a more Alpine character; there are several 9,800-feet (3,000-metre) peaks to scale. The highest mountain in the Drakensberg range is just over the Lesotho border, the 11,386-ft (3,482 metre) Thabana Ntlenyana. Most of the mountains in Natal which are interesting for climbers lie within nature reserves; before beginning, climbers have to register with the Natal Parks Board. Montesiel, between Durban and Pietermaritzburg, is held to be the best region in South Africa for hobby climbers. Information: Mountain Club of South Africa, Natal Section. Tel: (031) 30 0129 (office), or Natal Parks Board. Tel: (0331) 47 1981; fax: 47 1980.

Cape Province contains the most popular and best-known mountains for climbers. Leader among these is **Table Mountain**, (3,556 ft/1,084 metres), which boasts more than 500 routes. North of Cape Town, the **Cedar Mountains** enchant visitors with their wonderful rock formations. The du Toits Kloof Mountains (Baine's Kloof and Sir Lowry's Pass) are also favourites of climbers. Information: Mountain Club of South Africa, Cape Section. Tel: (021) 45 3412 (10am–2pm, Friday until 7.30pm).

For further information, contact the Mountain Club of South Africa, 97 Hatfield St, Cape Town, 8001. Tel: (021) 45 3412 (10am–2pm, Friday until 7.30pm). For Cedar Mountains, contact Directorate of Forestry, Private Bag 9005, Cape Town, 8000, or call the Algeria Forestry Station (tel: 02682).

Caravanning & Camping

Those who wish to get more intimately acquainted with the country and its people and who wish to remain independent at the same time might opt for a holiday with a camper or a tent. South Africa is ideal for this type of travelling, because there are countless out-of-the-way but beautiful nooks, the weather is mostly sunny and warm, and the campsites are clean, well looked after and comparatively cheap. It is possible to rent the requisite vehicle in the larger towns. Just about any reasonably sized village will maintain a campground. SATOUR publishes a comprehensive *Guide to Caravan Parks* in which a good 350 of the country's 700 campgrounds are listed. Booking is advisable, particularly during the school holidays.

Many of the caravan sites have huts with bed linen, cutlery, pots and pans etc. You only have to do your own catering. In addition, many sites have swimming pools and offer various sporting activities, from sailing to riding. Larger campsites may have restaurants or at least fast food. The two holiday resort chains are Overvaal Resorts and Club Caraville and their sites can either be booked directly or through a central booking office.

Overvaal Resorts (OV), PO Box 3046, Pretoria 0001. Tel: (012) 346 2277; fax: 346 2276.

Club Caraville (CC), PO Box 139, Sarnia 3615. Tel: (031) 701 4156; fax: 622 3587.

One normally reserves places in the game and nature reserves directly with the camp concerned. Telephone numbers can be obtained from a central authority such as the National Parks Board. You can also find a list of the campgrounds in each of the regions at the end of the chapter *Where to Stay*.

Motorhomes and campers of every size and price category are available for rent. The price usually includes 1,400 km (870 miles) free, with every further kilometre costing extra. Here are some rental firms:

Campers Corner (motorhomes & campers; 4-wheel drive vehicles for Botswana), PO Box 48191, Roosevelt Park 2129. Tel: (011) 789 2327; fax: 787 6900.

Leisure Mobiles (motorhomes and campers), PO Box 48928, Roosevelt Park 2129. Tel: (011) 477 2374; fax: 477 2321.

Capricorn Tours and Campers (motorhomes and campers), PO Box 1530, Somerset West 7130. Tel: (024) 55 2331; fax: 55 4062.

C.I. Caravans (motorhomes, campers), PO Box 137, Pinetown 3600. Tel: (031) 701 2203; fax: 701 2200.

Four-Wheel Drive Rental

Four-wheel drive vehicles are advisable for journeys into Botswana or the more remote beaches of Northern Natal. Vehicles for rent are fully equipped with long-distance tank, special jack, fridge, 1–2 tents on the roof rack as well as camping requisites (bedding, cutlery, gas stove and gas lamps). The price includes insurance and unlimited mileage, and vehicles are available from Campers Corner (see address above). If you have your own camping equipment, you can take a Toyota Double Cab with four seats and a cover over the back. Contact **U-Drive-Rent-a-Car**, Box 23802, Joubert Park 2044. Tel: (011) 331 3735; fax: 331 7116.

As tenting equipment is seldom available for rent, tents are best brought along from home, although camping and hiking equipment is available for hire in Johannesburg. Contact Camping for Africa, PO Box 1938, Randburg 2125. Tel: (011) 787 3498; fax: 787 3524.

Other Attractions

Johannesburg

The African Herbalist Shop, 14 Diagonal St, Newtown. Tel: (011) 838 7352. Open Monday–Friday 8am–5pm.This "variety store" for medicine men sells bones, animal skins, herbs, and the like.

Northern Transvaal

God's Window: a few miles outside Graskop on the R534 loop road. This site is very aptly named: here the escarpment drops 2,600 ft (800 metres) and more down into the Lowveld – a breathtaking view from any of the many "windows".

Dzata: ruins in the Nzhelele valley which was the capital of the Vha-Venda; the biggest Baobab tree in Africa, estimated to be more than 4,000 years old, is near the Sagole hot springs; there are also the Holy Forest and the Scared Lake, as well as the Nwanedi National Park in beautiful surroundings.

Western Transvaal

Bakerville: located 12 miles (20 km) north of Lichtenburg, on the R52 from Rustenburg, and 143 miles (230 km) from Johannesburg, Bakerville was overrun by nearly 100,000 prospectors when diamonds were found there in 1926. Today, some still hope to strike it rich, inhabiting, in the meantime, simple huts of corrugated tin, like their predecessors.

KwaZulu/Natal

Minitown: Snell Parade, Tuesday–Saturday 9.30am–8.30pm, Sunday 9.30am–5pm. Minitown presents miniature replicas of Durban's most famous buildings, including moving ships, airplanes and trains.

The Garden Route

Port Alfred: the Three-R Tour (River, Road, Rail) includes a boat trip on the Kowie River, a coach ride to Bathurst and a train trip on the Settler Express back to Port Alfred. Tel: (0464) 41514. For further information also contact the Port Alfred Publicity Association, tel: (0464) 41235.

Cape Town

Cape Town on Foot (Walking Tour): discover the city on foot, led by a tour guide. Visit, among other sites, the Malay quarter for a traditional lunch, or wander along the beach from Muizenberg to Kalk Bay. Arnoni Tours. Tel: (021) 762 3262 or 794 5505.

North of Wale and Buitengracht Streets, the Malay quarter was originally home to Malays who were brought to the Cape as slaves in the 17th century. Sunk to the level of a slum, the area was rehabilitated, thanks to a generous clean-up effort, into a picturesque residential area with coloured, flat-roofed houses, minarets and mosques.

In the Bo-Kaap Museum, 71 Wale St, you can see objects from the life of the Malays. Open Tuesday–Thursday 10am–4.30pm, Saturday and Sunday 10am–4.30pm.

Planetarium, Victoria St, City Centre. Tel: (021) 243330. The starry heavens are projected onto a dome 49 ft (15 metres) in diameter, while sound and pictures conduct you into outer space. Tours Tuesday and Thursday at 1pm, Tuesday 8pm, Saturday and Sunday 2pm and 3.30pm.

Signal Hill: 1,095 ft (335 metres) high, this rise affords a wonderful view out over Cape Town. At midnight the Noon Gun is fired, once a signal to ships in the bay so that they could set their chronometers correctly. You won't soon forget the spectacle of the lights of the city at night.

Table Mountain, open daily 8.30am–6pm, December–April 8am–10pm. Don't forget to travel by cable car up to this 3,551-ft (1,086-metre) high hallmark of Cape Town. The view over Table Bay and the city is breathtaking. Unfortunately, the height is all too often veiled by a "table-cloth" of cloud, even on sunny days. You can either ascend by cable car (where there's usually a crowd) or walk up from Kloef Nek. It's about a three-hour walk to the top, and there are 300 routes to choose from, ranging from gentle footpaths to trails for climbers with ropes and picks. (Table Mountain Guide by B. M. Quail, or Walking Guide for Table Mountain by Sh. Brossy.) Tel: (021) 24 5148.

Victoria and Albert Waterfront: the area along the historic Victoria and Albert Docks has been transformed into an entertainment district with shopping, restaurants and bistros, cafes, theatre, hotels, fish markets, boat trips and helicopter rides.

Northern Cape

Kimberley: there are still two unique drive-in pubs operating in Kimberley; in bygone days, gentlemen imbibed their drinks on horseback. Today, you're served in your car (Kimberlite Hotel and Halfway House Hotel).

Kuruman: bus tours will take you to Roaring Sands, some 124 miles (200 km) to the south; when the sand of these dunes begins to slide, you'll understand where they got their name.

Vintage Cars

Who knows how many worn-out, rusting, stripped-down car bodies are slumbering in dark corners of out-of-the-way farms, only waiting to be discovered and lovingly restored by some old-timer car fan. But it is certain that

3,500 automobile enthusiasts have registered their classic cars in 22 clubs. There are supposedly around 10,000 vintage cars capable of driving the Cape's roads. Top honours go to the member with 54 of the vehicles – all, of course, in the very best condition. See and be seen: the clubs organise around 60 meetings and tours every year (virtually every weekend). Motorcycles, too, receive their due: every year in August, there's a rally held in Transvaal, while March/April sees a tour from Durban to Johannesburg.

The Kleinjukskei Motor Museum, on Witkoppen Street in the North of Johannesburg, tel: (011) 704 1514, displays Africa's best collection of veteran and classic cars; moreover, it's located on a small river in an attractive neighbourhood. Every weekend, 50 cars are exhibited. Nearby, an Italian restaurant is on hand to still the pangs of hunger. Open Wednesday–Sunday 10am–5pm.

Visitors are welcome to come in and browse around all the clubs. The largest of these are:

Johannesburg: Vintage and Veteran Club, tel: (011) 783 2808.

Cape Town: Crankhandle Club, tel: (021) 686 3915.

Port Elizabeth: Eastern Province Veteran Car Club, tel: (041) 35 4275.

Durban: Veteran Car Club, tel: (031) 75 1558.

Further information is available from the South African Veteran and Vintage Association, PO Box 331, Jeppes Town 2043, Johannesburg, tel: (011) 614 8624.

Nightlife

Johannesburg & Sun City

The night life in South Africa is diametrically opposed to that in Europe. An exception that proves the rule: Sun City, the Las Vegas of South Africa, with nightly extravaganza revues in which pretty girls, ostrich feathers and glitter, often flown in from America, take over the stage. In the night club Lipsticks, the dancers are for the most part "clothed" only with high-tech light effects. Dance fans should check out the two discos.

In Johannesburg, Ziggie's Restau-

rant Theatre in the Ascot Hotel in Norwood (Tel: (011) 483 1211) and the Village Manor Theatre in the Balalaika Hotel in Sandown (Tel: (011) 884 1400) both offer cabaret. Jazz lovers convene at Kippie's near the Market Theatre (Tel: (011) 832 1641) or at Red's Jazz Bar in the Riverside Shopping Centre in Bryanston (Tel: (011) 463 2220), both of which present different musicians almost every night. The younger generation can dance to the music of rock bands in the Roxy Rhythm Bar in Melville (Tel: (011) 726 6019) or Late Night Al's in Fisherman's Village near Bruma Lake (Tel: (011) 616 2206), or to disco music at New Jaggers in Rosebank (Tel: (011) 788 1718) or Caesar's Palace in Braamfontein (Tel: 403 2420). Certain restaurants, for example Greystone in Sandown (Tel: (011) 783 5262), Owen's (Tel: (011) 435 3546) near the Wemmer Pan, a mining lake, or Berlin's in Randburg (Tel: (011) 787 6519) offer, in addition to good food, an opportunity to dance.

Musical Fountains in Wemmer Pan are an unusual theatrical event: fountains which dance in a colourful play of water to the sound of music. Performances are held every night except Monday from 6.30–8pm. In winter (July and August) there are no shows. Tel: 407 6833.

Pretoria's best-known disco is Jaqueline's (Tel: (012) 326 1798), while you can shake a leg to live music in Monroe's (Tel: (012) 341 4637).

Cape Town

In Cape Town, there is cabaret iat Blake's Restaurant and Nightclub (Tel: (021) 21 7839) in the Nico Malan Complex. The Base (Tel: (021) 23 3667) in Shortmarket Street (city centre) has special offerings for jazz-lovers on Sunday.

At After Hours in Wale Street (Tel: (021) 23 1804) you can dance to disco music; or, choose Tattler's (Tel: (021) 44 9531) in the Don Hotel, Main Road, Sea Point (jazz on Sundays) or Idols (Tel: (021) 22 2315) on Loop Street (city centre).

Live bands play at La Med (Tel: 438 5600) at the Glen Beach Country Club in Camps Bay, as well as at Tom's Cabin (Tel: (021) 49 3637) on Main Road, Three Anchor Bay.

Durban

In Durban, you'll find the Monte Carlo nightclub and disco on Stanger Street (Tel: (031) 323 880). There's cabaret on Tuesdays and Thursdays at the Royal Prawn (Tel: (031) 328 844) on West Street. Disco dancing takes place in the Knights Disco (Tel: (031) 211 241) in the Berea Inn Hotel, Berea Street; while a small dance band plays on Wednesdays, Fridays and Sundays at Saltori's in the 320 West Street complex (Tel: (031) 322 804). There are also several dinner-dance restaurants. For information, look in the daily papers or the information brochure of the Durban Publicity Association.

Shopping

Diamonds, Gold & Jewellry

In South Africa, diamonds can be bought at reasonable prices. Local diamond-cutters offer their wares for a fraction of the price one would pay in Europe; you can save the 12 percent Value Added Tax (VAT) – as long as you remember to bring along your passport and plane ticket. Ask at your hotel, or look in the Yellow Pages under *Diamond Merchants and Cutters*. You're likely to have particular luck in the larger shopping centres in Johannesburg and Cape Town, or in Smith and West Streets in Durban.

Clothing

You can find a wide range of good **bush- and safari-wear** in the shops of the national parks, or in many city curio shops. Peppy, bright pullovers are knitted out of mohair wool, as are attractive stoles and shawls, made in Lesotho.

It's best to buy your **saris** in Durban (Greystreet and the surrounding area), even if all you want to do is sew a pretty dress out of the pure silk fabric.

Shoes on the Cape are cheaper than in Europe, but they aren't always the best, in terms of quality.

Leather clothes are generally imported from Europe, and therefore cost considerably more. An exception: locally-made, high-quality leather goods, which are available at specialty stores in any large shopping centre. Items include handbags, usually reasonably priced, of ostrich leather and other natural leathers.

Souvenirs

The various native tribes on the Cape have developed their own individual crafts and styles. The **Ndebele** paint their houses with certain specific patterns, and produce magnificent, large pearl jewellery as well as copper and bronze bracelets. The filigree-like chains of **Zulu** pearl work have an entirely different character. Shops also offer grain baskets or sieves woven of grass and reeds, as well as stylised woodcarvings of animals.

The **Vha-Venda** produce brightly-coloured clay pots, while the Toriga weave mats from coloured sisal. In East Transvaal, along the Panorama Route, you can find *Leiklip*, a soft, shale-like stone with light and dark layers, found in the valleys of the jungles, which is used to make ashtrays and animal figure carvings.

Probably the best-known training centre for black craftsmen is **Rorke's Drift Arts and Crafts Centre** in Natal, some 24 miles (40 km) southeast of Dundee. Here, you can buy top-quality products from the pottery, weaving and embroidery workshops, as well as works by some of the best graphic artists (Tel: 03425 627). **Katlehong Art Centre**, near Johannesburg, is a similar centre (Tel: 011/825 3235).

In the cities, you can find African handicrafts in the many curio shops or at one of the weekly markets. Best-known among these last are the **Johannesburg Market** by Market Theatre, and **Greenmarket Square** in Cape Town. If you're still looking for last-minute purchases on the way from Kruger Park to the Johannesburg Airport, you'll find a large selection at Kraal Craft (Tel: 01311 32228) a few miles from Whiteriver on the left-hand side as you drive towards Nelspruit.

Antiques

Sotheby's and Christie's have branches on the Cape – a clear indication that there's a thriving market for antiques in South Africa. Most of the treasures came from England by way of the 1820s settlers and later immigrants. Also worthy of mention is Cape Dutch furniture, usually rustic in style and made of the valuable yellow-wood. Cape silver, too, has a good reputation. Antique and used jewellery can be had for a song in comparison with prices abroad (particularly in light of favourable exchange rates).

Cape Town and Johannesburg are the best cities for antique-lovers.

In Cape Town, most of the shops are located in the area around Church and Long Streets; the narrow alleys by the Link and Cavendish shopping centres can also be fertile hunting grounds. Ashby's Gallery in Church Street holds auctions every second Thursday (Tel: 23 8060).

In Johannesburg, Rosebank is the centre of the antiques scene. Flea markets, too, can yield wonderful treasures.

In March, Cape Town puts on the Antique Fair; in October, there's the Antique and Decorator's Fair in Johannesburg.

The visitor should take care to buy truly valuable items only from dealers who are members of the South African Antique Dealers Association (SAADA), a chapter of the international CINOA, which provides a guarantee of the object's authenticity.

Information: SA Antique Dealer's Association, Box 52801, Saxonwold 2132. Johannesburg, tel: (011) 463 3754; fax: 706 4434; Cape Town, tel: (021) 794 5489; Durban, tel: (031) 368 1414.

Markets

108 weekly and monthly markets have become tremendously popular in recent years. They offer arts and crafts (usually from small, cottage industries), used books, jewellery, flea market knick-knacks, or Far Eastern bric-a-brac.

JOHANNESBURG

The best-known bazaar in Johannesburg is the Saturday **Flea Market** (9am–4pm, in the large car park near Market Theatre on Bree Street). It's worth a visit simply to watch the activity. For information tel. (011) 832 1641.

On weekends, the **festive atmosphere of the Bruma Lake** market (9am–4pm, Saturday and Sunday) attracts hordes of shoppers. Bruma Lake is an old mining lake in Kensington, in the east of Johannesburg (not far from East Gate Shopping Centre). For information tel. (011) 786 0776.

A different kind of market: the **Organic Village Market** in Culross Road, Bryanston. Nearly 100 stands compete for the visitor's attention with hand-sewn clothes, jewellery, African batik and pearl creations, minerals and crystals, glass-, leather-, and woodwork, and even organically-grown vegetables. Everything offered here is made of all-natural materials. Thursday and Sunday, 9am–1pm. For more information tel. (011) 706 3671.

Apart from these, most shopping is done in the large shopping centres in and around Johannesburg. Some of these centres contain as many as 200 shops, ranging from baby clothes shops and hardware stores to a post office and bank.

Elegant and popular: **Carlton Centre** in Commissioner Street, at the heart of Johannesburg and **Sandton City** in Rivonia Road. Two smaller shopping centres which contain chic boutiques: Rosebank Mall and The First, located a stone's throw from each other on Oxford Road in Rosebank.

Bree Street's Oriental Plaza, past the Market Theatre, is still largely undiscovered by tourists. Customers are mainly either Indians or people with a flair for the unusual: here, they'll find light Indian cotton dresses for a song, curtain fabri, or cooking pots. Patience is the key to success: some of these tiny shops are bursting at the seams with a riot of goods.

The two "Exclusive Books" shops in Hyde Park Centre, Jan Smuts Ave, Hyde Park, tel: (011) 788 0724, and on Pretoria Street in Hillbrow, tel: (011) 642 5068, offer a broad selection of books about South Africa: literature, politics, cooking, animals, plants, picture books and the like. Open Saturday and Sunday 9am–10.30pm.

CAPE TOWN

Cape Town's largest and best-known market is at the city centre: Green Market Square, Monday–Saturday 8am–4pm. The market offers clothes, jewellery, antiques, leather goods and much more.

On the Green Point Common and in

Hout Bay, near the Hout Bay Hotel, Sunday markets are held on the first and last Sunday of every month. Tokai's Waldorf School also holds regular monthly markets.

Every December, a Medieval Craft Market is held in the gardens of the Groot Constantia Vineyard: artists and craftsmen present high-quality products.

Information about all markets is available from Captour, tel: (021) 25 3320.

A new shopping and entertainment centre is rising near the old harbour: the Victoria and Albert Waterfront Development could become as much of a magnet for tourists as the sea and the mountains.

Tradition lives on in the underground Golden Acre, a complex reaching beneath Adderly Street to the Cape Sun Hotel. Claremont is a consumer's paradise: the modern shopping complexes Cavendish Square and The Link present an elegant ambience characterised by marble and mirrors. And clothes as far as the eye can see, from bargains to haute couture. Outside, in the quiet streets and alleyways, antique lovers come into their own.

DURBAN

On the first and last Sunday of every month, 10am–5pm, the Amphitheatre on the Marine Parade in Durban is transformed into a flea market where you can also watch Zulu dances When the old railway station was moved out of the city centre, the locomotive repair shop was left standing; today, it's become a highly original shopping mall, called, symbolically, The Workshop. Dozens of small, often intriguing shops make window-shopping and browsing amusing pastimes. It's also open on weekends.

The Wheel on Point Road is an unusual shopping centre with cinemas, restaurants, and friendly shops. Inside, it looks like an old ship. Its name derives from the giant Ferris wheel on its facade.

When Durban's Indian Market moved from Warrick to its present location between Victoria and Queen Streets (near the mosque), it became known as the Victoria Street Market. Oriental haggling is virtually required: in this way, you can get discounts of up to 30 percent when buying jewellery, woodcarvings, hand-embroidered clothing or Indian spices. But don't feel guilty: these reductions have been calculated by the salesman as part of the sale price.

At the lower (beach) end of West Street you'll find many shops geared toward the tourist trade.

Sports

As clearly demonstrated by the number of top sporting names it has produced down the years, South Africa is a very sports-orientated country. This is not surprising when one considers the sunny weather conditions, easy access to space and general outdoor way of life.

The umbrella organisation which represents a broad spectrum of sporting bodies is COSAS. Their list of the administrators of dozens of sporting disciplines is the most up-to-date in the country. For information on any sport not covered in this little summary, contact COSAS, 814 Park St, Arcadia 0083. Tel: (012) 343 2470.

Participant

GLIDING: the Transvaal is renowned for its perfect gliding conditions. It offers endless blue skies, stable weather all year round with lots of sunshine and thermals that facilitate very long glides. Gliding tours are offered and clubs may be helpful in organising equipment privately; there are no commercially organised hiring facilities.

Contact the following two clubs in the Transvaal for more information:

Magaliesburg Gliding Club, PO Box 190, Tarlton 1749. Tel: (011) 716 5229.

Witwatersrand Gliding Trust, PO Box 6875, Johannesburg 2000. Tel: (011) 615 2461.

Lifestyle Gliding Adventures, PO Box 67, Randburg 2125. Tel: (011) 705 3201/2; fax: 705 3203. Lifestyle Gliding Adventures take you up on a soaring experience from the Parys airfield. The rates vary depending on the number of passengers.

HANG-GLIDING: to practise hang-gliding in South Africa, you need to be a member of the South African Aero Club, thereby incurring a liability insurance, but temporary membership is available. Also check whether your licence system is valid here. The Aero Club will be helpful in that respect. Contact The Aero Club of South Africa, PO Box 898, Kempton Park, 1620. Tel: (011) 394 4974 Fax 394 4977.

Equipment may present a problem should you need to hire it. Clubs may be able to help, but there are no regular hiring facilities. For further information contact the national body, or clubs directly:

The Hang-gliding & Para-gliding Association, PO Box 76241, Wendywood 2144. Tel: (011) 804 4210.

Hang-gliding is very very popular in the Transvaal as a result of good weather all year round:

Thermal Riders Eastern Transvaal, PO Box 203, Nelspruit 1200. Tel: (01311) 5 4371.

Natal offers coastal stretches, sugar cane plantations and rural isolation, but the most popular area for hang gliding is around the Drakensberg.

Natal Hang Gliding Society, PO Box 175, Durban 4000. Tel: (0323) 9 8726 (Darrel Moody).

The scenery in the Cape makes for fantastic glides; while the weather is agreeable in summer, in winter the conditions along the coastal strips are stormy and wet. However, in summer the scenic grandeur is unrivalled, making for memorable glides.

Cape Albatross Club, PO Box 342, Sea Point 8060. Tel: (021) 462 2660 or Rob Rademeyer, tel: 797 8347.

PARACHUTING: again the weather (especially in the Transvaal) and the superb scenery of Natal and the Cape make for fantastic parachuting/skydiving.

The sport involves a very active social club life. Below are listed some club contacts which offer courses and may also be helpful in other ways.

The Free Fall Factory, PO Box 87509, Houghton 2041. Tel: (011) 393 1020 (J.H. Visser).

Pietermaritzburg Parachuting Club, PO Box 798, Pietermaritzburg 3200. Tel: (0331) 52 2790 (home Kevin Moore).

Western Province Sport Parachuting, PO Box 7017, Roggebaai 8012. Tel: (021) 75 6161 (Alan Murray).

CYCLING: as there are no cycling paths, the sport is more hazardous than in Europe. However traffic on the smaller roads is not heavy. Despite the distances involved, people do cycle from Johannesburg to Cape Town, from Durban to Johannesburg, along the Garden Route and most of all around the Western Cape, which is wonderfully suited for fun cycling as it has magnificent scenery and there is no rain during the summer months (October–April). For organised rides contact:

The Western Province Pedal Power Association, PO Box 23190, Claremont 7735. Tel: (021) 794 2268.

Natal affords great cycling during the winter months as there is no risk of rain and it is pleasantly warm. Contacts:

Natal Pedal Power Association, PO Box 1048, Durban 4000. Tel: (031) 83 1598 (ask for Jan Hutchinson).

Drakensberg Mountain Bike Club, PO Box 60, Winterton 3340.

Southern Transvaal Pedal Power Association, PO Box 3521, Randburg 2125. Tel: (012) 345 4534 (Clive Anderson).

Johannesburg Mountain Bike Club, PO Box 1697, Halfwayhouse 1685. Tel: (011) 315 1285.

Hiring of bikes:

The Great Outdoors, Victoria and Albert Waterfront, Cape Town. Tel: (021) 419 9410.

Linden Cycle and Canoe, 63b 3rd Ave, Linden. Tel: (011) 782 7313.

In the eastern Orange Free State on the farms of the Jacana Country Homes a cycle trail of about 35 miles (60 km) has been established in a very beautiful area where you cycle on farm roads and upgraded hiking trails:

Jacana Country Homes, PO Box 95212, Waterkloof 0145. Tel: (012) 46 5365.

Tri-Cycling Magazine is a helpful contact for cycling, rowing and canoeing in South Africa Tel: (011) 887 6500

The Argus Tour is the biggest one-day cycling event in the world – in March 15,000 cyclists take part in the race around the Cape Peninsula.

GOLF: very popular in South Africa. A total of 400 golf clubs are to be found all over the country, offering a wide range of challenges. Many seem to have retained some of South Africa's colonial past, thus membership often requires more than "just" paying subscription fees. Many incorporate the natural habitat to stunning effect. From the Milnerton or Mowbray greens you have a splendid view of Table Mountain, while the Wild Coast Course is laid out with sea water, dunes and plants. The Royal Cape and Royal Johannesburg are graced by beautiful old trees, dating from 1882 and 1890 respectively. The Royal George and the Durban Country are claimed to be the most beautiful golf courses. For further information on golf courses that are part of holiday resort accommodation consult SATOUR's publication on golf and accommodation.

SATOUR, Private Bag X164, Pretoria 0001. Tel: (012) 347 0600; fax: 45 4768.

For further information – possibly the planning of a golf safari – contact the South African Golf Union, PO Box 1537, Cape Town 8000. Tel: (021) 461 7585.

Major Golfing events:

Sunshine Circuit, January–February, several venues throughout SA; South African Open Championships, January, various venues; Lexington PGA Tournament, January, Johannesburg; SA Amateur Golf Championships, March, not fixed.

Million Dollar Golf Classic, December, Sun City.

HORSE RIDING: the diversity and spaciousness of the South African landscape, together with the temperate climate lends itself ideally to horse riding and horse riding trails. Horse riding is within reach of many more people here than it would be in Europe since the means are relatively affordable. Trails are available in various parts of the country, thus offering visitors an experience of this land at a "grass-roots level" – the sensations of what South Africa is about are immediate and alive. Trails in the Drakensberg are organised by the Natal Parks Board and Drifters and take you through a scenic grandeur across natural streams and grassy plains along the escarpment. The area appears untouched by the twentieth century. You may come across rural dwellings or Basothos (people of Lesotho) pursuing the rhythm of their traditional lifestyle. Contact the following addresses for details:

Natal Parks Board, PO Box 662, Pietermaritzburg 3200. Tel: (0331) 47 1981.

Drifters Adventures, PO Box 4 8434, Roosevelt Park 2129. Tel: (011) 888 1160; fax: (011) 888 1020.

Equus Trails, PO Box 926, White River 1240. Tel: (01311) 51 998; fax: 5 0383. They offer rides through the bushveld in the Eastern Transvaal in the Songimvelo Game Reserve, which lies on the Swaziland border. There are no predators in this game reserve, but there is a wide variety of game and the trail takes you through magnificent mountain scenery (they also offer a Wilderness Trail for hikers):

Another trail in the Transvaal is the Glendwoods Magaliesberg Mountain Trail. The Magaliesberg (only two hours from Johannesburg) is one of the oldest mountain ranges in the world. You are likely to see smaller game and the range also has a breeding colony of the endangered Cape Vulture.

Glendwoods Magaliesberg Mountain Trail, PO Box 568, Britz 0250. Tel: (01211) 3 1404 (after hours).

Trails in the Cape are scenic, offering a different landscape altogether, lush green surroundings, rolling hills, forests, vineyards etc. Equi Trailing have organised a trail near Plettenberg Bay in a conservationist paradise and Amatola Trails take you through the Eastern Cape on horseback.

Equi Trailing, PO Box 1373, Plettenberg Bay 6600. Tel: (04457) 9718 (Mr and Mrs Rowling).

Amatola Trails, Hogsback 5721. Tel: (0020) ask for Hogsback 32.

Competitive horse riding is a popular spectator sport since it offers a form of legal gambling, namely betting, (gambling is illegal in South Africa). Some of the major horse racing events attract large glamorous crowds, amongst which are many high profile personalities (e.g. Rothmans July Handicap).

MARATHONS: road running is one of South Africa's most popular sports both amongst the white and black population, ranging in distance 6–55 miles (10–90 km). Events are held in almost all major towns and cities on weekends. Temporary licences are available for races up to 10 miles (15 km). For more information contact The South African Road Running Association, PO Box 11131, Dorpspruit 3206. Tel: (0331) 94 5413.

The highlight is the 55-mile (90-km) Comrades Marathon which alternates annually from Durban to Pieter-maritzburg on 31 May. The race has an 11 hour time-limit and attracted 13,000 participants in 1991. The runners have to endure a 2,300-ft (700-metre) altitude difference. The 31-miles (50-km) Two Oceans Marathon on the Cape Peninsula every Easter Saturday also attracts many runners. Another popular event is the City to City Marathon from Johannesburg to Pretoria.

TENNIS: enjoys a very large following amongst white South Africans as it is one of the sports offered at most schools. Tennis is very accessible both financially and practically since clubs are situated densely all over the country. Visitors are very welcome to play at clubs. Many hotels also have tennis facilities. For any information contact the South African Tennis Union, PO Box 2211, Johannesburg 2000. Tel: (011) 402 3580.

Water Sports

CANOEING: South Africans engage enthusiastically in all forms of canoeing: white water, slalom, sprint and long distance. Olympic canoeists and trainers regard the Highveld as a good training area because of the sunny climate and high altitude (Johannesburg lies at 1,700m) There are also some very challenging rivers in this country. Some clubs hire out equipment. For information contact:

South African Canoe Federation, PO Box 5, Mc Gregor 6708, Western Cape. Tel: (02353) 733.

Transvaal Canoe Union, 61 Dorsett, Parkwood, 2193. Tel: (011) 788 6693.

Western Province Canoe Union, PO Box 484, Milnerton 7435. Tel: (021) 551 1770.

Natal Canoe Union, 290 Bulwer St, Pietermaritzburg 3200. Tel: (0331) 45 4664; fax: 42 1562.

Major events are held in Natal in summer and in the Cape in the winter months (water level):

Umkomaas Canoe Marathon, 3 days, Durban, March; Orange River Canoe Marathon, 2 days, Hopetown/ Cape, April; Berg River Marathon, 4 days, 300–400 participants, Western Cape, July; Fish River Marathon (international), 2 days, 400 participants, Craddock, Eastern Cape, October; Vaal

Kayak Marathon, 400 participants, Johannesburg, December.

Duzi Marathon, 2 days, 700–1000 participants, Pietermaritzburg, December/January.

RIVER RAFTING: another popular way to enjoy the large African rivers, especially the Orange River. For 4–6 days let this gentle giant take you in rubber rafts or canoes through the most spectacular, unspoilt Richtersveld – cooking on open fires and sleeping under the African desert sky – a unique way of letting go of the stresses of civilisation. The wonderful thing is that no canoeing experience is required and even children can take part (especially in the rubber raft trips). There are a few organisations which offer rafting and canoeing trips:

Felix Unite (Tugela, Orange, and Breede Rivers – canoes), PO Box 1524, Sandton 2146. Tel: (011) 463 3167/8; fax: 706 1614.

Orange River Adventures (Indian Mohawk canoes), c/o 5 Matapan Road, Rondebosch 7700. Tel: (021) 685 4475.

River Rafters (Orange River – rubber rafts), PO Box 1157, Kelvin 2054. Tel: (011) 82 5407.

River Runners (rafts, canoes, kayak), PO Box 583, Constantia 7848. Tel: (021) 705 6229.

Sunwa Ventures (Tugela River and Vaal Dam), PO Box 41952, Craighall 2024. Tel: (011) 788 5120.

DIVING in the waters around South Africa is a great way to explore the rich marine life (2,000 species) from the icy waters of the west coast (the Benguela current of the Atlantic) to the subtropical east coast (the Agulhas current of the Indian Ocean).

On the Atlantic coast divers can harvest rock lobster, perlemoen, black mussels and others. As the warm Agulhas current can be felt further up the Eastern Cape coast the marine life changes: flame coral, starfish, feather stars and other exotic and colourful sea creatures abound. People without diving experience might consider making use of diving courses offered here to acquire diving qualifications. For further information contact the South African Diving Unions:

South African Underwater Union, PO Box 557, Parow 7500. Tel: (021) 930 6549; fax: 930 6541.

Border Underwater Union, PO Box

1201, East London 5200. Tel: (0431) 3 0320 (Mr Spat).

Natal Underwater Union, PO Box 251, New Germany 3600. Tel: (031) 72 5730 (Gordon Smith).

From Cape Vidal (on the level of St Lucia Lake) to the Mozambique border, an aquatic reserve stretches for three miles out into the sea. Divers are drawn by the world's southernmost coral reefs and the colourful marine life. At Sodwana Bay there is the Sodwana Dive Retreat and Sodwana Lodge Charters. These diving resorts offer training, sale and hire of equipment, speciality diving (such as night dives) and accommodation. The area used offers a beautiful sandy beach with a dune forest. The bay is sheltered by a ridge jutting seaward from the dune headland. Contact Sodwana Dive Retreat, tel: (031) 86 6266 (ask for Don Rennie); fax: 305 7430, or Sodwana Lodge Charters for Diving, tel: (031) 29 0972; fax: 29 4805.

The region between Umhlanga Rocks and Salt Rock with its shallower reefs close to the coast lends itself especially to spear fishing. Vetch's pier is more for beginners.

The Durban Underwater Club, tel: (031) 32 5850, offers excursions from Umkomaas and Rocky Bay. Trident Diving School in Durban, tel: (031) 305 3081, organises dives to the Aliwal Shoal 2 miles (4 km) off the coast of Umkomaas just south of Durban. Underwater World in Scottburgh, tel: (031) 32 5820; fax: 37 5587, offers diving excursions.

The diving businesses in East London are good places to organise diving trips. Countless reefs between the Great Fish River and Kidd's Beach provide excellent diving. Diving is popular around East London on account of the many vessels to have foundered along this stretch of coast. For further information tel. (0431) 2 6015.

The area around Port Alfred is only suitable for experienced divers. Information can be obtained from the Kowie Underwater Club in Port Alfred. Less experienced divers can brave the deep around Algoa Bay. The Dolphin Underwater Club in Humewood offers courses.

At the Tsitsikamma National Park east of Plettenberg Bay a snorkelling trail and a scuba diving trail have been established which explore this silent world. It is like diving in a gigantic aquarium. For information on the Tsitsikamma diving trails contact the National Parks Board, PO Box 314, Knysna 6570. Tel: (0445) 2 2095.

The numerous rugged stretches of coast in the southwestern Cape make diving a fascinating proposition almost everywhere. You may well discover old wrecks between Danger Point and Waenhuiskrans. Further information can be obtained from the Bredasdorp Publicity Association, tel: (0284) 4 2584. Cape Hangklip near Cape Town is another popular diving area.

SPEAR-FISHING: much the same can be said about spear-fishing as about diving. The best marine fauna is found in the area where the warm Agulhas current meets the cold Benguela current off the south coast. The best overall month for diving in South Africa is March. However, there are regulations that need to be observed such as the closed seasons on particular species, protected areas, size and number restrictions on the fish caught and also permit requirements. For such information contact the SA Underwater Union.

FISHING: trout fishing is pursued by many South Africans as there are streams all over the country that are home to trout. You need a licence, which is not transferable from province to province. The licence is issued by a magistrate's court or sometimes by the office of the nature reserve where the stream is located. You also require the prescribed trout tackle. The season is all year round, peaking in autumn and spring. In the Transvaal the favourite areas are Dullstroom, Pilgrim's Rest, Graskop, Sabie and Lydenberg, all in the Eastern Transvaal. For further information contact Transvaal Nature Conservation Division, Private Bag X209, Pretoria 0001. Tel: (012) 201 2469.

The Natal trout areas are all along the Drakensberg Escarpment and rivers in the Umgeni and Himeville districts. For further information contact Natal Parks Board, PO Box 662, Pietermaritzburg 3200. Tel: (0331) 47 1981.

In the Cape popular trout fishing are around Stellenbosch, La Bain's Kloof and Maden Dam ing Williams Town. For further ion contact the Department of

Nature Conservation, PO Box 9086, Cape Town 8000. Tel: (021) 45 0227.

ROCK AND SURF ANGLING is a favourite past-time all along South Africa's interesting coastline with its varied conditions concerning water temperatures, winds and currents, all of which affect the type of marine life. Fishing permits are required for particular areas such as Table Bay (obtainable from harbour authorities). No licences are required to fish off the Natal coast or in estuaries. Taking rock life such as crayfish does require a licence. For further information contact the South African Rock and Surf Angling Association, 28 Silverleaf Ave, Wynberg 7800. Tel: (021) 219 2629 (Mr Kollner).

Popular coastal strips include Durban Harbour, North and South Pier, St Lucia, Mapelane, Cape Vidal, Mission Rocks, Umfolozi, Sodwana Bay. The best season here is June–November.

The Garden Route coastline, the Peninsula coastline and False Bay up to Milnerton (north of Cape Town) and from Gordon's Bay around Cape Hangklip are popular areas. The season is all year round.

Major events are the Fredrick Old Brown National Championships in March and the Mossel Bay Boland Friendly in October.

GAME AND DEEP SEA FISHING has a special thrill for many anglers. June marks the famous Sardine Run which is accompanied by hundreds of game fish, while in the Cape the two main runs are the tunny run in October and the runs of snoek in autumn and winter. Equipment is privately owned while boats are available for charter. For further information contact the Ski Boat Light Tackle Game and Fishing Association, PO Box 4191, Cape Town 8000. Tel: (021) 21 3611 (ask for Mr Steyn).

The best areas of the Natal coast include the south coast, off Durban harbour and the north coast at Sodwana, Richards Bay and St Lucia (season December–June). Cape areas include Hout Bay, Simonstown and Hermanus, while the season stretches mid-October–November and March–mid-May. In Natal the best season for marlin and sail fish is November–April, while in the Cape the long fin and yellow fin tunny are in season September–April.

Major events are:
Cape Boat and Ski Boat International Tournament, October, Cape; Master Angling Tournament, mid-March, Cape Town; Eastern Transvaal Billfish Tournament, November, Sodwana Bay.

SAILING: with its 1,860 miles (3,000 km) coastline of sandy beaches, bays, lagoons, cliffs and rock shorelines the South African seas offer the sailing enthusiast the full spectrum of challenges from conditions such as the Cape of Storms to calm seas bathed in sunshine. On average the winds are in the 15–25 knots range. Yacht club facilities are excellent, from clubs with 50 to those with 3,000 members. Most yachts in South Africa belong to the cruising category in the 50–80 ft (10–15 metres) range, of which the majority are produced locally to stringent standards. Offshore sailing requires that you belong to a recognised yacht club and that you comply with harbour regulations (licence, permits, registration, etc.). The national body to which you can turn for information is situated in Cape Town:

The Cruising Association of South Africa, PO Box 5036, Cape Town 8000. Tel: (021) 439 1147; fax: 434 0203.

The organisations listed below offer courses in sailing, as well as chartered tours that are scenic and offer activities such as fishing:

Table Bay Sailing Academy, PO Box 32296, Camps Bay 8040. Tel: (021) 438 8242.

Lifestyle Travel Luxury Yachting Adventures, PO Box 67, Randburg 2125. Tel: (011) 705 3201; fax: 705 3203. They offer from lunch and sunset charters to 5-day cruises in 45-ft (13-metre) and 53-ft (16-metre) sailing boats off the Cape coast and in South Africa's best wetland and wildlife sanctuaries.

Major Offshore events:
Wilbur Ellis da Gama Ocean Race, 250 miles (402 km), Durban, 2 days at the end of April; Indian Ocean Racing Circuit Durban–East London and Algoa Bay, one week in June; Mainstay Week "round-the-buoy", off Durban, July; Keelboat Racing, Table Bay, one week, December; Castle Agulhas Race to Mossel Bay, December; Cape Town–Rio de Janeiro, every 2 years.

Dinghy sailing: referring to an under-20-ft (6-metre) boat with raisable centreboard, dinghy sailing is popular mainly on the inland dams. Clubs welcome visitors and may be helpful in getting you a "sail". In the Transvaal the Vaal Dam is the largest venue (260 miles/420 km), with some 430 miles (700 km) of shoreline, the season being year round. Major event is the Lion Week Vaal Dam, October. For further information contact the South African Yachting Association, Private Bag 0004, Germiston South 1411. Tel: (011) 827 3508; fax: 827 0538.

SURFING: South Africa has beautiful sandy beaches and great surf. Durban, South Africa's surfing centre, hosts most of the surfing competitions since weather and water are warm all year round. Further south lies Jeffrey's Bay, which is well know for its dangerous but exhilarating waves: "Super Tubes" – the best right hand wave world wide – "a breathtaking ride inside a vortex of clear water". Even more challenging are the legendary St Francis Bay waves known as "Bruce's". However they are not as consistent as the waves at Jeffrey's Bay (may only work on a few winter days a year). Then down from Port Elizabeth the long breakers abound right down to Cape Town's big solid waves. While the landscape is spectacular, the waters are freezing (e.g. Camps Bay). Major events are the National Amateur Championships, venue changes, July and the Gunston 500 (international) in Durban, July.

Equipment and information on local conditions is available from surf shops in major urban centres. For further information contact:

South African Surfing Association, PO Box 617, Umtentweni 4235. Tel: (0391) 2 1150.

WINDSURFING: South Africa's sunny weather all year round, together with the many beautiful sandy beaches along its coasts and the huge expanses of water of the inland dams offer many opportunities for the windsurfing enthusiast. Not only are temperatures ideal, wind conditions, too, facilitate the sport. Access to the water is very good and finally South Africa's rescue operations need to be mentioned, since they are located not only directly at the prime surfing areas, but involve a network that is so well organised that help is always at hand. All you need worry about is whether you can handle the strength of the wind. Some coastal areas require permits for offshore windsurfing. Below are listed some of the popular areas in the Transvaal, Natal and the Cape.

Transvaal: Bona Manzi Dam (near Bronkhorstspruit), Vaal Dam, Ebernezer Dam (near Tzaneen).

Natal: Midmar Dam; Suitable coastal areas are few: Warner Beach (Scottburgh), Amanzimtoti (for experienced windsurfers), lagoon at Zinkwazi, northern Richards Bay, lagoon at Mtunzini.

Cape: Plettenberg Bay, Struisbaai, Swartvlei (inland near George), and many many more. For further information contact the South African Windsurfing Class Association, Private Bag X16, Auckland Park 2006. Tel: (011) 726 7076.

Inland sailing, windsurfing, speedboating and water-skiing can be enjoyed at the Midmardamm lake, 15 miles (24 km) northwest of Pietermaritzburg on the N3 and at the Hartebeesport Dammk, an hour north of Johannesburg on the R511.

Spectator

CRICKET is one of the major team sports in South Africa. The standard is very high, and the game is strongly promoted. Cricket has led the way toward integrated sport in South Africa by hosting Rebel Tours, While at the same time trying to break the international sanctions which were imposed on all sport before apartheid began to be dismantled. Now sport is theoretically open to all South Africans.

The game was introduced to the continent by the British colonials. The fact that from 1858 the Queen's Birthday was officially celebrated by a cricket match testifies to its popularity amongst the English community of the time.

Major events are the Castle Cup Cricket Final in February (venue changes) and the Benson & Hedges Cricket Final in March (venue changes).

For more information contact the South African Cricket Board, PO Box 55009, Northlands 2116. Tel: (011) 880 2810.

FOOTBALL: soccer is played especially by black South Africans, who consider it the "number one" sport. Black children grow up kicking a ball around in their backyard or on the streets in their neighbourhood. Once they find themselves a job, football is usually pursued since it serves as a major recreational pastime. Wherever black South Africans are employed there is bound to be a football club or at least a team in the near vicinity.

At club level football is well organised. There are many clubs which are all a part of the league structure. The clubs represent all sections of the population from varsity students to manual workers in a township. Soweto boasts a few large football stadiums and three professional clubs. For information contact The Football Council of South Africa, PO Box 21, Sharpeville 1933. Tel: (011) 474 3522.

Major events:

Iwisa Charity Football Spectacular, round robin with four teams from the 1st league Soccer City Johannesburg, date not fixed.

J.P.S Knock-out series Soccer City, August.

Bop Save Super Bowl Cup Final Soccer City, November/December.

RUGBY: despite international sanctions on South African sport, rugby has remained strong and competitive. This appears to be the result of the high standing that rugby has at the school level which then channels its players into club rugby which then feeds into provincial rugby. Thus the foundation from which rugby draws its players is very solid. In both English and Afrikaans speaking schools this sport is given preference over other sports. For more information contact the South African Rugby Board, PO Box 99, Newlands 7725. Tel: (021) 685 3038.

Major events:

Currie Cup (senior provincial teams), league ends in a final in October.

Lion Cup, senior provincial knock-out, July.

Sanlam Bank Trophy (also called Piennar Competition) played by provincial teams not in the Currie Cup, October.

Gold Cup sub unions, ends not fixed.

MOTOR RACING: South A are enthusiastic supporters o

racing. Kyalami, a world renowned venue up until the late 70s, hosted a Grand Prix in Formula I every year. Many drivers have today voiced their support for the re-admission of South Africa to Formula I. Some famous names have come from within South Africa: former Formula I World Champion Jodi Scheckter; former 250cc and 350cc motor cycle champion Kork Ballington and rally ace Sarrel van der Merwe.

Rallies are facilitated by rugged terrain. Conditions are many and varied from the dry conditions of the northern Transvaal to wet muddy conditions of the Natal midlands.

Major events:

Roof of Africa Rally, October.

Paris to Dakar (to Cape Town!), end-December. A major bonus for South African motor sport is undoubtedly the changed format for the Paris Dakar which is now to finish in Cape Town. This will attract vast overseas interest and spectators.

Westbank Motorsport Rally, October, Kyalami.

For more information on motor sport and the events, contact the A.A. Motorsport Control, PO Box 596, Johannesburg 2000. Tel: (011) 403 3160.

Language

Afrikaans and English are the official languages in South Africa. Afrikaans being the mother tongue of the Afrikaners and the principal language used by coloureds. It derived from Dutch, and was brought to Africa by early settlers. More Afrikaners are bilingual than English-speakers.

Most urban black people speak English and Afrikaans in addition to their native language.

Further Reading
Other Insight Guides

There are nearly 200 Insight Guide titles to cities, regions, countries and continents of the world. Other *Insight Guides* which highlight destinations in this region include: *Insight Guides: Namibia, Kenya* and *Gambia and Senegal*. Also available is *Insight Pocket Guide: Kenya* which provides short itineraries for visitors with limited time.

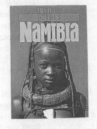

South Africa's neighbour is a fascinating, unspoilt region just beginning to be a major tourist destination. Its wonderful wildlife and dramatic scenery are all caught by Apa's photographers in this impressive guide.

Insight Guide: Kenya covers one of Africa's best-known safari destinations, ranging from a detailed guide to the capital, Nairobi, to coverage of all the top game reserves.

Complementing the Kenya book is a separate title, *Insight Guide: East African Wildlife*, which give a complete rundown on the the world's great game reserves of Kenya, Uganda, Zambia and Somalia.

Topical, authoritative and beautifully illustrated, *Insight Guide: The Gambia & Senegal* reveals an African gem. Expert writers introduce its resorts, fishing beaches and captivating music, backed up by Apa's customary high standard of photography.

☞

Robert de la Harpe/ABPL cover
Shaen Adey/ABPL 63
Daryl Balfour/ABPL 119
Andrew Bannister/ABPL 164, 166
Anthony Bannister/ABPL 12/13, 20,
61, 62, 114/115, 117, 134/135, 141,
144, 145, 146/147, 148/149, 191,
195, 202,203, 242, 252, 259, 264R,
274, 275, 280, 282, 283, 285,286,
287, 290, 299, 311
Daphne Barew 277
Courtesy Bloomsbury 100
Bodo Bondzio 1, 9, 64, 142, 152,
158, 173, 174, 184R, 185, 218, 229,
230, 245, 246, 247, 253, 278L,
292R, 293, 306/307
David Bristow 268L, 269, 282
Susanna Burton 60
Vincent Carruthers 122
Christian Barnard Museum 75
Ron Clark 69, 186
Gerard Cubitt 56, 76, 77, 79, 81,
116, 118, 120, 121, 123, 124, 127,
128, 129, 130, 132L, 132R, 133,
138, 156/157, 167, 178/179, 180,
184L, 194, 196/197, 201, 214, 219,
220/221, 237, 250, 268R, 271,
278R, 281, 284, 292, 294
Thomas Dawson 22/23, 91
Peter Devereux 109
Don Edkins/Laif 97, 301
Ellen Elmerdorp 238
Denis Farrell/AP 46
David Goldblatt/South Light 300
Roger de la Harpe/ABPL 14/15,
143, 206, 210, 211, 232, 240/241,
291, 302
Heiner Heine 52/53, 57, 65, 67,
70L, 70R, 71, 74, 82, 168, 175, 181,
183, 188, 192, 193, 210, 212, 267,
270, 312
Herin von Horsten/ABPL 243
Irvin & Johnson Ltd 104/105
D. King 261
Chris Van Lennep/ABPL 10/11
Tim Liversedge/ABPL 198/199
Eric Miller/South Light 80, 98L
Steve Milton-Barber/South Light
98R
Jean Morris 295
Natal Performing Arts Council 92,
93, 94,
95, 96
NCHOM 190
Christian Pehlemann 304/305

Gonsul Pillay 58, 83, 204/205, 207
Rob Ponte/ABPL 72
Herman PotgieterBPL 187, 222, 234,
256/257, 263, 266, 293
Phillip Richardson/ABPL 150/151
Joan Ryder/ABPL 18/19, 288/289,
303
SA Museum 24
Wayne Saunders/ABPL 189
Spectrum Colour Library 159, 162L,
162R, 163, 165, 170, 172, 209, 226,
227, 228, 231, 254, 255, 279
Lorna Stanton/ABPL 139
The Star 42
Peter Steyn 125, 126
Guy Stubbs/ABPL 2, 45
Colla Swart/ABPL 73L, 73R
Sun International 48/49, 176, 177
Christopher Till 88, 90
Guy Tillim/South Light 113
Gavin Thompson/ABPL 309
Topham Picture Source/AP 40, 41,
43
Transvaal Archives 36
Lisa Trocchi/ABPL 47, 66, 78, 86/
87, 108, 164, 219
Rudi van der Elst 249, 251
Chris van Lennep/ABPL 50/51,
296L
Dieter Vogel 223, 248
Hein von Horsten/ABPL 16/17, 54/
55, 136, 233, 235, 236, 239, 272/
273
Paul Weinberg/South Light 44, 85,
259
William Fehr Collection 28
Graeme Williams/South Light 99,
214
Gisèle Wulfsohn/South Light 106,
111, 171, 264L, 265

Maps Berndtson & Berndtson

Visual Consultant V. Barl